MEET ME AT ELBOW BEACH

MEET ME AT ELBOW BEACH

COLIN BIRD

Troubador Publishing Ltd
Unit E2 Airfield Business Park
Harrison Road, Market Harborough
Leicestershire LE16 7UL
Tel: 0116 279 2299
Email: books@troubador.co.uk
Web: www.troubador.co.uk

ISBN 978 1 80514 234 8

British Library Cataloguing in Publication Data.
A catalogue record for this book is available from the British Library.

Printed and bound by CPI Group (UK) Ltd, Croydon, CR0 4YY
Typeset in 12pt Minion Pro by Troubador Publishing Ltd, Leicester, UK

MIX
Paper | Supporting
responsible forestry
FSC
www.fsc.org
FSC® C013604

For Janet

Who joined me on life's highway, on which we have managed nearly fifty years of loving collaboration. We have encountered a few pot-holes and road works on the way, but the journey has been mostly smooth and memorable – thanks to that Bermuda magic.

'You can go to Heaven if you like. I'll stay right here in Bermuda'
Mark Twain

A WORD FROM THE AUTHOR

Even before I left Bermuda, I was making frequent notes about the daily goings-on in that earthly paradise, in the vague belief that one day I would consign it all to paper and even have the effrontery to submit it to a publisher.

This activity increased during my time in Pennsylvania, and had become an almost daily exercise when I set foot back in the mother country; I could often be seen stopping whatever I was doing, to make notes in a pad I always carried around with me. It was somewhat embarrassing at the check-out in Tesco, or the gents in the cinema – especially in mid flow – but I knew that if I did not get it all down then and there, the thought might retreat into one of those dark locked rooms in my brain, and be lost. I bought scrap pads in bulk from a newsagent in Bury St Edmunds, and filled box files with bits of paper, each one denoting an event or conversation by way of bullet points and memory jogging key words, and often filling several sides of paper with more specific details. All of this carried on while the Bermuda episode was still relatively fresh and active in my mind. I mention this only to answer a question that has often been levelled at me: *'How can you possibly remember all this stuff?'*

Although the note-taking carried on over many years as new recollections manifested themselves, the real work began during the very strict covid lockdown here in Spain that dictated we stay in our homes for three long months. It can be said therefore that our forced confinement was responsible for the completion of *Meet Me at Elbow Beach*; although there was also the encouragement from my old Bermuda pals and the constant nagging from my very good friend Douglas Dewar, who features large in this book.

Anything to get him off my back!

I want to emphasise that although written out of necessity through my own eyes and experiences, it is primarily a story of others who were part of my life and the daily events, during those far-off days in the early seventies. And of course Bermuda itself, which merits pride of place here, and perhaps will serve as an introduction to those who have never had the good fortune to explore those wonderful islands for themselves.

Thank you for purchasing, borrowing, or purloining this book, and I hope it will raise a smile or two if you did not personally experience those most wonderful years; and happy memories revived if you were fortunate enough to be there.

CB

ONE

As my brain slowly surfaced to consciousness and the cerebral gears began to mesh, the first sensation I became aware of was the absence of cotton sheets and instead the gritty feel of cool sand beneath my back. I was also aware of the muted light that signalled night becoming day, with the sun's stunted glow indicating the impending dawn and the earliness of the hour, and I cleverly deduced that I was not at home in my bed.

A cool breeze played across my body, gently ruffling my hair and causing soft rustling in some nearby bay grape and palmetto palm, and the delicate but distinct perfumes of sub-tropical flowers and shrubs gently carried in the clear Bermuda air. I raised my slowly awakening body on one elbow and before me were the familiar features of the secluded Church Bay, the small beach where I had spent my first Sunday having newly arrived on the island of Bermuda two months earlier, and was obviously where I had just spent the night. The glass-like sea close by shone like a polished gem, and the tiny wavelets shushed and sighed as they gently lapped the pink flecked coral sand.

A solitary juvenile cloud seemed to be searching for its parents in an otherwise unbroken and suffused gilded sky before dispersing as if by magic, and a lone petrel swooped dramatically low over the water before arcing gracefully away and disappearing inland. It was the coolness of the hour that had stirred me and as I surveyed the scene, gingerly rubbing the patina of sleep from my eyes with my free hand, I absently registered the sound of a dog barking somewhere close by.

Squinting, I took in the golden orb of the waking sun, poised on the far edge of the ocean as if undecided whether to bother making the journey west, and having experienced the Bermuda dawn after a recent all-night party, it was not an unfamiliar sight. But in those few seconds I absorbed it all and reminded myself, not for the first time how blessed I was to have all of this in my life – goose bumps notwithstanding. I felt content and poetic, a poor man's William Wordsworth… minus the daffodils.

It was perfection.

Except for one teensy detail… I was stark bollock naked and there was no sign of my clothes.

TWO

It took me a second or two to take in my predicament, and then in full wide-awake mode I looked around in a panic, attempting to remember why I was here and where the hell my shirt and strides were. My shoes and the rest of my kit could wait; barefooted and bare arsed were two entirely different things. Then I noticed that there was something blue right there on my chest. What was that? Writing, it was bloody writing. Oh my God, I had been tattooed. Completely forgetting my nakedness for one disquieting moment, I jumped to my feet and began rubbing at the script like a maniac and what sweet relief when my hand came away with a smudge of blue ink. It was only a felt tip or ball point pen, it really didn't matter which. It could be erased.

'Thank you, thank you, thank you,' I murmured into empty air, and I suddenly realised the absurdity of the notion that I had been tattooed while I slept… on a beach for goodness' sake. How likely was that? But what did it say? What was the message that somebody had taken the trouble to write on my chest? I craned my neck forward attempting to read what was written; whoever had scrawled the message had written it upside down. Well not upside down to them of course, but looking at it from my perspective, that's exactly what it was. It must have been a strange sight, me straining to see what had been written and twisting my head first to the right and then to the left as if this would get me a better view, and trying to creep up on it by shuffling forward at the same time. It was ludicrous. Then a voice behind me:

'Nice morning.'

What. Oh no.

'Lost something?'

I whipped round, perhaps an unfortunate phrase in view of my somewhat exposed condition, and came face to face with an attractive woman standing with hands on hips, doing her very best not to laugh out loud, and maintaining a lopsided grin due to the fact that she was biting her lip determinedly in an effort to keep control. I guessed she was a few years older than me, early-thirties perhaps, and with a pleasing figure that had all the curves in the right places. Her skin appeared smooth and flawless, and she gave an impression of confidence and sophistication that I reckoned you would only find in a lady of more mature years – not that I knew much about sophistication. All this I took in with that initial glance. It's amazing the detail that can be gleaned whilst standing naked as Adam on a secluded beach at dawn. But where had she come from and how long had she been watching me? It was embarrassing. I mean, I hadn't even brushed my hair.

Her smart white shorts and nice legs were hard to ignore, as was the pastel blue polo shirt on which I noticed an embroidered badge over the left breast: a white and gold sailing boat logo, probably representing some yacht club or other. Under normal circumstances I might have made some witty remark about it, something like: Looks like your boat is riding quite a swell, or: Do you need extra hands on your yacht? After all, I prided myself on having quite a way with my sparkling wit and repartee, even if it wasn't always appreciated by others – well, hardly *ever* if I was being honest. But wit was not something that seemed appropriate at that particular moment, because they were definitely not normal circumstances. The circumstances in fact were these: that I was standing alone on a deserted beach, or so I had thought, confronted by an attractive stranger as naked as a day-old rat (me not her unfortunately) and devoid of any means to cover myself apart from both my hands that were tightly clasped over Uncle William and the twins. This was obviously the owner of the dog I had heard earlier, and by way of confirmation, a soaking wet springer spaniel pounded past us, barking like a demented, er, well, springer spaniel I suppose, and eagerly leaped into the gentle surf chasing some, as yet unseen, object that had attracted its attention. So, I did the first thing that came to me in a sudden flash of irrationality and simply played it cool; acting as if this sort of thing was a daily event and was no big deal. Stupid I know, but I had not had time to formulate a logical plan.

'Oh hi, yes, I seem to have mislaid my clothes,' I coolly informed her, stating the bloody obvious as smoothly as my exposed situation allowed. As relaxed as I hoped this sounded, I thought it might have come across slightly more convincing if my bits had not hitherto been on full display, and so followed closely by her inquisitive eyes (which were a brilliant blue by the way), I hurriedly adjusted my hands around the exposed family group as I talked. Looking back later of course, I realised that this was a pointless and pathetic exercise, because she had already copped a really good eye-full as I was performing the tattoo waltz. I searched for some plausible excuse why I would be on the beach at this hour without a stitch of clothing, but all that came out was: 'Look, can you read this for me?' indicating with my chin the message that had been the cause of my bizarre sand dance. I was hoping that there might be a clue here as to the whereabouts of my missing clothing. There was the briefest of pauses during which I assumed she was searching for some smart answers that would have been calculated to add to my embarrassment, but obviously finding none that were fitting or even necessary, she donned a snazzy pair of specs that had been hanging on a silver chain around her neck, and tentatively approached me to study the message emblazoned on what passed for my manly chest.

At this precise moment, the spaniel rushed up wagging his tail furiously, and proudly presented the object that had been the centre of his attention in the surf. When I say presented, a more precise description would be that the bedraggled hound shoved it up my rear end forcibly and I nearly took off when I felt the cold and very wet nose prodding where no spaniel had been before. A Labrador or two yes, but definitely no spaniel... I would have remembered. One moment I could quite happily have deprived him of future parenthood on the spot had two rocks been handy, the next I felt like giving him doggie hugs and kisses because what he had brought was the bottom half of a bikini – a bright emerald-green bottom half of a bikini – and one that had obviously belonged to a lady of a larger persuasion if you get my drift.

'Good boy,' I enthused, as I gently teased the item of swimwear away from his jaws with one hand and gratefully swapped grips to hold the garment against my overexposed parts. Any port in a storm I thought as I turned my back on my unwelcome spectator and forced myself into the garment, back to front as it happened because the rear panel was of a larger dimension. And ever mindful of the exploratory nature of the spaniel's nose and the possibility that it might lock on to other more tender parts of my anatomy, I thought this to be a wise move. I knew it was farcical, but this piece of fabric had the effect of restoring my confidence slightly, and with the crown jewels once more locked safely away– more or less – I suddenly felt ready to again face the new lady in my life, even though emerald-green is not really my shade if I am being totally honest.

'Sweet dreams, blondie, call me... and *he* is a bitch,' yacht-club woman informed me, over emphasising the word 'he'.

'What?'

'It's a bit smudged but I think that's what it says,' she went on, edging a bit closer in order to confirm her translation. 'The message says "sweet dreams, blondie, call me",' she repeated. 'And my dog is not a good boy, she is a good bitch.'

I was tempted to suggest that perhaps it was a match made in heaven, but instead just mumbled: 'Oh right, that will have been Esther.'

'Her name is Roxy.'

I sighed. 'Nice name for a dog. No, Esther… the girl I was with last night,' I patiently informed her.

'Ah the message,' she smirked. 'If you say so, it isn't signed.'

This woman was beginning to annoy me.

'No,' I started to explain. 'Esther, she's the…' but then thought better of it. 'Look, I don't suppose you have seen a shirt and slacks lying around, have you?'

'Nope,' she said, and then nodded in the direction of the area further up the beach. 'But I think he has.'

I hadn't seen him in my haste to locate my clothes, but there he was, Richard, my erstwhile party companion, sitting on a large rock at one end of the beach holding my strides aloft with one hand, and with the other, waving a stick on which was tied my underpants like some outlandish pirate flag. Classy as always, but an action that I felt was somewhat tasteless given the circumstances. He was sporting a big grin and obviously enjoying the whole spectacle enormously.

'I take it that's not Esther then,' Mrs Yacht Club quipped. Then chuckling she turned and called her dog, who was now woofing up a storm at something else she had found in the shallows further along the beach. Hopefully an unexploded World War II mine, I thought darkly. The bikini bottom – and my own – were obviously now thankfully long forgotten by the hound, but then as a parting gift, my polo shirted friend shouted over her shoulder: 'You have a nice day now,' and with a wave she moved on, closely followed by the excitable Roxy.

I had no idea how long Richard had been watching all this, or how long he had been sitting there in total, and I didn't care, he had my clothes. My visions of having to flag down a passing car, or worse still a Mobylette, began to rapidly fade at the welcome sight of my friend. The thought of being labelled Bermuda's nude hitchhiker was bad enough, but having to endure 50cc's of throbbing Moby between my legs the whole trip home was too much to contemplate, and the possibility of making the front page of *The Royal Gazette* with pictures, was just *too much* to envisage.

'I thought you were never going to wake up,' Richard told me as I trotted up the beach towards him. 'I was just getting ready to come down and give you a kick when I saw your friend and her dog.'

'She's not my friend,' I corrected him.

'No, but I bet she'll remember you from now on; you seemed to have had her close attention,' he laughed, holding out my gear and straining forwards to read what was written on my torso.

'I see the lovely what's her name left you a note too. That's cool.'

'Stop taking the piss,' I muttered, 'and give me those. Oh, and as a matter of interest, how come you've got my stuff in the first place?'

He presented me with a mock frown of concern: 'Didn't want your nice new threads to get mussed up, you only bought them from me last week.'

Richard, it should be explained, was the manager of the family's men's clothing store Gentleman's Quarter, a smart men's boutique, and one of two in Hamilton, and from where I had purchased quite a few items since meeting him. He was lean and fit looking, with a mop of professionally cropped hair that he wore as a shortened version of an afro, and fashionable sideburns. And as you would expect from a men's boutique manager, always rigged out in the latest gear.

'So I thought I'd take care of them for you. Your shoes are in the car,' he went on.

'Oh man, why didn't you wake me?' I wanted to know.

'Are you kidding, man? That would have been too easy; I wanted to see your reaction when you opened your eyes. Then the dog lady showed up and I thought I'd wait around for the show. It was great. I only wish I had a camera with me.'

'Bastard,' I muttered. Then after the briefest of pauses, we both broke into hysterical laughter at the whole farcical episode. We both knew that I would have done the same thing if our positions had been reversed – then I had a sudden thought.

'She was the only one, wasn't she?' I asked. 'The woman I mean. Nobody else saw me on display, did they?'

Richard put a finger to his lips, looked skyward adopting a thoughtful pose, and after a second or two of mock concentration said: 'Nah, no one else… not counting the bus load of Japanese tourists.'

'Yeah right, very funny.'

'I would hate to meet the chick who owns those,' Richard chortled as I hastily discarded the outsize bikini bottom and screwed it up ready for disposal at the first litter bin to come along. I quickly slipped into my own clothes, ran both hands through my tangled hair and asked: 'So you haven't been home?'

'Nope. I wasn't getting anywhere with what's her name's friend, so I took her home and came back here to get you.'

'That's nice,' I told him, trying to sound sincere.

'Yeah well, I knew you couldn't get home without me and I wanted to check on your progress with… what was she called?'

'Esther,' I reminded him. 'Esther Chan.'

I had met Esther at a previous party, and I was pleased to see that she had attended the shindig the previous evening, and we had hit it off… obviously. She was born in England to an English mother and Singaporean father she had told me, and was far and away the most exotic girlfriend I had known. She was also only in Bermuda for a few weeks, en route to her next destination in her quest to travel the world, and would be leaving the island in the near future. Daddy must be worth a few bob, I remember thinking.

'Esther. Right,' Richard nodded.

I froze. 'You weren't bloody watching us, were you?' There must have been a note of panic in my voice. I mean, who wants to have his performance checked out, close mate or not.

'No, you were out cold on the beach and umm, what was her name again?'

'*Es-ter,*' I repeated, carefully enunciating the name.

'Yeah, Esther, she was just leaving. She left her bike parked up there if you remember,' and he gestured towards the road.

I did remember. It was all coming back to me.

'Did she say anything?' I asked as we made our way up the sloping pathway near to where Richard had been sitting, and which ascended to South Road above – leaving Mrs Yacht Club and Roxy examining something else they had discovered on the beach.

'Not really. Just asked if I had a pen she could borrow.'

We reached the road and after a quick glance in the car's wing mirror to make sure I wasn't too much of a disaster, which turned out to be a less than reassuring exercise, I clambered into the car beside him and a belated thought hit me.

'You gave her a pen? So she could scribble all over me?' I protested. 'How did you know she wasn't going to mutilate me with it, or write something, you know – somewhere else?'

Another big grin broke out on Richard's face. 'I didn't and anyways, there wouldn't have been room anywhere else,' and he slapped the steering wheel, breaking into more laughter.

'Bastard.' A repeat – but then so was the follow-up laughter as I shared the joke with my friend.

When we had composed ourselves, Richard made a smacking noise with his lips and announced, 'It's getting on for seven; somewhere for breakfast I think.'

'I'm up for that,' I agreed, smacking my own chops in response. I suddenly realised I was famished. 'Then I can get this crap off my chest too.'

'Good party wasn't it,' Richard grinned as he put on the specs he often wore.

'Must have been,' although to be honest only a sketchy trailer of the events of the night before was tumbling haphazardly through my still semi-functioning brain.

The windows of the tan coloured Austin 1100 were down and I breathed in that exceptional Bermuda air as we drove along South Road. There was a change in its perfumed quality, which I had learned, came from the flowers of the Sago Palm. It was said that sailors were able to smell the plant way out to sea even before they caught sight of land. We travelled sedately north-east along the South Shore, Richard strictly observing the 20mph speed limit that was the norm for the island, with the exception of certain marked built-up areas, where it was a mere 15mph. But there was no hurry; it was Saturday morning, almost no traffic at such an early hour, and the weekend stretched tantalisingly ahead of us – besides, the Paraquet restaurant did not open its doors until 8am. Perhaps Richard knew of somewhere else, I mused. Then I suddenly had another thought.

'We've got plenty of time,' I said. 'Pull in. Just up there ahead.' We had passed the entrance to the Bermuda Regiment's barracks and I had a sudden spur of the moment impulse. Impetuous was my middle name.

'What's the problem?' My startled friend asked.

'No problem. Just give me a few minutes please, the restaurant won't be open for a while.'

He pulled the vehicle into the side of the road where I had more or less indicated, his expression of puzzlement turning into one of resignation as I climbed out of the car. I could almost hear an audible clink as the penny dropped. I had done this before you see, and from this particular vantage point there was a breathtaking view of the shoreline through to Horseshoe Bay Beach, Warwick Long Bay and beyond where I knew from my limited experience, lay Elbow Beach and other tasty morsels of pink sand paradise. To the right were the sparkling waters of the Atlantic Ocean and just as I had reacted that very first day when the aircraft I was travelling in circled the island, I once more marvelled at the variety of stunning shades of blue and green that were displayed in the shallow waters surrounding these idyllic islands. From ultramarine through violet to turquoise, it would be a spectacular sight as the sun steadily rose to mark a new day, and I knew from my days already spent at the beach that these waters were the home of equally spectacular marine life. The following day, when we would be making our way to Horseshoe Bay for an afternoon of fooling around, swimming, and generally cooling out; in short not having to give a thought about work or the rest of the world, there might, with any luck, also be plenty of attractive females in evidence.

I will not take you for granted, I will not take you for granted, was the familiar mantra that I often murmured to myself and ran on repeat-play through my brain like one of those eight track recordings that Richard played in the car. My work contract was for two years, and I had no idea what the future held for me after that, but I had assumed Bermuda would not be my permanent home, and I was determined therefore to enjoy its delights every single minute of every day that I was there.

'Bermuda,' I whispered to myself, 'you are beautiful.' And I meant it.

Richard had been watching me patiently, arm casually draped out of the open car window, but then having finished the cigarette he had lit up anticipating my few minutes of reflective contemplation, he decided that I had been given more than enough time for my little ritual.

'Come on you love struck son of a bitch,' he shouted to me. 'We'll cruise down to Elbow and kill some time there – maybe even get breakfast if we are lucky. I need coffee badly.' And I needed a very large mug of strong tea, which had always been my preferred wake-me-up to get the day kick started. I took a last look at the marvellous vista before me, and gave a deep satisfying sigh before ambling back to the car.

As we resumed our leisurely progress along South Road, I reflected again on my luck and how it had all started. Not with the job interview I had attended in the industrial town of Slough in England six months before, or even the job advertisement I had seen for a roofing specialist in the *Construction News* a month before that in the pretty little fishing village that had been my adopted home in Cornwall. No, it had really all started in Mr Fry's third-year class at Whitley Park Primary School in my home town of Reading way back in 1956.

THREE

Whitley Park School was one of four primary schools on the sprawling council estate where I was brought up as an only child and lived with my parents. It was a typical Victorian structure divided into infant and junior sections, each half a mirror image of the other and divided down the middle of the central playground area with a solid fence. On the juniors' side was a flagpole that saw use on days celebrating the Monarch's coronation and birthday, Empire Day, and of course on those sombre occasions when the flag, at half-mast, had signified the death of somebody notable – usually a person we little-ones knew nothing about.

The whole school formed a perfect quadrangle except for a low wall topped by a wrought iron railing at the entrance end and fronting each playground. Adjacent to these either side were the staff rooms which in turn adjoined the offices of each of the two heads of school – the formidable Miss Laskey in the Infants and the bespectacled Mr Luxton in the Juniors. The other three sides comprised an unbroken covered walkway, or cloister, that completed the enclosure for the playgrounds and off which were situated the classrooms. At the back end of the complex, detached and standing slightly apart to left and right, were the two school assembly halls, again both protected and accessed by off-shoots of the covered walkway.

Looking back on it, it was a very practical set-up. You could walk from the entrance of either section and traverse the squared 'U' shaped structure right the way through to the entrance of the adjacent school, completely protected from the elements and with total access to all classrooms and the two school halls. Talking to the few ex-pupils who are still breathing and through the miracle of the internet I have reconnected with over the years, they seem amazed that I can remember any of the teacher's names after so many decades (most of those ex-classmates couldn't even remember my name). But for some strange reason, I can remember every one of the teachers from the Junior School: the Scottish Mr Burns, the games teacher, who sported red hair and a beard; the rotund spinster Miss Smith who provided the morning tinkling of the ivories at assembly and who wobbled to school on her ancient bicycle; Mr Capel; Mrs Durbridge with the legendary hair; Mr Croaker; the fiery Welsh dragon Miss Jones, and the rest. I can visualise them all as clear as day. I can even remember all of my classmates – but hey, don't rush off, I don't intend putting you through the tedium of that.

Stay with me…

I am not usually revered as someone who has a particularly good memory, but for some weird and inexplicable reason I can instantly bring to mind all the irrelevant, useless and boring facts from my distant past. Ask me anything of importance that might have a crucial bearing on current life, improving my financial prospects or my opinion on the changing climate, and mostly all you will get back from me is a gormless, open-mouthed stare with the suggestion of drool about to leak onto my chin, and holding out my glass for a refill.

During my time at Whitley Park Infants, I had begun to experience the joy of reading and the exploration of the wonderful world of books. Most kids in those days were introduced to the children's classics early on in life. Books such as *The Water Babies*; *Black Beauty*; *Treasure Island*; *The Wind in the Willows* and the Famous Five and Secret Seven books by Enid Blyton to name but a few. Usually this was during the early years at junior school, but looking back and thanks to my dad,

I developed my bookish interest earlier than most whilst I was still in the infants' section. My father would regularly read to me from the time I was a toddler, with me sitting on his lap or next to him on the sofa, so that I could follow everything on the page closely as he traced the sentences with his finger. These are some of my earliest memories and thus I learned to read and master relatively complicated stories at a very young age. I was also taught how to use my dad's dictionary so that when an unfamiliar word cropped up, I could look it up for myself and add to my vocabulary and spelling prowess. It was a ponderous volume as dictionaries tend to be, and I was so small at the time, it was all I could do to lift it down from the shelf without doing myself a mischief. On the debit side my maths was, and always has been, total crap.

Books were given to me by my parents and various aunts and uncles on my birthdays and at Christmas. I devoured them. Most of the usual classics were disposed of early on and at age nine, on my birthday, I was given a copy of *Nicholas Nickleby*, and a love affair with the works of Charles Dickens began. When I think back, it amazes me how, not only could I have enjoyed the book at such a young age, but how I was able to understand and get to grips with the Victorian vernacular and the sometimes-complicated language and moral lessons that the stories contained. But I did, and I was soon asking for more of the same.

So what has any of this got to do with finding myself in Bermuda many years later? Well, so far very little except that, at the same time I was reading about the heroics of Mr Nickleby in the face of the sadistic and bullying headmaster Wackford Squeers, I was given another lesser known children's classic that had somehow, up until then, escaped my attention. The book was *The Coral Island* by R.M. Ballantine. Our third-year teacher at that time was a certain Mr Fry, and I can picture him now. Although all teachers appear ancient to a nine-year-old, Mr Fry, with the power of hindsight, was probably no more than thirty. He was tall and lean, with an exceptionally long neck and a protruding Adam's apple that you were compelled to watch as it shot up and down as he spoke. He always wore a light grey suit, I remember, and of course as with all male teachers then, the obligatory collar and tie. He also took games on occasion and he was a strange sight in his football boots with striped football socks over his suit trousers; shirt sleeves rolled up and still sporting his tie that was now tucked into his shirt between the second and third buttons.

But it was actually our previous year's teacher, the totally bald and moustachioed Mr Sellers, who actively encouraged me in my reading and to even write stories of my own. He was something of a comedian and all the kids loved him. I was as pleased as punch when he held up a story that I had written one day in class and declared that he enjoyed it so much, he had taken it to bed with him. I glowed with pride. It was about a little Mexican boy who had managed to stay on a donkey that nobody else was able to ride. The method he used was to put glue on the saddle, making it impossible for the mule to throw him off; not what you would call an elaborate plot. But what neither Mr Sellers nor the rest of my classmates knew, was that I got the idea from a story in one of my Christmas annuals and with a bit of tweaking presented it as my own. Luckily nobody else seemed to have seen the original and I got away with my first and only attempt at plagiarism.

But getting back to Mr Fry (be patient, I'm getting there)…

The Coral Island had been a present from one of my aunts, and was given to me during Mr Fry's time in my third junior year. It was under his tutelage therefore that I had discovered *The Coral Island* and so I have come to always associate him and my time in his class with the book.

The significance of *The Coral Island* was the central theme that revolved around three young friends – all cabin boys on HMS *Arrow* – who had been shipwrecked on a Pacific coral island. They had been the only survivors, and the story describes their exploits in the struggle to survive in that tropical paradise. The vivid description of the island with its pristine beaches and other wonders, interwoven with the many adventures of discovery by Ralph, Jack and Peterkin, the three fictional friends, entranced me so much that it became my dream that one day I would live in, or at the very least, visit such a place. This was a dream that I maintained into my teens and early adulthood to such an extent that I had at one point written to the consulates and embassies of many of the islands in the Caribbean, requesting information and things like trade directories and local newspapers and any other useful information that was to hand. But with no formal qualifications, I didn't quite know how to take things further and it remained just a very appealing dream. It was the South Pacific islands that had been featured in that kid's book, but with a world atlas being a treasured item in my book collection, I could see that the Caribbean islands were a lot closer.

Then out of the blue some years later, an advertisement in the *Construction News* and the dream became a reality that manifested itself the day that my plane landed at Kindley Field, situated in St George's parish on the mini archipelago called Bermuda. Perhaps not the tropical south sea coral island I had read about as a boy, and not even located in the Caribbean as most people imagined, but in splendid isolation in the north Atlantic, actually sitting almost one thousand miles from the northernmost islands of the Bahamas, and six hundred and fifty miles from the nearest US landfall of Cape Hatteras, North Carolina. No, this was better, much better as it turned out; moreover, there were not as many cannibals in Bermuda – just a few man eaters that hung out in the Hamilton pubs and bars.

It was a sub-tropical paradise nonetheless and one that was to provide me with the most joyful, eventful, and memorable years of my life. It also gave me something much more precious: my wife and soul partner, and firm life-long friends who, in spite of their subsequent chosen places of residence in various far-flung places in the world (the selfish bastards), have been as close to me as family and have always been there should the need arise.

FOUR

It had been a difficult and strange few years prior to my arrival in Bermuda; a roller coaster of a time in fact in a very real sense, with my life being yanked in several different directions within a relatively short time.

I was married on Christmas Eve, 1966. I was twenty years old and my wife eighteen, and it was arctic cold in the church where we took our vows. Everyone told me it wouldn't last, but what did they know? We went months with not so much as a cross word… I rarely had the chance to use any of mine. But after a year, I found myself the proud and puffed-up father of a gorgeous baby girl, Emily Joy. Now everything looked rosy, and my vision of the future included at the forefront, a golden-haired daughter sitting on my knee, and with the picture of my own childhood in vivid colour forever lodged in my mind, I could see myself reading Emily stories, tracing the words with my finger and passing on my love of books and the written word at an early age, just as my dad had done with me.

But it wasn't to last, as barely six months after my daughter was born and completely out of the blue, my wife announced she was leaving, having met a bloke more to her taste, in her sister's public house – the Boar's Head in Reading – where she worked part time. In one fell swoop, my marriage was terminated and I lost my wife and daughter. The only word I could find to describe my feelings and state of mind at that moment was panic. Sheer blind bloody panic. Any plans for the future were obliterated; my dream of sitting my little girl on my knee, reading stories to her, evaporated. There was no plan B, and each day brought on deeper and deeper feelings of anxiety and the fear of an unknown future. I was in a dark place and had no idea what to do. A solicitor I had hurriedly consulted, had sympathised with me, but explained that only under exceptional circumstances would the child be placed in the care of the father. Those circumstances were: where criminal activities could be proved, or when the child was seen to be at risk.

Then a chance meeting with Ray Lawrence – the brother of an acquaintance – and through him a guy called Jim Anderson, meant that my life began to slowly transform into a new and more agreeable phase. Those two guys were life savers and I hope I have managed to convey that fact to them over the intervening years and let them know how important they were at that point in my life.

Having met my wife when I was just seventeen, with just one girlfriend under my belt (so to speak) up to that point, I was pathetically inexperienced in the romance stakes, and not having the advantage of film star looks – with the possible exception of a few Disney characters – I was a very late developer. But with a growing confidence helped along by my newfound friends, I quickly got the hang of things; after all, our teenage years are supposed to be the formative years with regard to dating and learning the ropes in respect of the opposite sex, and for me there had been a huge hole in my education. So once the jagged wounds of loss and betrayal had begun to soften at the edges, I made up my mind to make up for lost time and try to put the lack of experience behind me. But I confess, there were a few setbacks on the way.

After a year of doing the rounds, I met a lovely young nurse by the name of Stephanie – Stevie to her friends – who was in the final phase of her training before qualifying as an SRN, and things took on a totally new look, because I soon realised that this was a very special young woman.

But there was a major problem.

Me.

I was still playing catch-up with my love life, and enjoying it, but I did not want to lose this lady. We talked openly about it and although she was prepared to commit totally to us, including taking on Emily, she understood that I still had time to make up for, and although it was not carved in stone, there was an understanding that I would get things out of my system and we would take things as they came. It could be looked upon as having my cake and eating it I guess, although I now realise that there was also an element of extreme caution on my part, having recently had one very bad and damaging experience. But it was a practical agreement and made sense in a strange kind of way. Looking back, I feel humble and yet saddened by Stevie's generous attitude, particularly in view of what came later.

The following three years are far too involved to record here, particularly with regard to my daughter, but that is another long and bitter story. Suffice it to say things had taken a turn for the worse and I needed to escape from the grip of my home town and the still painful memories.

In 1971 I decided to move to Cornwall, a place I had never visited, but had been totally enamoured with when I saw a photograph of the village of Polperro. It was a calendar picture for August that was hanging on the wall of my local chippie and had caught my eye one evening as I queued up trying to decide on whether to have a nice piece of haddock or a couple of battered pork sausages with my chips. I fell in love with Polperro immediately and I decided there and then that was where I wanted to live, and a month or so later I stepped off the train in that lovely county. Not Polperro at that point it has to be said, but Penryn, the only place I had been able to find work within the roofing trade. Nevertheless, it was Cornwall, a county that was new to me, and it had given me a foot on the ladder that would eventually lead me to that prettiest of all pretty Cornish fishing villages.

This meant of course that the meetings between Stevie and myself were seriously curtailed, but we had agreed that given time for me to become established, and her wanting to put in a full twelve months with the nursing agency where she then worked having left the NHS, Stevie would join me later. I had not fully exorcised my wanderlust, but all things considered I told myself that enough was enough, and that perhaps it was time to finally settle down again. I felt I could not afford to lose such a loyal and generous individual as Stevie.

Six months later, having left Penryn, and via the delights of a five-month winter sojourn in the attractive harbour town of Looe, I found myself finally ensconced in my dream village, and after a suitable time to secure a furnished ex-holiday flat and find a job (dead easy in a place like Polperro where seasonal staff to cater for the summer tourist hordes are desperately needed) Stevie joined me.

Then one morning not even a month after her arrival, she discovered a pea sized lump in her neck, which followed the development of a vicious cough. She immediately took herself off to the village doctor and was later diagnosed with Hodgkin's lymphoma. Because time is of the essence in treating this disease, she transferred at her request, from Freedom Fields Hospital in Plymouth where the diagnosis had been made, to our home town of Reading, and from Reading to a specialist unit in St Bartholomew's Hospital, London. All of this over a frantic three-day period. As it happened this coincided with my applying for and securing the job in Bermuda that I had seen advertised in the *Construction News*, a publication I took regularly in order to keep abreast of what was going down in my neck of the woods and with a view to pursuing any roofing work that might be in the offing. The cruel irony was, that in the short time between my being told I had been selected for the position in Bermuda and Stevie's illness, she had made enquiries with the Bermuda Hospital Board, and was informed that State Registered Nurses were always required and that should she wish to apply, there was an excellent chance that she would be accepted.

The upshot of these life changing events was that I had quickly decided to contact my would-be employer in Bermuda, explain the situation and why I could no longer take up the position. It was the only decision to make. But Stevie was adamant that I should not do this and asked that I delay making the call at least until I visited her again in St Bart's, to which I reluctantly agreed. Then just after I arrived at the hospital two days later as I was about to enter Stevie's ward, the nursing sister intercepted me and told me that the consultant, a brilliant man, Professor Gordon Hamilton Fairley, would like to have a word with me. It shook me rigid of course. What the heck was he going to tell me?

I need not have worried because he explained that having been informed by Stevie of my situation with regard to the job offer in Bermuda, she had requested that I be briefed on the Hodgkin's and to give me his professional opinion. He assured me that what I did was entirely my own business and he was by no means attempting to influence my decision one way or the other, but he agreed with Stevie, that it was only fair I should be told what the prognosis for the disease was.

The initial radiotherapy and subsequent punishing chemotherapy had been very successful and based on her age and otherwise good health, plus his first-hand experience from past cases where there was a high long-term success rate, his feelings were that given time – in fairness, he emphasised, probably a year – there was no reason why Stevie could not eventually join me and take up a nursing job in Bermuda should I change my mind and continue as originally planned.

And so the decision was made for me.

FIVE

Another new year had been seen in and promised to be an exciting one, as I found myself on the way to the paradise islands of Bermuda; thirty-five thousand feet over the Atlantic, on my longest ever flight, in surely the noisiest plane in existence – a Vickers VC10. My excitement was as fresh as the day I first received my clearance from the Bermuda Immigration Service two months earlier in the chocolate box village where I lived – Polperro in glorious Cornwall. But there was a certain amount of trepidation too. The memory of my girlfriend Stevie and I saying a tearful and reluctant goodbye at the airport just hours before was still fresh in my mind, and had me yet again questioning my decision to accept the job. It was a two-year contract in what was, I reminded myself, a foreign land and I had absolutely no idea what to expect. But hey, it was Bermuda and the very name was enough to send tingles down any man's spine and get his M&S boxers rippling.

The one large cloud that had appeared on the horizon just after accepting the job, was the devastating diagnosis that Stevie had received after being taken ill in Cornwall.

With the prospect of my new job relegated to a remote area of my brain, and having looked forward in anticipation to Stevie joining me later in the year to take up a nursing position at Bermuda's King Edward VII memorial hospital, I turned my immediate thoughts to visions of talcum powder beaches, warm waters, and sun-soaked days ahead.

There was a daily BOAC service to Bermuda and the route taken was Bermuda-Bahamas-Florida-Mexico, terminating in what was then regarded as the millionaires' playground of Acapulco. I occupied an aisle seat immediately behind the bulkhead separating first class from economy, and my two travelling companions in the adjacent seats were, it transpired, a Harley Street doctor and his wife on their way to the up-market Mexican resort for their annual four-week break. How the other half live, I mused. I was also puzzled why they had not booked themselves into first class and were content to mix it with the hoi poloi, but they seemed to be a very nice down to earth couple and we struck up a conversation early into the flight. We got talking about this and that, but whenever the conversation slackened off, and deferring to their obvious pedigree, I refrained from taking out the copy of *Playboy* magazine I had bought at the airport terminal. Instead, I settled down to attempt to plough through the more cerebral *Daily Telegraph* that I had purchased at the same time, and I thought was in keeping with my new international traveller status. Then having pretended for fifteen minutes to knock off the crossword as a routine task, I gave it up as a bad job when I realised that I was not even able to understand the darned questions. They might as well have been written in Swahili, so I sat back and instead thought I would catch up with events in the sporting arenas and update myself on world affairs, but found myself reflecting back on my time in Polperro and a strangely prophetic message I had received whilst there.

In fact it was as a result of a visit to a fortune teller, which started out as a bit of a laugh, I mean, who takes them seriously? Although I gave it no credence at the time, I was told, along with the usual stuff that could apply to just about anybody, that within a year I would be living on an island. Bermuda was still several months in the future, and it was only after I had been accepted for the job that the incident came back to me. Perhaps the lady had just got lucky with her prediction – although she was most emphatic – but it made me wonder, because there I was jetting towards my new island home.

Those were the days before in-flight movies, iPads and Kindles, and you had to make do with whatever reading matter you could pick up from W.H. Smith at London Airport – which was how it was referred to before the place became known as Heathrow. World affairs to me at that time you have to understand, were way down on my list of priorities. Visits to see my young daughter; evenings spent with Stevie at her home in Goring-on-Thames, and Saturday nights in Southampton at Tiffany's-on-the-Pier, or that Reading hotspot the Thingamajig Club, with the boys, were far more important. Then in Cornwall, busily working ten-hour shifts at a restaurant and partying with the rest of the seasonal workers and local inhabitants most evenings.

Drinks on board had been served by the pristinely uniformed female cabin crew, or stewardesses as they were then called, and I was feeling mellow and suitably content with life as the BOAC staff began to serve lunch. Here I was, a long-haul traveller on my way to Bermuda of all places; moreover, I was in the company of some seriously well-off people, even though they obviously preferred to save their hard-earned cash and travel economy. They appeared to be genuinely interested in me and my new job and admitted that they themselves had never visited Bermuda, which left me feeling smug and quite superior. Then without warning, just as one of the very attractive stewardesses was attending the passengers across the aisle, that delectable young thing with the face of an angel, softly but audibly broke wind.

My mouth dropped open in utter disbelief, but like a true professional she carried on as if nothing had happened and it was obvious that those she was serving were completely oblivious to her delicate almost genteel fart, thanks to the fact she was facing them. Unfortunately her business end had been pointing immediately in my direction, and due to my having been allocated the aisle seat, a bit too close for comfort. I looked round to see if my fellow travellers had noticed, and observed that Dr and Mrs Harley Street were eyeing me with extreme distaste. It took a few seconds for the penny to drop and for me to realise what was going through their minds. My God, they thought it was me! And as if to reinforce their belief, I made the mistake of emitting a nervous girly giggle, raised my eyebrows and nodded my head in the direction of the culprit as if to say: *Did you hear that?* Well, they had, but obviously interpreted the eyebrow manoeuvre as a: *Whoops, sorry about that*, admission, because they were glaring at me with open disgust and accusing eyes.

Having finished her duties with the adjacent passengers, the young angel in question then turned to us and with a sweet smile began to serve the meals. My eyes locked on to hers desperately and they pleaded: *Say something*, while her own merely smiled sweetly back: *Not on your life matey*, with those of my two fellow passengers drilling into the side of my head accusingly as if to say: *You dirty sod.*

Angel face had left me to take the rap.

To attempt to deny it would have been a case of: *The bounder doth protest too much, methinks*, to misquote the Bard, and would only have reinforced their belief that it was me who had let rip. Then in addition to being the BOAC phantom farter, I would also be labelled a cad by my well-heeled travelling companions. I couldn't win.

To hell with it I thought; that had killed the friendly atmosphere stone dead along with any prospect of future conversation, so after a silent lunch and with nothing left to lose, I discarded the poncy *Daily Telegraph* and whipped out my *Playboy* magazine, immersing myself in the very interesting articles therein. And very revealing they were.

One of my most treasured memories is the first view of Bermuda from the window of the VC10 as it circled the islands preparing to land at Kindley Field, the airport that shared its runway and air traffic control amenities with the resident American naval base. It was a gloriously clear and sunny day, strikingly different to the appalling January weather I had left behind in London. For at least seven of the eight hours' flying time from London to Bermuda, and having cleared Land's End and the Isles of Scilly, the view from the cabin windows had been of the featureless wastes of the Atlantic Ocean stretching as far as the eye could see in all directions nearly seven miles below. Then as my ears started to pop and my hearing became strained – as did my internal organs – our aircraft began to rapidly lose altitude with the announcement from the pilot that we were approaching the beautiful island of Bermuda.

Bermuda, a British overseas possession, is tiny, a mere twenty-one square miles in area, and not one single island as many people assume, but a pygmy archipelago of over 130 islands and islets with the seven main islands linked by causeways and bridges. Nevertheless, the place is usually referred to in the singular, even by the inhabitants.

Then as the VC10 swung in a graceful turn and the starboard wing dipped, the spectacular view below was revealed. The whole of the Bermuda island chain shaped like a reclining, elongated letter 'J' was laid out beneath us and it is a sight I shall never forget. To say it took my breath away is a well-worn cliché, but there was a sharp intake of breath from me for sure when this marvellous vista came into view.

The lush verdant sub-tropical landscape with its many shades of green flora, interspersed with patches of vivid colour, showcased the white roofed buildings that seemed to sparkle in the January sun. And the twinkle of a myriad blue sapphires denoting swimming pools in the grounds of domestic properties and larger structures, that were probably hotels, accentuated Bermuda's affluence. On the long south -eastern edge was an extended ribbon of sand that made up the famous pink beaches I had heard so much about, but from that height seemed to have a golden glow about them. Like a magnificent brooch set into a liquid gown of many shades of blue – from pale turquoise through azure and cobalt to a rich indigo – this was to be my home for the foreseeable future.

As the aircraft stabilised to gain distance in order to approach the airport at the north east end of the island chain, Bermuda was temporarily lost from view. Then minutes later and losing altitude swiftly we swooped low over the sea where small boats criss-crossed leaving creamy trails in their wake and suddenly from nowhere, just as it appeared we were descending into the ocean itself, the land appeared and we touched down on the finger of reclaimed land that was the runway at Bermuda's airport.

I had arrived.

SIX

As we taxied to a halt some way out from the terminal building, those of us who were disembarking collected our bags from the overhead lockers, and prepared to leave the plane. My erstwhile travelling companions, Dr and Mrs Harley Street, seemed to have forgiven me for the misappropriated fart, wished me well in my new life, and having returned the good wishes for a pleasant holiday in Acapulco, I made my way to the open door of the aircraft with the other passengers whose journey also ended there. Had I been able to summon it, I would have loved to let go with a rip snorter by way of farewell, to show Doctor and missus Harley Street – and the guilty hostess – just what gold medal flatulence sounded like. But that would have been childish and was just a fanciful thought. Still...

As I stepped out of the aircraft, the unfamiliar sunshine and humidity enveloped me like a warm moist blanket. It was still January but the temperature outside was nudging seventy the pilot had earlier informed us, and having left a miserable and debilitating icy cold, wet London just a few hours before, it felt tropically warm to my pale and sun starved body as I walked across the tarmac squinting into the Bermuda sky.

There were no more than fifty of us that had deplaned, the remaining passengers on the VC10 now joined by others from Bermuda, who would be travelling on to their Bahamas, Florida and Mexico destinations. Nevertheless there was the usual queue and long wait for the luggage to arrive as with any airport, and once having secured my own bulging suitcase and heavy package that I had been asked to bring over for my new boss from the manufacturers of the roofing system I was in Bermuda to take charge of, there was another similar queue to clear customs which was, I found, a very thorough and long winded affair. And then it hit me. I had been told the package, which weighed almost ten pounds, contained one of the special heat guns that we used in the execution of the work that was my speciality – but was it? I mean, I had not seen the thing packaged at source and I only had someone's word that's what it was. Bloody hell, it could contain a stash of coke for all I knew, and my dream job would end right there with me being carted off to the nick as a drug smuggler. At best I would be deported and at worst, get a ten to fifteen stretch for…

'What's in the package sir?'

My thoughts were abruptly terminated; I had reached the head of the line and the customs officer was querying me about my suspicious looking box.

'Um, tools… a tool… for my work,' I said, hoping that the staccato waver in my voice was not too pronounced.

'And you are in Bermuda to work?' he went on, fixing me with a steely gaze.

'Uh, yes. Yes, I am.'

'Right. Well, I am going to open the package sir; I need to confirm what the item is. Do you understand?'

'Uh, yes.' And I have no idea why, but what also came out was a pathetic guilty sounding giggle – my second one of the day since the plane took off in London. Oh God! Whoever had prepared the package knew what they were doing and it took the officer, with the help of a colleague, minutes to cut through several layers of cardboard and industrial tape to get to the contents, which spilled out onto the counter forming an elicit, glistening white mound…

…Just kidding.

The heat gun was mercifully all it contained and exactly as specified... but you should have seen your faces.

'Thank you, sir, I will leave you to repack. Anything else to declare?'

'No,' I cleared my throat for a more manly reply. 'No nothing.' A pause and another steady gaze in my direction. *Oh, please God, don't let him ask me to open my case*, I silently prayed. Not that it contained any contraband, but if I unlocked the damn thing and flipped the catches, the place would suddenly look like a Chinese laundry. It had taken me an age to cram in all my stuff.

Then happily and with much relief: 'Welcome to Bermuda,' and I was waved through with what, if you have a vivid imagination, was an approximation of a smile from the customs officer, but was, I later learned, an exuberant greeting compared to the experiences of others. Then immediately, as if it had been deliberately timed, my name was announced on the terminal's public address system and I was instructed to go to the information desk where there was a message waiting for me. *What now?* I thought. It was with some relief therefore I learned that my future boss had called to say he had been delayed, and would be another half hour or so, but if I would be so kind as to wait outside the main entrance, he would collect me in due course.

Having hastily gathered together the pieces of the wrecked package and without bothering to use one of the luggage trolleys, I struggled to the entrance with my ballooning case, shoulder bag and other odds and ends, to be met with a simply wonderful panorama.

The inviting waters of Castle Harbour stretched out before me, and on the opposite side an imposing and elegant looking building, which I later learned was an establishment bearing the same name as its location: the Castle Harbour Hotel. It was stunning and I sat on a low stone wall to catch my breath and take it all in. My feelings were mixed. I was in what appeared to be pure paradise, but at the same time it was alien to me and I was thousands of miles from England for the first time in my life. As beautiful as this place undoubtedly was, would I settle in and adapt to my new environment? What about Stevie who I had reluctantly left behind, looking so vulnerable huddled in her long winter coat as we parted company in a cold, rainy, windswept London Airport? And would I ever see my infant daughter Emily again and under what circumstances?

My tumbling thoughts were interrupted by the chirping of birds hopping around at my feet, obviously in the hope of a bit of leftover passenger food. Sparrows! Sparrows? Here? Amongst all this sub-tropical beauty the humble sparrow, and suddenly those little fellers became a bridge between what I had left behind and where I now found myself, and as crazy as it sounds when I reflect back, my mood lightened, my confidence rose and I suddenly began to feel that this could well become home.

SEVEN

My boss, who I had met just once before at my interview in the town of Slough weeks before, arrived accompanied by a young Welshman, David, who it turned out was the superintendent – as the managerial position above foreman was termed – for the painting side of the business. Although the franchise for the new roofing had been acquired by my employer's company, the business was predominantly a domestic and commercial painting operation, and that's why there was a need for someone who was familiar with the system.

With introductions over at the airport, they gave me a short tour and commentary of the surroundings on our way to my new abode which had been pre-arranged for me. We stopped off at a grocery store en route so that I could get a few provisions paid for with some of the dollars I had purchased from my bank in England – the Bermudian dollar I learned, was tied to the U.S. version and were both acceptable on the island. Then I was taken to Netherlands on Harbour Road, Paget; a large house that had been converted into a number of apartments by the owner who just happened to be an acquaintance of my boss. In order for me to compensate for the jet lag that would undoubtedly overtake me, I was told to rest, have a good night's sleep, and I would be picked up late the following morning so that I could be taken on a more comprehensive tour of the island, and receive a briefing on work contracts that I would be tackling in the near future.

But before that, I was introduced to a bright new Honda moped (all 50cc's of it), that was waiting for me in the driveway at Netherlands, resplendent in its showroom red and cream finery, also courtesy of my employer. Then an introduction to my accommodation, and a quick look around to determine that everything was to my liking before I was handed the keys to both the apartment and the Honda. With a last assurance from me that I had all I needed for the immediate future, and a reminder from them of the time to be ready the following day, I was left to it with a further *Welcome to Bermuda* from my departing hosts.

I had been up at crazy o'clock that morning in England and a cab had been ordered which took Stevie and me to the station where we caught the red-eye shuttle bus from Reading Station to the airport. She had stayed with me at my parent's house in order for us to make the journey together; Stevie had insisted that she accompany me to wave me off so to speak, even though I had my doubts. I knew that it would be a painful and tearful separation, but I understood her feelings and of course had the situation been reversed, I would have wanted the same thing. Then with the usual organised chaos at the terminal – although the airport in January 1973 was an old folks' tea-dance compared to what it was to later become – added to the near eight-hour flight, it had become a long tiring day and now that my destination had been reached, the adrenalin pump dropped to a gentle idle, and exhaustion began to kick in rapidly. At least Bermuda was four hours behind the UK, and so I would have extra time to recuperate.

I unpacked my things, leaving most of them un-hung and un-drawered until the next day; bunged my just-bought provisions in the refrigerator, quickly explored my new surroundings which gave the word *compact* a whole new meaning, and put the kettle on for a much-needed mug of tea. Waiting for it to boil, I did a quick recce of the property immediately outside my door, which amounted to a huge entrance hall and an impressive staircase to the floor above, then I returned to my brew and began to unwind into my new surroundings. There was a large 1960's radio in the room, which I appreciated as a very thoughtful touch, and found that it was already tuned to ZBM, one of the Bermuda stations. It stood on a small table along with a telephone and a note attached telling me that the phone was connected in my name, and with my new number written in large print. Brilliant, they seemed to have thought of everything.

I later remembered finishing my very welcome mug of tea, and listening to what appeared to me to be an American accented plug on the radio for some burger joint or other (I was yet to learn and recognise the distinctive Bermudian dialect) which was followed by another advertisement for a beer I had never heard of called St Pauli Girl. Then I remember very little. I was zonked and away with the fairies.

I awoke with a start. It was full dark and I scrabbled for the light switch which in my hurry earlier I had failed to locate for later reference; then having accomplished the mission with some difficulty and painfully stubbing my toe, closely followed by my knee, on a blockading piece of furniture, I saw with surprise that it was barely 6.30pm. I had slept for only two hours, but it must have been a very deep satisfying sleep because I felt surprisingly refreshed. But something had disturbed me for sure and it immediately became obvious what it was: the noise of crickets that seemed to be parked right outside my window. It wasn't an unpleasant sound in itself, but having come from less subtropical climes where there would only be the sound of the occasional dog bark or the woman next door throwing things at her husband to disturb my sleep, it was an alien sound. In fact, to say that it was a cacophony of sound would not be an exaggeration; there seemed to be a million of the things going at it full pelt.

Not until the following day did I learn that in fact the chirpings I had heard emanated not from crickets, but from tree frogs, each one no bigger than an adult thumb nail, and as soon as the sun sank below the horizon each evening, as if by prior arrangement, they all began their chirrupy song on cue. This acquired knowledge was imparted to me by one of my neighbours at Netherlands – Tom Belvin. He had knocked on my door on his way to work that morning, in order to introduce himself and welcome me to Bermuda. He had learned of my impending arrival from our landlord, and having heard my story of the *crickets* and put me right on that score, he took a quick look at his watch, and assuring me that I could give him a knock any time if there was anything he could help me with, he rushed off. He was a lovely bloke and in the days ahead he was happy to answer the many questions I had about my new home. Later, when I had become established, we sometimes shared a beer or two together, but as we moved in increasingly different circles, our socialising became infrequent at best.

Incredibly it only took a few days to acclimatise to the sound of the tree frogs and it quickly became a calming reminder of my new exotic and exciting location. Conversely, but perhaps not totally surprising, when I eventually returned to the Mother Country two years later, it took me much longer to re-adjust from those little blokes who had kept me entertained musically night after night, back to the dogs and cats in the neighbourhood. I still miss their froggy song to this day.

Before Tom's visit, I had awakened with the lark that morning… well not literally with the lark; I don't think there are any in Bermuda, but it was about the same time I would normally start to come to life. I had heard all about jet lag and was quite looking forward to the experience, but I suppose with only an eight-hour flight, it really didn't come into play and I felt strangely cheated and let down.

After my brief conversation with Tom, I switched on the complimentary radio, which, as the DJ insisted on repeating at regular intervals, was *ZBM Bermudaaaa* and accompanied by a merry little jingle that was never going to make an impact on the charts. Pondering this, I filled the kettle and put it on the small two ringed hob for my first tea pick-me-up of the day. I cannot really get going until I've had that first cuppa, or should I say mugga, and it's a necessary regime I have always preferred.

'My God, they have a rush hour,' I murmured to myself as I opened the blind and saw the unexpectedly busy Harbour Road. Cars, vans, mopeds and more muscular two-wheeled vehicles, if you can call 125cc motorcycles muscular – which was nevertheless the maximum engine size permitted I later learned – all proceeding into town. But of course with Bermuda being such a prosperous place and everyone able to afford motorised transport, coupled with the fact that there is barely twenty one square miles of land on which to build roads, perhaps it was to be expected. One car per household was the law, and it was easy to see why this had been a necessary requirement.

With my brain now clear after the frenetic day previous, I began to take stock. I was here – Bermuda. Actually bloody here, and for the first time I threw any misgivings I previously had aside, and looked forward to the immediate future. I could take my time that morning because my boss had indicated that I would not be picked up until eleven when I would be given a further tour of the island and then back to the office for a chat and a run down on what to expect in the coming weeks with regard to work.

Top of the list, I had already been informed, was the roof to a new conference centre being built on top of the sixth floor of one of the wings of Castle Harbour Hotel, the edifice I had admired across the water the day before as I chatted to the sparrows outside the airport. But that was later. Right then breakfast was at the forefront of my priorities and suddenly feeling famished, I took out a handful of the top-round I had purchased the day before (minced beef to a Brit), seasoned it, formed a large patty and threw it onto a griddle pan also thoughtfully provided, and whipped up a few eggs with an added dollop of mustard for a special kick – all this to the sound of the O'Jays singing *Back Stabbers* on the radio, and with whom, in my euphoric state, I joined in enthusiastically.

I felt good.

EIGHT

The 'revolutionary' new roofing material and system that we employed was ideal for the climatic conditions in Bermuda, and at the same time conformed to the building regulations regarding water catchment areas. With no natural springs or rivers, fresh drinking water in Bermuda had originally been a continuous and worrying problem. Through necessity therefore, and many decades before, they had come up with a sound and intelligent solution. The distinctive white roofs catch and direct the rainwater into large basement tanks, which is then pumped automatically as required through purifying charcoal filters. If this sounds very third world, think again. Bermuda was and still is a modern society and sustaining a very high standard of living, but natural water supplies are scarce and necessity being the mother of invention, an efficient way of utilising rainwater was needed. Somebody later told me that the recommended ratio for tank capacity was linked to the roof area, and one square foot of roof space would equate to eight gallons of tank volume. But don't quote me on this.

In the unfortunate event that your tank ever reached rock bottom, water could be purchased and delivered – but it didn't come cheap. Nothing came cheap in Bermuda, I soon found.

During the brief familiarisation period I spent in England with the British company that had developed the roofing system, I was introduced to one of their operatives Tony, who had been lucky enough to spend time on the island where he had been involved with the new hotel project at Grotto Bay. As he obviously possessed the experience and had already spent a good deal of time in Bermuda, he was the first to be offered the permanent position there, but as a family man with certain commitments that he was unable to ignore, he reluctantly passed up the opportunity, much to the relief of his British employer. They had, after all, gone to the expense of training him in the first place and he had been part of the team that had undertaken the company's flagship contract on the new concourse at Kings Cross Station, and as such was a valuable employee.

We arranged to have lunch together three weeks before I was due to leave the UK and he gave me a few pointers about my upcoming relocation. These pointers, it transpired, were not to do with roofing, but exclusively about what bars to drink in, beaches to visit and what the local talent was like, even generously providing me with the names and phone numbers of two specific members of the opposite sex that he had met in his time there. For a happily married man who apparently took his responsibilities seriously, this was a guy who had put himself about a bit and was a serious party dude – if only half of what he had told me was true. His excuse was that, as a family man, he was not able to get out much at home, so had pulled out all the stops to fill his boots when given such a golden opportunity. But who could blame him. Certainly not me.

I thanked him for his kindness and duly slipped the piece of paper with the ladies' details in my wallet, and forgot all about them to be honest, until finding what had become a ragged piece of scrap paper several weeks into my Bermuda sojourn. I had very much got my foot in the door of the social scene by then anyway, so I binned the thing having made a mental note of the two female names.

During my initial foray into night life of nearby Hamilton, I had chanced on the Ram's Head, a very pleasant pub much to my liking and, because it was comfortable, I did not venture any further or to the

Robin Hood – an establishment that had been highly recommended to me by my erstwhile Slough luncheon companion Tony. The reason for my decision to continue to prop up the bar at the Ram's Head was that I had been instantly identified as a newcomer and was engaged in conversation by two of the local lads. This was a feature in Bermuda, I learned, where everyone you met for the first time seemed genuinely interested in hearing all about you and why and how you came to be on their island. I found later that it had rubbed off on the British ex-pat community also, and the friendly and easy-going atmosphere that prevailed was in stark contrast to the natural aloofness that could often be found in many British towns and cities.

Three interesting hours and an indeterminate number of beers later, I decided to call it a night and slurring a promise to my two (or was it four) new Bermudian pals that I would drop by again at some point, I took my rickety leave. I told myself as I made my cautious way home that, as enjoyable as my evening had been, it was important that I explore the Hamilton night life as thoroughly as possible before I found my regular watering hole.

Consequently, I decided that the Robin Hood would be my priority venue the following evening.

Being a fairly fit bloke, I decided the next evening to walk from Netherlands to Hamilton which turned out to be a rash decision on my part, with the ever-present threat of becoming a bumper sticker on someone's car as the traffic hammered past me at high speed – up to twenty-five miles an hour at times – and being berated by the many Mobylette stroke scooter riders that seemed to be competing to see who could whiz past me the closest without actually inflicting bodily harm. But I managed the journey without mishap, vowing that in future I would call upon the services of my shiny Honda to get me anywhere.

It was probably near 9pm when I eventually climbed the steps to the Robin Hood main entrance, and the contrast with the relatively quiet and relaxing bar at the Ram's Head was strikingly obvious. Two guys on guitars, Rab and Gibb, were giving it large with folk songs in one of the two bars, and the place was heaving with revellers. This was definitely the 'in place', and was right up my particular street, particularly as the predominant accent, judging by the smattering of conversation I picked up, was British in one form or another.

As with the previous evening, two guys in the quieter of the two bars which I had decided to honour with my presence – the term 'quieter' being relative – recognised me as a newcomer and struck up a conversation, and insisted on buying me my first drink which was my introduction to that wondrous beverage, Cockspur rum, or Dirty Bird as the locals sometimes referred to it. The more talkative of the two introduced himself as Richard, and right there began a friendship that had a big and important influence on my early life in Bermuda. Richard was Bermudian and managed one of the family men's clothing stores in Hamilton he had informed me, and discovering that I had walked to town from Harbour Road, generously offered to drive me home. But that was before he and his companion spotted two likely ladies enter the bar. Assuring me that he would still give me the promised lift home, they left me to chance their arm with the girls. No problem. I became involved in conversation with some ex-pats who, like me, had recently arrived on the island. In the meantime, another person who was to play a key part in my future joined us at the bar.

Mary had arrived with her best friend Lee, and they were obviously a popular duo at Robin Hood, even though I later found out that they also had only arrived in Bermuda that month. Mary in particular seemed to take an interest in me and before she and Lee sloped off to the adjoining bar, we made a date to meet for coffee the following Saturday at the Washington Mall in Hamilton.

It was close to midnight, still one hour before closing and many of the drinkers had departed (work in the morning), and seeing Richard and his colleague still heavily engaged with the two females, I approached them and told Richard I would leave him to it and walk home.

'No, no, Harbour Road is unlit and risky, give me ten minutes and we'll go,' he promised.

I was becoming very impatient with this, after all, if it hadn't been for the appearance of Mary and Lee and others at the bar who engaged me in conversation, I would have been hanging around alone for what was then approaching three hours. On the other hand, the two ladies he and his mate had understandably latched on to were not hurtful to the eye.

It was a slightly inauspicious beginning for Richard and me, but having chatted at some length sitting in the car outside Netherlands, we arranged to meet up again, and thus began a period of discovery, as far as Bermuda was concerned, courtesy of my new friend – not to mention a few adventures along the way.

NINE

There were three distinct systems for playing recorded music in the mid-seventies: vinyl, cassette, and 8-track, but before Bermuda I had never actually encountered the 8-track system and had in the late sixties converted my vinyl collection to the 'state-of-the-art' cassette arrangement. Looking back, I can hardly believe that I took such a Philistine action, sacrificing long-players with their aesthetically pleasing album covers, for the small functional box, whose only advantage was its compactness. How could I? But those were different times and cassettes seemed to be the future. It didn't help that I loaned my entire vinyl collection (just fifteen albums) to my then girlfriend, only to have her disappear with the lot, but leaving me with fifteen pre-recorded cassettes (plus one cassette filled with *Pick of the Pops* recordings hosted by the legendary Alan 'Fluff'' Freeman) containing all those precious tracks. But it didn't feel like such a loss at the time.

Bermudians seemed to favour the bulky 8-track devices and Richard's mother's car – which Richard frequently borrowed in preference to his smart Suzuki motorcycle – had one such machine fitted. So on an early March Sunday morning, at a time when the sparrows were still scratching their balls and rubbing the sleep from their eyes, we were listening to the Doobie Brothers' new album, *The Captain and Me*, at full volume and 'China Grove' belting out from the Austin 1100's sound system, as we raced along North Shore Road at an unlawful 22mph en route to Flatts village. Richard was such a daredevil.

He had arranged with a boat-owning friend to take us out for a day's fishing, and his vessel was moored at Flatts Inlet. I had to admit, after the residue of sleep had finally evaporated with the rising of the sun and I was feeling less cranky, that it was good to be alive and out and about on such a fine morning on a virtually traffic free road.

There was a noticeable contrast between the north and south shore areas of Bermuda; the south had larger beaches in greater number, whilst the north, although with less of an abundance, still had its fair share and could be just as spectacular in its own way – in fact Flatts Inlet itself was, for my money, the most idyllic and breathtakingly beautiful spot on the island, and that was saying something.

The boat was already being loaded when we arrived, and I was not surprised to see that the equipment for the day comprised ninety per cent booze and grub, and ten per cent fishing gear. Richard and I had taken along a couple of six packs and two bottles of our favoured Cockspur rum, but we need not have bothered because already there was a large tub on board, filled to the brim with ice, cans of beer and a number of bottles of various spirits.

'Blimey,' I remarked, 'that's the size of a rubbish bin.'

'That's because it *is* a rubbish bin,' our host informed us, and he chuckled.

'How much do you think we can drink?' I asked, realising that there would be just the three of us, plus one other who had at that moment appeared from below.

'All of it,' was the reply.

'I'm up for that,' Richard threw in.

Oh well.

The day was a great success… I think. I managed to piece together a jigsaw of images involving several medium size fish that had been caught, and later grilled on the portable barbecue that had been thoughtfully added to the vessel's cargo, plus some very thick mega steaks and sundry items of meat products that had also been piled on to the barbee. I knew Bermudians could drink, but boy, could they eat too. But then so could I.

I obviously enjoyed myself. Richard told me so later. But if I had to provide a detailed description of the day, it would be in disjointed single framed scenes. It was revealed that I had almost fallen overboard – twice – and had dropped my shorts and mooned at a passing boat of disapproving middle-aged people. I was told we were on the water for ten hours, but if I had been told twenty minutes, I would have been unable to contradict it such was my level of confusion. I remembered the beginning and the end, the latter consisting of falling onto my bed fully clothed and jabbering to myself, but everything in between was a collection of seemingly unrelated cameos. How on earth, I mused, could Richard have safely driven me home?

As time passed, I found that such drunken episodes subsided exponentially as my intake increased. The wonders of nature!

The following day, Monday, I had to be in St George's to start a job on the ancient looking St George Hotel. It could not have been further away from Paget, and I would much rather have been in bed, but I was meeting my boss on site, and needed to be on time. It had been reported by the hotel management that there were a number of annoying long-standing leaks in the roof and we had been asked to 'patch things up', but on inspection it was impossible to know where to start. The bituminous felt roofing was so old that water could be finding its way through in dozens of locations, and it was a miracle that more had not found its way through to the rooms below. The hotel had been built in 1906 overlooking the old capital of St George's, and it appeared to me that the roof covering could have been the original, albeit showing the evidence of a succession of repairs. There was only one remedy I told my boss, and that was to strip the lot off and lay a new roof, and judging by the bouncy sensation as we walked across it, so too would the substructure be in need of replacing. But it appeared that the hotel was having financial problems and my submission was out of the question; the important thing was to get the hotel through the upcoming tourist season. Our hands were therefore tied, and having assured my boss I would do what I could, added that no guarantee should be given on the work I was able to carry out. He shrugged resignedly and told me to do the best I could and, due to a price limit being imposed by the hotel authorities, I had just two days to carry out the works. It was a hopeless case, and even if I had not been hungover and had all my wits about me, the story would have been the same. The building was literally disintegrating.

The once grand hotel that had hosted celebrity guests such as F. Scott Fitzgerald and his wife, had just a short time to live as it turned out, and was later demolished to make room for the smart new St George's Club.

TEN

Bermuda was, and still is, an incredibly expensive and exclusive destination for tourists. In automobile terms, if Bermuda was an Aston Martin V12 Vantage, then Skegness would be a Reliant Robin with one wheel missing. But of course, if you were fortunate enough to live or work in Bermuda back then, the salaries reflected the stratospheric cost of living with the added bonus of no income tax, so it was never a problem for the residents, and in fact, the country had one of the highest per capita incomes in the world.

It was a different story for British tourists however, which is why they were few and far between in the mid-seventies, with the Yanks and Canadians constituting by far the biggest proportion of visitors to the islands. The few Brits we encountered in those days were usually friends or relatives of ex-pat workers and therefore had accommodation provided and did not have to have to fork out the equivalent of second mortgages to stay at one of Bermuda's expensive world-class hotels. Cheaper, first-class guest house and bed and breakfast accommodation was also available of course, but by British standards, they were still inordinately costly.

Now imagine that you are an American thirty-something housewife and you have booked a glorious week in this sub-tropical paradise with your best friend. Both husbands are still back home in the States because they have offered to martyr themselves and stay at home to look after the dog whilst secretly rubbing their hands together in contemplation of a few days fishing, or daily rounds of golf with the boys. There is also the prospect of slobbing out in front of the TV together night after night, watching endless football or baseball games over bottomless cans of Budweiser, which being an American brew is not proper beer of course, merely gnats pee. But you get the general picture – and all this without fear of receiving GBH of the ear-hole from the good ladies. Bliss.

So you, the lovely Rita and friend Alma, have arrived in Bermuda, and no sooner have you breezed in to your swish hotel, unpacked your bikinis and enjoyed those almost obligatory first Rum Swizzles, you then hit one of those darling pink sand beaches you have read about. This is what you came for, and this is what you intend doing each and every one of your seven glorious days in the sun – interspersed with a spot of shopping of course.

Then every night, you set out determinedly to deplete the stocks of lobster to the point of extinction, along with other endangered species. In other words, you eat yourselves stupid at some of the island's excellent eateries and put your diet on hold… That's the diet you have imposed on yourself for the last three months in order to get yourself in trim for your Bermuda trip. You have also met a couple of local Jack the Lads at the beach, one English, one Bermudian.

Enter Richard and yours truly.

You have participated in a bit of harmless flirting and joshing around, but nothing you can't tell Henry and Bert about; although only if you absolutely have to, after all, what they don't know can't hurt them. In short, the usual holiday shenanigans that two temporarily unattached ladies inevitably get up to when let loose in such surroundings, and who could resist two such fun guys, especially with those cute accents.

It was a Sunday, some weeks after my close encounter of the naked kind at Church Bay. I had not yet phoned Esther, the girl who had obviously excited me so much on that Friday night, that I had managed to nod off after a round of horizontal jiving. There were still blank areas in my recollections of that evening. But she had left a message on my chest to call her, and I still hadn't done so. I probably wouldn't telephone… I thought. But on the other hand… maybe. *Sweet dreams blondie, call me*, it had said. On balance it sounded like a promise unfulfilled, in which case it was probably a good idea to get back in touch, make a grovelling apology if necessary, arrange to meet up for a drink – non-alcoholic just in case – and make up for falling asleep in the saddle.

Yes, I should call her.

Though… maybe not. She had probably left for her next destination on her global trip anyway.

If decisions like this were all I had to worry about, I concluded, then who would I be to complain? So still pondering that minor dilemma, Richard and I hit the beach at Horseshoe Bay, nicely full after a gourmet lunch of cheeseburgers with the works at the infamous Roach Coach on South Shore. This was before I became aware of the burger stand's reputation and the fact that it was even referred to by the locals as transportation and full board for crawling things. It was just a convenient place to grab a bite as far as I was concerned, and it was only after a nasty case of arsequake and the screaming Eartha Kitt's that were still to come, that realisation would dawn, and purchases thereafter would be confined to cold cans of soda and any other products in airtight containers. But all of that came later. It didn't seem to bother Richard though, who never thought to inform me of the food wagon's renown, and who anyway seemed impervious to the mass attacks from its sinister bacterial life-forms.

It wasn't a particularly busy day at Horseshoe. But then it was still only March and most Bermudians would be hesitant about spending time at the beach so early in the year. There were a number of small groups dotted along the length of the bay, but the tourist season had not yet started in earnest, even though the temperatures were in the mid-70s. The much-vaunted annual invasion of hundreds of

American college girls was soon to come, covering the Easter period, which, the way Richard told it, was going to turn Bermuda into sex city.

I had been in Bermuda only a little more than three months and I was still finding my feet and my way around, but in a strange way that defied explanation, it felt as if I had always been there; it felt right and it felt as if I belonged, even though my blood had not yet thinned sufficiently or whatever it is that happens chemically to the body during the acclimatisation process, the temperature still felt pretty darned good to me.

We became aware of Rita and Alma even before we pitched camp with our towels, and after a conspiratorial look between us, decided on a spot just a few yards from the Americans. It was Richard who kicked the proceedings off with: 'Hi girls, on vacation?'

Wow what a killer opening line. But it worked and the response was immediate and encouraging.

'Sure are, how 'bout you?'

'Nah,' said Richard, 'we live here.' Then jumping right in, the smooth-talking dog informed them, 'I'm Richard, he's Colin,' and he inclined his head toward me.

They responded in kind with, 'Great; I'm Rita and this is my best friend, Alma.'

'You Bermudans?' asked Alma.

'Bermud-*i*-ans,' Richard corrected her.

'He's Bermud-*i*-an and I'm English,' I added.

'Cool,' said Rita demurely, lengthening out the oooo in cool, although I wasn't sure if it was Richard being Bermud-*i*-an, or me being English that she found so refreshingly chilly. Hopefully both: Richard with his dark afro style hair and me with my long blonde curly locks and full beard. Both very seventies – but then, it was the seventies, and of course there were our cute and appealing un-American accents.

'What do you think of the brunette?' Richard whispered to me.

'Well, I wouldn't crawl over her to get to Yoko Ono,' I whispered back.

'I'll take the other one then,' he said, 'you know me.'

I did. Blonde, red head or bald, Richard never much minded, I had often jokily told him. Mind you it didn't much matter; both of these ladies would have received seven or eight on a one to ten scale. It would have been a definite eight for Alma if it had not been for an irksome pimple on the side of her nose. Not that I was overly concerned. What's a zit between friends?

We took our cue and moved over to the girls, plonking ourselves down on their beach towels, which meant having to sit very close of course. We chatted about this and that, mostly made-up stuff on our part and designed to make us appear to be more worldly wise than we were. Richard suggested places to visit and we filled them in on our favourite bars, with the highly recommended Robin Hood at the top of the list. Then I described parts of England that I knew would appeal to two American girls who, we discovered, had travelled no further than Pizza Hut before their trip to our islands… see what I did there? … *our* islands.

Names like Stratford-on-Avon, Stonehenge and Buckingham Palace elicited exclamations of *oohs, ahhs* and *oh my Ghaaads,* from our new American friends. They chirruped on like two canaries that had overdosed on hemp seed about their home town in New Jersey; how great egg McMuffins were; the exciting activity of baby showers – whatever the hell they were – pet poodles; make-up and their houses. We were enthralled. Then they talked about their husbands.

Husbands? Effing husbands!

This had us looking over our shoulders and at each other, both thinking the same thing. But no, it was pretty obvious that these two were on vacation without their other halves present, which was quickly confirmed.

'Hey, we're going for a dip,' chortled Rita changing the subject abruptly and away from telling us about her sporty Chevrolet Corvette back home in Jersey, to going for a swim. 'Wanna join us?'

'Maybe later, we'll just cool out here and get some rays,' Richard told her. 'You go ahead.'

'Cool out,' the girls said... 'Cute.'

I had better explain that back then, nobody ever said 'chill out' in Bermuda; it was always 'cool out'. No really, I just don't want you to think that we were unhip and not cool dudes, ok?

After the ladies had dashed off and were squealing and giggling like two juvenile school girls as they splashed each other in the still relatively chilly Bermuda waters, I turned to my friend.

'What do you reckon?'

'They're married.'

I nodded. 'Yeah... but what do you reckon?'

'Could spell trouble,' he said.

'Mmm... so what do you reckon?'

'Dunno. What do you think?'

'They talk a lot,' was my observation.

'Boring too,' Richard added. 'Nice melons though.' And I nodded sagely at the thought; something akin to an antique collector weighing up the price of a pair of early French candlesticks, rather than a lecher pondering a nice pair of late American Bristols. (OK, just for the Americans among you: Bristols... Bristol Cities... English rhyming slang... right?)

'Sooo... what do you reckon?' I repeated.

There was a lengthy pause as we looked at each other, then at the two females cavorting in the surf, then back at each other again.

'Nah, too much hassle,' Richard said at last.

'You're right,' I grudgingly agreed. 'I've got an idea though, fancy a laugh?' And I outlined a plan I had been cooking up for the last few minutes, when we were debating whether or not to make a move on our two New Jersey lovelies. Richard listened intently as I told him what I had in mind, and then laughed out loud.

'Let's do it,' he said.

Being typical females, our two new acquaintances had brought enough stuff to the beach to ensure their survival for a whole weekend.

Not so much food – although there were some candy wrappers in evidence – but sun tan creams; make-up; changes of clothing; books and bits of costume jewellery. But crucially and in line with my plan, amongst this collection of bric-a-brac was an expensive looking Nikon camera. This had been the object of my attention and had been instrumental in formulating my dastardly plan. It was all a bit risky because short of going back to the car park, there was very little cover, apart from some small dunes on the section of the beach where we had settled, so we would just have to be quick and hope we didn't attract any attention.

Making sure the two bathing beauties were fully occupied and taking it in turns, we photographed each other in an imaginative variety of lewd poses and in various stages of undress. I was painfully accustomed to appearing nude on a beach if you remember, so it all came relatively easy to me and by the time we finished, the girls had an interesting collection of snaps tucked away in their camera to remind them of their time in Bermuda and the two nice lads they had met there. The problem with this sort of wheeze of course, is that you never get to see the fruits of your labours and you are left to rely on your imagination – which is one thing we had plenty of – what the reactions would be when the film was exposed so to speak. Would the girls get to see the snaps first and be able to keep them away from their men folk, or would they all be sitting around when the holiday photos were previewed for the first time?

We saw Rita and Alma one more time before they left *de Rock*… okay, another explanation here: *de Rock* refers to Bermuda, and is a local expression. In other words, *The Rock*, pronounced in the way most Bermudians express themselves, and Rock being the affectionate title they have given to their homeland which, encompassing only twenty one square miles of land area, seems a fair description.

It was at the Robin Hood where we saw the girls again. It was their last night in Bermuda and they had decided to check out the place based on our recommendation. Although they didn't come out and say it, they had obviously secretly hoped that Richard and I would be there and had decided that they simply had to see us one last time. At least that's what we told ourselves. Our friend the Nikon was in evidence and after a not unpleasant evening in the company of our two American friends, Rita insisted on a photo or two. She snapped Richard and me against the bar appropriately enough, and asked one of the regulars if they would shoot the four of us together. I couldn't help thinking that this is precisely what might happen at some point in the future if Henry and Bert got wind of our photographic prank – though not with a camera. Then promising to send us copies via the Robin Hood, they made their fond farewells and the two took a cab back to their hotel, waving manically from the rear window as the car disappeared towards town.

We both agreed that we had some regrets about the little surprise we had prepared for them, and several times had been on the verge of spilling the beans and giving them prior warning. But we didn't. It would have spoiled their final evening in our scintillating company.

Perhaps not surprisingly, we never did hear from the girls again and no photographs ever materialised at the Robin Hood – and thank God, no Henry or Bert turned up on our doorsteps wielding baseball bats or worse. Hell, it hadn't occurred to us at the time, but those guys could be cops or professional wrestlers, even members of the mob. It didn't bear thinking about, and our feelings of guilt made us wish like hell that only Rita and Alma had seen the artistic photographs – genuinely for their sake as much as ours.

They were pleasant enough ladies and good company, and we had seemed such nice boys.

ELEVEN

One of the venues that Tony, my erstwhile luncheon companion and fellow roofer back in England, had recommended and for some reason stayed in my memory, was the 2001 night club in Hamilton. I still missed my weekly jaunts to the Thingamajig club in Reading, and it seemed a lifetime ago that I had last laid down some moves on the dance floor (hark at me –'moves' where I was concerned, covered all manner of strange manoeuvres and gesticulations), so within the first month of my entering the islands, I took myself along to the venue only to be turned away because I was not wearing a jacket and tie. My red knee length Cuban heeled boots were okay, but with no jacket and tie, well that was a definite no-no.

I jest… I didn't own any red ones.

Anyway, I learned early on that practically all clubs, restaurants and hotel bars had strict dress codes that involved jackets and ties for males, which was irritating at times but refreshing in a strange kind of way. All very colonial. The laughable part was that having acquired some suitable clobber in the form of a snazzy grey denim jacket and lime-green kipper tie from Gentleman's Quarter, and having presented myself at the door of 2001 on a second visit, I noticed that the first thing all the blokes did on entering was to take off their ties and stuff them in their jacket pockets and as the evening wore on, jackets would themselves often be discarded. This anomaly seemed to be perfectly acceptable to the management and was one of the quirky little ways of Bermuda life.

The 2001 was not a disappointment and my first impression of the place was very favourable and held all sorts of promise. The atmosphere was reminiscent of my favourite hang-out back in Reading, the only difference being that The Jig, as we called it, was a cellar club with bare wooden stairs leading down into it, and bizarrely was an ex-chapel of rest with alcoves lining one wall that housed tables and bench seats, but were once used as receptacles for the departed. The 2001 on the other hand, was tastefully modern, situated on the first floor and accessed by a flight of carpeted stairs from Bermudiana Road. The sound system there was resonantly brilliant, and I can still vividly remember what was playing when I arrived on my first evening. As I ascended the stairs, the wonderful and extended introduction to 'Papa Was a Rolling Stone' by The Temptations, hit me between the ears. I still regard it as one of the very best intros, and certainly one of the longest, which to this day whenever it is played, instantly sucks me into a wormhole and I am taken back to that night when I first set foot in the 2001 with its flashing multi-coloured light show, and the music reverberating around the mirrored walls.

It was on that first evening I met a roguish gang of three: Brian, Malcolm, and a Scottish character friend of theirs called Roy. These were in fact some of the very first male ex-pats I met socially, and they were forever popping up at the same bars, same parties and same everything throughout my time there, and later, through other acquaintances, Brian, Malcolm and I came to be on very friendly terms. Brian was something in town planning, I was informed, and he joked about the fact that his office was immediately opposite the island's clinic that dealt with sexually transmitted diseases, or as Brian put it – the pox doctors.

'You need to be careful,' Malcolm told me, 'he knows everyone who goes in to that place,' and he and Roy laughed as Brian gave me an exaggerated wink.

There was a fourth member with them that night who, it transpired, had also recently arrived in Bermuda: a young man called Ian. The trio had temporarily taken pity on him being alone, and invited him to join their little group. I say temporarily because duly noting that I also was a newcomer, and after introductions and chatting about nothing in particular, they cleverly off-loaded Ian on to me, and drifted away.

It wasn't a problem; Ian was a very pleasant, though shy, fresh-faced young man in his early twenties and was in Bermuda on a short contract working for a firm of accountants, being himself a fairly newly qualified number cruncher. We had a few drinks, and as he was far too bashful and introverted to get up and dance with one of the many attractive females in the club, he left me to it after an hour or so. But not before we had arranged to meet up the following night for a few drinks at one of the popular bars, and if I had my way, go on to other establishments until we scored. I had immediately liked the guy and although it was none of my business, it seemed to me that Ian needed taking out of himself.

He surprised me by admitting that he had never learned to ride a bicycle, so he had no two-wheeled moped-style transport and asked if I could pick him up on my machine, which was still the hot red Honda 50 provided by my employer. He had been taken into town that night by his work colleague with whom he was lodging, and would be getting a taxi back. The colleague and his family resided in Smith's Parish, but it was no problem. Bermuda is so small you hardly ever have to go too far out of your way for anything; at least that's how it felt in the early days, but as I became fully adjusted to the speed limit/distance ratio, even travelling three miles to the beach sometimes became a bind.

The following evening after collecting Ian, we started out as I had planned at the Hog Penny pub and within a very short time, I had persuaded two young American tourists to join us for a glass or two. They were from Rhode Island and were waitresses called Candy and Cathy Sue (we would never have guessed the nationality from their names), but later Ian and I moved on to another slightly quieter setting at the Ram's Head minus the girls, and it turned into an okay evening with Ian relaxing into a more talkative mood now the strain of trying to impress our two waitresses had been removed. We told each other our life stories and I have to say that his was by far the more interesting.

Ian's family lived in Friern Barnet, London. His dad was in the diplomatic corps and there was a large family with a number of siblings, all of whom were older than Ian and had settled in the Cayman Islands where their father had once held a post. At least that's what I assumed. They were all doing rather well for themselves by all accounts, and I asked Ian if that's where he was headed after Bermuda, but he had not yet decided where his future lay. We rode back to my apartment at Netherlands and talked into the early hours about our past lives and our ambitions and expectations for the future. We listened to my limited selection of music cassettes played on my recently acquired twin Sony cassette deck and tuner – a machine I had coveted in England, but could not afford. In those days, electrical items in particular, did not go out of style for some time, and updated and newer versions did not appear as soon as the last model had barely seen the light of day in Curry's window. I even shared some of my cherished bottle of Courvoisier Napoleon with Ian, and feeling suitably warm and affable, just before dawn I took him back to his lodgings.

The sun was coming up as I made my way home after dropping Ian off, and still feeling right with the world and not a bit sleepy, I stopped on Harbour Road and took in the surroundings. Having propped the bike up onto its stand, I sat on a low stone wall at the side of the road and marvelled for the hundredth time about my extreme good fortune to find myself in that place, and in deep contemplation absorbed the scene in detail. I did not want to take for granted or miss even the smallest detail of this island paradise.

It was just after six thirty; there was no hint of traffic at that time on a Sunday morning, and as I took in the marvellous view across the glass-like waters to the city of Hamilton, with the rising sun behind me illuminating the pristine white roofs, I sighed deeply with contentment. There was an all-encompassing silence but the symphony of its beauty was deafening. I watched as a small flock of birds, a species I was not familiar with, fly erratically north, seemingly following the line of Harbour Road, before my attention was diverted to a disturbance in the water beneath my feet, as a huge shoal of tiny fish nosed the surface, presumably in search of breakfast. Even then, it still seemed surreal and hard to believe that I was living the dream in that wonderful place. After a good few minutes, I took a deep even breath, grabbed one last lingering look at the marvellous scene before me in an effort to indelibly print it on my brain, then reluctantly mounted my bike and made my way home. It was a scene that has stayed with me in brilliant detail down the years, and was the first of many such experiences that were to follow.

Ian left the island three weeks later and having exchanged addresses, we promised each other that we would keep in touch. We upheld that promise for a while, then after I left Bermuda we seemed to lose contact completely, but although I didn't know it then, we were to be thrown together again seventeen years later in what was to become just one of a series of strange coincidences associated with Bermuda and the people I met there.

TWELVE

I had been in Bermuda for less than two months and the long-awaited prestige contract at Castle Harbour was only now approaching the roofing phase. As with most building projects there had been unconnected problems that affected our part of the contract and had necessitated long delays. I had completed several jobs in various parts of the island and a week before we were due to commence work on the hotel project, I had been sent to a warehouse-cum-office building in Serpentine Road in Hamilton, where the company had been contracted to re-surface the ageing corrugated asbestos roof over the storage section. The dangers of asbestos used in buildings and elsewhere were relatively unknown in those days, and the material was still a health time-bomb waiting to explode.

It was a fairly large area, and because my boss was anxious to complete the job as quickly as possible and get me on to the new conference centre at Castle Harbour the following week, a crew of two was sent out to work alongside me – Clyde and Nobby. We had been there for no more than an hour, when I spotted in the distance, a slow moving, and decidedly wobbly moped advancing towards us. The rider was obviously female, perched precariously on the machine, ramrod straight and wearing what looked like a several sizes too large crash helmet, giving her a disproportionate top-heavy appearance. Her concentration was palpable as she endeavoured to stay upright and roughly pointed in the right direction. Obviously a newcomer to the world of formula one moped riding. I cannot explain why I was so fascinated by the spectacle, but I could not tear my gaze away from the slowly advancing figure. Perhaps it was just that I was intrigued to see who was hiding under that ludicrous helmet, or perhaps it was because I had never witnessed a dramatic moped crash. But for some reason I needed to know the identity of the rider, and I was delighted to note that having come to an abrupt stop outside the building on whose roof I was standing, she had obviously reached her destination.

There then followed a complicated procedure as she tried to kick the bike up onto its stand, and having been unsuccessful after several attempts, she proceeded to manually force the stand down by hand. Not an advisable operation, because leaving just one hand free to steady the moped, there was a serious threat of it falling on top of her. But to my relief, she eventually figured it out and managed to get the machine stabilised and secure without incurring serious injury to herself or damage to the bike. A cheer went up from my work colleagues that, unbeknownst to me, had joined me to see what I was finding of interest, then silence as the rider slowly removed her helmet.

'Whoa, that is *fiiine*, Big Bird,' Clyde, one of my colleagues decided, as a mop of blonde hair was hastily shaken into place by the gorgeous young thing standing below us. Big Bird had been the assumed name that the company's Bermudian workforce had re-christened me with, having learned that my family name is Bird, and thought it a great joke to associate me with the Sesame Street character. They could see that I had been taken with the new arrival, and there was much good-humoured ribbing and banter as they resumed work, but I carried on spying and almost laughed out loud when blondie finally managed to open the entrance door to the building. She had pulled on the handle for some time, only to realise that there was a printed sign on the door, that even I could see from my position on a spur of the roof where I stood, that clearly said: *PUSH*. That was the clincher, and I resolved to find out just who this quirky young lady was and if possible, acquire a phone number at the very least before the day was out.

As lunch time approached, which with my gang could have been any time between 11am and 2pm – we drew lots to see who would ride into Hamilton city centre and purchase the lunch time beef pies at DeGraffe's mobile lunch counter in the City Hall car park. Subsequent to that day, it was always a must-have if I was working in the area because they were the best beef pies I had ever tasted. Still are for that matter. But actually, the day in question was the first time I experienced one of those beauties, and although it was Nobby, another of my work colleagues, who was nominated to collect lunch, I decided to tag along and see what all the fuss was about. Although it was a short ride into the city centre, I reasoned that it would be safer if I rode shotgun in Nobby's car to ensure the goodies arrived in one piece.

I let Nobby order for himself and Clyde, whilst I stood back observing and waiting my turn. The server – DeGraffe himself, I wrongly assumed – asked me what fixings I wanted, and not knowing what the hell a fixing was, I asked him what he had. Mayo, ketchup, mustard and relish he reeled off, and not even knowing what relish was, I simply told him I would have *the works*, having learned the expression from previous dealings with the orders of hamburgers and hot dogs. He gave me a strange look, shrugged and deftly sliced the top off the crust and squirted all four concoctions from plastic containers into the pie. Then replacing the pastry lid, he slid my lunch into a grease proof bag and took my money.

It was the first and last time I asked for the works for one of his pies.

Firstly, there was little space for anything within the pie case, which was packed with prime tender beef chunks and thick gravy; and secondly, in the absence of a table with plate and eating utensils, the pie became impossible to consume without the need for protective clothing and a bucket of water in close proximity. It was delicious and as tasty as described, but the most difficult and hazardous street food I have ever encountered. From my first gungy experience that had me looking like the victim of an explosion in a paint factory, I simply settled for a small squeeze of relish from that point on, even though I remained ignorant of its constituent parts.

I had promised myself that after lunch and on the pretext of using the office bathroom, I was going to introduce myself to the lovely young thing that must be working somewhere below, and make my move. It was therefore imperative that I clean up after the DeGraffe's pie experience, and did not present myself looking like a second-hand oven glove.

Having done my very best to remove the technicolour smears from my chops with the aid of some water from a convenient tap at ground level, and being egged on by my mickey-taking colleagues, I ascended a flight of stairs to where I assumed the young lady was situated. I found myself in a huge area with no dividers that seemed to constitute the one and only office in the building. It was devoid of furniture and fittings, except for a bank of filing cabinets and a desk that sat dead centre in the massive space. This supported two telephones, a typewriter and an open lunch box, behind which was the object of my attentions.

'Hi, I'm Colin,' I said. 'Do you have a bathroom I can use please,' belatedly becoming aware that asking for the bog was hardly an ideal opener.

'Hi, yes it's over there,' she told me between chews, pointing to a door with her half-eaten sandwich, and giving me a big smile in the process. Then as I made my way over, making a point to give it my best loose-limbed walk, I heard: 'And I'm Penny.'

'Hi Penny,' I said, turning my head in her direction. 'Yes,' I whispered to myself clenching my victorious fist in front of me in celebration as I resumed my trek to the distant amenities. Phase one, the breaking of the ice, successfully concluded. I was unsure how long we chatted after I emerged from the bathroom, and I didn't really care. The boys on the roof knew what to do, and anyway, if they took exception to my absence they could do one. I had already worked out that we would require less than two days to complete the work and were well ahead of schedule. I was in charge, and some things were far more important than fiddling about on roofs. As it happened when I eventually emerged into the sunlight, they both gave me a cheer and a brace of thumbs-up, and hurried over to ask me if I had pulled.

Penny, it transpired, was English and had only arrived in Bermuda a few days earlier, and this had been her very first assignment from the agency she worked for: Services Unlimited. This was an agency that hired out temps, most of whom were ex-pats, to businesses across the island. She was disappointed to find that the job she found herself on that day was simply to sit and answer the phone, which had been ominously silent thus far, she told me. But she was heartened by the fact that it was for one day only and she would be placed elsewhere the following morning, which would hopefully be a bit more challenging.

She came from Sudbury Town in London I learned, but had lived with her parents in Bushey before leaving on her new adventure. She gave me a perfunctory résumé of her very brief time spent thus far in Bermuda, and rather than pussyfoot around, I plunged right in and asked her out. She was also above pussyfooting it seemed, because she immediately agreed and we arranged for me to pick her up two days later and I would take her to the Bermuda Culinary College for dinner. I knew from a previous visit that we would receive first-class food prepared by trainee chefs and attended to by keen waiting staff, all at an affordable price. It would be the perfect first date.

There was just one tiny fly in my smooth-talking ointment. As I turned away having made the arrangements. She called after me.

'Oh, by the way.'

Uh oh… 'Yes?'

'There's a piece of pastry in your beard.'

Shit!

THIRTEEN

I found myself on my own and unattached the following night and decided that another visit to the 2001 was a splendid idea. Visiting the nightclub had to be planned in advance, as I have explained, because although the Robin Hood and other watering holes were strictly casual when it came to dress, and men wore almost exclusively simple shirt and slacks – in the 2001 and similar establishments it was strictly jacket and tie. Like many other venues, there was always a drawer full of ties at the door ready to loan out for the evening for clients should they have forgotten that particular piece of neck-wear.

There were a number of familiar faces present including the ubiquitous Brian and his little band, who seemed to be at just about every drinking establishment I had thus far attended. I spent some time chatting to them whilst eyeing up the female clientele; then having passed the time with one or two people who were known to me as regulars at the Hood, and enjoyed a couple of dances with a pretty young lady from Newcastle, before returning to the bar for a freshen up, the place seemed suddenly to come to a standstill as every face turned to the club entrance.

Three gorgeous young women had entered; all immaculately and expensively dressed and made-up, possessing the sort of figures blokes like me salivated over. All were stunning, but one in particular held my intention, due mostly to the fact that as an ardent leg man she had a perfect pair that went all the way up to Sandys Parish, and she was obviously intent on showing them off at their best, with her black and gold hot pants outfit. Be still my palpitating heart I thought.

They were all top class and very, very special, and made the lovely young thing I had been dancing with look like Popeye's girlfriend. Sorry Olive. I glanced at Brian and saw the calculating look in his eye; I just knew he would be the one to make a move first, so pre-empting him I glided over in my best man-about-town fashion and smoothly welcomed the girls, asking if I might buy them a drink. All this was done with aplomb I felt, and if aplomb had not been to hand, I would have done it anyway. I was actually relieved that Brian was right behind me at the head of a queue of other would-be Lotharios because they removed the necessity for me to buy all three drinks, which came as a great relief and a real bonus for my overworked wallet. All three ladies were striking as I believe I have already indicated (but cannot be stated often enough) but the one I had targeted was simply breathtaking and I could feel my heart rev up to ramming speed as she accompanied me to the bar… I wasn't about to leave her sitting there surrounded by half a dozen other lechers I can tell you.

I bought the drinks and finding two vacant seats, we talked and talked for a half hour or so and I could not take my eyes off her. Her name was Geri and it turned out that all three were the resident singers with The Ray Anthony Band who were appearing at one of the island's top hotels later that week, and were known as The Bookends. Ray Anthony, she informed me, was one of the original members of the legendary Glenn Miller Orchestra and had performed all over the world. She told me that she was from Milwaukee, Wisconsin and seemed proud of the fact for some reason – but what did I know except that it was famous for brewing. Also, that she had replaced Viki Carr in the group, who went on to become a star in her own right, and that she – Geri – was engaged to be married.

Bummer!

My hopes for the evening were flushed down the toilet, although in fairness, I probably wouldn't have stood a chance with such a lovely young thing. But she did say she thought my hair was groovy.

However, there was sufficient flirting taking place for me to agree to buy a ticket for the upcoming Saturday gig at Bermuda's premier hotel, The Southampton Princess, although I made the condition that she had a drink with me after the show, which to my surprise and joy, she readily consented to. Great, I was doing mental back-flips. I would persuade shy young Ian Wight, who was still on the island at that point, to splash out and come with me... it would blow his socks off when she joined us at our table.

You should have slipped the maître d' ten dollars; I was reliably informed – after a previous trip to see The Drifters where I had to make do with a seat near the back – and he would have got you a table at the front. Something worth knowing because under the circumstances this was a must; it was going to be so good to see Ian's face when the stunning Geri joined us.

Everything turned out as expected and then some. The show was a knockout and as far as I was concerned, and in my heavily biased eyes, the girls were the stars. Ian was suitably impressed with our front row table, and became almost crimson with embarrassment when Geri arrived for what turned out to be a very brief visit. Never mind, I had made my point.

I never saw or heard of Geri, The Bookends, or Ray Anthony again, and I do not flatter myself that the thought of me ever crossed the mind of that beautiful lady, but it had been a memorable hour or so in her company with a superb show thrown in, and I was content with that.

FOURTEEN

I had known from day one that the company had secured the contract at the Castle Harbour Hotel involving the new roofing system. This was the first roof of significant size and prestige that we had undertaken, and was therefore important that everything proceeded well.

Castle Harbour consisted of several flat-roofed wings, each six or seven stories high, enclosing a large open-air swimming pool, gardens, and an al fresco paved dining area. A new conference centre was to be built on the hotel entrance block and this was where we came in. The roof would be gabled and sloping on three sides, with a flat walkway area at the apex for maintenance access, and running the complete length of the building. Working from scaffolding would be a necessity... or so I had assumed. The fact was, no scaffolding was to be employed. Although Bermuda was a very modern and forward-thinking place in other ways, when it came to health and safety, it was obviously lacking far behind – at least it was as far as the building trade and the Castle Harbour contract were concerned. Scaffolding would have come at a huge extra cost of course, but nevertheless, having no scaffolding on a building of this height, and crucially, one with a pitched roof, would never have been tolerated in the UK, and in fact would have been illegal. I protested long and loud when I was taken to the site for the first time. 'How the hell do you expect me to work on a pitched roof this far from the ground with no scaffolding?' I protested.

'Don't worry,' the boss told me, 'you will be wearing a harness.'

'Attached to what?' I asked in agitation. As far as I could see, there would be nothing to hitch it to.

'Whoever we put you with,' was his answer, as if this was explanation enough and the obvious solution.

So it was not going to be a *what* but a *who*. He obviously had no idea just how hazardous an operation this would be, and if he thought I was going to spend several weeks (it was that size of job) working on what would amount to a slippery and dangerous sloping surface seventy feet from the ground, he could bloody well think again. But the fact remained: there would be no scaffolding and I was the only one that could do this work. Then Brian Lunnon, the site agent, who had been listening with obvious interest, intervened.

'It shouldn't be a problem,' he told me. 'The roof substructure of marine ply is not going on in one piece but a section at a time so that you can access each section from a mobile scaffolding tower on the inside of the building, keeping the need to work outside to a minimum. When each section is complete, we will assign a carpenter to you and he will erect the substructure on the next section and so on,' he elaborated. But I was not convinced even though I knew each section would only be the width of a sheet of marine ply – four feet. But I was at least satisfied that the most precarious part of the operation – working on the eaves and the very edge of the roof – could indeed be negotiated from inside the new structure. After that though, there would be no choice but to complete the remaining section fully exposed outside.

Fully exposed at Church Bay weeks before, was a doddle compared to this.

What had I let myself in for? The hotel that had looked so inviting in January when I had arrived and sat waiting for my pick-up from the airport, now took on the menacing aspect of Dracula's castle. I had a further meeting with the Brit site agent Brian, who I had to say, was an extremely affable and accommodating bloke and he fully understood my misgivings. But it amounted to this: that after the first eaves section had been secured, I would then have no choice but to lay and seal the remaining strip from eaves to ridge virtually unprotected on the outside of the roof. If none of that makes sense to any laypeople, let me just say that in a nutshell it was going to be a challenging and testicle-testing few weeks, requiring my complete and uninterrupted concentration at all times, and always making sure to have with me a change of durable underwear.

The operation entailed a carpenter being assigned to me for the duration, as Brian had promised, who would take care of the preparatory work one step ahead of me, and I was introduced to Dez Maillet, a moustachioed native of Cape Pele, New Brunswick in Canada. I guessed he was in his forties and he seemed to be a rather shy man and a somewhat dispirited individual. It didn't help that he had a very thick accent, due to the fact, I had been told, that both French and English were official languages in the province, and his accent was a garbled version of both. But he was good at his job and seemed keen to have me as a friend. I liked him a lot.

Shortly after this meeting, our part of the contract began and I was introduced to my new partner, the safety guy, Felix Brown, a young Rastafarian with impressive dreadlocks that he normally kept hidden under a multi-coloured knitted rasta-cap the size of a pillowcase. Although Rasta's had their origins in Jamaica, the movement had rapidly taken hold of the imagination of young black men in many of the Caribbean islands and beyond. Felix seemed an okay guy although worryingly laid-back to the point of unconsciousness. Even communication was difficult at first, with me failing to comprehend most of what he was saying, always referring to himself as: *I and I*, greeting me with *Wa gwaan* every morning, whatever the hell that meant, and shouting *Yes I* at me if he happened to see me in town – or at least *Yes I* is what it sounded like to my un-rasticised ears. At other times he reverted to pure English-Bermudian, and I got the impression that Felix, bless him, was simply learning the ropes and still serving his Rastafarian apprenticeship. But we got by and the important thing was that he understood me, because at times all that was between me and becoming strawberry jam on the patio below, was a four inch by four inch triangular timber fillet called a water glide, designed to direct rainwater into downpipes situated at intervals along the roof, and thereby into a massive storage tank beneath the building. The glide was where I would place my feet, with Rasta Felix sitting on the flat roof section holding on to a rope that was secured to my safety harness. With my heels dug into the water glide I quickly rediscovered religion, knowing that apart from a bit of timber, it was Felix and his God *Jah*, who held my fate in their hands.

One morning Felix arrived carrying a pair of binoculars, and having tried hard to understand his explanation, I eventually learned that as he was bored just holding a rope, he wanted to see what action there was in the hotel rooms of the block opposite. Forgetting that he would have to release at least one hand to do so, he shrugged off my instructions that even ignoring the obvious illegality of it, this was definitely something he should not do, he assured me that even with one hand, 'I and I got yo ass man.'

Then one week into the job, a world-shattering event took place. An unknown assailant or assailants had assassinated the Governor Sir Richard Sharples and his ADC, Captain Hugh Sayers in the grounds of Government House. The resulting knee-jerk heavy-handed actions by the police when they smashed their way into properties in a notorious and predominantly black area of town called Court Street, predictably and perhaps understandably, caused serious rioting. There was absolutely no evidence to support their actions and it was rightly seen by the black community as an excuse to cover the fact the police had no idea who was responsible for the killings. At least, that's how it seemed at the time.

In spite of Felix's constant Rastafarian philosophising about peace and love and the brotherhood of man under the beneficent rule of Emperor Haile Selassie (Lion of Judah, King of Kings) for the previous seven days, he was now muttering things about acquiring guns and shooting the whites, as I hung suspended over a sheer drop.

It was at this point that I decided enough was enough.

Clambering back to the safety of the flat roofed walkway, and refusing point blank that morning to resume work supported only by my heels, a length of rope and a raging Rasta, *I and I* decided to invest my time in an effort to calm my colleague down and take him for some caffeine and a no-holds barred reading of his horoscope. I forcefully spelled out to Felix that my life was definitely in his hands, and if he had any doubts about that responsibility and could not give it his one hundred percent commitment, then I needed to know before I even thought about getting back on that bloody roof with him. We sat in silence for some minutes over our coffees in the Castle Harbour staff cafeteria, and then finally Felix looked at me with doleful eyes and said, 'Everyting irie with I and I.'

'What?' I snapped. To be honest I was getting tired of this crap.

There followed a long thoughtful silence, then: 'You and me bro, we good,' he told me in more or less plain English, and leaning across, and putting a placating hand on my shoulder, he gave me a reassuring grin, 'Yeah man... we good.'

I let out an inaudible sigh of relief, and decided to have an early day and let my work mate go home to mull over our conversation, and hopefully calm down some more with a hit or two of Jamaican herb.

For the duration of the contract, Dez Maillet and I had shared a few evenings at several of the city's drinking establishments, on one occasion latching on to two American tourists and making a date to pick them up from their bed and breakfast establishment the following night. Des hardly spoke a word the whole time I was giving the girls the chat-up routine, he was obviously far too bashful and inexperienced to know what he should say... even if they could have understood him. I was a bit confused, Dez had told me he was married with a wife back in Canada, which normally would have accounted for his reluctance, but he had agreed to accompany me the following evening, and all things considered, it was a reasonably enjoyable time.

Two weeks later, just before I was able to hand over the completed roof to the main contractors so that they could officially sign it off, Dez informed me that he had notification that all non-Bermudian carpenters were required to leave Bermuda within a set time period. It appeared that there were now enough Bermudians able to do the job and outside help was no longer needed. There was a good deal of controversy surrounding what amounted to banishment from the island – from carpenter recipients and other trades, but also from Bermudians themselves. The principal was not the bone of contention, but it was the cold and arbitrary manner in which the department of immigration handled it, and the short time that was given to those concerned to leave Bermuda. It appeared that many had put a good few years' service into their time there, and in one well publicised case, a man who had married during his residency, had two children who were born on the island and were therefore deemed to be Bermudian. Be that as it may, poor Dez had no choice in the matter, and near to his time of departure I called at his rented apartment in Hamilton to wish him bon voyage, only to be met at the door by a formidable looking female with an expression like two turds mating – harsh, but she was that depressing. This was, I discovered, Dez's wife who had flown over to take her husband back to Cape Pele. No wonder the poor bugger looked downtrodden and so dispossessed of self-confidence; she was obviously the boss and evidently there to make sure he didn't do another runner. Dez had been upset about leaving Bermuda and it was no wonder why. Her manner mirrored her physical appearance, and she made it very clear that I should say my goodbye quickly and leave, which I refused to do and presented my friend with a bottle of the best stuff in order to say our goodbyes properly. He agreed enthusiastically much to the witch's disgust, and we took our time, toasting and wishing each other good health… and to him the best of British luck.

I never saw or heard from Dez again, but I have often thought about him down the years in the hope that things improved for him, and that perhaps he was able to find a priest who was prepared to perform an exorcism.

I was in town anyway, so I strolled over to the Robin Hood for an early aperitif… or three, before dinner.

All three partners were in attendance: Richard Floyd, Tinny McCann and Jack Harris, and for some reason we got into a conversation about cockroaches. I told them I had seen a few in and around Netherlands, and asked what was the best way to deal with them. Bermuda cockroaches were big buggers, and could be a problem, but Jack's opinion was that they were only insects after all, and no worse than their creepy-crawly cousins.

Tinny disagreed, and said that the best way, was to spray any one of the anti-roach products liberally around your pad, and gave me the name of ones he reckoned were the best.

Richard just chuckled and told me that whilst the sprays might be effective, the chemical they contained stunk to high heaven, and was more of a curse than the bugs. 'Try this' he said, and handed me a copy of the previous days' Royal Gazette that had been lying on the counter. 'Open your front door carefully; make sure the newspaper is rolled up, then hit the lights and whack them with it. 'You need to be fast because as soon as they see you, they hightail it under the furniture, or into some hidey-hole or other. And hit 'em real hard, because they are tough little fuckers and don't roll over easily.'

I tried the spray later, and Richard was right. It was definitely worse than the bugs, so the newspaper method was adopted with some success. But it has to be said, that the islands resident giant toads and cute geckos also did a sterling job, with roaches being number one favourite on their menus. And a lizard on your bedroom ceiling was a welcome and sure sign that you would not be bothered with those pests. Not sure about having a toad as company though.

FIFTEEN

Amy was a young lady I had been introduced to via my friend's girlfriend three years before I departed England for the pleasant pink sands of Bermuda. She was a petite, attractive girl with a great sense of humour and a warm personality. She wore her auburn hair long and had a figure that would have been the envy of any female of the same age and she dressed simply, but with taste. In short, she could justifiably be classed as very pretty, except for one significant and unfortunate imperfection… she was cross eyed. That's to say she had a cast in one eye.

What this meant was that whilst one eye appeared to be focused on one thing, the other seemed to be looking elsewhere, and I remember with shame, feeling slightly uncomfortable when I was first introduced to her; it looked as if she was only giving me half of her attention (a common enough occurrence it has to be said) and glancing over my shoulder at someone else. It was the sort of disfigurement that people make jokes about, and her days growing up must have been difficult, knowing how cruel kids can be, but on the face of it she seemed to be a tough little cookie, and laughed it off simply as just a cross (or cross eyes to be precise) she had to bear. But after that first meeting, even I hardly noticed it, because Amy's cheerfulness and genuine love of life shone through. Looking back, I became quite protective, particularly when I caught sight of someone staring at her, and I would glare back until they realised their rudeness and hastily look away. I once almost came to blows over it. There was never anything serious between us, but I saw her on several occasions, often making up a foursome with my friend, Les, and Amy's pal Yvonne, who according to Amy was, and I quote: still being rogered by Les at the time – a humorous assessment of her pal's relationship that had me spluttering over my beer one night when she volunteered the information.

Fast forward three years to Bermuda…

I had dropped by the Modern Mart to pick up some essentials on my way home from work one afternoon; the essentials being a box of English breakfast tea bags, a quart of milk, and most importantly, a dozen or so packs of Club biscuits for which I had a fondness bordering on addiction. The trouble was, no matter how many I purchased in order to theoretically last me the week, I always managed to snack my way through my stash in a couple of days. They were extremely moreish and thank goodness I was not inclined to gain any weight, no matter what or how much I put inside me. The advantage I suppose of a youthful active metabolism. But also a good deal to do with genes inherited from my dad who could not have weighed more than a hundred and twenty pounds soaking wet and carrying lead weights in his pockets. He measured only five feet two inches in height, unlike my own sparse one hundred and fifty pounds eked out into a skinny six foot one frame. My Mum was also a short-house, and it has just made me recall that when I was a very young lad, I can remember that our baker was a long lanky bugger and a regular visitor.

Hmm. Anyway, back to Amy…

As I was browsing the tea section, I happened to glance across to the adjacent aisle, and almost dropped my PG Tips in abject surprise, because not twenty feet away was Amy. But surely not. How could it be? It was more than three years since I had last seen her in England, three and a half thousand miles away; but there was no mistaking the face, the hair and the killer giveaway – those trademark eyes. As I looked in disbelief her gaze fell upon me, and after a long pause her face broke into a smile of recognition and she rushed across from the neighbouring aisle and ran towards me. I was just about to open my arms in preparation for an almighty hug of reunification, when she continued on past me, and grabbing a jumbo box of sugar frosted pigeon droppings or whatever, from the nearby cereal display, held it aloft and shouted across to her male partner, 'Here they are hun, your favourite,' in an unmistakeable American accent.

I had placed my bet on the wrong eye.

Close up I could see that although seemingly identical from a distance there were one or two minor tell-tale signs that indicated that this was not in fact Amy but a near perfect doppelganger. The accent was the clincher.

It is said that somewhere in the world, we all have a double, but what are the chances of an almost identical young woman with the same rare optical flaw as my acquaintance in England, turning up on a speck of rock in the North Atlantic and in the same supermarket as me? It all qualifies as a subject for the Twilight Zone, particularly as there was yet more to come on the subject of strange coincidences during my time on *de Rock*.

SIXTEEN

I had seen Penny on a couple of occasions at the Robin Hood since our original meeting in Serpentine Road, including a fun-filled night at the Bermuda Culinary College that consisted of excellent food at an affordable price, and much laughter. She had let on that she had spotted me on the roof that day in Serpentine Road, and had me pegged as some sort of rock star, with my long blond hair and John Lennon shades, which pleased me no end, and I asked her to put it in writing. We had found out about each other's past albeit in abridged form, and it was obvious to both of us that this could well be the start of a close friendship at the very least. I had taken the next step and invited Penny to dinner at Netherlands, all prepared by the inexpert hands of yours truly. I had decided on chicken curry, which must be easy enough to knock up I told myself, and although I had never cooked any sort of curry before, I was fairly confident of making a decent job of it: chop up some chicken breasts, a few vegetables, maybe some mushrooms, bung it all in a frying pan, add curry paste and toss it around a bit. What could go wrong? I was looking forward to Saturday, which was the designated day of the Indian feast, courtesy of head chef Colin – particularly so as it had not been a good week for me thus far.

It had been a bad Monday. I had started to feel queasy, which soon developed into stomach spasms and had come to a head during a site meeting with my boss and a client in Riddell's Bay which was – *A paradise within a paradise,* I had been told. And it was. Unfortunately for me, I was unable to take it all in and appreciate the gorgeous landscape because I was doubled over in pain, and my boss was so concerned, he insisted I go home and make a doctor's appointment *tout suite.* 'Tell them it's urgent,' he yelled after me as I sped away on my Honda racer.

I arrived back at my apartment in the nick of time and rushed to the bathroom where there was an arsequake of super seismic proportions – ten on the Richter scale. I didn't dare go to the phone to call a doctor; not that I had a doctor's number handy, never having had the need for one during my brief residency in Bermuda. But daring to leave the sanctuary of the bathroom and spending desperate minutes leafing through the telephone directory would have been far too risky. I must have spent the best part of thirty minutes in the smallest room, wondering just where it was all coming from – how could I have eaten that much, and what had caused such an onslaught? Then the image of the Roach Coach flashed through my mind, and realisation dawned. It wasn't called the Roach Coach for nothing, and all the stories I had heard about the place and had waved aside, now came home to roost. So to speak. I had munched on a burger from the place on Sunday – the day before.

At last, feeling tentatively confident to uncouple myself from the bog, and make it to the fridge for a cold drink, because by then I was feeling dehydrated and parched, and no wonder. But having attempted to flush several times, I realised to my horror, that the loo was blocked. Shit!

…Well, yes.

I wasn't up to doing anything about it right then, and I most certainly could not bring myself to phone the landlord; I mean… what do you say? So I downed a gallon of water and laid on the sofa to rest, hoping that given a bit of time, the offending X-certificate blockage might have eased itself through the plumbing system – and also mine. Some hope. It was still there and unflushable an hour later. I even tried two bucketsful of water to assist things, but it didn't budge and the only thing I managed was to compound the matter by flooding the bathroom floor.

I'm sensing that this is becoming a story with too much information, so suffice it to say that having mooched around looking for some sort of tool I could use, I happened to glance through the window and noticed a trowel someone had left unattended in a flower bed, and desperately holding my bubbling rear end, rushed outside to retrieve it. Long story short; after some intense excavating, I managed to breach the bunged-up pipe work. Although I felt somewhat better, I decided to play safe and find a doctor's surgery, my recent experience having convinced me that at the very least, I probably required some sort of medication to firm me up. I now needed to drop by the supermarket anyway, to stock up on my now, depleted toilet paper supply, so leafing through the directory and finding a surgery number in Hamilton that appeared to be the nearest to me, I was surprised and pleased to be told that there was a gap if I could attend within the next twenty minutes.

No problem. I hoped.

I arrived more or less intact (no explanation needed here) and the doctor, who looked as if he was a sixth former on work experience, asked me with a straight face if my excretions had an aroma. I was astonished. 'Yes,' I said, 'just like Old Spice actually,' thinking: what sort of question is that? Then after an uncomfortable pause, with me hoping against hope he would not ask me to lower my strides, the unsmiling medic put it down to a mild case of food poisoning and prescribed medication. If this was mild, I thought, what the hell would a severe case feel like? The whole process with the doc took no more than five minutes… I had never been relieved of twenty dollars so quickly before.

The rest of the week went by without too many complications; the pills that had been prescribed seemed to do the trick, even though they were given without even a cursory examination of my abdomen. Then having been told by my understanding boss, who had phoned to see how I was, that I should take twenty-four hours to recuperate, I was back at work on Wednesday feeling empty, but reasonably secure.

Saturday afternoon saw me preparing the bits and pieces for my chicken curry which I had decided to get ready in advance – just in case. I saw nothing wrong in heating it through after Penny had arrived.

Now I know what you are thinking; that it all turned out to be a catastrophe, and as a result, both of us having a repeat performance of the screamers. But you would be wrong. It was err, quite tasty, and Penny enthused about the meal, although I doubted that it was that good. Nevertheless, God bless her anyway for enthusing. There was one small problem, however. I imagined that all you needed to do with rice was add water and boil, which of course is true, except that specific quantities are crucially important and was something I failed to check on. Consequently what came out of the saucepan was a rice Ayers Rock, which, if dropped, would have done serious damage to the tiled floor, not to mention my foot. Still, Penny didn't seem to mind the mashed potato with her curry, and personally I think it's a whole lot better than rice… even properly prepared rice.

All in all, I told myself, another promising evening.

SEVENTEEN

Although I had placed my feet firmly under the table at the Robin Hood during my first few weeks of residence, I would still occasionally drop by the Ram's Head for old time's sake as a precursor to the evening before moving on. But also because it was a welcome oasis of calm in the early evening that I sometimes required if there had been a trying day at work, or I simply needed a quiet drink on my own for whatever reason. I liked the place; it was definitely a great way to unwind before succumbing to the vibrant magnetism of the Robin Hood which was still, and would remain by far, my favourite tavern and meeting place.

On this particular evening I was surprised to see Richard Floyd at the bar talking animatedly to several fellow drinkers. He seemed to know everyone wherever he went, I had observed, and was instantly recognised whenever he put in an appearance. He told me later that he would often call in to the local competition, in the form of Hamilton's drinking establishments, to see what was going down. A popular bloke and a shrewd businessman was my opinion of Richard.

The conversation that night, however, appeared to be centred on the depressing news circulating across the island, that only weeks after the still unsolved killing of the governor and his ADC at Government House, two men, the co-owner and an employee, at a popular supermarket, had been brutally murdered in a robbery. How could these things be happening in this tiny slice of paradise I asked myself? Would those killings be the tip of an iceberg? Was there more of the same to come?

We soon began talking of other lighter matters concerning the Robin Hood, mutual acquaintances, and the topic of musical preferences, where we found that we had very similar eclectic tastes – a contradiction in terms perhaps, but best sums it up. We had been talking about the relative merits of certain progressive rock bands, and the harder rock groups such as Black Sabbath and Led Zeppelin, when Richard made a suggestion.

'Tell you what, come back to my place for a drink, and we can listen to some Deep Purple', he suggested in his distinctive drawl. 'I've got their latest release and it's really far out.' I knew the album which I had recently acquired from Sounds Plus, and I had been a fan ever since seeing them as an unknown band in 1968, performing in the backwoods of Berkshire.

Having arrived at the Floyd residence I was introduced to Richard's charming wife Barbara, known to everyone as B.D. I had seen her at the Hood on several occasions, but had never made her acquaintance. I also met their massive slobbering hairy lodger, Hash, their lovable and soppy St Bernard dog. Richard selected the Deep Purple *Who Do We Think We Are* album that had been under discussion and which featured the track 'Mary Long', the song that mocked Mary Whitehouse who was a well-known UK voice at the time, and constantly in the news for her criticisms and condemnations of the attitudes of the younger generation in particular. Along with her pal Lord Longford, they had taken it upon themselves to seize the high moral ground based often on outdated views and standards. The band had been one of her targets and as a reprisal Deep Purple released their aptly named album, echoing one of Whitehouse's pronouncements about them.

As the opening track got underway with the introductory guitar riff to 'Woman from Tokyo', Richard produced a familiar looking bottle. 'Have you tried this?' he asked, showing me the label: Goslings Black Seal Rum. Well, yes, I had seen the bottle behind various bars, but had to admit that I had not tried it, having been engaged in my mission to sample as much Cockspur Rum as possible since my introduction to the Barbadian spirit on my very first visit to the Robin Hood.

'Here, try it,' and he poured a tiny amount into a shot glass.

'Be careful, you don't want to give away too much,' I quipped as he handed me the small glass.

'No, it's a serious drink and this is just a taster for starters. One hundred and fifty-one proof,' he told me.

'Did you say a hundred and fifty-one?'

'Yep, just try it and tell me what you think. Roll it around your mouth for a bit before you swallow.' This was not my accustomed way of drinking, but I didn't say that and cautiously sipped the brew. One hundred and fifty proof? Bloody stroll on.

The strength of the rum is evident immediately, but strangely smooth for such a strong drink. But it's when it hits the back of the tongue that it really comes alive and delivers a flavour punch Muhammad Ali would have been proud of. 'Wow this is something else,' I enthused, 'but I wouldn't want to drink too many of these.'

'No, no, you don't drink it neat; I just wanted you to taste it straight to get the full flavour, but there is an eighty proof version which most people drink.'

'Pansies,' I joked as Richard produced a couple of Collins glasses from his drinks cabinet and proceeded to fill them with crushed ice from a conveniently full ice bucket, whilst giving me a running commentary...

'First ice, then about two thirds full of ginger beer, not ginger ale,' he stressed, waving his forefinger. 'Then top it off with a third of Black Seal. It's not written in stone and it depends on your taste, but it should be about two to one. You can add a wedge of lime if you like, but I don't have any so, cheers,' and he handed me the two-tone cocktail which was totally delicious.

The second track on the Deep Purple album, the aforementioned 'Mary Long' had just got going, and we chuckled at the insulting lyrics as we enjoyed our drinks. By the time 'Our Lady' was being played at the end of side two, we were chuckling at just about everything.

It was the start of a life-long love affair with *Black Seal*, although having introduced it later to the friends I was yet to meet, it was a drink that we kept or ordered for special occasions – aka any day of the week with a *Y* in it – and always, always, the one hundred and fifty proof version if we could get it. Ambrosia with attitude is how I described it. It was also the start of a long-standing friendship with one of Bermuda's more colourful and interesting characters.

EIGHTEEN

Although the studio apartment that my boss had found for me at Netherlands prior to my arrival in Bermuda was adequate, it was never intended to necessarily be my permanent home – at least not by me.

Netherlands was a large house on Harbour Road in Paget that had been converted into several studio apartments, which is the posh term in Bermuda for what is known as a bedsit in the UK. But it was okay, a good base close to Hamilton, and not that far from Mills Creek where my employer had offices, which in any case, I had no great need to visit on a regular basis.

The design of the furnishings looked as if they had been installed about the time that Fred Astaire was tripping the light fantastic with Ginger, but they were in excellent, almost new, condition and had obviously been purchased by someone with a penchant for the nineteen forties. Apart from the overall size of the place, I had no complaints, it was clean and serviceable and it was my own space.

From the outset I had made it known at the Robin Hood and the Ram's Head that I was in the market for a house or apartment-share even closer to town. Then not long after, Richard Floyd approached me to say that one of the regulars at the Hood was looking for someone to share a house with him in Woodbourne Avenue. Not only was it in town, but Woodbourne was tucked away in a small street just a very short walk to the Robin Hood. How lucky was that?

I jumped at the opportunity and duly met the guy, one Colin Marshall, the following evening at the Hood, and having satisfied ourselves over a drink or two that we would probably be able to tolerate each other's company, the rent was agreed and we shook hands on it. I had not even seen the property concerned at that point, but it later proved to be a very pleasant cottage – in British parlance, a bungalow – with three reasonably good equal size bedrooms, a smart shower/bathroom, an adequate kitchen and a cosy and comfortable living room. It was close to amenities and the city centre, but tucked away in a quiet neighbourhood and quite literally a stone's throw from the all-important Robin Hood. There was a small lawned area at the front and a medium sized garden at the rear which looked as if it had never been informed about the invention of lawn mowers and rakes and was certainly not amenable to sunbed lounging and socialising. It wasn't a tip by any definition, but what I prefer to call a nature reserve for insects, shrubs and our feathered friends, just this side of unruly and in estate agent speak – 'mature'. There was a plus side in the form of a large avocado tree, and several banana plants that produced miniature versions of the familiar fruit and which made it interesting. But as neither Colin M nor I had a taste for avocados which we both agreed resembled unflavoured soap in a skin, the interest was minimal. I moved within days, having paid up my monthly commitment at Netherlands, along with my telephone and various services bills.

It seemed silly to have a bedroom going begging, so Colin and I agreed that we should advertise in *The Royal Gazette*, Bermuda's premier newspaper, for a third housemate. We were paying a rent of 400 dollars per month (remember this was 1973), and split three ways it would be a much better proposition and leave us with some leeway regarding our bar requirements. The evening of the day that the advertisement appeared, we were inundated with phone calls, mostly ex-pats, but a fair dusting of Bermudian sounding voices as well, and all males. Goodness knows how many missed calls had been made during the day when we were at work, and although we did not have the luxury of owning a recording machine, it was a safe bet that the phone had been ringing non-stop. From the moment I came home just after five, I found Colin already fielding enquiries from would-be roomies. We had not expected such a response; obviously this sort of accommodation was in great demand, and we had not discussed a strategy for choosing the most suitable person. That is until we received a call from Tricia.

Tricia had been the first female to enquire, and because her telephone call was late in the day, she was convinced, she told us later, that we would have received many more enquiries and consequently the room would have already been taken. In fact, she had decided it was probably a hopeless case and almost didn't bother to ring. It appeared that she had applied for other properties and each time had been pipped at the post. She was a hairdresser; had a posh accent, and we hoped other attributes which rendered our need for a strategy a non-starter. Who needed a strategy – she was a girl.

'So when can you move in?' I asked.

'When do you want me to move in?'

'We'll wait in for you,' I told her. 'It's seven thirty now – see you soon.' I gave her directions and that was that. She arrived even before I had poured myself a third pre-dinner drink (a very short time, but one I was in training to improve) and Colin M and I did not need any convincing that we had found our third housemate, when a tall, blonde, well-spoken female arrived on our doorstep. Actually, it was not until the following weekend that Tricia arrived with all her girly gear in transport provided by her Bermudian boyfriend, a well-to-do young businessman who ran a motorcycle dealership on the island. We duly welcomed her into the fold and the three of us drank a toast of Cockspur (what else) to a successful partnership.

It turned out to be a good arrangement. Tricia had what appeared to be a serious relationship with her boyfriend and so was otherwise occupied most evenings and weekends, with the guy often staying over, which was fine by us. And although Colin M and I managed somehow to find ourselves in the Robin Hood most evenings, thus becoming good friends, we nevertheless lived our own lives and tended to gravitate to different groups within the Robin Hood community. We bought our own provisions and with a few exceptions, managed to keep our hands off our housemate's goodies in the fridge and elsewhere. The two things Colin and I agreed to share were his small portable TV and my Sony cassette deck and tapes, both of which were installed in the lounge for general use. Then most weekends he would disappear and spend the majority of his time on the water sailing, although he always seemed to manage to find his way to the Saturday night parties. But I have to say that, initially at least, I met far more people through Colin than he did through me; after all he had been on the island much longer and living previously on a houseboat of all things.

Bermuda had a startling effect on me and although I had always been naturally gregarious, it had been stifled by events that had left me with a fractured confidence and a good supply of emotional baggage. I never forgot those I had left behind in the UK and I had arrived with a sizeable degree of guilt, but it wasn't long before I began to come to terms with those misgivings, and saw no reason why I should not embrace the new lifestyle which fortune had favoured me with.

NINETEEN

It was a normal night at the Robin Hood, or at least our definition of normal as far as the pub was concerned. Colin M was obviously sharing a joke with two of his work colleagues, Dave Revell and Alistair Anderson, when I walked in, who were rolling up with laughter at one end of the bar. Terry, a new friend I had met at the Hood, and had been subsequently invited to his twenty-first birthday bash – and of whom you will hear more of – had the attention of two attractive females who looked as if they might be tourists, and were smiling in wonder as he regaled them of his life experiences. (I had heard his chat-up lines on several previous occasions, and he was *good*.) The tall figure of Ian Crawford was in evidence in one corner with Wendy in attendance who, as usual, was looking up into Ian's face with scarcely concealed love and admiration, all apparently going over Ian's head as he gazed dead pan (his usual expression) around the bar seemingly unconcerned. Then Mary and Lee had just entered behind me, and immediately homed in on a group of guys who were well known faces in several of the various drinking dens in town.

Penny had told me about two other girls that had signed up with the same secretarial agency, and that night I was duly introduced to Jane and Sandra which was, it turned out, their first outing to our favourite ex-pat hangout. They were a fun duo and along with

Penny, later became regular faces in the Hood soon becoming familiar faces at the frenetic party scene, and of course at the beach. To save time and valuable breath when referring to the glamorous trio, I later referred to them collectively as the *Dazzler Sisters*.

Sandra was a stunner and a magnet for the many slobbering Casanovas who regularly supported the alcoholic beverage industry by way of the Robin Hood bar, and she was obviously relishing the enthusiastic male attention as any female would. My newfound friend Terry who, with his fashionable threads, afro hair, and horseshoe moustache, was, as stated, something of a ladies' man and popular with the opposite sex, had watched Sandra enter, and detaching himself from his two admirers, joined the rest of us, and introduced himself. He was never going to have problems pulling.

'Looks like you're in love again,' I whispered to him, suspecting that an assignation was in the pipeline.

'I have always found it hard to recognise the difference between love and lust,' he whispered back. Not that Terry ever boasted about his exploits, and unless asked, never let on just who he was taking out. There was a rumour regarding him and a set of triplets, who were fairly regular faces at the Hood. But that's Terry's story to tell, not mine. The dog.

Jane was also very attractive and getting a lot of attention that night; softly spoken and with a cut-glass accent, she was the epitome of a genteel and very correct young woman. That is until one ever-so-slightly drunk young Romeo must have said the wrong thing because it elicited a very firm: 'Why don't you just fuck off, you little prick,' from Jane.

My mouth dropped open in shocked surprise as she continued laughing and chatting with the rest of us as if nothing untoward had happened. What an eye opener. But it was a feature of Jane that she could curse with the rest of us if the time was right and if she felt a situation demanded it. We quickly learned not to mess with Jane and witnessed many a scene in the months ahead of would-be suitors being cut down to size and slinking away with bowed heads. In between her 'gollys' and 'hurrahs', there were plenty of 'bastards' and 'arseholes'... but delivered with poise. We all liked Jane a lot.

Richard Pedro was also taking a great interest in her, even though he was currently seeing Belinda, who was one of the part time bar tenders at the Hood, and on duty that night. She was giving Richard an icy glare – not that he noticed as he homed in on Jane. I had taken Belinda out on one occasion, and it was memorable for her choice of tipple which was Parfait d'amour and pineapple juice. I never even knew there was a liqueur of that name. But I digress...

For my part, I still had the hots for Penny, that little blonde bombshell I had fancied ever since I had seen her swaying menacingly towards me on her moped that day in Serpentine Road. But I had to admit, along with Sandra and Jane, the three of them added up to an impressive triumvirate of lustful possibilities.

TWENTY

There is no heavy industry in Bermuda as such, and there are three things that Bermuda is well known for: onions, Easter lilies, and Bermuda shorts.

Seeing grown men sporting tailored almost knee length shorts and smart blazers hurrying to work, was not exactly a culture shock, but certainly a significant blip. Their ensemble was usually completed with a plain coloured shirt and club tie, knee length matching colour coordinated socks, and highly polished brogues. Colours for shorts and jacket ranged from pastel blue to heart stopping yellow. But I not only came to accept the sight, I admired the ability to wear such clothing and look ultra-cool in the process, and I harboured a secret longing to be able to adopt the same style. There was a necessity to be in the possession of a half decent pair of legs in order to get away with the look however, which therefore excluded yours truly because I had an understandable phobia about my own limbs; a left over from my school days when they were once described as Woodbines in water pipes. Please note to all those out there who believe that their baggy, arse sagging, psychedelic monstrosities are real Bermuda shorts – they are not. Go to Bermuda to see the real thing and how it should be done. On second thoughts, if you really do have the effrontery to drape your body with such fake clobber, go to *Soufend* or *Great Yarmuf* – you'll feel more at home.

Oh, and the other two famous items: Easter lilies grown specifically for that time of year, and as far as I know, still exported to the United States; and Bermuda onions, renowned for their sweet taste and sometimes eaten like an apple or pear, at one time in great demand and exported to the US. But those grown on the island in more recent times were not even sufficient to meet local demands, resulting in Bermuda becoming a net importer of the common or garden version of the vegetable.

I was fortunate that my job took me to practically every corner of Bermuda. There were contracts that ran for a week or two, but in the main they were few and far between, and there were times when I could be in Spanish Point on Monday, say, and Somerset Parish the following day, then on to the US naval base for the rest of the week. Not only did this provide for a great variety in the jobs that I did – although they would invariably require me to be perched on a roof somewhere or other – but more importantly, it allowed me to explore the many fascinating nooks and crannies in that small but glorious speck of verdant rock basking in the North Atlantic sunshine. I was able to take in the stunning world-famous pink sand beaches as I purred my way along South Road; ranging from the well-known Elbow, Horseshoe Bay and Warwick Long Bay beaches, so popular with tourists, to the more secluded and intimate settings like Jobson's Cove that were more in favour with the locals. And of course, the location very close to my heart (and other parts of my body), the small beach at Church Bay. In other parts of the island, names like Crystal Caves and the nearby Tom Moore's Tavern, Tobacco Bay, the camp-sounding Fairylands and Gibbs Hill Lighthouse, had all been mentally targeted as places to visit as I travelled between jobs. There was also Hidden Beach, but I was never able to find it.

I became accustomed to seeing that popular Bermudian landmark, the Moon Gate, in several of the hotels and private estates I had cause to visit for my work. These were as you would picture from the title: circular stone or rock structures, sometimes free standing, sometimes as part of a wall, and with a triangular or trapezoidal cap-stone in the centre of the arch. The story is that a sea captain returning to Bermuda sometime in the eighteen hundreds, had the first moon gate built on the island after seeing one in a Japanese garden during one of his travels, and as time went by the feature was copied by others and gradually absorbed into Bermudian culture. Part of the tradition that has grown up around them is for newlyweds to walk through the moon gate in order to bring good luck and fortune, but I made a point of walking under several, and they never brought a raise in salary. I didn't trust the custom enough to bother finding myself another wife.

Travelling to work every morning was like having a leading part in a travel video. It was only after moving from Harbour Road to Little Arches that I explored Hamilton city centre in depth. It had been a regular destination for me on Saturday mornings, when I would ride into town and drop by Sounds Plus in the Washington Mall to see what new releases or old favourites were on the cassette racks. I occasionally called into Music City where there was more to browse, but less of the type and vintage of music I was seeking. I kept an on-going list of albums I wanted, and if they were not on display in Sounds Plus then they could be ordered and ready for collection the following weekend. I had a much depleted cassette collection on my arrival in Bermuda, and I was determined to remedy the situation in the shortest possible time. After the musical inspection I would drop by a nearby coffee shop for some mid-morning refreshment. This routine was adhered to after I left Netherlands for Little Arches and crucially, I no longer needed transport. The city centre was just a few minutes' walk away.

Although tea had always been my beverage of choice, it tended to have an inconvenient effect on me. Not to put too fine a point on it, tea went straight through me – it did not pass go, did not collect $200, and notably required several visits to the khazi. I could never figure out why there always seemed to be more going out than coming in, a bit like my weekly budget. Conversely coffee just did its coffee duty and circulated leisurely around my internal parts leaving my kidney's looking longingly at the clock, bored out of their adrenals with nothing to do. Hence my preference for mid-morning coffee on my Saturday expeditions into town. But it was still that mug of tea first thing in the morning that re-sharpened my pencil for the day ahead.

It was during one of my forays into Hamilton that, having dropped into my usual coffee watering hole after purchasing the brilliant *Chicago IV, Live at Carnegie* album, I had a noisy encounter with what I can only assume was a ladies club gathering. Although I had never witnessed one at first hand, I imagined it to be akin to a British Women's Institute meeting. No sooner had I sat down, than a flock of twittering flamboyant starlings invaded the place. They were ladies of a certain age and they presented a colourful scene of sun hats, bright lipsticks, and varicose veins, and although I was not sure if such a thing as the WI existed in foreign parts, had they broken into the patriotic strains of *Jerusalem* and proceeded to get out their knitting and pots of jam, I would not have been surprised.

Realising that the calm of my surroundings was irreparably damaged, I quickly downed my coffee and departed for a more tranquil location, but having gained my liberty onto the street, I had second thoughts and gave up on the idea of more coffee, opting instead for a very early lunch at the Dick and Tickle – aka The Cock and Feathers. I was addicted to their shepherd's pie and chips, which apart from anything else, satisfied my love for the humble potato.

I was looking forward to the following day, when I would experience my first Sunday brunch, accompanied by a young English lady I had met the previous week with the highfalutin name of Suzanne Bennett-Trigg… an unnecessary use of double letters if you ask me, especially as she preferred to be known simply as Sue. She had been in Bermuda since the previous year and knew the ropes as far as where to eat was concerned, and so Ariel Sands had come highly recommended. She also knew the ropes involving several other matters, but that's another story.

It was during our delicious brunch that the real reason for taking me to Ariel Sands became obvious.

We had just made ourselves comfortable at a table near to the pool, when Sue poked me hard in the ribs and said, 'look over there,' She was pointing excitedly to the other side of the pool where a family were just sitting down with their drinks.

'Yeees,' all I could see was a happy family gathering enjoying their holiday.

'The lady on the right is Diana Douglas.'

Another 'Yeees' (so what) from me as I rubbed my bruised ribs.

'And look who is sitting next to her.'

'Look I don't recog— Holy shit it's wosisname Douglas… Streets of San Francisco…' I almost shouted, standing up to get a better look. 'He's Kirk Douglas's boy.'

'I know, it's Michael Douglas, silly,' Sue laughed and pulled me back down before I drew too much attention to myself.

'They must be staying here,' I said, stating the bloody obvious.

'That's because they own Ariel Sands.'

'Wow, really.'

Later after asking around, I was informed that Ariel Sands Hotel had belonged to the Dill family since it was built in the fifties, Dill being the family name of Kirk Douglas' Bermudian wife Diana.

It was surprise after surprise. Bermuda just kept on giving.

What a place.

Having the first ever Sunday brunch in Bermuda was something most people remember well, and was comparable to remembering where you were when President Kennedy was assassinated, or when man first set foot on the moon. Well, all right, not quite, but it tended to be a significant event in most ex-pats' minds, and that Sunday afternoon was no exception for me, with it living up to expectations and then some. Later I wondered why it had taken me so long to experience that Bermudian tradition, and I put the matter right immediately, by trying out the many establishments offering similar good value deals. Like most things, you arrive at your favourites, and the Henry VIII, Waterlot Inn and the Hamilton Princess became three of the most revered, although I can honestly say that I was never dissatisfied, wherever the chosen venue was. All you could eat for as little as five or six dollars plus occasional live entertainment and breathtaking views. I mean. And although it was not exactly a Sunday brunch, the *Hangover Special* at the Robin Hood prepared by chef Dave Weedon, consisting of steak, eggs, black pudding, chips and Bloody Mary for $8.50 was a sure-fire winner with a guaranteed captive market.

TWENTY-ONE

Richard P had introduced me, via the car's 8-track player, to two American hippy comedians, Cheech and Chong, whose humour was largely based on booze and marijuana. I had to admit that at the time, it was right up my alley, and we spent a good few hours before embarking on our nightly bar crawl, laughing at the pair's antics.

Richard was also responsible for introducing me to the Elbow Beach staff club, which was to become an integral part of my life. It was a month after we had met and it was obviously where many of the ex-pat community, and an equal number of young Bermudians, spent their Friday evenings. There was always a party-like atmosphere, and as an added incentive, all the drinks were half price at fifty cents.

On that first night, we had started off at the Bermudiana staff club in Hamilton, where Richard had several friends, and although it was a friendly atmosphere, it was a stark contrast to our next destination at Elbow Beach. The trip to the Bermudiana was a pleasant change from our usual haunts, but it transpired that it would be my one and only visit, because although at that point in my Bermuda experience Elbow Beach had not yet become an almost obligatory Friday night venue, it was still the watering hole of choice should we have the urge to leave the Robin Hood early. It would be later, along with friends that I was yet to meet, that the Elbow Beach staff club scene would become the mandatory setting for our kick-start to the weekend and achieve iconic status for many of us.

Little did I realise in those early days what a significance our Friday forays would take on, not only as a meeting place for the young set, but one where lasting relationships were born, including my own experience. It was also where the coming weekend was planned and information about the following night's party, or indeed parties, was telegraphed around the Friday night throng. There were occasions when we would leave the club and along with others, a mixed bunch of male and female, we would make the short walk along the beach, and throwing modesty to the wind, splash around in the diamante spangled water.

It was always somewhat of a mystery how the management of the staff club were able to host so many people who were in no way connected with the hotel industry, but we were all signed in as temporary members each week, or at least that's my recollection. It didn't really concern us how it was done, because the only thing that mattered was the pursuit of pleasant diversions in the form of good company, brilliant music and cheap drinks.

It was not long after my Ariel Sands/Michael Douglas experience that I was in town after work one afternoon, having stopped off for a few much-needed supplies. Retrieving my bike from its parking spot, I looked up and recognised a very familiar face passing close by. It was Ringo Starr. No doubt at all – there was no mistaking that famous profile. He was deep in conversation with another not quite so familiar face that I was unable to immediately put a name to. I was so gob smacked that I just stood for a few seconds gawping, before collecting myself and shouting after them: 'Hi Ringo, how's it going?'

What a scintillating greeting I realised. But all due respect, he half looked back and shouted over his shoulder in that familiar Scouser twang: 'On top of the world, man.'

My noisy salutation had attracted the attention of other passersby, and it was obvious from the pointed fingers and people turning to stare, that they too had recognised Ringo. Then it hit me. His companion was Harry Nilsson, I should have known because I owned his album *Nilsson Schmilsson* that had Harry's picture plastered on the cover. I had bought the long player, I remembered, purely for the single it contained, 'Without You', that reached number one in the music charts, and which was written by guys from one of my all-time favourite late-sixties British bands – Badfinger. Recognition had occurred a few seconds after twigging Ringo, and consequently the pair were a few yards further on, so I hollered: 'How're they hanging, Harry' – a slight improvement on my Ringo greeting. On hearing this, they both stopped, looked round and gave the thumbs up, whilst those who had been rubbernecking trying to get a better view of the Beatle, had resumed whatever they had been doing. But then, there are plenty of Harrys around and not worth the bother to look, I guess.

Although it was not advisable, it was legal to carry a pillion passenger on most 50cc mopeds, including my own Honda. I say not advisable because even though the seating arrangement was just about adequate there were no passenger foot rests as standard, necessitating the person on the back keeping their feet well away from the rear wheel. On reflection I could have had some fitted I suppose, but it didn't seem worth the expense; I would rarely have had need of them. There was also the question of power, but as long as the road was fairly level, the Honda carrying two would putter along without too much effort.

I had invited Penny out the following day, Sunday, with a view to taking her on a picturesque ride along the South Shore with its wonderful panorama of pink sand beaches, to Somerset, a trip that she had not yet made. But I should have known better.

She had been excited to learn that Ringo Starr was on the island, and hoped that she would get the chance to see him, being an ardent Beatles admirer. Admittedly we had only known each other a short time and her strange little ways and idiosyncrasies had not yet impacted fully on me. Apart from the confusion over whether or not a door that she had attempted to open by pulling, sported a sign saying 'push,' she had also informed me that it was quite a regular occurrence for her to forget food that was cooking, with it ending up as burnt offerings. In fact, before I had picked her up that morning, she had been cleaning the shower, she told me, then when sluicing it down, remembered too late that it was always advisable to do so from the outside.

Two things about Penny: she was self-deprecating… and clean.

But embarking on our afternoon ride out, having emphasised the danger of holding her feet too close to the wheel, I assumed that she would take note. This would mean stopping to rest periodically in order to stretch aching muscles, but hey, it was Sunday afternoon, we could explore the beaches and coves one by one and we had all the time in the world. Then just past the impressive and fairly new Southampton Princess hotel, the bike and I parted company abruptly as the Honda came to a dramatic stop, sending me sailing on for a few extra feet in the general direction of Somerset Parish and beyond. Penny had stuck her foot in the back wheel and the effect was instantaneous and dramatic.

I landed heavily and sat by the side of the road examining my injuries: two grazed knees with matching elbows, and mourning the loss of my almost new white jeans that now had splits around the knees and which, had I known it, in a few more years would become fashionable. The back wheel of the Honda resembled a chromed pretzel and Penny almost in tears and obviously distressed at my sorry state, hobbled towards me with concern on her face, then pausing to pick up a piece of mangled footwear from the middle of the road, shouted at me:

'Look what your bike's done to my shoe.'

'Triffic,' I mumbled, taking in the mutilated Honda and ragged pants… 'Just bleeding great!'

TWENTY-TWO

Stevie and I kept in close touch, and it was heartening to know that her treatment had been a resounding success and there had been every reason to be optimistic about the future. Much of her old energy had returned; she was working again, albeit part time on her doctor's advice, and her once luxuriant shoulder length hair that she had lost during the harsh chemotherapy treatment, was growing back. She had booked a flight to visit Bermuda in October and would be staying for several weeks. Things were looking good.

Having anticipated that by the end of that year she would be able to join me permanently and take up a position at the Edward VII hospital in Hamilton, Stevie had completed an application for employment. It was an involved and in-depth application as was to be expected, but she was a qualified State Registered Nurse – a necessity – and had all of the other prerequisites needed for a position. But fate and the gods of malevolence had other ideas.

Meanwhile life rolled on unhindered at Little Arches and we had all settled into a comfortable routine. As ever, by and large Colin M, Tricia and I led separate lives and had relatively little contact within Little Arches itself. But one night, after a party in Warwick, not far from the South Shore, Richard and I, and Jane and Anita – a lovely young girl I had met for the first time that night – decided to do a bit of frolicking in the sea at one of the nearby beaches. Obviously we had not planned this, so surprise, surprise, we did not have swimwear to hand. Never mind, we were happy to let it all hang out, and cavort a bit in the altogether to our heart's content. It was extremely liberating and a first for me, but this was something that became a fairly regular event over the months to come, and I can thoroughly recommend it.

I invited them all back to Little Arches, where we showered off the surplus sand in pairs – so as to conserve water – and I invited the lovely Anita to stay the night, but stressed that there were no strings attached. It was the first time that I had slept with an attractive female, and *really* just slept. It is something that I have looked back on over the years, and thought: *You prat!* But at the same time, I feel very proud of my gentlemanly conduct that night. I hope Anita feels the same way.

Early on and having accustomed herself to living with two guys, Trish announced that she would like to cook Colin M and I dinner one evening as a belated thank you for inviting her to join us. She had been searching for somewhere suitable to live for quite some time, it transpired, and she was delighted to find herself sharing with 'two lovely guys', as she put it.

'Bloody 'ell,' Colin had whispered, 'she's easily pleased.'

But it was a nice gesture and greatly appreciated; we certainly were never going to turn down the offer of free grub prepared and served by an attractive woman.

It was a good evening; I bought the wine – two bottles of Hock (my palate was in its early days of development with regard to wine), which Tricia and I drank, and Colin bought the beer which he was happy to neck unaided. I have no idea what I had for dinner yesterday, but I remember on that night half a century ago, that Tricia prepared a dish called bobotie, a South African concoction she told us, made with curried minced meat, herbs and other mystery stuff, with a creamy baked egg topping. Easy to make she said, which was correct because I have prepared it myself several times since, and very tasty it is. I have no recollection what the pudding was, or even if we finished up with coffees – probably not – but we expressed our appreciation in the time-honoured way by toasting Tricia: me with German wine and a smile, and Colin with Heineken and a belch of appreciation, both of us declaring that she could cook for us as often as she liked.

Bermuda brought a succession of new experiences and ideas. The camaraderie and bonding between so many people in such a short time; the wonderful openness of the ex-pats and Bermudians alike, and the sheer joy of living – it was unique in my own limited experience. Yes, I had several good friends in England, some of whom have remained close throughout my life right up until the present day, but in Bermuda there were none of the usual hang-ups or personality clashes for the most part to inhibit us; life was for living and by God that's what we did. We had been provided with the right tools for the job: Cockspur Rum; Goslings Black Seal, and fabulous surroundings. The beauty of the islands was outstanding, with their pristine pink sand beaches, the sparkling white roofed, pastel-coloured houses, the absence of grinding poverty, and of course the ever-present (well almost ever-present) glorious sunshine. There was just one aspect of the climatic conditions that was, at first, difficult to adjust to: the extreme humidity. Each morning the day's forecast was broadcast on the radio, giving air, water and humidity figures, and on at least two occasions I was aware of, the relative humidity for the day was given as a sweltering one hundred per cent. But with Bermuda's sub-tropical climate the flora was breathtaking and having spent just one day in Little Arches I had encountered a sight that has stayed in my memory.

By the evening of that first day in my new home, I had successfully unpacked my belongings and deposited them in the array of cupboards and drawers that had been allocated to me; lovingly placed my new super-duper Sony twin deck cassette player (with radio receiver) on a polished wood table in the living room, and feeling suitably pleased with myself decided that some alcoholic sustenance and a bite to eat was called for. So where better and more convenient than the Robin Hood just a short walk away.

We were situated at the end of the street where the road did a sharp right-hand turn, before exiting on to Richmond Road, close to our favourite bar, and as I turned the first corner I was met with a fabulous sight. A hedge of a variety I had seen many times before during my tenure at Netherlands, but never as spectacular. The whole of the front boundary of the property was a mass of purple, coral, salmon and red flowers. It was stunning, and although I have in subsequent years seen the plant many times in my travels, it was my very first sight of such a glorious and breathtaking example of Bougainvillea. It was not only the blaze of mixed colour, but also the combination, and loving and artistic way it had obviously been cared for. It is a sight that I have never forgotten.

But then a few weeks later, and coincidentally in the same garden, an even more spectacular sight if that were possible, where a tall tree with an impressive spread that I had seen many times on my nightly pilgrimages to the Hood, had suddenly exploded into life and was a mass of magnificent bloom. There is red and there is very red, and then there is blinding red, but the intensity and denseness of the blossom was such, that it almost hurt the eyes. The homeowner, who was pottering in the garden at the time, saw my astonishment and seemed proud to inform me that it was a Royal poinciana, a native of the far east but equally at home in Bermuda's sub-tropical climate, thank you very much. It was simply magnificent.

What a place this Bermuda was.

TWENTY-THREE

In their quest for generating interesting side projects, the Robin Hood team of Tinny, Jack and Richard Floyd, looked at the darts scene, and had decided that Bermuda darts required a kick up the jacksie, and flew over two top professional players from the UK. They played a number of exhibition games and the response was immediate, with the Robin Hood forming a darts team and joining a rejuvenated darts league. As Richard P and I had played regularly in between drinks rounds just for the hell of it, we were automatically press-ganged into the team. Our teammates were Dave Lovelock, Colin Marshall (when he was standing), Bob Alley, Dave Jansen (when he remembered), either Jack or Richard Floyd (when available) and the star of our team, Ian Crawford, who was light years ahead of the rest of us, always up for it, and our sure fire, at-least-one-leg-certainty player. But there was always one or two of the RH regulars who would be dragged away from the bar to make up the numbers, and quite often when we were playing at home, the popular bar-keep Michael Correia, who it turned out was a mean player when the mood took him. His shout when he played a good dart was: '*Ah my boooy!*' and he would punch the air enthusiastically. In fact, this was his cry whenever Richard P and I and others he knew well, walked into the bar. Michael was a popular guy with everyone, looking like a cross between Frank Zappa and Jim Croce, but better looking than either of them.

Sadly though, a good friend and character who was taken from us far too young.

We surprised ourselves at the end of that first season, when up against such teams as Vasco da Gama; Moose; Spanish Point Boat Club and RAFA, all of whom had some pretty tasty players at their disposal, we finished near to the top of the league table. It was obvious that Cockspur and Black Seal played a very important part of our game plan, so we of course continued our association with the two products. The games were not always as laid back as they were meant to be, and on one notable occasion, a player who shall remain nameless, from the opposing team, which also shall remain nameless, was so pissed, he threw his remaining dart (having scored a one, and then the wall with his first two darts) at our main man Ian… he missed of course. This was a definite no-no, and several of us had to physically eject him from the Robin Hood. Forefront in that exercise was an athletic looking guy who was new to us and just happened to be in the bar that night. He seemed to enjoy the task of bouncing the player out of the door, even though he had not been involved with the melee or even the game.

Two evenings later, the same young guy arrived at the Hood, looking crestfallen and despondent; it seemed he had failed his driving test that morning, because the examiner turned out to have been none other than the bloke who had hit the pavement two nights before courtesy of our self-appointed bouncer. We tried to console him, these things happen we said, but at least, courtesy of the management and ourselves, he went home that night with an untouched wallet and a full bladder.

The following day was a Friday, and the office had received a call from the Deepdene Manor Hotel to report a roof leaking over one of the corridors that for obvious reasons, with the comings and goings of guests, was regarded as urgent, and a request was sent out requesting our immediate attention. Having had no rain for some time it did not take a Rhodes Scholar to figure out that this was highly suspicious, and I was sent along to investigate, taking all my gear with me just in case it was something I could attend to on the spot. I had often ridden past Deepdene on my travels, making a mental note to self each time that I would stop off and check the place out as I had with several other establishments during my time in Bermuda. So it was fortuitous that I could now do so in work's time, which was a bonus. It was late-morning and even if the survey took longer than expected, I would still be justified in having a spot of lunch on site and I could work in a bit of nosing around. The place had always fascinated me because, whilst the hotel proper was on one side of Harrington Sound Road, a bridge spanned the thoroughfare and linked up to an iconic tower and boat house opposite on the Harrington Sound shoreline, which, I was later told, was a leftover from the days when the hotel was a family residence.

I was directed to the roof in question by the hotel's maintenance man, and it became obvious straight away that he had not bothered to investigate the problem himself, because whilst the roof was obviously in need of repair, the source of the water that was seeping through was from a corroded water pipe that ran across the flat roof. There was nothing I could do with regard to roofing repairs until the leak in the pipe was remedied, which to my eye, looked as if it would be a complete replacement job, and I reported my findings to the embarrassed maintenance guy accordingly. Had he taken the trouble to get up on the roof earlier, it would have been immediately apparent. I also told him that after the pipe replacement, and because of the roof's age and general condition, I would strongly recommend complete renewal. I did a quick measure-up and left him with the promise of a quotation for the required works within the next twenty-four hours.

Mentally smacking my lips so to speak, plan A swung into action and I looked for the hotel's dining room in the hope that non-residents (and contractors) were welcome. It had been a long time since breakfast. But no sooner had I made my decision when I spotted a very familiar figure advancing toward me from the reception area togged out in kitchen garb complete with stripey pants and a toque, aka a chef's hat (I looked it up).

On several occasions at the Robin Hood, Richard P and I had noticed a guy that always seemed to have several females clustered around him, damn it. With his impressive mane of dark fashionable hair, teeth like enamel headstones and Mediterranean good looks, he was – and I say this grudgingly – the living definition of a babe magnet. There was no doubt in my mind that the bloke was Italian, it was written all over him, and Richard reckoned that he had seen him at the Waterlot Inn waiting on tables. So imagine my surprise when the same guy approached me that day and in broad Newcastle vernacular said: 'Hiya, seen you a lot at the Hood, how are you doing? My name's Rob.' And he held out his hand. I took it and laughed out loud – I couldn't help myself. Rob looked at me with a hurt expression before I was able to reassure him that it was just that I had him tagged as a spaghetti bender, as I termed it, which once it had sunk in, elicited laughter from him also.

'I'm Colin,' I told him, 'exceptionally pleased to meet you.' And I was. I learned that he was already firm friends with Terry, and before we parted – him to work and me to eat – we arranged to meet that night in the Hood before travelling on to Elbow Beach.

It was the start of another firm friendship and added one more face to a group of Brits who would remain close in spirit, if not geographically, for the rest of their lives after forging that close Bermuda bond.

TWENTY-FOUR

One of the more colourful traditions in Bermuda was kite flying on Easter weekend, or more specifically Good Friday. It was like a carnival of the air, with the simplest shop-bought kites mixing with the more intricate and convoluted home-made variety, in which were contained a variety of complexity and colour; with the more adventurous and passionate kite fliers experimenting and building their contraptions months in advance. To say that it was an obsession with some would be putting it mildly, and the term applied to serious kite fliers, I learned to my surprise and amusement, is 'Pilot'.

I had thought that this pastime would be a relatively quiet affair, but apart from the obvious gleeful shouts from excited children, many of the kites were fitted with 'hummers,' that gave out a cacophony of whirring sounds as they waltzed and sashayed through the air. It wasn't quite my thing, but I had to admit it was a beautiful sight, and I was glad to partake of the other Bermuda traditions available on the day, of hot Bermuda cod-fish cakes. Yummy and highly recommended.

I was informed about College Weeks by an eager Richard Pedro, in the build up to Easter. The way he told it, the island would be inundated with American college girls crowding the roads on their rented Mobylettes for a whole month surrounding the Easter recess, looking for likely lads and not to put too fine a point on it – gaggʲ for it. Particularly if you had a Bermudian or better still, an English accent. But first of all, what was this College Weeks thing all about, I wanted to know?

Some say it started in the 1930s, but the popular opinion is that it began in earnest in the fifties as Rugby Week, when teams from North America and beyond flew to Bermuda in the spring holidays to compete with Bermudian and British teams. But the whole thing took on the appearance of a Roman Bacchanalian knees-up, with partying taking precedence over the actual sporting events and college students from across the US, and particularly the east coast, making it an excuse to get their summer season off to an early start.

The Bermudian government sponsored the occasion by providing free passes for the students to everything from boat trips to dances at some of the island's hotels, and from steel band concerts to beach parties, and it soon became *the* spring holiday destination of choice, and the island was stormed annually by large numbers of students, the greater proportion being young *female* students.

The dishing out of all these goodies was not, however, a purely munificent gesture on the government's part, but was designed as a taster of what Bermuda had to offer with a view to attracting those youngsters back at a later date, and more particularly portraying itself as *the* Honeymoon Island.

The whole experience lasted for almost a full month, and travelling became a nightmare for Bermudian drivers, because the roads and lanes were filled with hordes of swaying, wobbling mopeds attached to which were raucous American teenagers. I learned a valuable lesson that spring, that far from being a testosterone pumped male dream, it could be a bloody nightmare. For a start, in the pubs and hotels, they hung around in large groups, and attempting to break one away from the herd was like trying to extract a dollar bill from Viv Tierney's wallet. And believe me, many men better than I have

 hard! Viv, I had better explain, was another ex-pat of the regular crowd at the Robin Hood and other hments, who had acquired a certain reputation for

112

being light on his feet in avoiding the front of the pack when another round was called for. But he was one of the lads and a well thought of fun character for all that. But getting back to College Weeks…

The other thing that struck me almost immediately about this annual female swarm, was that age for age, American girls seemed to be several years behind Europeans in maturity. Those sixteen and seventeen-year-olds seemed to be, for the most part, the equivalent of third-year secondary and grammar school girls in England – they were, in the main, a giggling flock of chattering canaries and quite frankly, the way I saw it, a pain in the backside. And you knew on first meeting what their conversation openings would be: 'Love your accent, do you know the Beatles?' or 'Are you from Liverpool?' Just how small did they think England was? But on the only occasion I managed to shoe-horn one of them away from her avian sisters, I was totally dumbstruck not believing my good fortune. An opinion that I had good reason to soon reconsider.

She introduced herself as Carolee Ann – even spelling it for me – and immediately added that her daddy was the owner of a newspaper in Boston, and feeling that because of her less than aristocratic demeanour and the rolling of eyes from some of her companions when she related this information to me, I had good reason to perhaps ever so slightly regard it as a bunch of steaming effluent that she had probably already spun to other would-be suitors. And I told her so in no uncertain terms.

But she didn't turn a hair.

'Oh wow, I just love your British accent,' she told me, obviously overlooking the fact that I had just suggested that the only thing rich about her was her imagination.

But naively thinking that I still had a shadow of a chance with this one, I went on to say: 'I have a bottle of Courvoisier Napoleon in my apartment (not entirely true, as it was now only half full), why don't we go back there and compare star signs over a drink.' Ok, ok, a pretty naff chat-up line I admit, but horses for courses and all that.

But I wasn't lying about the brandy. That bottle cost me an arm and a leg at the London Airport duty free, but it was bought purely as show (apart from my generosity in sharing some of it with my friend Ian weeks earlier), and a talking point for any would-be overnighters – at least those who might have an inkling what Courvoisier Napoleon actually was, and what followed illustrated that this particular female most definitely did not. I might as well have told her that if she came back to my place there was a Big Mac and fries on offer with a strawberry milkshake to follow, for all the interest she took in my cellar credentials.

All I got was: 'Wow, that is such a cool accent. I just love the Brits.' But nevertheless, she said 'yes,' and I wanted to shoot off with her on the Honda before she invited all her mates along. I had actually prised one away from the flock, and I had scored.

Well, no, I hadn't.

I was fumbling my bike keys in my haste to get on the road when she stopped on the steps from the bar and asked: 'What about your buddy?'

'Oh, he's okay,' I told her, even though Richard had also been struggling with the rest of her crowd and puzzlingly seemed to be enjoying it. But it was every man for himself in these circumstances, and there was an unwritten understanding that if you pulled, then good luck mate and get to it. 'Don't worry, he's enjoying himself with your friends,' I told her truthfully.

'What did you say?' she queried.

Thinking she must be a bit hard-of-hearing, I upped the volume and repeated: 'I think he's enjoying himself with your friends.'

'Oh wow, that really is such a far-out accent. Say something else.'

I looked at her in total disbelief. This wasn't an act, was it? Did I really want to spend time with someone who's only interest in me seemed to be the way I spoke? And instead of the angel face and trim figured individual I had latched on to at the bar, all I could see now was a good-looking girl with a fixation on dialects.

'Alright I will,' I told her, and speaking slowly and exaggerating every syllable as if talking to a school kid, which of course I was, said: 'Look, I tell you what, let's go back inside and have a few more drinks with your mates. It was a bit cruel on reflection, and somewhat egocentric on my part, but it was how I felt at the time.

But it didn't faze her and her face lit up. 'I love the way you said that; it's so cute,' then turning around as instructed, and seemingly unaware that I had just dumped her, she made her way back up the steps to the bar. But there was just one more gem of an afterthought she honoured me with when she reached the top, and turning she presented me with an all-time classic.

'Your friend Richard...'

'Yeees?'

'For a Bermudan he sure speaks good British.'

'Oh, sweet Jesus and the angels take me now,' I muttered under my breath.

That Easter was the first and last time that I would even consider chancing my arm with one of these girls, although in fairness, I had simply been in the wrong place at the wrong time, and I know many others (well alright, *everyone*) who had, had more success than me and through sheer determination and resolve, had many a juicy tale to tell. In one instance that I heard about, a guy actually married his college girlfriend and as far as I know – and I do hope so much that it's true – they lived happily ever after.

TWENTY-FIVE

Greg was a well-known face at the Robin Hood. He would often drop by at the ex-pats' preferred watering hole and tell us about his day at the office. With anyone else, that would have been the time to make excuses and leg it… the last thing any of us wanted once we were let loose, was to talk about work. Work was an irritating inconvenience and moreover an unwelcome intrusion into our far more important social lives. But Greg was different; he was lucky enough to have what many of us would have termed the best job in the world: he worked with, and trained, dolphins at the Blue Grotto dolphinarium. Greg was in fact an American who was a professional dolphin trainer, and was in Bermuda to help the resident Bermudian duo of 'Nollie' Robinson and Ronald Darrell with the dolphins.

He would describe the day's work and we would all listen avidly. There is something about these creatures that make even the hardest of men turn gooey with pleasure; they were Greg's children, and his pride and love for them was self-evident. He and his two colleagues had been training the dolphins ready for the upcoming season, working out complex routines that were designed to amaze and confound the paying customers, but no matter how involved they were, he told us, these highly intelligent animals always grasped the new choreography with consummate ease, and seemed to genuinely enjoy it.

The opening day duly arrived, and we waited to hear how things had gone. Greg eventually appeared at the Hood, but instead of the expected look of self-satisfaction, his expression was non-committal. He marched up to the bar and without acknowledging his friends, he ordered a very large drink… something had obviously gone very wrong. None of us had the courage to broach the subject and ask the obvious question, we just hovered in gloomy anticipation and waited for Greg to bare all.

He downed his drink in silence and ordered another.

The tension was killing us, and eventually not able to contain myself, I asked him as gently as I could what had happened.

'How long have we been training them?' he asked.

'Oh, weeks I expect,' I said, not really having a clue.

'Yeah, weeks and goddamn weeks,' he acknowledged. 'It would have been a great show, and do you know what they did?' We all shook our heads dumbly. 'They had worked out a whole new routine for themselves – nothing like the one we had rehearsed. And do you know what was worse?' More head shaking. 'It was even better than ours.'

But the twinkle in Greg's eye, and the pride in his voice, belied the stern words.

TWENTY-SIX

During the summer that year, the island had the dubious honour of hosting the Gunners, aka the Arsenal football squad. Two years before, the club had completed the League Division One and FA Cup double in great style, and following a lean year after that, had to be content as runners up to Liverpool in the recently completed 1972-3 season.

But that didn't stop them letting their hair down and partying big time as if they were once more the champions, and apart from dedicated Arsenal fans and many of the young female contingent who thought they had died and gone to heaven, the rest of us, aka the young male population, were somewhat jarred off with their presence. There was a good reason for this because, regrettably for some of us, the boys from North London had discovered the Robin Hood early on in their tour of the island, and they had determinedly set out to sample just about every facet of Bermudian nightlife. Consequently, some of them became regular faces in our favourite drinking den, ergo, the centre of attention as far as the female customers were concerned. We blokes were livid; just who did they think they were? Well, er, good looking, over sexed, over paid football stars, I guess.

Not all of the squad had come to Bermuda and although I was not a team fan, one player I would have liked to have met was Charlie George who was sadly not one of the group that had made the trip –

either that or he simply never made it to the Hood. I never did find out. I would not have been able to identify many of the team anyway, but Peter Storey, Peter Simpson, Ray Kennedy and George Armstrong were some that were pointed out to me, as I recall, but I would not have known or much cared one way or the other. One exception and a face that I did instantly recognise was the Arsenal keeper Bob Wilson who went on to become a TV pundit for the BBC covering a span of many years, and I had good reason to remember him thereafter or more accurately perhaps, he had good reason to remember me.

Having the need for a leak in the Robin Hood gents, and without thinking who might be on the other side of the door as I exited fully relieved, I collided with Bob who was leaning against the door jamb giving it large to a small audience of female admirers. Being a smoker in those days, I had just lit up after zipping up, and had one of my favourite Kool ciggies on the go, and purely by accident it made contact with the back of Bob's hand. You could not inflict anything worse on a goalie. I apologised at the time of course, and did not approve of the stifled laughter from some of my friends who had witnessed the event. No really… I didn't! Anyway, having suffered the glares from Mr Wilson who failed to accept my sincere regrets I'm afraid to say, I would like to state again here and now, many years down the line, that it was a genuine accident, Bob.

The only other Arsenal player I had any interest in meeting was Peter Marinello – the glamour boy of the squad. Apart from being a brilliant player that Arsenal had purchased from Hibernian in 1970 for a staggering one hundred thousand pounds at the age of just nineteen, he was also a poster boy and modelled clothes with the singer Lulu amongst other extra-mural activities. He even appeared on Top of the Pops later, handing out prizes for the best dancing. He was dubbed by the press as the next George Best; however he was another Arsenal player who was never seen at the Robin Hood and I assumed he had stayed at home for whatever reason. But then one evening, having decided to eat out at the Little Venice, we were surprised to see him enjoying a meal with an attractive young lady who, we were later led to believe, had accompanied him on the trip. He was charming and gave us the time for a brief chat without displaying the air of self-importance which was a trademark of many others in his position, and certainly his teammates at the Robin Hood. So it came as a shock that his behaviour later became synonymous with a playboy lifestyle which was eventually to become his undoing. He freely admitted in interviews many years later that he had wasted his talent and the earlier pronouncement by the press, that he was the next George Best, had been prophetic for the wrong reasons. A great shame and a loss to the game, but I shall always remember him as a polite, somewhat humble young man.

That was the only highlight of the Gunners visit for me, and most of us were relieved to see the back of them with some of us even discussing the possibility of getting together at the airport on their day of departure with Liverpool banners and other rival football club accoutrements, expressing the basic and popular sentiment that they could bugger off and not come back. But their flight back to London being on a weekday, it was felt that it would be better served if we went to work as usual and reflect with satisfaction on the fact that whilst they were having to return to a dreary and colourless England, we were staying on in our earthly paradise.

Yeah... see!

TWENTY-SEVEN

Weather patterns have changed since those days, but back in the seventies hurricanes rarely hit Bermuda with full intensity because their favourite hunting grounds were much further south, centred in the Caribbean and often venting their full force on the Caribbean islands, Florida, and the US South-Eastern seaboard. However, they did on occasion come dangerously close to Bermuda and in 1973 a hurricane warning was issued for Wednesday the 4th of July – ironic if you happened to be American. The eye-wall of the storm was due to brush the islands during the early evening and being young, adventurous and stupidly reckless, a deadly combination, I was determined to get up close and personal with hurricane Alice as she had been christened. It could very well be my one and only opportunity to witness such a thing, and would surely be a story I could dine out on in years to come.

To my surprise, it appeared that there wasn't a sense of trepidation and anxiety amongst Bermuda's inhabitants, but one of excitement and anticipation at the approaching storm. Many hurricane parties were hastily arranged for that night I later learned (Bermudians need very little excuse to party), and the liquor stores were doing a brisk trade throughout the day. Businesses closed early; buildings were secured, and as a loss of power was envisaged, stores experienced a run on hurricane lamps, torches and candles.

As it happened, I had a dinner invitation that evening with a new acquaintance and his wife at their home on Trimingham Hill, but if I left Little Arches early enough I figured, it would give me time to ride out to the North Shore and watch Alice pass by before returning to Hamilton.

Big mistake.

This may not have been one of the big ones as far as hurricanes were concerned, but the sight of Alice as she approached was pretty awesome and had me mesmerised. The brilliant blue-green waters surrounding the island were transformed into an angry black seething mass of hostile waves that lashed the shore, and the voice of Alice was a hair-raising banshee howl. I should have been content with just a fleeting look and skedaddled on my Honda, pronto, but I wanted to see just a little bit more before I departed, totally confident that I could outrun the storm if necessary.

But these things travel fast and wanting to get every ounce of excitement from the event, I underestimated Alice and badly misjudged the timing, leaving it a little too late. Before I knew it, I was whipped off my bike and all hell broke loose around me. I was blown to the ground and felt parts of my clothing being tugged violently by the vicious wind as I scrabbled to find a handhold somewhere. If somebody had told me years earlier that one day, I would be in Bermuda having my clothes ripped off by someone called Alice, I would have said bring it on, but this foreplay was a bit too rough for me. Goodness knows how I managed to retrieve my bike but I did, and eventually, having miraculously started the damn thing, I rode a squiggly and hazardous line back to Hamilton and my friend's house where I arrived bedraggled, but safe, sometime later.

The door was opened by my friend only to encounter a forlorn and sodden figure dripping in the porch; wearing a shirt that was torn and filthy, muddy chinos, and hair standing straight up in gooey rods – but triumphantly clutching a somehow intact bottle of red wine.

'You needn't have gone to so much trouble,' my host said, deadpan, as he slowly eyed me up from head to toe.

'Sorry,' I told him, 'Alice got a bit pissed off because she wasn't invited.'

TWENTY-EIGHT

I had been in Bermuda for several months before my boss informed me that it would be necessary for me to be able to use a company vehicle at certain times, in order to transport materials and other items of plant etc., to the various sites where I was posted. Hitherto I had made my way to wherever I was working on my now not-so-shiny Honda 50cc moped, but with the increase in the firm's order book, it had become necessary that from time to time, I would need to transport the items I needed for my own use instead of tying up our superintendent David, who was required to keep close supervision on the many painting contracts that were in operation. The problem was that no driving licences issued in countries outside of Bermuda for cars and goods vehicles were valid, not even international driving licences. Mopeds which constituted the majority of the means of transport on the islands were no problem, but for anything on four wheels, a Bermudian licence was needed and the company had therefore applied for the necessary driving test on my behalf.

This was not necessarily good news; I had taken my test in England more than nine years previously and I had certainly picked up a few bad habits in the interim, but my work colleague David assured me that it would be a piece of cake, having taken his own test before I had arrived in Bermuda, and within a few days I received confirmation of the date of my test. The one thing in my favour was that Bermuda was a British island and therefore the traffic drove on the left. But fate had played a cruel trick on me because the date of my test was the 5th of July, the day after hurricane Alice had kissed the island and given me a titanic blow job on the North Shore. What would the state of the roads be like I wondered? Surely they would inform me that my test would have to be postponed until after a clean-up operation had taken place. But no, I duly arrived at the test centre in Hamilton, having negotiated all sorts of debris on my way in, including considerable flooding in low lying areas, and was informed that it was business as usual. Heck.

David had already arrived at the centre ahead of me with one of the company's vehicles in which I would take my test. To say it was interesting would be an understatement, with fifty per cent of my time driving on the wrong side of the road in order to avoid fallen trees, broken down vehicles, bits of buildings, assorted garbage and amazingly, a semi inflated blow-up doll in one street sporting (I could not help noticing) a larger than life mouth surrounded by a pair of pouting crimson lips – presumably designed for lonely, sad, fellatio obsessed men. I was convinced the test was a lost cause as my tester remained silent and impassive in the passenger seat throughout, occasionally making notes on his clipboard.

The last part of the test was back in the large yard at the centre, where I was required to back into a limited parking space, avoiding touching the high kerbstone that marked out the back and ends of the bay. Just one instance of coming into contact with said kerb and it was a fail, David had informed me prior to the test. *Thanks for telling me, Dave*, I thought – no pressure there then.

Well, what the hell, it looked as if I was heading for a second test anyway, and not giving a toss, I manoeuvred quickly and effortlessly into the required space without a hitch. After a bit more scribbling in silence, my tester suddenly smiled and informed me that I had passed with flying colours. I had? Really? But I was not about to argue. Obviously he was prepared to look beyond the obstacle course of detritus left from the night before, and realised he was dealing with a cool, calm and highly proficient driver. Right on. Then having accompanied him into the office, he issued me with the necessary documentation and still, somewhat bemused, I had become a bona fide Bermuda driving licence holder.

'Give Dick my best,' he called after me as I left the building.

'Sorry?'

'Dick… your boss. He's a good friend and he told me you would be coming in today.' Then he winked before turning away to prepare for his next customer.

TWENTY-NINE

Colin Marshall's work colleagues and regulars at the Hood, Ian and David, lived in nearby Richmond Road, but their back garden opened out onto Woodbourne Avenue directly opposite our house, Little Arches. We had talked previously about throwing a party, and one night in our local – the Robin Hood where else – we firmed up on the idea and decided that we would jointly host a party with the said garden of Ian and David being the focal point for the event. This was something to look forward to as it was to be my introduction into the party scene as host, or co-host in this instance, and the first of several such parties over the next two years.

It was to be a busy and illuminating weekend, with our party bash being held on the Saturday, then up to Ferry Reach the following day to watch the start of the annual *Round the Island Power Boat Race*, although depending on what state I was in, perhaps only able to watch the race finish. In any event, Richard Pedro would be picking me up, so it would be entirely in his hands.

I was totally taken aback by the number of people who turned up at Ian and Dave's place, and it became obvious to me why Little Arches had not been chosen as the venue; with its average size garden, it simply could not have coped with the extent of the multitude that descended on us, and in any case Ian and Dave's large plot was mostly lawn which, although slightly bedraggled, was nevertheless sufficiently navigable and better suited to an outside knees-up.

There was always a new face or two appearing at the Robin Hood or at the numerous weekend parties I had already attended, and that night there seemed to be more than the usual quota – many of them to become familiar faces and regulars at future events and at the Robin Hood and other bars. It was probably due to the house being situated just steps from the Hood that made it the perfect add-on to the evening's entertainment for many people.

The usual suspects were present, one such being Ron Robinson who was the maintenance engineer at The Inverurie Hotel situated on Harbour Road. He was a distinctive figure, lean and tall, sporting thin long black hair with a beard to match and always... always, arriving with a case of two dozen beers on his shoulder accompanied by a broad good-natured smile. Looking back, I do not remember attending a single party during my time in Bermuda when Ron did not put in an appearance, and always with the mandatory case of beer and grin. With the benefit of hindsight and the passage of years, I have always thought of him as a carbon copy of Mick Fleetwood of Fleetwood Mac some three decades later; a much younger version then of course, but the similarity was striking. Ron was often at one of the glorious beaches that were a trademark of Bermuda, and seeing Ron emerging from the sea, with wet hair clinging to his face, always reminded me of a latter-day Neptune; he only needed a trident, with a mermaid on each arm and the image would have been complete. He had a close pal who always accompanied him, yet another Colin – Colin Thomas – and one of the many people whose presence was almost guaranteed at the many events over the next two years.

Notably, there was a trio of characters in attendance, one of whom, I learned, worked at one of the major international insurance or reinsurance (whatever that is) companies that were registered in Bermuda. They were to become a regular sight at the various parties in the months to come, and for some reason seemed to find Richard

P and me amusing; not in the acceptable way that they thought we were a couple of happy, humorous lads, but they were often to be seen sniggering in corners like adolescents, and making it plain that we were the object of their simpering attention. Sticks and stones and all that, but it became increasingly irritating as time went on, and we referred to them as *the insurers*, by virtue of the fact that it was the known occupation of one of their number. As for the two companions, we neither knew nor cared where their place of employment was. It all came to a head many weeks later when, because their antics became more than just schoolboy sneering, we decided to take action. But that was still very much in the future.

Early in the morning when the party was still in full swing, we were honoured with a visit from two of Hamilton's finest who nosed their patrol car into the open gate. 'Uh oh,' I muttered to a companion as the cops made their way through the throng asking whose property it was and who was in charge, 'looks like the party is about to come to an end.'

I saw David push Ian forward which made sense as he was by far the largest of us and like me, David was a fully paid-up wimp. There followed a few minutes of what seemed intense discussion, then a shrug from Ian and a word in David's ear who rushed off towards the house followed seconds later by a sharp reduction in volume from the Edgar Winter Group who were belting out *Free Ride*. The two boys in blue seemed satisfied, made their way back to the car and drove away. It appeared they had received a complaint from an un-named resident in the vicinity about the noise, but no more than five minutes after they left I noticed that the volume had started to gradually increase until it reached its pre-plod dimensions and we were back in full swing with the heavy dirge-like, *In-A-Gadda-Da-Vida* by Iron Butterfly hammering out into the Bermuda night. Ian had a particular fondness for the group along with the strange folky-psychedelic sounds of the Incredible String Band. But we were spared that at least.

There was a re-run an hour later with the same two cops pulling up at the gate and this time wearing sterner expressions, they zig zagged through the crowded garden to much good-natured cat-calling and rude hand signals that resembled shaking invisible ketchup bottles, until they found Ian. There was more debate, this time including myself, David and Richard (strength in numbers and all that) with raised voices from the two cops and once again the volume was turned down until the Old-Bill were satisfied, then with a few final words of warning and pointed fingers directed at all of us, they drove off.

The rest was predictable and right on cue, because The Hollies were giving 'Long Cool Woman in a Black Dress' some welly only seconds after our uniformed friends' departure.

It was inevitable I suppose that the complainant would have been on to the police once again and giving them a right old ear-hole bashing, because policemen one and two duly arrived at the gate and having been met by the four of us, darn near pleaded for us to do something permanently about the loud music. The heavy approach had clearly not worked and so having accepted a couple of beers for their trouble, they seemed more than ready to enter into a compromise agreement. We would terminate the party in one hour at about 4am, we told them, probably cutting it short by two or three hours if things were allowed to run their usual course. All they had to do was stall the irate resident for sixty minutes and we would call it a night. How was that?

'Or we could arrest you now for causing a disturbance,' one of the cops ventured, although in a rather half-hearted manner I felt. Thinking they were gaining the upper hand, they both took a long swig of their beers and waited for our response.

'Okay,' said Ian, holding his hands straight out mockingly as if waiting for the cuffs to be slapped on… 'Arrest us.'

'But you had better do something about that beery breath before you take us in,' Dave added.

There was a long pause; I think pregnant pause is the term because the atmosphere was filled with swollen possibilities. Then Richard broke the silence: 'Another beer?' The cops looked at each other, gave capitulating shrugs, and plonked themselves down in two garden chairs.

'Bugger it… go on then.'

The party had wound down in accordance with our promise to the local constabulary, and although there were still a number of characters chatting and swigging beer in the garden, and several more sleeping off their excesses in garden chairs, at least the music had been terminated. Richard had left, Dave and Ian were nowhere to be seen and I made my way back across the street to Little Arches. There seemed little point in going to bed; I was still wide awake and as it was getting on for breakfast time, I decided to have a good old full English to start the new day. I could grab forty zeds later on if I needed them. I had no idea where Colin M had got to; he was at the party of course, being one of the hosts, but at some point he must have wandered off to pastures new, because having peeked around his bedroom door I saw that the bed was empty and unslept in. Perhaps he had decided on a very early start on the water and was having breakfast at the clubhouse or whatever it was the yachting types used for their H.Q. Equally likely, he had crashed out somewhere in Ian and Dave's apartment, and was loudly driving the cows home. As for Trish, she had gone out with her boyfriend the night before, having shunned the party and was, I assumed, shacked up at his place for the weekend, something that had happened before.

I always liked music first thing in the morning at the weekend; it put me in a good mood and the post-party spirit, so selecting my new purchase, Elton John's brilliant album *Goodbye Yellow Brick Road*, I jacked up the volume on my Sony tape deck, secure in the knowledge that I was alone.

I was in the kitchen preparing my food, warbling along to 'Saturday Night's Alright for Fighting', when Trish appeared in the doorway. 'Oh no, I'm sorry,' I shouted over the music. 'I thought you were still out. Hold on, I'll turn it down,' and wiping my hands on my Fred Flintstone and Barney Rubble apron (stop sniggering) rushed out to attend to it. Trish looked awful and appeared as if she had been up all night, which as it turned out, she had. I sat her down on our well-worn sofa and made her a cup of strong coffee, then plonked myself down beside her. 'What's happened?' I asked.

It all came pouring out. Her boyfriend had taken her out for a candle-lit meal somewhere, then by way of an after-dinner chat and completely out of the blue, he had dumped her without ceremony. She was given the usual bull about it being 'time to move on' and, it's 'not you but me,' and 'hey, it's been great hasn't it?' The usual crap dished out by guys who had led their women on giving them the false impression that it would be a long-term relationship. Then he had brought her home, given her a kiss on the cheek at Little Arches' gate, and said, 'See you.' Or something like that, and that was it. It had been two months, during which time Trish had fallen for him hook line and sinker, now just a memory and probably another notch on the bastard's bed post.

Colin M and I always had our doubts about the guy. It wasn't as if he had done something that many of us would not have repeated if an attractive young woman showed an interest in us. But we could see how she had fallen for him so completely, whilst knowing by reputation what his history was. We had kept quiet in the hope that we were wrong and that things would work out for them. Stranger things had happened and what could we have said to Trish anyway whilst she was wearing those rose-tinted spectacles. I tried to comfort her, but there was nothing I could say except that I was there for her, without even knowing myself what the hell that meant. Both Colin and I liked Trish and I knew he would feel the same way as me when he heard the news, but there was little of anything practical that we could do except make ourselves available with sympathetic ears. It wasn't a unique situation, far from it; I had been blown out more times than a second-hand trumpet, so I knew what she was going through.

It just so happened that the following Saturday I had been invited to a twenty-first birthday celebration at The Breakers Club. The lovely Sue Measures, whose party it was, had been introduced to me by Penny some weeks earlier and as a result I had been included on the guest list. I asked if it would be in order for me to take along a partner, which Sue readily agreed to, and so I had taken Trish in an attempt to lift her spirits and forget, at least for one evening, her troubles. It wasn't much in the scheme of things, but we had a good time and it was a great relief to see Trish laugh again, and I hoped, begin to get her life back together.

The following weekend, Trish had arranged to go to the beach with some work colleagues and it was a treat to see her so upbeat and cheerful. It really did seem that she had begun to shrug off the misery of the last few days and get on with things. To add to her more optimistic mood, there had been a welcome message from her brother John in England, to say that he would be visiting her in the near future. It all seemed to be coming back together for our lovely housemate.

THIRTY

I had dropped by Gentleman's Quarter to see Richard as I often did on a Saturday. One of the downsides of being part of a family-owned menswear shop of course, was weekend working. We chatted in between customers, and just as we were thinking about going out for some lunch, Richard became somewhat excited when a well dressed looking dude came into the shop and started to browse the range of shirts on display. He wore a white Fedora, and a polka dot shirt with a collar like the wings of an albatross. His tailored jacket seemed to be of the softest of leathers, and his flared jeans were so wide at the bottom, no trace of his shoes could be seen. But it worked, and he had that confident swagger of a man who knew it.

'You're Billy Paul, right?' Richard said.

'Right on,' said the dude.

'Man, I've just bought your new album – *War of the Gods*.'

'Hey that's cool, what do you think?'

'Cool... really cool.'

I almost started to shiver it was becoming so cool, but I had no idea who this guy was, although the name rang a very distant bell that was on a par with a budgie pecking away at his plaything with a rubber beak.

'Hey, great to meet you,' I said, faking it.

'You too, man,' and we all slapped palms like really cool dudes do.

It was only after Mr Paul had left the shop, Richard told me that he was the guy who recorded 'Me and Mrs Jones'. Of course, that's where I had heard the name. Why hadn't I thought of that a few minutes earlier; I could have impressed Billy with my knowledge of his songs, well, *song* to be precise. The fact was of course, Billy Paul was much better known as an artist in his homeland, and apparently Bermuda. He was just visiting the island, he told us, and getting away from the pressure of his work. Nice guy though and surprisingly softly spoken and modest with it... super cool too.

I reminded myself again just what a great place Bermuda was for famous faces; first Ringo and Nilsson, now Billy Paul. And although I had not laid eyes on her, it seemed Twiggy was a regular visitor and even owned her own small island. Wow upon wow.

When it looked as if Richard could leave Frank, his second in command, to handle things, he announced that we should go greeze, and we walked the short distance down the steps of Chancery Lane to Richard's favourite café. I had become accustomed to many of the Bermuda colloquialisms including greezing, which meant to eat – greeze being a distorted version of the word grease... obviously. Well, it made sense in a strange sort of way.

'They make the best cheeseburgers in town,' Richard would often tell me, and although I believed him, I preferred to stick with my regular bacon burger with the works but definitely not cheese, I stressed, when I gave my order. 'Why not have both?' he often admonished me, so I had told him: ever since my early childhood I had hated the taste of cheese; some of my earliest hazy memories were of nursery school where I was forced to eat grated cheese on salad, thus, I believed, it had put me off all cheese for life. On that particular Saturday, however, I gave in to Richard's entreaties and ordered my first cheeseburger having already made up my mind that I would probably be hastily discarding the dairy product. But wonder of wonders, it was delicious. Obviously melting the stuff had made all the difference; the aversion had left me suddenly after more than

twenty years, and I resolved to make it a cheeseburger from then on...
but still with bacon and the works. *Always* with bacon and the works.

Richard had left me to it in a hurry, having seen a group of locals who
were known to him pass by the cafe, and who he hoped were on their
way to his store. It was his turn to buy and before rushing off, he paid
for both our meals. But I was enjoying my lunch so much I ordered
another beer and took my time over the remains of my burger. I
finished with a sigh of satisfaction at the awakening of my cheese
friendly taste buds and I proffered a twenty-dollar bill as payment for
the beer.

'That all you can do?' grumbled the proprietor. Surprised, I simply
nodded.

This was 1973 and a twenty was probably the equivalent of
tendering a fifty today, but it really should not have been a problem.
But judging by the scowl on the proprietor's face, it did not go down
well. He was obviously having a bad day and trouble making change
as he delved into the cash register, but after much scrabbling around
he returned to me holding out two clenched fists, but this time with a
wily smirk on his face.

'There you go, bro,' he said as he opened his hands and off-loaded
two piles of small denomination coins. 'Sorry, man, this is all I can do'
he said. 'Y'all come back now,' and he turned, chuckling to himself as
he made his way back to the counter. He had made his point, but not
wanting to appear put out or concerned in any way, I trousered the
coins and casually as possible strolled out of the café.

But it's hard to look nonchalant holding up bulging strides using
both hands and with two pounds of shrapnel in the pockets.

There was a party that evening that Richard had got wind of, somewhere
on middle Road not far from town. But first he said he was taking me
somewhere that I had not been to, or even knew existed – the Four
Aces bar in Hamilton. We lined our stomachs first with a few drinks
at the Robin Hood, then travelled the short distance to where the bar

was situated. I should have guessed that Richard had a surprise for me knowing his sense of humour, and the caterpillar of doubt had started munching into the cabbage that was my brain as we left the Hood. The penny finally dropped with a clang as we were about to enter the said bar when Richard declared:

'Don't worry, we'll be cool, quite a few of these guys are Gentleman's Quarter customers.' I really should have cottoned on much earlier. To say that everything stopped as we entered and every head turned towards us sounds like an exaggerated claim and is something only seen on TV or movies, but that's what really happened. It looked as if ours were the only white faces in the place, and just call me intuitive, but it seemed to me that there would be no red-carpet welcome, or any warm smiles of greeting. Richard was not phased one little bit, however, and he acknowledged several of the patrons as we made our way to the bar, receiving cursory nods and unsmiling faces in reply. Customers are customers you would have thought, but the 'Yep?' from the unsmiling bar tender only reinforced the impression that we were about as welcome as shot-putters in a glass factory. But with no other choice than to go along with it, I ordered our drinks, secretly hoping that we would be asked to leave by the sullen barman.

To say I was relieved when Richard suggested we go after just one drink, would be a monumental understatement, and so forcing a smile, I followed my pal through what appeared to me to be a gauntlet of hostile faces, but on reflection were probably expressions of simple curiosity (yeah, right) to the welcoming doorway that represented escape. Outside, and with a straight face, Richard asked: 'Enjoy that?'

'Yeah, about as much as piles,' I told him, at which he couldn't hold it in any longer and laughed himself silly at the look on my face. His wind-up had been a success.

We located the party venue in Paget not too far out of town, and Richard seemed to know exactly where we were going; but as he pointed out, all born and bred Bermudians knew the layout of their tiny country like the backs of their hands. It was hard to ascertain just who was throwing the party, but the host residents were an irrelevance anyway; as with practically all parties it was an open affair and as long as you brought along sufficient liquid sustenance to get you through the night, then – welcome one and all!

I was still getting to know people from my evenings spent at the Hood and other establishments, also the ubiquitous parties and there were a number of familiar faces present that night, including Marilyn, an attractive lady I had met not long after I had moved into Little Arches, and with whom I spent a large part of the evening dancing and chatting with. She had already tagged me with a nickname, 'The Viking'. Not because of my build, which was more of a Viking flagpole (if I turned sideways, you could cut bread with me) but because of my mass of long curly blond hair she had informed me. Richard had sloped off doing his own thing with various friends, mostly females, and I saw little of him until the early hours when he told me he was feeling a bit the worse for wear, and would be making tracks. Did I want to stay on and if I did, would I be able to find my way home, he asked. We had both arrived courtesy of Richard's Suzuki trail bike and thinking I might find it difficult to get myself a lift home later, I decided to join him. It was getting on for 3am after all, but having witnessed sunrise at the previous week's bash, an 'early night' might be in order.

The downside to the evening had been the presence of the three smirking individuals we had labelled *the insurers*, who as always, seemed to find our appearance amusing. It was harmless albeit annoying, and on the last occasion I had to calm Richard down and talk him out of wading into them, even though I came close to a confrontation myself. It was all wearing a bit thin with us, and we sensed that something had to be done, and soon, and that evening, it all came to a head in no uncertain manner.

Richard's bike was stationed along with others, on a gravelled space at the rear of the house that served as a parking area for the partygoers, and as we approached his machine I glanced back and saw the three stooges watching us from the open French garden doors of the house. The parking area was unlit, and it was difficult to see much which accounted for what happened. After Richard had straddled the Suzuki, kicked the engine into life and been joined by me on the pillion seat, he released the clutch and almost immediately there was a thud and a sharp jolt, powering me into the back of my friend, who had been thrown against the handlebars. *What the…?*

On inspection we found a length of wood had been placed through the spokes of the front wheel, so that when we moved forward, it jammed against the front forks and stalled the engine. We were shaken but unhurt, and as it turned out the bike had received little serious damage, but having had my head ricochet off my friend's back, I had inadvertently glimpsed in the process, the three tormentors laughing at our misfortune, before quickly moving away from the open doors. They had clearly anticipated the dramatic event and it became instantly obvious who had placed the offending item in the wheel of the bike.

Keeping uncharacteristically calm and having removed the offending article from the wheel, we remounted and rode back to Little Arches where, over several brandies, we decided that action had to be taken. Satisfied with our decision, but still unresolved as to what we might actually do, Richard left me just before dawn to return to Spanish Point.

A red line had been breached and accountability was on its way, although we were still clueless about what to do, and had not come up with a suitable plan of action.

THIRTY-ONE

Richard and I had been discussing the possibility of purchasing some land in the British Turks and Caicos Islands, that he had got wind of from one of his customers who was someone big in real estate. Geographically the islands are effectively an extension of the Bahamas group, and lie north of Hispaniola – the large island that comprises Haiti and the Dominican Republic.

My ears had pricked up when Richard had brought the subject up, because Brian Lunnon, the site manager at the Castle Harbour Hotel project I had been involved with a few months before, had indicated that the Turks and Caicos would be the next boom area in his opinion, and all it needed to set things off, was for the British government to approve the building of an international airport on the islands. Brian had his own plans to look into the possibility of investing in a breeze block manufacturing facility, obviating the need to import the product once the anticipated building boom had begun. I didn't know much about breeze block manufacturing, but I could see the sense of his idea.

The land for sale was a seven-acre parcel on the island of Providenciales, which meant nothing to me, and was on offer at ten thousand US dollars. It was mostly scrub, Richard told me, but was ocean fronted. Like Brian, he could see the potential and the demand for land taking off once the tourists started pouring in courtesy of the new airport.

I could see two major obstacles: firstly, there was no date for the building of the airport, and if it failed to get off the ground (see what I did there), then it would turn into a massive white elephant. Secondly, and closer to home… how the hell was I going to put my sweaty mitts on my share of the ten grand? Richard tried to assure me that getting a loan for such a project would not be a problem, and although I had discovered early on during my stay in Bermuda that acquiring credit was a simple process (I had procured my Sony piece of audio kit that way), there was a gigantic difference between a few hundred dollars and five thousand. So reluctantly – because it really did sound good – I told him that I would not be applying to the bank for a five grand loan. Despite Richard's assurances, I knew what the answer would be.

It would turn out to be one of those *If only* moments, because in the not-too-distant future from the day we had the conversation, the go-ahead for an international airport was finally given by the British government. Land was acquired, and building started.

I was back in England when the centre page spread of one of the UK tabloids at the time was focused on some T&C islanders thanking the government for making them millionaires overnight, when their previously worthless land was bought for eye watering sums.

Never ask me for a stock market tip.

It was around this time that a Russian cruise ship, having strayed a little too close to the islands, had run aground on the outer reef and being Russian, the help offered by the Americans to tow the embarrassed ship off the reef, was refused. The captain's only hope was that the ship could be floated off at high tide without the assistance of the imperialist Yankee war mongers and their Bermudian lackeys. In the meantime, it was reported that dozens of Bermudian pleasure boats had powered out to the ship and, finding that it was full of Cubans, had exchanged American beer and cigarettes for Cuban cigars. But I had no personal experience of any of that, more's the pity. I was quite partial to a good cigar.

That weekend turned out to be yet another hectic time, with two parties to attend, and a tour of three, or was it four, of Hamilton's finest taverns before the Saturday night rave, and I had been introduced to a concoction called a Bullshot… and that's not a typo! This is a drink designed for the few who are in need of some urgent therapy, consisting of vodka and beef consommé or bouillon, and made more interesting (if that's possible) with lemon juice, tabasco, Worcestershire sauce and any other condiments that come to hand. I have never slurped stagnant water, but I reckon it would run a Bullshot close. Never again!

I had managed only a little sleep after the regular Friday night get-together at Elbow Beach – something I had eaten I supposed, though not from the Roach Coach – so the boisterous Saturday parties were taking their toll.

I had been talking to, and dancing with Kathy, one of the seemingly endless supply of nurses that we were always bumping into. She was a petite red-head from somewhere up north *tha knows*, and had been around for some time. So, she was a familiar face, and had been pleasant company. I made the almost customary offer of coffee and cocktails back at Little Arches, and in view of the fact Woodbourne Avenue was not a million miles from her own apartment, she accepted. The problem for me, however, was that I was out on my feet by the time we arrived back at the house. It had been a physically and mentally exhausting week which was nothing out of the ordinary, but with the lack of meaningful sleep, it meant that I was feeling well below par, and it had suddenly caught up with me. So having downed a large black coffee after our arrival, in an attempt to freshen myself up, and provided Kathy with the same along with a brandy chaser which she seemed to enjoy very much, we chatted about this and that… which inevitably became less about *this* and more about *that*. Even though I was seriously beginning to struggle, I pointed Kathy in the direction of my room, excusing myself for a few minutes in the process, ostensibly to pour more brandy and make another strong coffee for myself.

Waiting for the kettle to boil, I ducked into the bathroom to give my teeth a wash and brush up, and looking in the mirror – which surely was not functioning correctly – I observed that the bags under my eyes would have been ample for a fortnight's holiday in Jamaica. So, Kathy or not, I decided to take five minutes shut-eye on the sofa. And that was it.

The next thing I remember was waking up and glancing at my watch, realising that I had been sparko for more than an hour, but figuring that Kathy would be asleep herself by now, I decided to snooze on, but I was vaguely aware in my semi-conscious state over the next hour or so that Kathy periodically peered round the arch leading to the lounge to see if there was any movement from the strange life-form on the sofa, then having decided it was going to be a no-show, she would retreat back into the bedroom. This happened several times, but for some reason I still do not to this day understand – because I had noticed she was wearing some very fetching frilly white underwear – I just could not bring myself to move from my comfortable couch.

To Kathy's credit, she seemed not to hold it against me – although that had originally been the whole point of the exercise – and she accepted my apology as I left her at the door to the apartment she shared with friends, but only after I had politely refused her generous offer to make me another strong resuscitating coffee and a hair of the dog.

Despite the fact my behaviour would have qualified as an insult in most people's eyes, we remained friends throughout the rest of my time in the islands and we never did get around to a re-match.

THIRTY-TWO

I have never understood or pretended to understand the complexities of cricket. The only time I was foolish enough to engage in conversation with a Bermudian cricket fan and thereby an expert (all Bermudian males are cricketing experts, I discovered) was during the Cup Match weekend. He hit me with so much unintelligible jargon which might as well been Mandarin Chinese, that to save embarrassment I made the excuse I was experiencing some bowel problems and urgently needed the facilities. This was not all together a lie, because his incessant chatter about leg spinners, short-arsed cover strips and googly Yorkie bars, had given me the screaming shits.

Cup Match weekend in Bermuda is the traditional battle with the bat and ball between Somerset and St George's cricket clubs, and is a combination of two national holidays: Emancipation Day and Somers Day (much later renamed Mary Prince Day) and are the Thursday and Friday before the first Monday in August each year. So, Cup Match weekend is actually four days. Got all that? Good.

Even as a cricket Philistine, I still found it to be a colourful and fun event. There were no casinos on the island, but with all that pent-up desire to gamble away the kids' college fund, the legal Crown and Anchor tables did a roaring trade – I even had a few goes myself. Predictably unsuccessful I might add... but the selection of food on display was mouth wateringly good, with many traditional Bermudian dishes on offer.

Roger, one of Richard Pedro's brother's, was taking his boat – a smart little fourteen-foot Shetland cruiser – to one of the many small islands in the Great Sound… or should that be, Roger's boat was taking *him* to one of the islands? Anyway…

He was spending a couple of days there with his other half, Suzie, and camping out overnight. Richard was taking his then number-one girl Jo, and I was also invited and told I could be accompanied by a young lady of my choosing (wished it was *that* easy). But I didn't hesitate, and invited my good friend Mary – one half of the Mary and Lee partnership – who was always good company.

It was a great couple of days, with a lot of food prepared invariably on the barbecue, gallons of beer and of course Cockspur rum supplied by Richard and me, and even a few drunken fireside sing-songs – mostly of the barrack room ballad variety such as The Ball of Inverness, and In the Street of a Thousand ars—… well, you know.

Lots of laughter that weekend too as envisaged, when during the night Mary and I decided it would be more comfortable on the boat, so being careful not to waken the sleeping shapes wrapped up in their bags around the remains of our campfire, we paddled out to the cruiser anchored a short distance off-shore. But it turned out that it was easier to imagine than actually execute, with me almost getting a hand hold then slipping back into the warm water a number of times. There was much stifled giggling from both of us, but after several minutes trying, I managed to haul myself up only to be challenged by a voice coming from the darkened cabin. It was Richard telling us to bugger off and find another boat. We were still giggling like school kids when Mary and I got back to shore and sat beside the dying embers of the fire drying ourselves off.

All good clean fun – damn it.

THIRTY-THREE

It was a strange time. Stevie was due to arrive the following day for an extended holiday and I was experiencing a spectrum of emotions, from excitement to apprehension, guilt to optimism, and trepidation to exhilaration. I was a mess.

The only preparation I had decided to make for her visit was to treat myself to a new camera and make sure I got as many pictures of her stay as possible. So I took myself off to Stewarts on Reid Street from where I had purchased my cassette deck the week after my arrival on the island. I was quite taken with one of the new Canon cameras, and could see myself as a bit of a David Bailey with such a professional looking piece of kit. The problem was the price. Seeing my interest, a young male assistant approached me with an offer of help, and I told him frankly that although I really fancied the Canon, it was probably more than I wanted to spend, hoping secretly that it would prompt a *today only* offer at a reduced price... which is what happened.

Well, not quite, but as good as.

He told me that he would be upgrading to the model in question, and therefore offloading his present camera, also a Canon, at an attractive price. It was less than a year old he assured me, and in perfect condition. He was obviously an aficionado, a keen photographer, and thoroughly convincing... also, easily contactable if things went wrong, so not likely to be less than genuine. Having agreed a price and my promise not to let on about our arrangement (his bosses would be slightly miffed if they found out, he said), we fixed a time and place to cement the deal, and I acquired a nice low mileage, late model Canon SLR.

I had been living the life of Riley, whoever he was, since arriving in January that year, but at the same time I had missed Stevie's presence. I knew this day was coming and although I had plenty of time to think and prepare for it emotionally, I still could not see beyond her visit and catch even a glimpse of what the future might have in store for us. We had kept in close touch, although if I was being honest with myself, not as frequently or as fervently as we should have – she, because her father had had the opportunity to move with his job to Newcastle, and it had been a chaotic and trying time for them as all moves are; and me because I never seemed to be able to find enough time to write as often as I should due to my new frenetic lifestyle. I did, however, call her as regularly as possible, taking into account the time difference and the fact that she always opted for night duty with the new nursing agency in Newcastle where she was working on a part-time basis.

Once Stevie had been cleared of the life-threatening Hodgkin's lymphoma that had prevented her from joining me in Bermuda at the outset, and she had been given the green light by her brilliant consultant, Professor Hamilton Fairley at Bart's Hospital, she had immediately reapplied for a position at the King Edward VII hospital just outside Hamilton.

That had been a month before.

It had been hinted at during the summer of the previous year when she had first applied and before her diagnosis, that as an SRN her acceptance would be almost a formality. But now ironically, with her medical record and her cancer experience, she had been told that the hospital authorities would be unable to offer her employment. It was a massive and unexpected blow and presented all sorts of problems and the need for some serious rethinking and decision making on both our parts.

I had already programmed in the fact that Stevie would be coming to live and work in Bermuda, and I had accepted that my pleasure seeking and party-going lifestyle (and that was before I had met a certain Dougie Dewar) would have to come to an end, but that was okay. Another year or two of the same wouldn't have gone amiss, but I could just about live with finally settling down, and I owed it to Stevie – or so I told myself. There was one major problem and that was Bermuda itself. It had got seriously into my blood and although I had spent a busy and exciting nine months there, meeting lots of interesting new friends and partying as if my life depended on it (apart from my first two wasted weeks *settling in*, I had not spent one evening in alone in all that time), but I longed for more. With over a year left on my contract, I was desperate to find a way of reconciling that to my responsibilities and emotional ties to Stevie. It was a classic case once again, of wanting to have my cake and eat it. But of course, it was irreconcilable.

My work colleague David had kindly offered to take me to the airport to meet Stevie when she arrived, and as it was in the middle of our working day, our boss had generously given us the time off along with a company vehicle to do it. Stevie and I had not swopped photographs of each other during our near ten months apart – neither of us even owned a camera – and although I knew what to expect when I saw her again, I nevertheless experienced a small shock as she walked from the aircraft across the asphalt towards the terminal building.

For the whole four years I had known Stevie, right up until her illness, she had worn her lustrous hair shoulder length. Then after the radiotherapy and the round of invasive chemo involving a powerful experimental drug called *mustine*, she lost it all. The NHS provided a wig of her choice, and she accepted the situation with good grace and incredible courage which left me in awe; but then that day at the airport in Bermuda when I saw her sporting a new jazzy short hairstyle (all her own), it still left me with a feeling of deep sadness. The important thing was she had been cleared by her consultant and was looking fit and well again, and seeing her walking towards me, I realised how much I had been looking forward to her visit.

I promised myself I would ensure that Stevie squeezed every last ounce of enjoyment from her trip to paradise and it was agreed she would stay as long as she wished, and with her open-return air ticket, it did not present a problem. For me it meant dropping out of my regular social routine for obvious reasons; not that I was hiding Stevie away or that I was keeping her away from hearing about my sybaritic lifestyle, of which I had kept very little back from her (although somewhat toned down I freely admit), but purely to ensure that we spent as much exclusive time with each other as possible.

I introduced her to the Hood, how could I not with the place being right on my doorstep, along with some of the many friends I had made, but sensibly avoiding some of the more intimate ones. I took her to dinner at various restaurants, careful to review the menus first, for Stevie had always been a vegetarian and not many establishments provided interesting and inventive veggie dishes in those days. Most evenings though, I knocked up something that I knew would conform to Stevie's preferences. I had become an average to fair cook since the curry and rice-brick episode, and had experienced my own brief period of vegetarianism whilst in Cornwall. That was before I began work in the Saxon Bridge Restaurant where the only vegetarian options were egg and chips or Welsh rarebit; besides which everything we ate was paid for.

I took some advanced holiday leave and we travelled around the island taking in all the wonderful scenery and stopping off for lunch at places like Castle Harbour where we had our picture taken beneath one of the island's many moon gates. We also frequented the Paraquet, Waterlot Inn and Henry VIII amongst others. I introduced her to the Bermuda custom of Sunday brunch at Ariel Sands and again at the dock at the Waterlot Inn, where we whiled away the whole afternoon at the water's edge, taking our time over the splendid dishes, many of them satisfying Stevie's veggie credentials, and listening to a band knocking out traditional jazz.

We did the usual tourist things as in: Crystal Caves, the Flatts Aquarium and Natural History Museum, and a glass bottom boat trip where we fed tinned dog food to the barracudas and other species circling the vessel, who had responded to a whistle from the skipper – it was obviously such a regular occurrence that the fish were conditioned to associate the sound with food.

With its sub-tropical climate Stevie fell in love with the flora of the islands evident in the myriad colourful gardens and small lanes that interlace Bermuda, and we spent time at the Botanical Gardens in Paget where many species of tropical and sub-tropical plants and trees from around the world were on display. She was enthralled with the quaintness and history of St George's, the islands old colonial capital, and the exclusive and varied stores in Hamilton, the present capital. The locals were somewhat incensed if you called Hamilton a town, and rightly so. As Bermuda's capital, complete with its own cathedral and belying its small size, it is nonetheless a city.

We spent time on Elbow, Horseshoe and Warwick beaches, and it seemed right to take her to Church Bay where I had spent my first weekend acquiring a rosy face. I decided not to relate my other adventure at that location, however.

At other times when I had no choice but to go to work, I managed to wangle the odd half hour taking her to this location or that on my trusty bike. At other times she was quite content to use public transport, or simply take the short walk into the centre of Hamilton, shopping and sipping a gin and tonic at one of the many bars. When I was able to obtain a lift to work with a colleague, she even chanced her arm at scooting off on my moped. In short, she was having a good time in spite of the hovering but noticeable change in the dynamic between us.

Two of my work colleagues were young men who went by the names of Stanley and Winston. Work colleagues in the sense that whilst we worked for the same company, they were exclusively involved in the painting side of the business with Stanley occupying the position of foreman. But on the odd occasion I was sent to the same job, or when no roofing contracts were in progress, we became friendly and over time I had got to know them quite well. They were not the flavour of the month with the Bermudian contingent because both were Jamaican émigrés and with Stanley having reached a certain position of authority, it did not go down well with the locals, even though he had earned his foremanship through hard work and dedication to the job. The Bermudian sobriquet for a Jamaican was *Jump Up*, therefore Stanley and Winston were regarded as outsider *Jump Ups* by their work colleagues, and although it never seemed to bother the pair, they always found themselves segregated at break times. On the occasions we found ourselves in the same location and during the lunch break – peas and rice for them, and sausage rolls and sandwiches for me – we talked about our past lives and I found them to be a lovely couple of blokes. They were both in their twenties, married with families, and very religious. They would constantly try to convince me that I should attend their church with them one Sunday because in Winston's words: 'We like you, Colin, you are a nice man and we want to save you.'

I felt both honoured that they liked me so much that they felt a duty to save me, but slightly peeved that they felt I *needed* saving. But I took it at face value and always politely declined their kind offer. I didn't want saving, I told myself; what I really *wanted* was to share my unworthy self around to the many joys of Hamilton, and help the struggling rum distillers of Bermuda and Barbados. That is until Stevie's arrival of course.

One night whilst regaling Stevie about my life in Bermuda over the previous months, I related the story of my Jamaican colleagues. She was always up for something different, a characteristic that had been further enhanced by her brush with death the previous year, and she asked me to pass on to the boys that she would love to attend their church if they would kindly collect her from Little Arches. I was a little surprised at her enthusiasm I have to admit, as Stevie was an agnostic bordering closely on atheism at the time. I was tempted to join her, but only briefly, and in the end felt that my time would be more enjoyably spent propping up the bar at the Robin Hood. My reasoning being that the pub was missing me, having been absent the previous two evenings when Stevie and I had dinner at the classy Newport Room restaurant in the Southampton Princess hotel, and the brilliant Fourways Inn in Paget – an eye-wateringly expensive couple of nights by anyone's standards.

Stevie duly arrived back from church, escorted to the front door by the gentlemanly Stanley; she was full of it, and had obviously enjoyed herself enormously. Hers had been the only white face in the Jamaican assembly and was such a rarity, that she was spoiled and fussed over by the congregation. She was persuaded to stand up and deliver her testimony, as they termed it. This meant that she was invited to tell them all about herself, and Stevie being Stevie, she did just that in her usual confident and I imagined, entertaining way. She came away having been saved, she was assured, and made many new friends in the process. She also returned with the plea from Stanley, Winston, their families and most of the congregation, for me to attend on any Sunday of my choice so that I too could be rescued for Jesus. But I genuinely regret to say I never did, and I guess that meant I was doomed.

The weeks slipped rapidly by and there was a growing sense of unease between us as the day of Stevie's departure loomed large. How could there be two such conflicting and diametrically opposed emotions sharing living space in my head? On the one hand guilt and the belief that I should never have left Stevie at her time of most need, in spite of her insistence that I go and take up my job in Bermuda. On the other hand, the feeling that Bermuda was turning out to be the best experience of my life and had I stayed in England, it would never have happened. It was puzzling, contradictory and crazy.

It was a sad and suppressed farewell when the day came. There seemed to be so much we should be saying to each other, but at the same time, both realising that there were no words suitable to express what we were feeling. I believe that we both knew in our hearts that this would be the end of our time together, and there was a wretched feeling of inevitability that we had become two entirely different people, shaped by the circumstances we found ourselves in, and who now needed to set out on separate paths.

On that beautiful sunny mid-October day, we said a sad goodbye at the airport, and later as I watched from the terminal building, Stevie paused as she walked across the tarmac towards the aircraft, now displaying its brand-new British Airways insignia, looked searchingly back in my direction and waved.

It was the last we would see of each other.

THIRTY-FOUR

It was ten days after Stevie's departure. I had not arrived back at the house until nine in the morning, having stopped off for breakfast at the Chicken Coop with Richard, another establishment that I had been introduced to, and had become a regular stop-off point for post party breakfasts. Perhaps we just struck lucky whenever we dropped by for something to eat, but the Coop seemed to be always open, no matter what the time of the day or night. It should have been named Schrödinger's Kitchen.

There had been a great shindig at a large house in Devonshire the night before with spectacular water frontage and large gardens, and it had been my first party since saying goodbye to Stevie and I simply had not the inclination to seek out any female company. But parties are parties and I had spent an adventurous hour or so in a hammock with a young Bermudian lovely before leaving, and I was not in much of a condition, or frame of mind, to spend the afternoon at Horseshoe Beach, which was the usual routine.

The hammock thing by the way is not to be recommended, at least not without insurance. Consequently, I did not intend to leave the house before our regular evening session at the Hood, and for the first and only time I decided to crash on the sofa and watch Colin M's TV in the full expectation that it would soon have my eyelids drooping, leading to me to doze off.

Trish had breezed past me as I entered Little Arches, full of the joys and setting off to meet friends for a morning at the beach, followed by brunch at the Whaler Inn, she informed me. It seemed she really had turned the corner and put the recent hurtful events behind her. It was good to see, and had me wondering seriously for the first time, whether or not to try my luck, but on reflection I was honest enough to admit to myself that Trish was probably a class above me. She had never shown the slightest bit of interest in that respect, and we had become good friends, so why spoil it. Best to keep things as they were, especially as she and Stevie had got on particularly well. It just wouldn't be right.

Fate can be a fickle creature and has a nasty habit of taking away what once has been given, because settling down to watch a television movie called *She Lives* starring Desi Arnaz Junior – a name I was familiar with having avidly watched *I Love Lucy* on TV in my youth – madam fortune decided that there should be a counterweight to Trish's newfound happiness by putting a serious dent in my own. There would be no couch shut eye for me as I became transfixed.

She Lives tells the story of two college students who fall in love, only to discover shortly after moving in together, a small lump in the girl's neck, which is subsequently diagnosed as terminal Hodgkin's lymphoma and for which no life-saving treatments were available. She and her boyfriend then frantically set about looking for experimental and alternative treatments for her illness.

An American singer I had hitherto been unfamiliar with and had discovered courtesy of the DJ's at stations ZFB and ZBM, was Jim Croce. A new name to me, even though he had been performing and recording for a number of years in the US, but I loved what I had heard from the American songster and I became an instant fan. The musical theme from *She Lives*, was Croce's *Time in a Bottle*, and although there is a happy ending to the movie, it was such a poignant reminder of Stevie's experience, I found that before the end, tears were streaming down my face.

I was saddened to learn that in fact Jim Croce had died in a plane crash with five others, just weeks before in Louisiana. He was on tour and they were on their way to the next gig in Texas. He was 30 years old.

THIRTY-FIVE

'Gas gangrene. You can actually hear it,' Liz Winter was explaining to me. I nodded my head and kept on chewing. 'We had this man on the operating table; he had huge black blisters on his leg and the surgeon was getting ready to amputate. You could hear the bloody gangrene hissing away... yes, really. Then when he went to make the first incision the leg just disintegrated. We had to take it out in buckets. And the smell... one of the theatre nurses vomited into her mask...'

'Yes, thank you, Liz,' I grimaced, cutting her short. I cleared my mouth and dropped the remains of my burger back onto the plate.

'Oops sorry, you're eating,' she smiled sweetly.

'I *was*,' I said, and took a long swig from my Cockspur and ginger, and an even longer look at my half-eaten hamburger. I was a baby boomer from the days when our parents were still recovering from rationing and the shortages that the second world war brought, and consequently I was taught never to leave anything on the plate. But on this occasion...

Liz was a nurse at Edward VII Memorial Hospital, and I had made the mistake of asking about some of her experiences in the operating theatre, not out of any real interest, but by way of making conversation until I had finished my lunch. Never let a pretty girl get away, was my motto, and although I had seen Liz at the Hood and at parties from time to time, I had never taken the opportunity to get to know her better. So when she plonked herself down next to me that Saturday in my favourite watering hole, I thought it would be the ideal opportunity to do just that and I gave her my best smile in between bites.

Before the gas gangrene thing, and not wanting to lose her, I had tried to charm her with my repartee by saying: 'I think I've caught your infectious smile,' delivering it with a hefty dollop of extra mature cheddar, which made her laugh. She obviously thought it was overly cheesy too. Then after I had discarded the remains of my burger, we chatted as several of the regulars began to drift in, including my Geordie chum Rob, who reminded me that the Hookers were playing their first football match that afternoon and we promised we would go and support them. So after another round of drinks, several of us, including Liz, rode off to where the girls were playing.

The proprietors of the Robin Hood were always thinking up new wheezes to keep their patrons entertained and quirky new ways of drumming up fresh business, and so a ladies football team – the Robin Hood Hookers – had been formed. They had been kitted out in a snazzy two-tone green and black strip, which later proved to have been an unnecessary expense, because it turned out to be their one and only game, but as it transpired it was one that produced more laughs than a Tommy Cooper concert. It wasn't so much their inability to play the actual game of football, but more their antics trying to kick, punch, chest, or head the ball, and in the process colliding with other players, mostly their own teammates, or falling on their delightful arses. They seemed to think that to put the ball into the back of either net was within the rules and it proved to be a hilarious sixty minutes… the referee having decided early on that he couldn't bear to officiate the circus through to the full hour and a half. But it was an entertaining afternoon with seven goals being scored in total, although it was anyone's guess who had won. Still, with it being a charity match, cash was raised for a good cause – whatever the cause might have been, I simply don't remember.

After the game I decided to cool-out back at Little Arches and decided to sun myself in our wildlife rear garden for a change. And I was so glad that I did. I had previously only shown a fleeting interest in the birdlife out back, and I was surprised just what a vibrant place it was as I watched the antics of the kiskadees and red cardinals that obviously called it home. I later learned that kiskadees, so named because of their distinctive call, were only introduced to the island in 1957, and the red cardinal cocks, with their raised head crest resembling a cardinal's hat and sporting brilliant red plumage with a black face mask, were also introduced along with their female companions, from elsewhere. I had seen the iconic longtails on many of my beach forays. Bermuda's national bird whose full title is White Tailed Tropic Bird, migrated to the islands early each year, and they could often be seen in pairs, their long tail feathers touching in a courtship dance as they swooped and dived above the coastal areas.

As well as becoming a budding horticulturist, thanks to my obliging and patient neighbours who were constantly answering my questions about their impressive gardens, I was now on the road to becoming a knowledgeable ornithologist. Ask any question on cardinals, kiskadees and long tails, and I'm your man.

That evening, Richard P and I struck up a halting conversation with two officers from the Russian-owned cruise ship, *Alexandr Pushkin*, which was currently docked on Front Street. A halting conversation because Jakobi, an East German, who answered simply to the name Jak, spoke almost no English, and his companion Alex, a Russian, had a limited but just about coherent, if comical, grasp of the language. Both looked to be in their forties, but with their weather-worn faces, it was hard to judge accurately. They were both tall, about six feet, but almost perfect opposites in other ways with Alex broad shouldered and bulky, and Jak lean and wiry. Neither wore any kind of uniform.

Alexandr Pushkin was an outdated looking vessel compared to most of the other ocean liners that visited the island, and was one of two Russian ships that called infrequently into Bermuda – the other being the *Maxim Gorky*. We joked about the ship being named after Alex (he had probably never heard *that* one before), Bermudian girls, and Bermuda shorts…

'Is true, grown mens vear shorts to vork in oriffice?'

Alex proudly spoke of the amenities on board his ship, including cabins that held six people and with three taps in each cabin: one for cold water, another for hot, and a third for sea water. Luxury indeed. We smiled politely. If only he knew. We naturally asked about their lives in the Soviet Union and their working life on board ship and whilst they were happy to give us lots of information about their families, they proved to be reticent about their positions in the shipboard hierarchy, only to say they were both engineering officers of some indeterminate rank, and the passengers were a mixture of Russian and Eastern Europeans, with a contingent from Cuba. Reading between the lines, we reckoned the passengers probably comprised the better off citizens from the Soviet Bloc and their buddies from the Caribbean – or perhaps they were being rewarded for being good little communists. We had seen quite a few of the Pushkin's inexpensively dressed passengers window shopping on Front Street, but there didn't appear to be much purchasing going on.

But they were a friendly couple of guys, and appeared to enjoy being in our company, which was probably in no small way due to the fact we seemed to be buying all the drinks. But to be fair, we had taken pity on them when we saw their reaction to the price of drinks, even though they were only drinking American beer.

'Vot! Vun whole dollar for American piss – how much wodka?… VOT!!!'

We had not realised just how valued the American dollar was to these guys, which had many times the buying power in the Soviet Union than we were used to.

During our jolly conversation with our newfound friends, who should stroll in but one of the Insurers – the group of wretches who always seemed to find the presence of Richard and me the height of hilarity. This was in fact the only member of the trio who had been identified as working in insurance, and on that occasion, he was accompanied only by a female. Quite attractive we had to admit, in a quiet Scottish Widows sort of way. Strangely, on that occasion without his usual back-up, he did not seem inclined to find anything to laugh at, but he still had that haughty sneer on his face that we were familiar with.

'Look at him, he's so far up his own arse, he carries a toothbrush in his top pocket,' I said to Richard.

Jak and Alex noticed the comment and the malevolent stare we were giving our antagonist and Alex asked: 'Not friend?' So we patiently told them the story and the fact we were devising some way of teaching the sods a lesson and getting them off our backs.

'No problems, get gun and shoot son of bitch.'

We explained that this was not the done thing in Bermuda, and although we had considered confronting them, we had decided that we would need to be a little more subtle – but there would definitely be no guns, or violence of any kind, we stressed, at the same time, not really taking him seriously. We ordered more drinks as Alex was jabbering away to his colleague and obviously translating what we had said. There followed an intense few minutes where the two of them were in deep discussion in what was obviously Russian, with Jak doing most of the talking along with much gesticulating.

'For you, we take care,' Alex reported, thrusting out his chin aggressively.

Then as we were about to remonstrate with him again about the inadvisability of even mentioning firearms, he held up one meaty hand for silence, and went on: 'For one hundred American dollar, we snuggle on board ship, and hide. Then when we are in ocean, we make so discover him and report to captain. Then he will be put in lock up, and pushed off at next port as stowedaway.'

It was preposterous, just about understandable, and almost laughable – surely he was joking. But in spite of myself I asked: 'So how we… sorry, how *do* we get him aboard your ship?'

'No big problems,' Alex shrugged, 'you drug, give dicky flynn, then leave him on streed by gangs planks, and we take on board. Easy.' He shrugged again and held out his hands palms up, as if to ratify the deal.

'What's the next port?' asked Richard.

What's the next port? Were we really considering this?

'No saw... place in Barmars... how you say?'

'Nassau, Bahamas?' I suggested after a thoughtful pause.

'Yes that.'

'When do you leave?' Richard wanted to know.

'Tomorrow in afternoons.'

'That puts the mockers on that then. There's no time.' I said, greatly relieved and yet strangely and worryingly disappointed.

'So when are you back?' Richard wouldn't leave it alone.

'In...' Alex held up three fingers.

'Three,' we both chimed.

'Yes, maybe tree, how you say?... munts... tree munts.'

THIRTY-SIX

In 1973, the celebration of Halloween was an alien concept if you were British. Sure, we knew what it was and that the American kids lost their tiny minds every October thirty first, dressing up as mini Draculas, werewolves and Frankenstein monsters, and blackmailing householders to either give them buckets of candy or suffer the consequences in the ritual trick or treat nonsense. But as far as I knew, it was not yet established as a popular event in the UK. But with its proximity to the American mainland and the resultant influence through tourism, Halloween in Bermuda was an accepted annual phenomenon, and in spite of my reservation about the whole thing due to a scary brush with Satanism in 1971 (don't ask), I decided to attend a Halloween bash at a large house situated on Harrington Sound that I had heard about through the super-efficient Robin Hood grapevine.

With Halloween falling on a Wednesday, the party was scheduled for the nearest Saturday which was the 3rd of November. It was close enough, and nobody wanted to wake up with a sore head and shuffle their way to work the next morning. None of the established gang would be going because, unlike me, they had other more interesting things to do, mostly involving games like hide the torpedo, knowing Terry and Rob, but there it was. There was bound to be plenty of hot young ladies at the bash.

Later, pondering what I should wear, it brought back a memory of a similar beano I had experienced eighteen months before when I was living in the quaint chocolate box village of Polperro in Cornwall.

There was to be a party thrown at a country house some distance inland from the village where there had been another wild bash some weeks before, and it suited the Halloween theme perfectly with its Gothic architecture and isolation, situated miles from anywhere. The views though were superb, I remembered.

Because it was the end of June, it was obviously not an actual Halloween party, but simply circulated amongst the flowered and unshorn young population of the village (which was most of us) as *The Monster Mash*, after the 1962 recording by Bobby 'Boris' Pickett and the Crypt Kickers, with everyone being required to dress as some sort of spook, demon or vampire. The more inventive the better, we were told.

Although I was a permanent resident in Polperro, the majority of those who worked in restaurants, gift shops and suchlike, were students on their summer vacation, or free spirits travelling the roads and getting seasonal work wherever and whenever the mood took them. There were a small number, who, like me, had come to Cornwall to live permanently or just to get away from city life and spend the summer months working in tourist-related enterprises. My own intention at that time, before Bermuda reared its attractive head, was to make a future for myself in that beautiful county, and although I worked in the kitchens of the largest restaurant in that lovely fishing village, my ultimate aim had always been to go into business for myself. Working in a restaurant in a tourist hotspot in the height of summer is not the easiest of occupations but I loved it. We worked our socks off for ten hours every day, then partied ourselves silly every night. It was the perfect life for unattached young people with outrageous hair, bell-bottomed loons, flowery shirts and a zest for living. Life was there to be grabbed by the scruff of the neck and shaken vigorously, and that's what we did. After all, I was still making up for lost time.

Jacko was a young guy from Manchester who simply wanted to earn a few pounds without the commitment of a career; to smoke a bit of weed, and generally drop out from the rat race. He worked part-time as a general dogsbody at one of the four village pubs – when he wasn't propping up the opposite side of the bar that is. I often wondered where his income supply came from because he seemed to spend far more than he earned and was never short of a few bob; perhaps there was a clue in his public-school accent, but I never pushed it, having asked about his background on one occasion and being steered by him, quite forcefully, away from the subject. There was probably an interesting story there, but I never got to the bottom of it.

He was perfect for what I had in mind with regard to my fancy dress for the party, but he had a very firm idea of his own and had decided to go simply as Dracula. 'Boring,' I told him. 'There will be more Draculas there than flies on a dog turd.' But in spite of my honeyed words, he was adamant. Until, that is, I outlined my idea.

Because Jacko could be described as rotund – as a small planet as it happened – and me being built like a galloping hairpin, he fitted the part I had for him perfectly, because my twist on the Dracula idea was to go as a vampire Laurel and Hardy. Brilliant or what? Moreover, I knew where we could get hold of the perfect ill-fitting suits, complete with bowlers, and Jenny, a waitress at another of Polperro's many excellent restaurants, had already volunteered to administer the make-up. Her only condition was that I take her to see the film Vampire Circus, that was still showing in Plymouth. What was it with the vampire craze that everyone seemed to be mad on? But Jenny was a nice girl and it would be no great hardship.

The Saturday night of the party arrived, I had cleared the decks in the kitchen where I worked, and met Jacko in the Crumplehorn car park, situated at the top of the village where he kept his ageing vehicle. It was just before eleven o'clock and he was waiting in his dented blue Volkswagen Beetle with the engine running, and barely waiting for me to adjust my safety harness, we blasted off in a rackety cloud of blue smoke.

The beat-up VW lurched round the many sharp bends in the unlit country lanes, and I was constantly shouting at him above the noise of the engine to slow down before we ditched the damned thing. He had already negotiated curves and bends in the narrow lanes like Jackie Stewart on laughing gas, but Jacko ignored my warnings insisting that there would be no traffic at that time of the evening. Then, as he tore round yet another sharp curve in the road, the inevitable happened. There in the glare of our headlights was a woolly overcoat on legs, one moment looking very sheepish, the next looking very unhappy as the car hit it full pelt. Too late, Jacko skidded to a stop, then pulled the now even more battered VW, over to the side of the road. We ran back to tend to the unfortunate animal, but as we suspected, it was way beyond our help. The only consolation for the poor creature was that it had all been over very quickly. I was raging at Jacko for being so bloody stupid, then as we started to drag the deceased animal off the road, we heard the sound of a car approaching in the direction from which we had just come. As the headlights appeared around the curve in the narrow lane, there was the sound of hastily applied brakes and the vehicle slewed to a dead stop a few yards from us. There was a moment of silence with us spot-lighted and frozen in tableau still gripping the sheep; then with a shrieking of tyres the driver of the car attempted a multi-point turn in the narrow road. After ramming a tree on one side and sending clods of earth into the air from the opposite embankment, it fishtailed off in the direction from which it had come, still in first gear and screaming like an Osmond Brothers groupie.

It had started out as a good evening. The lovely Jenny had painstakingly made us up as two blood sucking comedians complete with pasty white faces, deep set dark eye sockets and fangs, and of course the obligatory gore running down our chins from crimson lips; all under two ludicrous bowler hats and dressed in rather worse for wear matching dark pin-striped suits that had come from a charity shop in Looe. Now here we were bent over a dead sheep in the middle of nowhere and some moron in a car was roaring off like a thing possessed without stopping to offer help. What's wrong with people I thought?

The Halloween party in Bermuda was a rowdy affair with the usual rivers of alcohol and loud music which aptly consisted of much Black Sabbath and Alice Cooper stuff and other heavy rock sounds – and of course 'Boris' Bobby and the Crypt Kickers giving it large. There was even a collection of pastries and other unidentifiable items of food, all craftily baked and prepared in the images of bats, severed heads, witches' hats and other typically devilish things; much as you would expect at a proper Halloween party I suppose. And of course, everyone was dressed in the appropriate manner; for my part as an undertaker, complete with grimy fingernails, blackened eye sockets and dirt encrusted suit.

It had taken me about five minutes to make up.

I danced with a female vampire and some sort of ghoulish figure that I hoped was female, but never did find out. I was felt-up by a zombie at one point, but jeez she was ugly, and I'm not sure that removal of the make-up would have made much difference. All told it had only been a moderately enjoyable evening for me – the absence of my group of friends had not helped – and even though I was a dedicated party animal, I left uncharacteristically early but, it has to be said, accompanied by a like-minded Cleopatra. What Cleopatra was doing at a Halloween party was beyond me, but at least she was original and very tasty in an Egyptian kind of way.

'Good thing we're leaving before sun up,' I told her. 'With the number of vampires here, they will probably combust and burn the bloody house down.' I occasionally come up with gems like that, and all credit to Cleo, she laughed like a drain and then followed me back to Little Arches on her Vespa. Modesty forbids me to go into details, but during our shower together, in order to help each other get rid of our make-up you understand, and of course, in the cause of water conservation, I was amazed to discover she had a tattoo on her backside.

'Did you know you have a beetle on your arse?' I laughed.

'That's a scarab.' She corrected me.

'That's another name for a dung beetle,' I informed her, displaying my in-depth knowledge of such things.

'Seriously?'

'Yeah really. They are well known for pushing balls of camel shite back to their lairs, burrows, or wherever it is they hang out.'

'Then what do they do with them?'

'Do with what?'

'The camel shit.'

'Good point… have it with chips probably.'

She laughed. 'I prefer the name scarab; they were sacred to the ancient Egyptians, you know.'

And that I realised, explained the Cleopatra connection.

THIRTY-SEVEN

In late October after Stevie's departure, two other significant events took place within days of each other. Firstly, I had sold the Honda at long last, having various dents and scratches attended to, and spruced up the paintwork generally, and purchased a new Suzuki trail bike, similar to Richard's machine, but the latest model, sporting the plate number: 3079A. With 100cc's between my legs after the Honda, it felt good, and before anyone starts tittering, let me tell you that by Bermuda standards where the maximum engine size allowable for motorcycles was 125cc, this was one sporty machine and, let's face it, with only twenty one square miles of land on which to plonk roads, it was more than adequate.

The second event, and of great concern to us at Little Arches, was that the owners had decided to sell the property and we had been given one month's notice to quit. Just one month to find suitable, alternative accommodation. The way the Bermuda rental market was, it promised to be a difficult job, and the likelihood that it could well be a sharing situation with strangers.

I was delighted with my new two-wheeled acquisition and took every opportunity to take it for spins around the island, introducing it to all my friends and points of interest. I had taken Penny for a ride out to Tucker's Town, which after the shoe-in-the-wheel incident with the Honda, was not an easy decision to make, but having purchased at great cost, extra Fully Comprehensive Penelope Insurance cover, I took the risk. But this was a 'proper' motorcycle with a pillion facility and fixed footrests for the passenger as you would expect. That didn't stop me considering having strong leather foot straps fixed as an extra precaution and perhaps a safety harness for good measure, but then I thought that knowing Penny, she would forget she was attached to them and when she came to dismount, take herself and the bike over a cliff.

No cliffs in Bermuda? Trust me, you don't know Penny.

Although initially the worry of needing to find another property to rent was a problem, the matter was soon resolved when one of Colin Marshall's sailing buddies, who happened to be in real estate, offered him a large property to rent on Pitts Bay Road, not that far away as the proverbial crow flew, and still very handy for Hamilton and our favourite hang-outs and crucially, the Robin Hood. However, another problem presented itself in the fact that it was a four-bedroom house complete with a detached one-bedroom studio apartment, which was all reflected in the hefty monthly rental required. Trish had already been offered, and had accepted, a house share with some work colleagues, which left Colin and me to find six hundred dollars every thirty days – an amount that would be a serious assault on our means if no other partners could be found. But we had been shown the house, Highclere, and had taken an instant liking to it, even though we had been informed that the property was also for sale. But having been on the market for some considerable time, the agent felt that with the Christmas season approaching, and with no viewings in the pipeline, there was little chance of it being shifted in the foreseeable future. So it was imperative that we start to look around for housemates, preferably three, but with only a short time to do it.

Luckily, I knew where we would find one new member, a bloke called Graham Blackshaw, a Brit who I had befriended earlier and had met on several occasions in the Hood and at the beach. The only thing I knew about Graham was that he was a printer by trade. Then one Sunday, we found ourselves in the same queue at The Phoenix in Hamilton. The Phoenix pharmacy on a Sunday afternoon was a tradition with the ex-pat population, because at 5pm, the doors were thrown open to signify that the British Sunday papers had arrived and were ready for sale. Scores of us, eager for the latest depressing news via the *News of the World, Sunday People, Sunday Times* etc., queued outside the drug store on Reid Street for our little taste of home. Graham and I got chatting on that particular Sunday and he graciously invited me to dinner at his place the following week. He seemed a good guy and I was happy to accept.

The evening of the dinner, we got to know each other pretty well, filling in the details of our past lives in England and how we had found ourselves in that earthly paradise called Bermuda. I was impressed with his culinary skills even though it was fairly simple fare, with a meal of fillet steak and oven roasted vegetables albeit cooked to a turn. I mention that only to enforce an earlier statement that I can remember a myriad of unimportant and insubstantial details from the past – not that I rated Graham's cooking as insubstantial, in fact I don't think I ever told him what good grub it was, so here you go, Graham… it was a great meal and if I was remiss in telling you at the time, belated thanks.

We talked of many things; our likes and dislikes, rating the women we had met at the Hood on a scale of one to eleven – there was always room for a number eleven – and our tastes in music. On that subject Graham produced his latest purchase; an album by a new British group – Uriah Heep. The track 'Gypsy' blew me away and I resolved to buy the album *Very 'Umble Very 'Eavy*, the following week. In fact, they proved not to be a new group at all, just new to me, and along with the said album, which had been their debut recording, I also purchased the subsequent *Demons and Wizards* and *The Magician's Birthday*, albums at the same time. Terrific stuff in my estimation and albums that I have played to death over the years, and still find them brilliant. Thus it could be said that my friendship with Graham was fused through the music of Uriah Heep and fillet steak. Crucially, he also let on that he was in the market for a bigger flat or even a house, was more than happy to share, and although it meant nothing to me at the time, the discourse took on a new importance later, with the acquisition of Highclere.

Remembering our conversation I telephoned him, hoping against hope that he had not found a new location, and I was delighted to be told he was still on the lookout for a new roomier pad, and it would coincide nicely with his securing a new job at the Castle Harbour Hotel where he would be in charge of all the hotel's printing requirements. This was music to my ears, and having explained the situation to him and the monthly rent requirement (though I have to admit, without letting on that the sum quoted was on the assumption five of us were sharing) we arranged a time for him to inspect Highclere the next day, which went swimmingly well. He seemed very taken with the house, but much to my surprise, having previously told me that he would be more than happy to share, he fell in love with the one-bedroom studio in the garden. No problem with that, however, it still gave us another share towards the rent and it left us with just two more housemates to find.

THIRTY-EIGHT

There was nothing remotely weird or creepy about Highclere. It stood in an elevated position off Pitts Bay Road and although it dated back to the nineteen thirties by all accounts, it was certainly not what you would call ancient. Because Colin Marshall and I were the first two people to occupy the property, and with him anticipating spending little time there except for sleeping and perhaps breakfast, and often – looking back to his time at Little Arches as an indicator – spending weekends elsewhere, I was privileged to be given the roomy master suite. This comprised a large double bedroom, an attached bath and shower room, and off to one side, another door leading to a large dressing room which, I envisaged, could be used as a first-floor cooling-out den for us all, and perhaps a storage area. The suite therefore took up the complete eastern front corner of the upper storey.

My bedroom was also the only room in the house to have an air conditioning unit installed, but I later found that there was little to choose between the high humidity and heat, and the noise of the air conditioning unit as it clattered into life, and so I opted for the heat. But I now look back on that old air-con unit with a certain fondness, not that I would want the darn thing chugging away again in my window and posing a constant threat to the stability of the house, but it's what it represents; reminding me of a time before all those supposedly labour saving and technologically advanced devices that are designed, we are told, to improve our lives, but in fact have given us more things to go annoyingly wrong and costing us far more than the advantages they promise.

The first indication that there was something seriously strange about Highclere was on Christmas Eve. Colin M had returned to England for the holiday and Graham was due to move into the studio immediately after Christmas and so for the time being, it looked as if I would be in the house alone. I have always enjoyed Christmas Eve ahead of the actual day itself – at least ever since I was old enough to be able to spend time in pubs and had discovered Courage Best Bitter at the popular Boar's Head Inn in Reading. Richard Pedro had a family gathering to attend and Terry and Rob would meet me at the Hood, as would Graham. The *Dazzlers* would also be present, and pretty much everyone else who were regulars. The intention was to then go on to whatever party or parties were in the offing and see in Christmas Day with a bang.

Christmas Eve! There had to be a party... didn't there?

Well as it turned out, no – at least not one that had come to our notice.

We had our usual boisterous evening at a packed Robin Hood which in fairness, was a great party in its own right; we did our fair share of flirting and networking with some of the usual suspects, and had taken full advantage of the generous buffet spread that had been put on, washed down of course with liberal amounts of Barbados' finest. But it was at the outrageously early time of one in the morning, that we found ourselves with only our homes to go to. Terry and Rob seemed already to have disappeared, and Graham and I, still in disbelief that there had been no indication of festive activities or parties to move on to, wished each other a gloomy Merry Christmas in the car park, then saddled up and went our separate ways.

I returned to a darkened and empty Highclere. No black clouded skies with the accompanying sound of thunder; no creaking door swinging on its hinges even though it had been locked when I left, and no eerie sounds of wolves howling at the moon; just an ordinary, common or garden empty house.

I made myself a large mug of black coffee in the kitchen, added a generous shot of rum, and after ensuring the ground floor was locked and secured, made my way to my room still sulking at the disappointment of a short-lived Christmas Eve and regretting for the first time, that I was not the owner of a television, Colin Marshall having sold his portable job before the move. Surely there must be something going on somewhere I thought, and because I was still fully awake and needing to see in Christmas in style, picked up the phone and called Graham who I had left not thirty minutes before, in order to share my despondency over our bad luck. Perhaps he could come up with an idea to perpetuate the evening, but as we chatted and came to the conclusion that there was no alternative other than to have an early night, I heard someone walking slowly but audibly across the polished wood floor of the landing outside my door.

The spacious landing was in the shape of a fat 'L,' with the largest section almost a perfect square, off which were Colin M's and my own bedroom opposite each other, and a family bathroom with the aforementioned dressing room between – the one that also had a connecting door to my bathroom. Then a narrower section alongside the stairwell pointing to the rear of the house, and the doors to the other two bedrooms along with a large cupboard between them housing a water tank and immersion heater.

My first thought was that Colin had not left for England after all, then immediately dismissed the idea. Colin had left for the airport early the day before. I would have known if he had changed his mind and, in any case, why would he? The house was locked up, I had made sure of that both before I had left for the evening and on returning a half hour before, so what the hell was going on?

ll on the phone to Graham and relating all this to him

otsteps seemed to come to an abrupt stop outside my

e was doing rapid half a crown-sixpence convulsions,

but I took my courage in my hands and only after a brief hesitation and arming myself with my Brut aftershave – the only thing to hand – I threw the door open.

The landing was empty.

I rushed back to the phone and told Graham quickly what had just occurred and to hang on whilst I looked in every room brandishing the bottle of Brut, which I was more than ready to use and quite prepared to aftershave whoever the bastard was, to death. Happily, there was no need, as the whole floor was deserted. It was a mystery and having satisfied myself that I had no uninvited guest, I retreated to my bedroom, shut the door, and picked the phone back up to report what had happened, to my friend.

I was feeling decidedly unnerved I can tell you, and had there been a lock or bolt on my door, I am not ashamed to admit I would have activated it double quick. Then almost immediately, as Graham and I were discussing the possibilities of what the sounds could have been, the footsteps started again, this time moving away from my room, and the sound receding as if heading for the furthermost bedroom at the far end of the landing. Then the distinct sound of a door opening and closing.

It was an intriguing albeit frightening experience, and having terminated my call to Graham perhaps twenty minutes or so later, I knew that I would not be able rest until I had checked out each room again – particularly bedroom number four, where it seemed to me the owner of the spectral feet had entered. Spectral I say, because by now I was convinced that we had a ghost. On close inspection, everything checked out of course, and I included another visit to the ground floor to satisfy myself that no one could have entered there, and eventually with nervous energy depleted, and the effects of the evening's intake of booze taking over, I returned to my room and slept without further interruption.

This was the first of a series of similarly inexplicably weird happenings that occurred during my time at Highclere that were later to be experienced by other members of our household.

THIRTY-NINE

I had always been a Christmas kind of person, so I was looking forward to spending my first ever Christmas in Bermuda, but not without reservations. For me there is something almost other-worldly about Christmas Day – and I am not referring to the strange experience I had encountered at Highclere – but something I would now describe as spiritual, although I would never have dared to put it that way to friends back in those days. They would have almost certainly looked at me in a strange way, or called me a soft bastard. That said, I strongly suspect that many of my generation have the same warm feelings and happy memories of their own Christmases past, if they were to be completely honest.

I had probably travelled the same route as many of my contemporaries where religion was concerned. At primary school I had marvelled at the telling of the Christmas story and looked forward each morning in our December assemblies where we would bawl out those well-known carols which we came to know by heart. Then later in secondary school and into my teens I went through the almost obligatory 'Doubting Thomas' time, when unless I could see, touch, smell or taste something, then it simply didn't exist – or more to the point, held no interest for me whatsoever. It's true to say that I was, to all intents and purposes, a non-practicing atheist during those early years (non-practicing because I simply couldn't be arsed), which through the many contradictions between belief and non-belief, had slowly developed thereafter into a frustrating and unsatisfactory state of puzzlement, which was precisely where I was at by the time I arrived in Bermuda. Nevertheless, every year as Christmas approached, I remembered with great affection childhood memories of what was then for me a magical occasion, and one Christmas in particular many years before, pre-teens, in the early 1950s…

Christmas Eve, the one night of the year when climbing the stairs to bed was accomplished with enthusiasm and without the need of encouragement from parents. Yet here I was tucked up securely, bursting with excited anticipation with still not a hint of weariness. I could just make out the time on the big old fashioned alarm clock sitting on the bedside table – nine o'clock – an hour when all young children should be fast asleep otherwise, we were told, Father Christmas might pass us by.

I lay there wide-awake waiting for drowsiness to overtake my alert body, squeezing my eyelids tight shut and trying to force the images of the events from the wondrous day ahead from my overactive mind. But try as I might, visions filled my head of the stocking full of the traditional fruit and nuts and the bulging pillow case which soon would appear as if by magic at the end of my bed.

Muffled voices from my parents in the tiny living room below drifted up to me, and the faint but distinct smell of hot cocoa wafted tantalisingly through my bedroom and only served to emphasise the late hour and the desperate need for sleep to take me.

The feel of soft, clean sheets beneath me, snug and safe under layer upon layer of coarse heavy blankets – no duvets to keep us snug then – and my mother's winter coat spread out on top for good measure. A rubber hot water bottle at my back and a stone one at my feet and knowing from experience to be ever so careful not to roll over and stub my toe; warm so very warm except for my nose peeking through the blankets and blushing red in the chill air of the room. Central heating to us was the open coal fire in the living room, and a paraffin stove on the landing between the two small bedrooms. Where was sleep? Where was tiredness? Was I the only child in the whole world who was still awake?

The glass in the metal-framed window was blurred with a filigree pattern of frost, inside and out. But strangely in the centre of one pane, a round unfrozen aperture, formed as if the Christmas angel had breathed gently on the glass until the thin layer of ice had retreated momentarily, and through this peep-hole perfectly framed, the full Christmas moon shining brilliantly down on the world from a clear star-filled sky, as surely it should on this special night, and in my childish imagination, how it must also have been on that very first Christmas Eve two thousand years before.

Then as I gazed in childish wonder, I promised myself that I would remember always this perfect moment, through every Christmas and every year of my life yet to come.

Somehow, miraculously, sleep finally came to take me as it always had in years gone by and I fell into a dreamless slumber, unconsciously awaiting the faint sound of tinkling reindeer bells somewhere above the eaves of the roof and the soft tread of fur boots on floorboards.

And so it has been, with the memory of that magical Christmas Eve remaining with me, undimmed, down the years.

Now in the unfamiliar Yuletide landscape of Bermuda, another Christmas was upon us and the recollection of that childhood Christmas Eve many years before returned to me as always with untarnished clarity; the enchantment undiminished by the passage of years and the childhood pledge to remember it fulfilled.

I still looked forward with enthusiasm through the intervening years to the Christmas holiday and carried on giving it large with those carols whenever I heard them played on the radio or long-playing records bought for the occasion. Of course enjoyment of Christmases since childhood was on a different level and particularly when I had reached my late teens, because the new highlights were mostly centred on the pub and nights out with friends rather than the Christmas tree in the living room, with Mum presenting us with turkey and the steaming Christmas pud that held threepenny-bits you could break your teeth on if you weren't careful. (We weren't in the silver sixpence league), then of course followed by the excitement and the ritual of opening presents. Nevertheless, for whatever reason, for me there has always remained a certain undefinable enchantment in the air at that time of year.

Now here I was in Bermuda in my mid-twenties, morphing into someone who felt like his brain had been kick-started into life and was suddenly thinking deeply about things that needed thinking about, but couldn't quite come up with any sensible answers. All this thinking conveniently thinly sandwiched between the many hours of unbridled pleasure that Bermuda had delivered. Gone was the assurance of kindergarten Bible stories and later the absolute teenage conviction that there was no such creature as God, or harp playing angels. Now I just didn't know what to believe. Welcome to the unsatisfactory world of the agnostic.

So with my first Christmas in my new home rapidly approaching, I wondered, with some trepidation, just what a Bermuda Christmas Day had in store for me.

But I needn't have worried.

From having the prospect of a lonely Christmas with just a few beers and a bottle of Black Seal rum, and perhaps roast chicken for company, I was suddenly thrown, within the space of a few days, from that sad scenario into one where I had been invited to not one, but three Christmas dinners. Fortuitously, they were all to be held at different times of the day and evening. What would I do? Well, obviously, I accepted them all.

Richard Pedro had received the same invitations, and naturally we decided that we would travel together and that it would be in Richard's mother's borrowed car. There was to be a Pedro family gathering on Christmas Eve, and so Richard had agreed to attend that, but then do his own thing on the big day itself.

It was an arrangement that suited me down to the ground of course, because it meant that as a passenger I could freely indulge myself with all the liquid Christmas cheer that would be on offer, with having to worry about nothing more serious than falling over and giggling a lot. But having experienced these things once before and waking up in a strange bed with amnesia (yet another story), I was determined to not only enjoy the day with my many newfound friends, but ensure that I remembered every single moment of it. I therefore promised myself that I would be sensible and pace myself through the many impending hours of making merry.

The first lunch invitation was from Liz Winter, the gas gangrene expert, who shared an apartment at Spanish Point with two female hospital work colleagues, and was not far from Richard's mother's house, where he still lived. It was a small fairly intimate dinner with just nine of us present. Everyone I knew except one guy, and although I was unaware of it then, he was someone who would play a huge part in the remainder of my time in Bermuda and beyond. His name was Douglas Dewar; he had been invited by one of Liz's work colleagues and it transpired that he had arrived in Bermuda the previous June and subsequently become a regular at The Robin Hood. This came as a surprise to me because I did not recall having seen him on any of the many evenings I had already spent there, but then astonishing as it seemed, I had to admit that the Hood was heaving most nights of the week, with new faces constantly appearing among the throng. And he had a face that was fairly memorable, my first thought being El Diablo – the devil. It was a picture I had seen somewhere along the line in some magazine or other. Not your regular Satan you understand, but a devil with a twinkle of mischief in his eyes and if I was any kind of judge, a bit of a lad. With his long face, high forehead and matching dark devil's eyebrows, beard and shoulder length hair, I reckoned that here was a bloke who was up for anything and would be interesting company.

We chatted a good deal and there was a strong feeling that we were kindred spirits. Apart from the fact that we were both bearded, smoked menthol cigarettes – the long American Kool brand – and shared what you might describe as a bizarre sense of humour; there was a compelling impression that there were interesting times ahead for both of us. We cracked a few jokes together and he regaled me with tales from past Christmases spent in his home town of Bedford, and I responded in kind with a story of my own – an incident that had occurred in Reading, five Christmases before, and is worth telling again…

My good friend Jim and I had met student nurses in one of the prominent watering holes in town sometime in November 1968 and had enjoyed their company through to December, which was in itself something of an achievement in longevity in those early days after wifey had left, having decided that the grass on the neighbour's lawn was greener. As December approached, we promised to find them the best Christmas tree they had ever seen, and what was more, it would cost them nothing. We had envisaged some worthwhile brownie points being awarded accordingly.

We planned to launch a raid on Burghfield Common, an area situated a few miles from town, and to bring home our prize in Jim's old Ford 5cwt Thames Trader van. The common would surely be awash with fir trees of different denominations, including Norway spruce, which was our tree of choice and would present no problems, we reasoned. A report in the local rag stated that wardens were on patrol in the area to deter Gypsy gangs from taking large numbers of trees, but we felt that a small van like Jim's would go unnoticed and just to be sure, we slopped mud over the number plate in an attempt to remain incognito. Unfortunately, we had overlooked the fact that emblazoned along the side of the van were the words: 'The Lincoln Greens Show Group'. This was the band for whom my mate played rhythm guitar and sang lead vocals. But you can't think of everything.

We prepared for our mission in the girls' flat by donning our fishing gear – camouflage jacket and trousers bought at the local Millets store, and Wellington boots. We smeared our faces with burnt cork and topped the ensemble off with dark woolly beanies pulled down low. We were ready to rock and roll and we looked the part. In today's parlance, probably two *right parts*.

An hour after reaching the common and wishing that we'd had the foresight to bring along a flask of something hot, we were still looking for a suitable tree amongst what appeared to be a forest of stunted and disfigured examples of coniferous growth. Burghfield Common at night resembled the set from *The Curse of Frankenstein*. It didn't help that no sooner had we parked up than an assortment of vehicles cruised past menacingly. There was no way to distinguish whether they were wardens, would-be Christmas tree robbers like us, or just couples looking for a place to indulge in a bit of festive nooky. Eventually we decided to continue our search on foot, so finding a narrow track we drove for several minutes deep into the woods. Jim turned the engine off and we waited, listening intently for sounds that would indicate we were not alone. But the night was still, with no sign of other human presence in the vicinity, and so grabbing our torches and a bow-saw, we renewed our search for the elusive Christmas tree.

Almost immediately we wandered into a small clearing and there before us as if by divine command stood the object of our assignment: the perfect specimen. It was the right height, had a flawless triangular profile and on closer inspection possessed a full complement of healthy branches. It wasn't adorned with glass baubles and tinsel and topped with a Christmas angel, but hey, you can't have it all. The girls were going to be so grateful.

We were about to get to work, when a voice boomed out of the darkness, 'Shine that torch over here cacker monger.' Both of us swung round and as instructed shone our torches on a lone figure standing at the edge of the clearing. It wasn't his gnarled face that had our immediate attention, nor was it the build of the man, well over six feet tall and almost as wide, but the double-barrelled shotgun pointing right at us.

'What you think you doin'?' he growled ungrammatically. It was no good telling him we were collecting mushrooms, it was obvious what we were about, so with a slight wobble in my voice, I confirmed it:

'Looking for a Christmas tree for our girlfriends.' As if sharing the blame with the nurses somehow mitigated the crime. Honesty is always the best policy when confronted by a gun toting giant I have always felt.

'Not here you not,' he said, 'now git off you pair of gishnuts for I pepper yer arses.' And we did, quickly... very quickly, without question. I didn't bother to ask what the heck a gishnut was, but I was certain it was nothing good.

As we were driving home, I asked my friend, 'Who the hell talks like that.' But I knew the answer as soon as the question left my mouth, and so did Jim. Our tormentor wasn't a warden, but a Gypsy. We had been out-manoeuvred by a rival Christmas tree bandit.

Dirty and dishevelled, and me with decidedly damp underwear from the sight of that twelve-bore, we were a pathetic sight as we shuffled treeless and heavily camouflaged up the stairs to the girls' top floor flat, and taking deep breaths we unenthusiastically rang the bell.

'How do you feel?' I asked Jim as we waited at the door.

'Like a knob,' he mumbled.

I nodded my head. 'Couldn't have put it better myself.'

I had added a few touches to give the story more flavour, but Dougie laughed at the images my tale conjured up, and he asked if I had discovered what a gishnut was. I had, and I explained it to him. He let out a hearty guffaw, which was to become one of Dougie's hallmarks – but we never used the term again, it was that disgusting. Unfortunately, the answer is unprintable.

We swopped other tales from our respective pasts before the dinner gong was sounded so to speak, and we sat down to what was potentially for me and Richard, our first Christmas dinner of three that day. Actually, it wasn't a gong that announced dinner, but one of our hostesses bawling out: 'Sit your arses down and get stuck in.'

Sheer class.

We placed our arses at the appropriate places as instructed and indicated by festive little cards on the table displaying our names, at the very civilised time of 1pm and over the next half hour or so, we enthusiastically tucked into a traditional turkey lunch with all the trimmings. Then nursing pleasantly full stomachs, we managed two or three more rum and gingers to go with our dessert, which was of course plum pudding, and over some after-lunch conversation I ascertained from my new pal Dougie that he was on the lookout for fresh living accommodation. Like Graham, he was also a printer – having two in the house might prove useful one day… but I really couldn't see how. More importantly, here was our potential fourth housemate.

Time was racing on, and having checked our watches, Richard and I made our heart-felt apologies and said our reluctant goodbyes to our hostesses and the assembled company, but not before Dougie and I had exchanged telephone numbers and it was arranged that he would meet me at Highclere in the near future to view his potential new lodgings.

FORTY

Christmas dinner number two was twenty minutes away on Middle Road in Devonshire and our hostess was Linda Jansen, the young lady I had met at the bank when opening my new account during my first week in Bermuda way back in January. She had made a remark at the time, saying I was obviously a newcomer due to the clear signs of having exposed my lily-white skin to the unaccustomed sunshine. I had walked into the bank sporting the tell-tale panda rings around my eyes having worn shades on the beach at Church Bay on my very first Bermuda Sunday, and by way of confirmation, my nose was a rather attractive magenta shade. Remember, that had been in January, in the depths of what passed for winter in Bermuda, but to a pasty-faced new-kid-on-the-block, the Bermuda winter sun had still been a force to be reckoned with.

Richard and I had been informed that we would sit down to dinner at 5pm but cocktails would be served any time after three o-clock, so naturally not wanting to miss a drink or two, we timed our departure from Spanish Point so that we would arrive at four o'clock as a suitable compromise. Another hour with Liz, Dougie and friends had been most welcome.

The huge table that Linda had prepared looked magnificent and decorated tastefully with beautiful Christmas baubles and set with classy silver cutlery and what appeared to be crystal glassware. Linda had really gone to town and I couldn't help wondering where such classy table settings had come from. She must have a contact at one of the big hotels, I remember thinking. The problem was that having finished eating barely two and a half hours before, and with the allotted time for this second meal set for 5pm, we felt that it was going to be difficult giving it the justice it would undoubtedly deserve. We had decided on the ride over, that as much as it irritated us to have to forego another excellent feast, we would make our apologies to our lovely hostess and regrettably pass on the food, but simply share a few drinks with all of those present – numbering at least fifteen by the look of it, most of whom we knew well.

It would not have been so bad, and we could probably have enjoyed a second meal had it not been for the fact that our third and final stop for Christmas dinner was scheduled for 7pm and would, we felt, be the highlight of our day. Crucially, we were told to arrive as early as we liked in order to indulge in some Christmassy fun and games, which sounded intriguing. The glamorous trio of Penny, Jane and Sandra were to be our hostesses and like meal number one, it was to be a relatively small group of invited guests. We should be about ready by seven for whatever food they had lined up for us we mused, and we knew that whatever fare was on offer, it would be scrumptious and there would be plenty of it.

Linda knew this and was not perturbed in the slightest, informing us that she was not at all surprised, because having felt honour bound to tell her in advance of our prior lunch engagement, she had mentally prepared herself for us having to pass on the dinner. In any case, there was no shortage of guests and our absence would probably not be noticed. So having enjoyed the wonderful Christmassy atmosphere, fantastic yuletide trimmings and the lively company, we once again reluctantly made our apologies and left for our final port of call.

We had probably downed a good few 'cocktails' since arriving at Spanish Point earlier in the day, but we both agreed that, thanks probably to the copious amount of food acting as a sponge, we felt good, totally clear headed and looking forward to our last stop which was in Grape Bay, Paget, and the aptly but unimaginatively named house, 'Bay Grapes,' where the three *dazzlers* resided.

Once again, the house had been decorated with colourful and exotic Yuletide decorations, including a real Christmas tree elaborately adorned with dozens of baubles and twinkling lights. Where the hell did they find a Christmas tree in Bermuda, I remember thinking.

The meal was a sumptuous affair with a variety of tasty dishes and the evening turned out to be full of laughter and goodwill to all men and all that stuff. The wine and other beverages flowed freely, and we regressed into a bunch of kids when we played charades. I was particularly proud of my antics in miming the Panto Characters' name, *Widow Twankey*, which my team made a meal of guessing, but nevertheless eventually helped win the game for us. Unfortunately the display of bodily contortions I had to go through to give us the win, had me feeling embarrassed for days after, as the whole routine was described to the Robin Hood crowd by some of my fellow party colleagues. Twankey. . . sounds like?. . .get the picture?

There was hilarity and much seasonal bonhomie as we all left the house sometime in the early morning of Boxing Day, so much so, that it was a full half hour before we had said our concluding farewells and departed in or on our various modes of transport. Richard seemed none the worse for wear, but I asked him anyway: 'How are you feeling mate? Okay to drive?'

'What if I'm not, do you fancy walking back to Highclere?' he said in a good-humoured way.

There were going to be no taxis at that time in the day, even on Boxing Day morning I reasoned, so his deduction sounded perfectly logical and I simply grunted my approval and got in the car. Richard had matched me drink for drink pretty much the whole day through, and I had stuck to my decision to pace myself, so perhaps with the volume of food we had got down us, my resolve had paid off. I felt ever so slightly tipsy and mellow and after an uneventful drive back to Pitts Bay Road, we arrived at 'haunted' Highclere unscathed, then after wishing each other a Merry Christmas for the hundredth time, I was dropped off and Richard resumed his short journey home.

I rolled into bed at just after three in the morning and slept the sleep of a satiated and thoroughly contented hog. It had been a good Christmas after all, in spite of my ghostly experience the night before, and I felt strongly that I had made a new friend in Dougie. I had no idea then that he would become such an influence in my life, and I had no perception of the many adventures we would share in Bermuda and throughout our later lives.

As it turned out, Dougie and I spent the whole of Boxing Day together – or what was left of it. He viewed Highclere with me in the late morning after I had secured a key from Colin M. Dougie had imbibed as much as me by the sound of the account he gave of the Spanish Point party Richard and I had left the previous day. But like me, he was a quick regenerator, so we agreed to partake of yet more Yuletide beverages over whatever food was on offer at the Hood, and as there was no point in going back to our respective abodes, only to have to make the journey back to the pub in the evening, we simply stayed put for the rest of the day and evening.

In those few hours together we prodded and pried into each other's lives; discussed our likes and dislikes; compared notes on the young ladies we had each come into contact with since arriving in Bermuda (one or two familiar to both of us), and we had come to the conclusion that we shared many things in common, not least of which was the ability to not take ourselves too seriously and laugh as much as possible at every available opportunity. Everything that life had to offer was up for grabs. Some weeks later, in a particularly loquacious mood, over a bottle of Goslings finest I hasten to add, we made a silly pact that although we could not influence the advancing years and, with a bit of luck and a following wind, grow old, we could on the other hand make the decision *not* to grow up. I am glad to say that we have honoured that agreement in style, and have adopted Keith Richards as our patron saint.

I was relieved to hear that Dougie liked the look of Highclere (I had carefully avoided mentioning the resident spook until a later date). He was more than happy with his room, and he found the rent affordable. In fairness to him, I had explained the potentially precarious position of our tenancy with the house being on the market, although, according to the agent, there seemed little likelihood of it being sold in the foreseeable future; but this did not faze him and he was prepared and happy to move in immediately. Brilliant. That left me with just one more housemate to find and the target for the ideal financial arrangement, but with four of us sharing the rent it was already a manageable situation.

FORTY-ONE

Early in the New Year we acquired Adrian Robson, and none of us remember how that happened. Even Adrian has no recollection of the event. One minute we were four-strong at Highclere, the next there was Robbo comfortably ensconced in our last vacant bedroom. We had wondered who was eating all the leftovers in the fridge, and stealing the beer. He had a habit of just turning up as we later discovered, but as a fifth rent-paying member at Highclere, he was nonetheless a welcome addition to our little group.

Adrian – rapidly christened as Robbo by the rest of us – was a sports journalist working for the Royal Gazette and had recently arrived in Bermuda, having spent three weeks in a small cottage in Bailey's Bay provided by the newspaper, before somehow joining our little gang. Not that it was a bad addition, far from it, he was as mad as the rest of us and constantly displayed it, so he jig-sawed in perfectly with the rest of the team. One of his favourite pastimes was swinging on a rope that someone had left hanging from a big cedar tree in the front garden. It had probably been hanging there for years, because one day it parted company with the tree at the height of its swing with Robbo still attached, and yelling 'Tits aliiiive!' (Robbo's trademark expletive) as he sailed through the air and bounced several times down the grassed slope that constituted our front garden. To be honest we were all pretty impressed with his dying swan act and the fact that he sustained only a few bruises for his trouble. Until the arrival of Robbo, I had not seen so many grazed knees and elbows since my days at infant school; he was always doing something daft that resulted in cuts and abrasions. He had landed heavily on his head a couple of times, falling off the terrace and once off his moped. So thankfully nothing vital was damaged. His story was that as a hot-shot sports journalist, he indulged himself in as much sporting activity as possible, but unless auditions were planned for another Tarzan film, his antics on the rope would go unnoticed by his editor.

It was about this time Dougie had a disturbing experience when, during the night, something crashed with an almighty bang against his bedroom door. As with my own strange experience at Christmas, we conducted an exhaustive search accompanied by a solemn promise from everyone that it had nothing whatsoever to do with them. It was relatively unspectacular, but nevertheless gave us more pause for thought, and Dougie to quickly change his soiled sheets.

Then a week later, having left Adrian in the house still getting himself ready for the evening and promising that he would meet us later, he turned up at the bar looking decidedly shaken and definitely stirred, that's to say, more than usual. He told us that as he emerged from his bedroom, there was, as he described it, a ball of light floating over the landing, which having hovered there for a few seconds, simply vanished. We were all a bit suspicious of this story as Adrian was becoming known as a prize leg puller who, apart from his tree swinging activities, seemed to be in training for the day when bull-shitting would become an Olympic event. But he continued to maintain the truth of his story, at least until some forty-five years later when having visited Adrian in his new home in England and during our reminiscences of old Bermuda days, I mentioned the incident. There was a blank look on my companion's face and having thought hard, he shrugged and submitted that he had no recollection of the event whatsoever. But the clincher for us all was to come at our big Valentines party in February.

It had been at least a month since our house-warming bash and we thought it high time we threw another party. We held a meeting one night before venturing out to do our usual rounds of the local haunts, to discuss what sort of party we should throw. Adrian suggested a Gypsy party, and receiving blank stares from the rest of us, he went on to explain that we could all go out and steal something.

'Is that it?'

'Er yeah.'

There was silence for a moment or two but then: ker-ching! The penny dropped; it was coming up to February, and the obvious choice would be to throw a Valentine's Day party, which we found actually fell on a Thursday. So side stepping that fact, we decided on Saturday the sixteenth for the event and made our plans accordingly. Graham volunteered to print the invitations at his new workplace – Castle Harbour – and we calculated how they would be distributed. Having printed invitations was a first; the normal method of inviting people to parties was to simply spread it around the Robin Hood and Rum Runners, and crucially the Elbow Beach staff club, and leave it at that. The ultra-efficient Bermuda grapevine would do the rest. In fact, that is exactly what we intended doing by leaving a bunch of invitations at each establishment and having them issued randomly but at the same time making it appear more of an exclusive event. To our closer acquaintances of course, we dished them out personally. Invitations or not, we would be inundated with partygoers. We just liked to be different and hoped the printed invites would suggest a bit of class.

'Bit of class... Did you see how I managed to keep a straight face there?

But to be honest, the pivotal reason and the deciding factor to have printed invitations, was that Graham could get them done for nothing.

We purchased a quantity of booze that was as always, more than enough for our needs: after all, it was a fact that almost everyone brought along sufficient for their own use and then some. Very few people took advantage by bringing cheap bottles of plonk or no booze at all whilst drowning themselves in the host's supply. Alcohol was one of the less expensive items in Bermuda, so it could be relied upon that plenty of booze would be flowing. In fact, without exception, after each party we had hosted up to that point, and those parties still to come, there was to be ample booze left over to re-stock our bar for some considerable time. The day after such events, our kitchen resembled a distillery, with us decanting part bottles into other part bottles in the name of economy and saving space. I have no idea what we supplied in the way of nibbles – multiple sacks of crisps, several gross of mini sausage rolls, a regiment of sausages on sticks probably – just the usual stuff and something to soak up the alcohol. It really didn't matter.

The day arrived and having tarted the homestead up, selected music for the evening and satisfied ourselves that everything was ready to go, we decided it would be in keeping and thoroughly deserving to relax before the onslaught over a few refreshing cocktails. But quite unexpectedly a couple of very early partygoers arrived in the form of Debbie, a Canadian who worked at one of the big banks in Hamilton, and her very attractive workmate Tanya, who none of us had met before. It wasn't that the girls had misunderstood the suggested start time, but they had simply not observed the accepted protocol of kick-starting the liver by sinking a number of large beverages at any one of the popular watering holes before making an appearance at whatever party was scheduled for the evening. Indeed, it was not unknown for people to turn up after the bars had closed at 1am; after all very few of the parties back then wound up before first light. Nevertheless, we made Debbie and company welcome and stuck a couple of drinks in their hands.

For some unaccountable reason, I can remember very well that the music we were playing at the time was from the album *Band on the Run* by Paul McCartney and Wings, and with every light in the house switched on, along with Terry's borrowed disco-light boxes weaving their multi-coloured way across the ceiling and walls, the atmosphere at Highclere was the antithesis of anything spooky or whoo whoo.

But it became obvious after a short time that Debbie's pal was having some problems and we asked if she was feeling ill.

'I'm sorry,' she stammered, 'but there is something wrong with this house, I think I need to go.' And with that she stood up, apologised again, and explained: 'There's a presence here… an unpleasant spirit.' Then apologising a third time, she hurried off. Debbie, obviously feeling responsible for her friend said that she had better go too, but not before telling us that Tanya was very sensitive to *that kind of thing* and similar incidents had happened before. Had Dougie and myself, and possibly Adrian, not had our own unnerving experiences, we would have dismissed the strange young lady as a bit weird, with a few loose screws, but under the circumstances it only confirmed what we had already come to accept.

Highclere was definitely haunted.

We never experienced any other spectral phenomena after that night for the rest of the time we were in residence, and we never delved deeply into the history of the house – there were far more important matters to put our minds to. Perhaps the ghost whoever he, she, or it was, decided on calling it quits after that raucous Valentine's party where, we calculated, at least two hundred people graced us with their presence. It could have been the loud music and flashing lights, and it could have been the volume of alcohol consumed, or as I preferred to think, it could have been the realisation that the five mad buggers who lived there had better things to do than give time to some restless spirit when spirits of a more liquid nature were a way of life and in constant use.

The party itself turned out to be one of the biggest and heaviest attended raves that Dougie and I had experienced up to that point, and was a great success. The ground floor of Highclere was jam-packed with revellers, with many dancing their backsides off to the carefully selected music. The rear garden, likewise, with hardly a square inch of grass to be seen – the green stuff growing on the ground that is – and the expansive front veranda was packed with people shoulder to shoulder. Even the steeply sloping front lawn that plunged down to

Pitts Bay Road had people stretched out beneath the palms, drinking, smoking and having a thoroughly good time. It was all told, a very Bacchanalian affair with a true Valentine's spirit. Not quite licentious, but not far off.

In short, it was just another typical Bermuda party.

It was no great surprise when I noted that the *insurers* had arrived at some point in the proceedings; there seemed to be no party that had not been *enriched* by their presence. But it was no problem. Richard had also spotted them, much to his disgust, but I told him to simply ignore them – they probably would not be staying. He looked puzzled by that, but not wanting to miss any of the action, he shrugged and disappeared into the crowd.

As hosts, the Highclere five circulated making sure everything was going smoothly, but not at the expense of our own enjoyment of course, and the haunted house rocked into the night. Much later, Richard found me and asked if I had seen the insurer 'jerk-offs' as he put it. After the motorcycle incident, he did not trust the trio one little bit and he had already checked his bike parked out front, on several occasions.

'No sweat,' I told him. 'They left about an hour ago, and they seemed in a hurry.'

'Why what happened?'

'Apparently the booze didn't agree with them,' I said.

Richard began to grin, 'Why?... Go on, what happened?'

'Let's just say they seemed to be slowing down a bit, so I slipped something into their drinks to help with their motion,' using the deliberate pun. Then I went on to tell him that one of our mutual nursing friends had given me some advice on the best laxative to use for fast results. 'It comes in little sachets,' I told him. 'Perfect for administering discreetly.'

Richard roared with laughter, 'How did you manage that?'

'With a little help from my friends,' I said, tilting my head towards Kathy the little red-headed nurse and her female companions, who seemed to be popular with several male partygoers across the room.

'How much are you supposed to give, because it must work quick if they've left already?'

'One sachet per person.'

'Yeah but…'

'They each had three, just to make sure.'

'Holy shit.'

'Yes, you could say that,' I laughed. 'They were in a bit of a hurry when I saw them, and they were walking funny.'

'In that case, I would check your bathrooms if I were you,' Richard advised.

Jeez, I hadn't thought of that, and I rushed around checking our two khazi's, which thankfully were just as you would expect, having entertained two hundred pissed-up revellers. Not pristine, but thankfully there were no obvious disasters of the excremental kind.

As was the norm, yours truly had not received one Valentine's card, which, I can reveal, was totally expected because I have to confess, I had never in my life up to that point, ever received such a thing. Not ever. But in fairness, there had only been two instances when I had actually *sent* Valentine's cards. The first did not even qualify as a true Valentine's, because I sent it to one of the teachers at my secondary modern school. He was an obnoxious man and seemed always to have it in for me, so having selected a suitable card and splashed it with a few drops of my mum's *Evening in Paris* perfume, I sent it off to him with a few suggestive words inside, being careful to disguise my distinctive handwriting in the process. I was very proud of my handwriting back then.

It wasn't hard to find his address because there it was displayed in full, in the telephone directory. I did not have the satisfaction of seeing first-hand the result of my little wheeze, but the teacher concerned did look a little ashen faced in school the following day, and appeared not to have had a very good night's sleep.

The second occasion was back in 1969, a few months after my marriage breakup. I was seeing a lady called Chloe, who I had met one night in the lounge bar of our regular watering hole in Reading, the legendary Boar's Head – commonly, but unjustifiably known as the Whores Bed – where my sister-in-law and her husband were landlords.

Chloe was a stunner and I had the feeling I was punching well above my weight. I was still regaining my confidence at that point and I was surprised that she had taken a fancy to me, but as always in my life there was a serious downside to the relationship because her particular tipple consisted of a pint of Guinness and a Babycham chaser. It was costing me a small fortune, although to be fair, she did on occasion take pity on me and buy her own drinks. But never mine.

It was the evening of Valentine's and I was meeting her in the Boar's Head, but as I entered the bar with my good friend Ray, Chloe was already there and I could tell by the expression on her usually smiling face, I was in trouble. The bar was barely half full and relatively quiet, and so when she held aloft a familiar looking card and raised her voice, all eyes turned to her.

'Oh look, here's lover boy,' she announced. 'Thank you very much for such a lovely Valentine's card.'

It was obvious to Ray that something interesting was brewing and he wisely detached himself from my company and made for the bar. Then to everyone in attendance, Zoe read from the card: 'Roses are red, violets are blue, when I fondled your mum, I was thinking of you… isn't that touching?'

I was conscious of a good many sniggers from the assembled patrons but I needed a way out of this. I thought my poem was pretty damn witty to be honest, and would be well received by anyone with a sense of humour and a forgiving attitude, but as I was about to find out, Chloe possessed neither.

'But whatever makes you think it came from me?' I asked innocently and trying to laugh it off.

'Well now, let me see,' she sneered as she held one hand aloft and began to count with her fingers. 'Firstly, it's the sort of thing that would come out of that brain of yours,' she said as she tapped my head none too gently.

'Secondly, there are beer stains on the card – look,' and she held the card out at arm's length, and walked around the bar for all to see as she jabbed her finger at the dark blotches dramatically. There was a pregnant pause.

'And thirdly?' I nervously prompted, hoping that I could still extricate myself from the ever-tightening noose that Chloe had placed around my neck.

'*Thirdly,*' she said, heavily emphasising the word, 'You bloody signed it, you dick!'

Oh… I had written the card the previous evening on the very bar where Ann my sister-in-law, having seen me enter, had just plonked my usual pint of Courage Best Bitter. Moreover, it was at the end of the evening when I had been ever so slightly three sheets to the wind, having met some friends in a nearby tavern before moving on to the Boar's Head, and I had no recollection whatsoever of signing the darn thing, which I must have done out of habit. But there it was.

The pub was silent as Chloe strode up to me, smacked the offending card on to the bar; dropped her half-smoked Rothmans (another expensive habit of hers) into my fresh pint, and stormed out, her red stilettoed shoes clacking menacingly on the stone floor.

'Well, I thought that went quite well,' my mate Ray hazarded after a long drawn-out pause, having kept his head safely down up to that point. 'Better get a fresh pint in… but tell me about Chloe's mum.'

FORTY-TWO

There was a massive bathtub in my en-suite at Highclere, and the great thing about taking a bath in Bermuda, was that you never needed piping hot water such was the high average temperature inside the house as well as outside. To me there is something luxurious and indulgent about taking a long, perfumed bubbly soak and letting the stress of the day melt deliciously away. Not that there were that many stresses to worry about, apart from the inconvenience of work that kept getting in the way. How pleasant to just fill the bath and plonk myself down; not like hot baths in the UK shifting from one leg to the other as the piping hot water rose up my legs, and working up the courage to lower my pale and trembling buttocks into the slowly rising magma. It was a Catch 22: if you filled the bath with water of a bearable temperature, you knew full well that within minutes of immersion, your body temperature would adjust and there was a need to top up with hot water. On the other hand, if you dared to drop yourself lobster-like into water that was likely to inflict first degree burns, there was a temptation to dilute it with something from the cold tap, thus defeating the whole object. Not so in Bermuda.

But, as appealing as a warm bath was, it was only on two occasions that I indulged myself. With water a precious commodity and the prospect of having to buy the stuff if the basement tank ran dry always a possibility, we were conscious of its conservation. But we had experienced a recent storm with a lot of rain, and so my reckoning was that it was justified, on the first occasion, to spoil myself after a particularly dirty job, and relieve my scummy body in a relaxing soak. On the second occasion, I just felt like treating myself for no particular reason.

But I enjoyed those lukewarm baths tremendously, and having fallen asleep both times, I only awoke when the level had dropped due to an ill-fitting bath plug, and I found myself wallowing in two inches of water and silt.

One of these immersions coincided with the house being uncharacteristically empty apart from my own presence. It was a Friday evening, Robbo and Colin Marshall had left early, and although Dougie, along with Terry, Rob and me, were rarely out of each other's company, this was one occasion when we all seemed to have separate arrangements. Dougie was helping with a private party on Hawkins Island scheduled for the next evening, and organised by American International, a large multi-national insurance corporation that had offices in Bermuda.

An acquaintance of Dougie, known simply as CB, owned a boat and for some unaccountable reason, it had become known as *the party boat* – actually not hard to see why of course, with CB and other rum-heads often giving it large on the water well into the early hours. The wife of Doug's friend happened to work at American International, and word had got out to her superiors about their boat which was a sizeable craft, and large enough to transport supplies over to the island for the party – supplies being predominantly booze and food. Dougie's friend was asked if he would do the business and he readily agreed, especially in view of the fact that he and Dougie had been issued with invitations.

This turned out to be a bad decision.

They managed to get all the supplies over to the island without too much of a problem, but it was on the return journey late the following night that posed certain challenges. The evening had progressed in the time-honoured Bermudian manner with the usual noisy, inebriated goings on and *bought-in* entertainment, progressing well into the early hours. When eventually it appeared the party was winding down, Doug and his colleague loaded the leftover food and alcohol – miraculously still a significant amount – back into the boat and headed off for *The Foot of the Lane* mooring where the vessel was kept. As they approached the mooring, Dougie had the brilliant idea with the help of Captain Cockspur, of jumping overboard, grabbing the chain from the mooring buoy and hooking it to the boat. There was a good reason for this because as the boat slowed, Dougie was unable to reach the buoy from the deck. There then followed three drink-induced silly mistakes.

Firstly, Dougie forgot to tell CB, who was busy at the wheel trying to keep the boat steady, that he was jumping overboard, so one minute Doug was on deck, the next, when CB turned round, he had disappeared. Second, having grabbed the chain from the buoy, Dougie sank like a stone, forgetting that twelve feet of steel chain was a bit on the heavy side, and it took him a few seconds to realise that it might be prudent to let go of the darn thing. Then, having swum to the surface he found that the boat was directly above him with the still revolving propeller missing his head by inches. He was now bobbing around in the water, yelling at his friend who eventually managed to drag Dougie out and between them they were able to manhandle the chain into position and secure the boat to the buoy.

For some reason they could not fathom, the dinghy that was needed to get to land was no longer tied to the buoy, so Dougie repeated his Desperate Dan act, swam to shore and grabbed a dinghy that happened to be propped up against a wall, then splashed his way back to CB's boat. This is where mistake number three came into play. They proceeded to load the booze and food residue into the dinghy which they had failed to notice was not equipped to carry such a weighty cargo, plus two hefty and very drunk passengers, although that didn't seem important at the time according to Dougie.

By the time they had finished loading and with both of them seated, the dinghy was sitting very low in the water, with only two or three inches of freeboard. It was a full moon and the water was very calm, so they proceeded to the shore at a slow pace, then for some inexplicable reason they started to giggle, and the more they laughed the more the boat rocked and the more it rocked, the more they took on water. By the time they were twenty feet from the shore the dinghy was totally submerged, but they continued to paddle.

Dougie said that he would always remember the sight of hundreds of little gold foil packets of butter floating around, twinkling in the moonlight. They managed to salvage all the booze but the steaks were a bit soggy, and Dougie's mate was never asked to use his boat to ferry any sort of comestibles again.

FORTY-THREE

When I left Ashmead Secondary Modern, I had no idea what I wanted to do. So I did what all the other no-hopers did... I applied to enter the Civil Service. It involved attending a half day of interrogation and an in-depth written examination at the University of Reading's Whiteknights Campus. The problem was we had been forewarned that the selection process took up to three months, which of course meant finding some sort of paid employment in the meantime, and no guarantee that there would be acceptance from the Civil Service, and a job offer at the end of it.

It turned out to not be a problem because a firm called Huntley Boorne & Stevens, where my dad had worked since the end of the war (the second war in case you are wondering) had a large rush order, and temporary staff were urgently required. H.B. &S. had been originally set up in 1832 to make the tins for the famous Huntley & Palmer biscuit products – the H.B. &S. Huntley partner, being the son of the biscuit maker who was half of the Huntley & Palmer company. Reading was once known as the biscuit capital of the world, with two hundred varieties being churned out at the height of their power. Not that any of that matters – well obviously it did to them, but anyway...

The company had expanded to manufacture other tin-plate products and I officially started my working life there, albeit for just four weeks, after which the rush order had been pushed out, and likewise the temporary staff. That left me kicking my heels and the need to find some way to earn a few bob, and quite by chance our next door neighbour was a manager at a busy roofing company, and having heard that I was looking for a job, arranged for me to attend an interview with his M.D. who was looking for a trainee estimator/surveyor. It was a boom time in the industry and it appeared they were finding it difficult to cope with the number of orders, such was the demand for new housing and industrial roofing at that time.

Luckily my neighbour had no idea that I was waiting to hear from the Civil Service, so I was well pleased that I could at least be earning whilst waiting, and I was subsequently taken on. It was a win-win, because if I failed to secure the position of Civil Servant, I already had a job. On the other hand, if I was offered a position, then I could just say roofing wasn't for me, and wave goodbye.

After three long months of waiting for the entry exam results, a letter bearing some fancy official seal pertaining to Her Majesty's Government arrived for me. I felt like Billy Elliott must have felt in the movie that day he received the envelope from the Royal Ballet School – except I can't dance.

To my complete surprise and, I have to say delight, not only was I offered a post, but I was given a choice of three ministries… the small Reading branch of the Ministry of Agriculture Fisheries and Food (nah, small time and no prospects); the Ministry of War, soon to be re-titled the Ministry of Defence; and the prestigious Home Office. Now that was more like it. It all sounded very grand and I had visions of me as a Whitehall Mandarin (whatever the heck fruit has to do with it), delegating earth shaking decisions; living in a front-line Georgian house at Sunningdale Golf Course, and retiring at age fifty with a pension that resembled an American telephone number. But having slept on it and mulled it over for a couple of days, the reality of the situation hit me, and it boiled down to this: did I really want to have to crawl out of bed at some ungodly hour every morning to get to the station; share a carriage with hundreds of other oiks all the way to Paddington, then travel across London in a sardine-like carriage on the underground in order to clock in at 9am? And I really couldn't see me in a pin-stripe suit, with a briefcase and brolly and God help me, a frigging bowler hat! It was a no brainer really, and I found myself comfortably ensconced in the roofing trade.

It was okay. I had the advantage of working in the office when it was wet, and outside in the fresh air when the weather was fair. As an estimator surveyor, I had the best of both worlds. Then after three years training, following a dip in the fortunes of the building industry and a nationwide recession, and a definite feeling of boredom with my job, I decided to get out into the fresh air permanently and went 'on the tools'. I became a sub-contractor and found myself staggering around on roofs for a living, and realising to my cost, that the 'fresh air' of England often involved getting soaking wet or freezing my nuts off.

It was a pretty dull few years to be honest and the reality was that my income was totally dependent on the vagaries and unpredictability of the British weather and the notorious roller coaster vagaries of the building trade, so I livened things up a bit by inadvertently becoming an arsonist, and being responsible for two very nice fires.

The first was on an office block in Reading. We had taken all the precautions with our propane burners that heated the boiler, that is to say a thick layer of sand, then a layer of asbestos sheeting, repeated three times. But several days into the contract, as I was eating my sandwiches – legs dangling over the edge of the roof – I noticed wisps of smoke beginning to appear from beneath the fascia. Moreover, it was happening along the full length of the building, which was almost the size of a small English county. My sandwich suddenly had the appeal of a caterpillar pasty and I legged it down the ladder and into the reception area yelling '*FIRE!*' Not very original, but the staff got the message. I could not help noticing whilst there, that the suspended ceiling was beginning to buckle alarmingly from the heat.

Once the big red lorries started to arrive, along with the boys in blue and ladies and gentlemen from the press, I discreetly retired to a nearby café and allowed my colleagues the honour of having their pictures splashed across the local papers. I have always been generous that way and a modest person to boot. Luckily thanks to the efficiency of the fire service, a major fire was averted, but I was informed later that had the ceiling panels been removed for whatever reason, then the updraft of air would most certainly have led to a conflagration.

In my defence however, it was found later that whoever had installed the original electrical system, had draped the live cables across the roof joists, instead of drilling through and avoiding pressure from the roof sub-structure. The extra weight and scaled-down heat from our boiler were enough to set in motion the melting of the cable casing which led to the timber joists start to smoulder, and the beginnings of a serious fire.

All in all though, it had been a successful practice run, and had prepared me well for my second effort which was on a military barracks at Kindley Field, the US air force and naval base in Bermuda.

Not having taken in my instructions on how to gauge when the bitumen material we were using became overheated, my colleague and friend Nobby, had loaded a large container of very hot bitumen on to the hoist, which half way to the roof, had suddenly ignited. I had an urgent choice to make: either lower it rapidly to the ground where there was a very real danger to my colleague, or bring it on up quickly where I hoped I would be able to deal with it.

I opted for the latter, which turned out to be a mistake. Bitumen expands when it burns, and when the container reached the roof it spilled over and quickly spread like a fiery blanket across the barrack's roof. My first concern was for the safety of the occupants in the building and I dropped through one of the hatches and yelled '**FIRE!**' I was getting good at this – my earlier incendiary activities in England had left me in good stead and in fine voice.

There seemed to be no sense of urgency judging by the absence of activity in the dormitories below, and I had noticed earlier that apart from the loud heavy rock music that had been blasting out from the open hatch since Nobby and I had first arrived on site, there had been a constant aroma of certain herbal substances emanating in an almost visible cloud. At times, if I had got myself close to the open hatch, I had to admit to experiencing a very good feeling that everything was right with the world and… you know… far out man and all that.

When the natty red fire trucks arrived, I stood to one side and let the base fire department deal with the blaze – which to their credit they did, quickly and efficiently. Once the incident had been dealt with leaving, surprisingly, only superficial damage I was relieved to see, I saw the base fire chief heading purposefully in my direction. I knew he was the chief because his helmet was white not black, and it sported a natty shield motif on the front.

'Now I'm for it,' I murmured to Nobby. 'The Yanks don't take kindly to people taking liberties with their property.'

'You in charge?' The chief challenged me.

I decided to tough it out and standing with my hands confidently on my hips replied: 'Yep, sorry about that, one of the hazards of the job.'

His face broke into a broad grin and holding out his open hand said: 'Put it there my friend… all we ever get round here are fucking drills and God-awful simulations. That's the first real fucking fire we've had and my boys did fucking good.'

'Yeah, they… did,' I agreed, and they had; it could have been a lot worse. I think he would have presented me with a medal if he had been able to. With hindsight though, I think I could have done a lot more damage as a civil servant.

FORTY-FOUR

The *Dazzlers* – our friends Penny, Jane and Sandra – had arranged an end-of-season lobster night at the aptly named Lobster Pot Restaurant in Hamilton, for the coming weekend and there were to be twenty of us in attendance. A number of prominent restaurants throughout the island had dedicated the whole weekend to mark the approaching end to the lobster fishing season, and we had opted for the Friday night as a prelude to the regular Elbow Beach get-together. Most of the regular clique of desperados were there including the ubiquitous trio of Brian, Malcom and Roy, the beautiful Angela, and several others. There were even place-name settings and predictably I found myself seated next to Dougie, which proved to be most enlightening. We had both typically ordered the Bermuda Fish Chowder to start, having done our very best to discourage others from doing the same in order to maximise our own shares, and had slurped down large bowls of the stuff extravagantly laced with our favourite Black Seal rum and Outerbridge's Original Sherry Peppers, the residue mopped up with several crusty rolls. Then the main course and the highlight of the evening arrived.

Believing that there was nothing more in the food consumption department, my friend could do that would surprise me; I was proved way out on that assumption. Having wolfed down the lobster meat and fixings, Dougie then proceeded to demolish the shell. Then with several pairs of astonished eyes looking on, he asked if he could have mine, and repeated the process. There was total silence in the room except for an impressive volume of decibels as Dougie munched his way through a second crustacean's overcoat.

'Handsome,' he declared, and rounded it off by holding up his glass of Cockspur and giving a toast: 'The lobsters. Cheers!'

At least Dougie will never have a roughage problem, I remember thinking.

Every week was the same... every week was different!

In theory, most weekday evenings spent at bars such as the Rum Runners and Robin Hood, with the occasional restaurant visit thrown in; then Friday nights spent at Elbow Beach with a guaranteed party somewhere on the island added to the mix would appear to be a boring routine. But not so.

There were always new faces on the scene, each with a story to tell – mostly ex-pats like us who had recently arrived on the island, or who had switched allegiances from other drinking establishments, such was the growing reputation of the Robin Hood. We never knew what to expect, and the proprietors of the Hood in particular were always coming up with new schemes and devices to interest their patrons. There was never a day that I can remember, when absolutely nothing out of the ordinary was going on, because apart from the rare uncharacteristic sullen mood by one or other of us because we had run out of Cockspur, Black Seal, Kool cigarettes, or a refusal to stop at the Chicken Coop for an early breakfast, the atmosphere was always upbeat and exhilarating. For me even work was varied and often interesting. How many people have clambered about on a sloping roof six stories up, placing their trust in a laid-back Rastafarian on the other end of a rope?

See what I mean.

None of us ever seemed to lose that sense of joy and sheer good luck from finding ourselves in that wonderful sub-tropical paradise with its hedonistic lifestyle, and with few exceptions we all realised that the fabulous adventure may not always be available to us and at some point we would be obliged to move on elsewhere or return to the Mother Country. *Live for the moment* was not just a glib observation, but very much the order of the day. And it was far from a male dominated scenario; all the young unattached ex-pat workers – male and female – as well as the Bermudian locals, went at life full pelt as if there was no tomorrow.

Excluding our inconvenient employment obligations, our Monday to Thursday default evening arrangements involved meeting up at our favourite drinking haunts and a half dozen or so other licensed premises where we would hang out with friends or members of the opposite sex (or not opposite, depending on your orientation), simply relating stories of recent exploits and swopping bawdy jokes, or getting to know new faces that were appearing on a fairly regular basis on the island as already mentioned. Above all, there was a constant barrage of laughter. We never talked about work – except for me, about a certain pitched roof seventy feet up. I dined out on *that* one.

There were a good many times when one of us had a prior engagement, shall we say, but even then, that usually still entailed dropping by one of the drinking establishments for a glass or two of whatever took our fancy and to meet up, albeit briefly with our good friends. During the summer months, we often found ourselves lounging on one of the beautiful beaches along the South Shore, acting the fool, then after dark, perhaps lying on the sand staring in wonder at the universe through the pollution-free sky. Only on two occasions were we forced to stay home, both times because of a tropical storm raging outside. But we consoled ourselves with large amounts of rum and beer, and a quantity of a certain home-grown substance that somebody always seemed to have to hand; and to lighten the disappointment of our confinement, we played very loud Bowie, Mott the Hoople and Jethro Tull tapes in serious competition with the rolling thunder, often indulging in our favourite card game: Crazy Eights.

The Friday schedule was slightly different to the rest of the working week because our final port of call for the night was of course, at the Elbow Beach staff club. The Robin Hood sojourn was almost compulsory as it was on all other evenings, but fortified with a few drinks we moved on and Friday evening at Elbow was where the young single ex-pats congregated in large numbers. For us the weekend always officially started at Elbow Beach staff club.

The fact that drinks were half the price of regular bar rates – that's to say 50 cents – was a great incentive, but over and above that it was where the forthcoming weekend was discussed and, of paramount importance, finding where the parties were being held the following evening. There was always a party or parties on Saturday night.

We could never figure out how it started, but at some point, Dougie and I became the recipients of this vital information and it became the thing for the organisers to notify us of their shindigs in advance so that we could circulate the news throughout the Robin Hood and beyond. By the same token, we would receive phone calls from those wanting to know where the weekend action was going to be. We were like unpaid ticket agents, except tickets were hardly ever required. Every single drinking party we attended was an open affair and everyone was welcome, and it was a common occurrence to have upwards of one hundred people arrive throughout the evening and early hours of the morning. Indeed, with the pleasant temperate Bermuda climate and being able to utilise gardens and outdoor spaces, double that figure was not unheard of, our earlier Valentine's party being one example.

The music was always good and loud at the staff club, and given that there was a lot of hair to let down in those days, we all did just that. It was a party atmosphere in its own right and we seemed to have no inhibitions in letting it all hang out on the dance floor and no doubt looking very silly in the process. The dance craze at the time was *The Bump*, at which Terry, Rob, Dougie and I reckoned we were the bee's knees, although to be honest we really didn't give a toss how good or bad we were, and week on week we inflicted a large amount of bruises and abrasions on our unwitting dance partner victims. We all agreed that Dougie was champion at this by far, and considered the possibility that he had a financial interest with the manufacturers of muscle embrocation.

On a really good night we would find ourselves hitched up with some mini-skirted lovelies and end up on the beautiful Elbow Beach itself where we would throw all caution to the winds, strip off and spend an hour or so skinny dipping and frolicking in the surf. Then delighting at the phosphorescence in the crystal-clear waters – that strange phenomenon caused by the luminescence of microscopic organisms, sparkling like millions of tiny lights – we splashed around like kids and played the fool before stretching out on the cool sand, staring in wonder at the canopy of stars that represented the Milky Way and beyond.

Elbow Beach staff club became something of a legend and for many an important landmark in their lives, with lasting friendships forged there and some even meeting their future lifelong partners, that perhaps had only started innocently with a bruise or two on the dance floor.

All in all, the memories generated would last the regular Friday night patrons for the rest of their lives and it was recognised as the place that marked in no uncertain terms, the beginning of another wild Bermuda weekend.

FORTY-FIVE

'What time did you get in this morning?' Dougie asked me between yawns, as I stumbled into the kitchen, desperate for that first mug of tea. Predictably he had a saucepan full of baked beans on the go and was buttering a slice of toast which he added to a pile already prepared on his plate.

'Did you score?' he enquired, not being a man to mince his words.

I yawned back, stretched and told him: 'Nah, well, sort of. I'm seeing her next week.'

'The one you were dancing with all night?… Her with the legs and long red hair?'

'Yeah… you don't often see red hair that long on someone's legs,' I said. 'How about you?'

'Not really, nobody worth bringing back anyway. Want some beans?'

'Might as well, bung some bread under the grill and I'll open another tin. Jeez, my mouth feels like the bottom of a bird cage.' Dougie appeared to be taking little notice of what I was saying as he loaded up his plate and slid it onto the work counter ready to get stuck in. Then Robbo put in an appearance, scratching his head with one hand whilst easing his shorts down and kneading his balls with the other, as if he was prepping dough for a loaf of bread.

'What's happenin'?' he greeted us between great noisy yawns.

It was obviously that yawning time of day. 'I need a coffee,' he said, and after putting the kettle on disappeared to the bathroom, passing Colin M on his way in, and judging by Colin's appearance he had experienced an equally demanding night somewhere.

'Morning,' he grunted and made his way to the fridge.

'Bit early for one of those isn't it,' Dougie cautioned as Colin returned to the table with a Budweiser.

'Breakfast of champions, haven't you heard.'

We wondered if Graham had made it back, and was sleeping his own hangover off in his studio at the bottom of Highclere's garden. 'See if his bike's there,' suggested Dougie, and I got up from the table, took another luxurious stretch and wandered over to the front door.

'Yep, he's in,' I reported back. 'That's a first.'

'What is?'

'That's the first time I can remember all of us being here on a Saturday morning, and with no strange bikes outside.' It had to be said that often, on a Saturday or Sunday morning, the drive at Highclere resembled a hotel car park.

'Alright, who's nicked my soap?' Adrian came storming back.

We all looked at each other in obvious puzzlement. Soap?

'I know one of you blokes has nicked it, because I had it hidden and now it's gone.'

More puzzled looks. Robbo had soon learned to keep his toiletries away from the rest of us. We were always running out of the basics like aftershave, toothpaste, soap, and it wasn't beneath us to nick someone else's gear, so Robbo had taken to hiding his stuff – he even had his own toilet paper stash.

'I need a slash,' Colin M cut in, and lurched out of the kitchen.

Nobody had owned up to the alleged theft of the soap, and Robbo had left the room grumbling to himself as he went. By the time I had scorched and buttered my toast and poured over the beans, Graham had appeared and Dougie was lighting up his first Kool of the day having demolished his own breakfast.

'Terry's party tonight.' A cheerful Graham reminded us, not that we needed reminding, it was bound to be a good bash. For some reason we could not figure, Graham always seemed to look as fresh as the proverbial daisy and full of beans, no matter how late he got in or what he had been up to the night before. The only way the rest of us would be full of beans at that time of day, was courtesy of Heinz and the tinned variety.

'Have you been to his place before?' he asked, looking from Dougie to me for an answer.

'I have,' I said. 'Last year for his twenty-first birthday bash, it was pretty much where I got to know him.' And I recounted the story, that in March of the previous year, having been in Bermuda for only three months, I had got to know Terry. We had been on nodding terms at the Hood, but it was at his twenty-first birthday party that we had hit it off and become friendly. But this second party that Graham was alluding to was in fact a kind of farewell do. For whatever reason, Terry and his housemates were going their separate ways and Terry had found himself a one-bedroom bachelor pad near Hamilton, conveniently close to the action. Knowing those guys, the party that night would be a very loud, very boozy and very long affair. Right up our street.

I was just about to tuck into my beans on toast when Robbo reappeared. 'Found it,' he said, brandishing a well-used bar of Camay. 'It was under the sink.'

'Camay? You tart,' Dougie chided him, making the two of us laugh. Colin M rejoined us and did his best to smile, but gave up on any idea of breaking his headachy silence, deciding to break wind instead.

Robbo had to have the last say, however, with a caustic, 'At least I don't wash myself down with bleeding carbolic like you guys; probably why you've got faces like this kitchen floor.'

'Yeah well, carbolics to you,' exclaimed Dougie, jumping to his feet. 'Let's go eat.'

'You just did and I still am.' I reminded him.

'Oh… right. Well let's go drink then.' And that was our signal to make what, even for us, was an exceptionally early start at the Robin Hood or wherever was open… once I had finished my beans on toast of course. Never leave food on a plate was our motto.

The house Terry and his cohorts shared was just off South Road in Warwick, not far from the ocean. We, as usual, arrived well after the party had got started and were surprised just how murky it was in the house. Although I had been there the year before, none of it looked or felt familiar, partly due to the passage of time during which there had been many diversions, but also, wasn't helped by the fact that the lads had decided not to use the new-fangled invention called electricity and had placed candles at various points around the lounge and kitchen. It was hard to discern the state of their soon-to-be ex-home through the gloom – although the smoky aroma of joss sticks was perhaps some sort of indicator. Even the bog had just one candle and a large incense cone stuck in a teacup on top of the cistern. Finding your way around and taking a whiz, was literally a case of hit and miss whilst in a sober state, but pissed as a parrot… I wouldn't have wanted to be the one to clean up in the morning.

Although Doug and I had pretty much the same volume of alcohol over the day, my friend seemed to be in a higher state of inebriation than me when we arrived, and was on one of his hyperactive dance floor trips, bumping the hell out of any female unfortunate enough not to have heard of his reputation. That's not to say that I was exactly walking in a straight line, but I was keeping the dancing down to a minimum – unless of course it was a soft sexy slow number with the chance for a bit of friendly canoodling whilst my female partner performed the important task of keeping me upright. But I remember later spending an interesting half hour sitting on the steps leading up to the house, and chatting with Mary, who was a friend of long standing in Bermuda, and was the same Mary I had known since my very early days on de Rock and had spent a fun-filled weekend with during the previous Cup Match holiday.

Dougie in the meantime had been talking to Terry about his

impending move, and he came outside to tell me that because the fridge freezer belonged to the boys and had not come with the house, they were looking to sell it at a reasonable price. I had glanced at it on my many trips through the murkiness to the bar, and remembered thinking what an unusual piece it was, having a very striking copper coloured door. I had never seen a refrigerator quite like that. Our own appliance was probably purchased around the time that Guy Fawkes had been nabbed as he was about to start his own party off with a bang, and it had already looked pissed off and down at heel when we moved into Highclere. So it seemed a good idea to make an offer for the classy copper job. The word classy and Terry in connection with the abode on South Shore, were strange bed fellows, and should have set the alarm bells of caution off right there.

Dougie told me on the way home that Terry and his mates would probably take thirty dollars for the fridge, which they needed to shift quickly, and seemed to be a steal. One of Terry's housemates had even offered to deliver it for us in a van he had access to. But we had nevertheless arranged to drop by the following day on our way to the beach, and give it the once over just in case.

Unsurprisingly Dougie and I had decided that due to the murmurings from our bellies, it would be rude not to interrupt our journey home with a call at our favourite eating establishment, the Chicken Coop. I once quipped that the only thing Michelin about the Coop, were the tyre marks on the roadkill they served up with eggs. But it was a light-hearted jest, and quickly taken back by me at the site of the proprietor approaching me menacingly with a cleaver in his hand.

Dougie in particular was well known at the restaurant, and on that particular early morning, he added further to his infamy by ordering a double large breakfast… twice!

'Okay,' the waitress checked; 'you want a double large breakfast, right?'

'No,' Dougie started to carefully enunciate, 'a… double… large… breakfast… twice.'

'But… that's four large breakfasts,' she protested.

'You got it.'

Even I who had witnessed Dougie's gargantuan appetite first hand on many occasions had my doubts, and believed that here at last he had bitten off much more than he would be able to chew – quite literally. One large breakfast at the Coop consisted of: two eggs, two sausages, two rashers of bacon, grilled tomatoes, beans, mushrooms, a pile of home fries and two rounds of toast.

But I shouldn't have doubted my friend, he had never let me down before, and that morning was no exception, and with the one deviation in the shape of a lone tomato, inexplicably being tossed on to my plate (literally) in the name of friendship, he polished off the lot, washing it all down with a third mug of tea. It made my own meal of double sausage, bacon, egg and home fries look pathetically inadequate in comparison, although I did indulge myself in two OJs … plus Dougie's generous and much appreciated tomato contribution.

Another incident in connection with Dougie and the Coop that is worth mentioning and will always cause me to smile, occurred later that same month when Dougie and company had arrived for the usual early breakfast. He gave his order then immediately put his head on his folded arms and fell asleep across the table.

No more than two minutes later he woke up with a start, looked around the room and shouted towards the kitchen: 'Where's my bleeding breakfast? How long are you expected to wait for food in this place?' It was one of those occasions that we have all experienced at some time or other, when we have been so completely exhausted, that on waking we have no idea just how long we have been asleep. It could be five hours or in this case, just five minutes, such is the depth of our unconsciousness. Dougie assumed that he had been out for some time and the service at the Coop had hit a new low and had – justifiably he felt – made his feelings known.

The following day, we arrived at Terry's South Shore residence about midday on our way to Horseshoe Bay for our regular Sunday beach liaison with the rest of the gang, and it was hard to recognise the house in full daylight. It was even harder to recognise the interior. The boys were still trying to clear away the results of the previous night's shindig, not that they were moving that fast or showing enthusiasm; it was a picture of lethargy from four extremely hungover individuals. They made three-toed sloths look like cheetahs on speed.

What the…

To say Dougie and I were shocked when we entered the kitchen was an understatement. Apart from the wreckage strewn across the worktops; puddles of beer and other beverages still on the tiled floor – and mystifyingly several colourful splotches on the walls and ceiling, which in fairness, could have always been there – it was the fridge freezer that stopped us dead in our tracks. What had appeared to be a state-of-the-art appliance with a snazzy copper coated door the previous evening in the candlelit semi-darkness, and enhanced no doubt by our merry condition, was in fact a piece of machinery that looked as if it had been wrongfully delivered to the house instead of being transported to the dump. Because what we took to be copper, was actually a dull shade of rust, with the whole door one unbroken area of oxidised metal. I had never seen, nor have I ever seen since, a door of a fridge or any other white kitchen appliance that was so comprehensively bolloxed. Our faces must have been a picture and for once, we were speechless.

'So, you don't want it then,' Terry said as he took in our open mouths and goggle-eyed expressions. We just shook our heads, still lost for words.

'I thought it was a bit weird when you said you would buy it last night,' he said with a phoney look of bemusement on his face.

The amazing thing was that Terry had had the bloody nerve to offer it to us for thirty dollars. But I guess if you don't ask, you don't get, and knowing Terry he was probably looking forward to our reaction when we saw the thing up close and in the daylight. Judging by the sudden grin on his hungover face, and the disbelief on ours, I didn't think he was disappointed.

FORTY-SIX

The roofing system franchise that had been acquired by my boss was ideally suited to the climactic conditions and unique architecture of those sub-tropical islands. It was a British innovation and prior to leaving England for my new exotic pastures, I needed to take a crash course in this latest product.

I was sent to Belvedere in Kent where the company were working on a new comprehensive school. My work colleague was a permanent employee of the company who lived in nearby Gravesend and it was he who recommended a *cheap and cheerful* bed and breakfast establishment for my seven-day sojourn in the area; indeed, he himself lodged there.

Well, cheap it was, but cheerful it most definitely was not. In fact, it was a greasy spoon transport café that also provided accommodation, and it transpired that two very good friends of my new workmate owned the place. Not only was it a dump, but having been shown to my room by a close relation to Lurch, I found to my astonishment that I was expected to share with a complete stranger.

'What do you expect for the money,' shrugged the Munsters' butler as he wiped his nose on the back of his tatty shirt sleeve. 'Bleedin' Holiday Inn?' And before I could answer, he had shambled off down the dingy corridor, no doubt to frighten some old ladies. I could have found myself shacked up with the Gravesend poisoner or Doctor Mengele, so I counted myself fortunate that I was co-habiting with a timid and pleasant little man, by the name of Colin Smith. It was a temporary arrangement; I only expected to be in residence for a short time so, hey, it could have been worse. But then again, not much.

Colin and I got to know quite a bit about each other over the next seven days (no, steady on, I know what you're thinking – there were *two* beds in the room ok?) and he even taught me the rudiments of chess; it turned out that he had been a schoolboy chess champion in his native town of Exmouth. He was currently unemployed, he told me, but was a skilled shoemaker and shoemakers as everybody knows, are cobblers.

No really, it's true.

Anyway, my interest was aroused by the name Exmouth because I had spent many childhood summers in the Devonshire town by virtue of the fact that my aunt and uncle lived there, and so accommodation was always provided for us. My dad would not have been able to afford a fortnight's summer holiday at the Devon coast or anywhere else for that matter, had this not been the case. I told Colin the names of my relations, but they apparently didn't ring any bells, although when I reeled off their address, he knew the location.

So there it was; ships that pass in the night and at the end of my time in Gravesend I moved on and I never saw or heard of the man again.

Fast forward twelve months.

With the exception of Robbo, the rest of us had been at Highclere for two months, then one evening at the Rum Runners the co-owner Roger Pedro asked us if we had any spare accommodation. He had engaged a new chef from the UK who would be arriving on the island shortly, and would be requiring a temporary billet whilst he got himself sorted out. All of our bedrooms were spoken for, but the dressing room attached to my bathroom was wasted space and quite roomy. Moreover, it contained a convertible sofa bed so could quite easily become a sixth bedroom. The extra rent coming in would be very handy and leave us with more dollars to squander.

The new guy, Steve Croucher, duly arrived and settled in with us very quickly. He was a good bloke, we all liked him and he was quickly initiated into our merry band and with our help, dipped his toe into the vibrant waters of Bermuda's social life. Over drinks one night, and having detected a West Country burr to his speech, I asked him where he hailed from, which turned out to be Exmouth in Devon. Naturally I asked him if he had ever encountered my relatives. He shook his head; their names meant nothing to him. Then remembering Colin Smith, I related the Gravesend saga.

Yet another of those strange coincidences that seemed to follow me around, was about to reveal itself.

The name obviously struck a chord and Steve asked me if I knew what the other Colin did for a living. When I told him that although unemployed at the time, he was a trained cobbler, his mouth fell open in amazement. Incredibly it turned out that Colin Smith was Steve's uncle who had simply left home many years before and was never heard of again by any of his family; and the clincher that put his identity beyond doubt? Uncle Colin had been a schoolboy chess champion.

What was the strange cosmic purpose that had tied me, a lad from Reading working in Gravesend, a town I had never visited previously – and having spent seven days there never wanted to visit again – to then meeting Colin Smith under exceptional circumstance, and finally culminating with me sharing a house with his nephew Steve Croucher on a tiny dot in the North Atlantic. And all bound to a common source: the town of Exmouth in Devon. Its purpose is even more of a mystery because it was later discovered by Steve's family in England that Colin Smith was long gone from the digs in Gravesend leaving no forwarding address. Perhaps the assurance to his family that he was alive and well was purpose enough. But it made me wonder.

I'll let you ponder that while I get on with the next chapter.

FORTY-SEVEN

Dougie and I had dropped by the Rum Runners one Saturday lunch time. We had a hankering for one of Steve Croucher's appetising lunches and of course a few obligatory cocktails, whilst whiling away an hour or so discussing such world shaping matters as whose party we would be attending that evening, and who, our mate Rob was currently shagging... or more to the point, who he wasn't. The subject of Dougie's footwear also came up and I asked what colour he intended painting his shoes that weekend. This was a ploy that my friend had devised in order to save on purchasing footwear for every occasion – simple. Just change the bloody colour!

Having eaten, we were sitting out on the balcony that overlooked Front Street, and my eyes went immediately to two ladies sitting at another table, deep in conversation. One was middle aged – although early forties was middle age to us at that point in our lives – and the other was a very striking blonde twenty-something, I guessed. Actually, both ladies were attractive and had distinct facial similarities. Mother and daughter, we surmised, but there was something about the younger one that took my immediate fancy.

'Got the hots for that one, have you?' Dougie whispered, having noticed my interest.

'Not 'arf,' I said. 'Haven't you?'

'Yeah, very tasty. Tell you what, you go and chat her up and I'll take the young one.'

'Knob head.' Although I had to admit that mum was a not hard to stare at either.

We went on like this for some time, but without either of us making a move, and to be honest we had pretty much given up on doing anything about it and backing up our phoney machismo. Attempted mother and daughter pick-ups, although intriguing, must be fraught with all sorts of problems, not least of which was the embarrassment of being laughed at and told to: 'bugger off sonny.' Not that we knew for sure because neither of us had had the experience except for the odd fantasy and wishful thinking. Then having finished their drinks, both women got up from the table and made their way inside.

'Well?' Dougie said. 'It's now or never.'

It was just a throw-away remark and not meant with any real conviction, but he's bloody right I thought, and quickly knocking back my drink, hurried after them much to my friend's surprise. I remember quite well the spiel I rolled out to the ladies, and it was along the lines of: 'I'm sorry, I can't let you go without asking if you would consider having a drink with me sometime (this to the twenty something) and before she could reply and holding up my hand, I went on: 'I realise you don't know me, but what's an hour or two wasted with a stranger compared to the chance that you may have found someone you would happily spend the rest of your life with? Please don't risk it.' What total bullshit.

That was pretty well it, chapter and verse, and having used this line once before to great effect, I was fairly confident of at least a smile along with a polite rebuff, but mum looked at daughter, then both looked at me before mum turned her gaze back to her girl to see what the reaction would be. I received an amused look from blondie (as expected), then gently biting her lip in a way that I found very stimulating to put it mildly, she smiled and said: 'Ok, when?' (Not expected.)

Ok, when? I mentally congratulated myself.

'How about tomorrow?'

'No not tomorrow or in the week, my mother goes back home to

England on Friday. How about this time next week?' *Mother*, she had said. We had been correct about their relationship.

'Right next week it is. Here at one o'clock. Is that alright?' And she nodded.

'Great, oh and enjoy the rest of your time here,' I addressed to mum who with an appraising raised eyebrow and the glimmer of a smile, nodded back in response.

I was about to turn away to impart the good news to Dougie who still sat on the balcony eyeing up passing talent on Front Street, when blondie asked: 'What's your name?'

Jesus, yes, name. 'Colin,' I told her (as in Mr smoothie Colin). 'And yours?'

'Glenda.'

'Wonderful, see you here… right here.' She laughed as I pointed to a spot on the floor. 'One o'clock next Saturday.' And that was it. Job done… well, half of it.

I had only ever known one Glenda, and that went way back to school days. So I thought it might be a great ice-breaker to relate the story to Glenda Mark II when we met the following Saturday. And that's what I did.

It was on my morning paper round in a better part of the council estate where I lived, and where most of the gates were still on their hinges and the postman had kept the use of his legs, that I first saw her. I was just thirteen going on nine, and to my inexperienced virgin eyes SHE was everything a young boy could want in a girl – the face of an angel with long blond hair, and riding a shiny new-looking red Raleigh bicycle.

SHE was a papergirl for a rival newsagent, and the happiest moment of my young life was when, after only four or five weeks I summoned up the courage to talk to her and say hello, and oh joy, SHE said hello right back. This could only mean one thing – SHE fancied me. After helloing for a week or two, I decided to take it to the next level and I asked her name. Glenda, she told me, and it seemed to my juvenile mind that there was never a more perfect name for an angel. Now I knew SHE loved me too. We had exchanged names.

I thought nothing of it then, but it was me who always had to seek her out for our morning exchange, and I figured this must be what was meant by playing hard to get. All part of the game I had read somewhere, but that was cool; I knew how SHE really felt.

Then the morning arrived when my goddess did a swallow dive off her pedestal and head-butted me in the crotch. It was a Saturday, known thereafter as 'Humiliation Day'.

I found her at the door of 44 Landrake Crescent where SHE was collecting money. Glenda saw me at the gate and there was a whispered exchange between her and the lady customer. The lady, who sported perm-rollered hair and a grimy apron, glared and without taking her eyes off me said to Glenda in an excessively loud voice, 'Why don't you just tell him to sling his bleedin' hook, love.' She hadn't even taken the cigarette out of her mouth.

If the road had opened up in front of me to reveal a set of stairs, I would have body-surfed down them. In one telling sentence, it all became clear to me. My education had begun. I mumbled something incoherent, and then with my face the colour of a whore's hat, I pedalled off as fast as my skinny legs could take me.

Unrequited love. Bitter sweet.

That was how I told the story to Glenda in the Rum Runners that following Saturday, which as I had calculated, entertained and amused her. It had been a perfect opening to what turned out to be a perfect weekend, because at the end of my tale, she leaned forward on the table we were occupying and said: 'That's very sad. I think we had better put things right and wipe out the memory of Glenda number one, don't you?'

I could not have agreed more, and that's precisely what we did.

Several times.

FORTY-EIGHT

'Where's the bash tomorrow night?' Rob asked in his celebrated Geordie accent.

It was Friday night and we were standing near the bar in the Elbow Beach staff club; Rob had just arrived and Terry was getting the drinks in.

'Usual, Rob?' Terry yelled across the bobbing heads between us. Rob stuck his thumb in the air.

'Wallingford... Pitts Bay Road,' Dougie informed Rob.

'Vicki and Lesley's place,' I added.

'Aye, we've been there before, haven't we? Should be good if the last one's anything to go by,' he said grinning. Rob had obviously pulled last time and Dougie and I nodded in agreement as Terry duly arrived with the drinks.

'Thanks for giving me a hand, chaps,' Terry admonished. 'I'll go back and get the other two, shall I?'

'Should have asked for a tray, mate,' Dougie told him.

'This is Elbow Beach staff club not the bleedin' Savoy,' Terry grumbled.

'Terry!' I called after him.

'What?'

'Hurry up.'

'Bollocks.'

'What's the talent like tonight?' Rob was never slow in getting to the heart of the matter. He was busy surveying the room.

'The usual crowd,' I said. 'Quite a few new faces too by the look of it.'

'Hey, look at those two tarts,' Dougie was gesturing towards two unfamiliar female figures at the far end of the bar, both looking in our direction.

'Don't like yours,' I told him.

He carried on sizing them up with his expert eye. 'Nah, neither do I,' he decided, before turning his attention elsewhere in the crowded room.

'I think I'm in.' Rob was looking at a group of five or six girls jigging around on the far side of the dance floor.

'Which one?' Terry had arrived back with our drinks and craned his neck to see.

'All of 'em if they're game, but the one in the red skirt fancies me I reckon.'

'You're joking,' Terry told him. I have it on good authority, that she hates Geordie accents.

'Yeah, I know her too,' said Doug. 'More pricks than a seamstress with hiccups.'

'Dougie's right, 'She's had more jumps than Beechers Brook.' I added.

Rob laughed. 'How would you Nancies know? Nah, I'm definitely in there,' and undeterred by the banter, he left us and made his way through the throng, flashing his killer smile and providing more work for the island's optometrists.

More pricks than a seamstress with hiccups? I mused. How does he think of this stuff? Not that it bothered Rob, who seemed to be doing well with the young lady in question.

We three circulated in the room, pausing to chat when we saw a familiar face, with an emphasis on female familiar faces. Then as if by magic our glasses were empty.

'Time for a refill. I'll get 'em in' I said, and made my way back to the bar.

I was still waiting my turn when I felt a finger gently poking me in the back. I turned expecting to see Penny who I had acknowledged on my way over and had intended to divert to for a chat and a dance after delivering the drinks. But my mouth dropped open when I saw not Penny, but a familiar face nevertheless.

'Buy a lady a drink, Colin?' she said. It took a second or two for it to fully register, but holy shit, it was the attractive dog walker I had encountered over a year before when I had found myself temporarily indisposed in the form of a bare-arsed nature on Church Bay early one morning.

Translating thoughts to words, I exclaimed: 'Bloody hell... surprise, surprise, fancy bumping into you again. I've never seen you here before.'

On the morning of our first encounter, I was aware of her attractiveness, even though my mind had been on other more urgent matters, but then, standing before me in the staff club, I could appreciate just how impressive this lady was. She was wearing a colourful blouse with ruffled cuffs and a multi-coloured ankle length skirt and sandals, all of which immediately reminded me of the hippy fashion of recent past times; she even sported a headband that matched the blouse. I have never been good at describing women's fashion, but I can remember years later in great detail how the lady looked that night.

I remembered that my first impression of her age was maybe early thirties and one year on, my altered impression was that she was probably a little older, and dressed as she was, almost certainly one of the original flower power people.

'Some friends told me about this place, so thought I should get out more and give it a try,' she said, and gestured to a small group of similarly aged females. 'I almost didn't recognise you with your clothes on... Bacardi and Coke please,' she said, holding out her empty glass. I raised an eyebrow and thought, Mmm, yes definitely a Bacardi type of woman.

'Right, coming up,' I said after a moment's hesitation; I was not used to being flustered in the presence of an attractive woman, but she had taken me completely by surprise. I gave my order to the bar tender who had directed his attention towards me at last, and I turned back. 'You remembered my name' I said.

'Of course, how could I forget under such unusual circumstances?' She raised one eyebrow in a mock expression of scandalous outrage. 'And how is the lovely – what was her name? Esther, wasn't it?'

Hell, she had even remembered the name of the girl that had scrawled a message in Biro on my chest. I laughed; I was beginning to enjoy this. 'She's okay, I think. She left Bermuda to see the world.'

'Nothing serious then?'

'Sorry?'

'Between you two.'

'Oh, fuck me no.' I assured her, forgetting myself for a moment.

'What about you, are you married?' I asked, thinking what the heck, I might as well get down to the nitty gritty of what was on my mind.

She looked me straight in the eye: 'Yes,' she said. That was it. This lady does not beat around the bush, I thought.

'Okaaay.'

We spent the next couple of drinks chatting about Bermuda generally and what I had been up to in my time there, and she, carefully avoiding giving too much information about herself. Then finishing her drink, she kissed me on the cheek and whispered in my ear before going over to her friends to explain I presumed, that she would be leaving early and gestured in my direction – the long-haired git at the bar wearing what I tried to portray as a confident out-of-sight look, but which probably came over as a big cheesy grin. She then made her elegant way to the exit.

Seeing all of this, my two open-mouthed friends arrived back at the bar, accompanied by Rob with miss red-skirt hugging his arm as if to prevent him escaping.

'Who the fuck was that?' enthused Dougie, furiously slapping the back of his neck.

'Just an old acquaintance,' I told him.

'Could be his mum... like older women, do you Colin?' Terry grinned.

'Only if they are still breathing. Anyway lads, I have an appointment to keep,' and draining my glass I made my way over to the door, giving a little wave over my shoulder as I went.

They say you should never go back. But I have to say that Church Bay revisited that night, was all that I remembered it to be.

Saturday was going to be a busy day, even by our standards. I needed to get myself down to Sounds Plus to pick up two albums I had ordered the previous week: an old LP, *Aqualung*, by Jethro Tull, that I wanted to get reacquainted with, and The Rolling Stones', *Goats Head Soup*. I was still playing catch-up and bringing my cassette collection up to scratch. Then, as I was in town, I decided to grab lunch at the Dick and Tickle, where, you will remember, they made a mean Shepherd's Pie and served draft English beer – another plus.

Dougie was going to see one of his current girlfriends in Hamilton, Dianne, the one with the little boy who constantly wanted to know from Dougie: 'Wos dat?' as he pointed to something that had caught his attention. Then when Dougie told him, the little lad would move on to some other object in the room or item of Doug's clothing, and ask: 'Wos dat?' It was constant, 'Wos dat? Wos dat?' Dougie told me. The little lad was relentless. I would like to have been a fly on the wall when things got amorous between Doug and his lady friend... *Oooh ... Wos dat?*

We had agreed to meet up later back at the house, and decide where to eat that night. Our other housemates were off somewhere doing their own thing, but it was odds-on that they would find their way to the evening's bash at Wallingford.

There was a casino evening at the Mariners Club that night which was a short distance from the Robin Hood, and so to save time and unnecessary travel, we decided to eat at the Hood, followed by a few drinks – quite a few drinks actually – spend a couple of hours at Mariners and then on to Wallingford which was also in the general neighbourhood being situated at the town end of Pitts Bay Road.

Our meal was good, supported by the usual Cockspur rum of course, followed by a very successful evening at Mariners, at least by my standards because I only lost twenty dollars, before taking the short ride to Wallingford.

As usual, we travelled courtesy of the Suzuki, and by the time Doug and I arrived at the party, we were feeling minimal pain. There was a circular gravel drive to the property and I applied the brakes of the bike a little too energetically as we pulled up at the entrance to the house, resulting in my passenger being thrown forward, bouncing off me and, almost in slow motion, rolling off backwards onto the drive.

'Heyyy look,' Dougie proudly announced, holding up a bottle of Cockspur in each hand from his prone position, 'didn't break one!' Two broken ribs, a sprained ankle and a fractured pelvis, but no sweat – the rum was safe.

Not really. Dougie was fine.

The girls had set up the bar outside, parallel to the front wall of the house. I was surprised to see a guy called Mike tending bar because although I had been seeing Vicki on and off for a few weeks, he had been the boyfriend before I came on the scene, and he obviously was not giving up and had been making it clear that he had high hopes of getting back together with his ex. Having checked that there was an adequate supply of Cockspur behind the bar, we handed over our contributions to the collection, asked for two large ones moderately flavoured with ginger ale, and went inside to say hello to everyone including, of course, our two hostesses.

The place was already packed with all the usual suspects present, including our little gang of five. There was the usual banter and silly talk from us four blokes, interspersed with dances with whoever took our fancy and in my case making a point of spending time with the lovely Vicki, our co-hostess. But in between, there was something strange going on between Penny and me.

We had been friends ever since she had arrived in Bermuda more than a year before. We had seen a good deal of each other in the early days, but this had morphed into a friendship which had developed and strengthened as time went by. She would call me to ask for my advice on various things, including amazingly, boyfriends, and what I thought of them. She had even asked me, in all innocence, to stay overnight at her place on one occasion because she was taking her driving test the following day and needed some moral support and company because she was as nervous as a cat in Barking. And genuinely that's what it was, me simply giving support to a friend when she needed it.

There was seven years' difference in our ages; I had still plenty of living to do and generally putting myself about following five lost years and a broken marriage behind me, and Penny had plenty of her own living and life experiences to discover, being just nineteen when I first met her. Therefore, as far as a long-term romantic relationship was concerned, it was a non-starter. But that night at Wallingford, there had been a subtle but distinct shift in the dynamic between us.

On one of our regular top-up trips to the bar outside, I told Dougie about it. He just shrugged in the time-honoured Dougie way and said, 'Just go for it, man, that's what I'd do.' That was the way I felt, but Vicki... It was at that point Matt arrived, obviously already pretty hammered and very vocal. As he banged a bottle down on the bar, he yelled at Mike: 'Barman, gi' me a large whiskey and a beer... an' wha'ever they're having,' referring to Dougie and me. Pretty generous in view of the fact that he wasn't paying.

'Wait your turn, I'm serving,' Mike snapped.

Uh oh! We knew Matt – Mike did not. But that was soon put right with the air temperature seeming to drop several degrees as Matt glared at the now uncertain and somewhat nervous looking Mike. Then in a softer almost gentle voice, Matt turned to us and said: 'Och, a'm aff tae be getting blud oan mah noo sherrt.'

Mike's Adam's apple took a noticeable and rapid ascent in his throat – reminiscent of the metal clapper on a fairground *Test Your*

Strength attraction after you whack the striker with a mallet. I laughed out loud, not because it was funny, but because I wanted to diffuse the situation and save Mike from a trip to the emergency room at the hospital, which was a distinct possibility.

'Yes, what he wants please, Mike, but we're in no hurry,' I said, trying to pour cold water on the tense moment.

A pointless exercise because Dougie chirped in, always ready to stir the pot – 'Yes we are in a hurry, make it snappy.'

Swallowing hard, Mike hurriedly presented Matt with his drinks, then as quickly as he could, mixed ours. As we moved back towards the front door of the house, and the source of the loud party music, Matt never took his eyes off Mike, and almost walking backwards, he made sure his head and eyes remained locked on Mike's face until we had gone inside.

'Scared tha' living shite oot o' him didnae ah?' Matt laughed as we got inside. It had all been a complete wind-up. 'Ah juist dinnae like him.'

There had been no arrangement with Vicki about whether or not I would be staying the night, just an unspoken acceptance that I probably would, but the unexpected, revived intensity between me and Penny threw up other possibilities. I discreetly handed Penny my house keys to Highclere and told her I would follow later – at least I thought I had been discreet. I did not want to make the whole thing obvious with the two of us leaving together, but as I turned and surveyed the room, I saw Vicki quickly look away and force herself to laugh at something that was said within the group of people she was chatting to. She had seen the exchange and I knew without a doubt I had just ensured my actions had effectively terminated our relationship, but more damaging than that, I had caused a very nice person, who I genuinely felt affection for, undeserved pain and humiliation. It had not been my finest hour.

FORTY-NINE

I had arrived home at my usual time, only to find that Dougie was not there and uncharacteristically putting in a bit of overtime. Colin M was already relaxing in the kitchen and enjoying his first beer of the day along with a doorstep sandwich of some description, and perusing a copy of the *Mid Ocean News*. There was no sign of Adrian and Steve, although Steve had probably already left for work at the Rum Runners to prep his kitchen in readiness for the evening dinner crowd.

I heard Graham drive up to the house shortly after, and he stuck his head briefly round the kitchen door to say hi, before retiring to his garden bachelor pad; presumably to freshen up and prepare himself for the evening. Graham, we had noticed, spent far more than any of us in his preparations for going out on the town, and just about in everything else for that matter. He was by far the best organised of any of the Highclere squad.

It was rare for any of us to make firm arrangements to meet up for the evening – there was no point. Weekdays it was almost obligatory that we would see each other at the bar of the Robin Hood, and only then would we hear what each of us had planned. Often we would stay together and either make a night of it at the Hood, or visit a number of establishments on our drinking roster. Sometimes we would call round uninvited to the houses of acquaintances, for free drinks, which was reciprocated just as often. On other occasions, some of us would have a prior arrangement elsewhere, or get lucky and disappear for the rest of the evening. Sometimes we would go as a group to the 40 Thieves Club, where there would often be international acts performing, such as The Drifters and Tom Jones amongst others.

To heck with it I thought, I'll take a quick shower and get myself off to the Hood where it was their weekly free spaghetti night. It saved on cooking and expense and was where I would have landed up anyway, albeit normally much later. My usual practice was to have a couple or three hours' relaxation after work before venturing out. Dougie would undoubtedly join me in his own good time.

It was just before six when I arrived at the Robin Hood and with all sorts of things going around my head, I was only vaguely aware that there were already a few diners in the restaurant as I made my way up to the bar. The place was less than half full at that time of day, and the glorious Olga, my favourite barmaid, was on duty as I entered. 'Hey, Colin, had a good day?' she greeted me, and stuck an already prepared Cockspur and ginger under my nose. She had seen me arrive.

'You know, just your average working day,' I told her, and eying the welcoming cocktail told her sincerely: 'You never fail to please. Thanks, Olga, cheers.'

'I caught the whiff of your scent when you left the house,' she said laughing.

I smiled back. Ever since Dougie, Rob, Terry and I had dropped by the Groove Tube2 store one Saturday a couple of weeks earlier, and had come away with a collection of essential oils, there had been a standing joke about it at the Hood. Rob had opted for frangipani; Terry fancied sandalwood and Dougie and I both took to patchouli. The oils came in small glass vials and were powerful concoctions, requiring only the faintest hint on a fingertip which was then dabbed on to the face and neck in lieu of aftershave, or in Dougie's and my case, no-shave. Strictly face and neck too, because I doubt there is a man from the sixties generation who did not make the mistake of squirting a bit of Brut or Old Spice inside his grundies at some point, never to repeat the mistake again. My own experience of the practice is indelibly printed on my brain, when I squirted a hefty dose of Tabac into my underpants just before I was leaving the house on a night out sometime in the mid-sixties. It took a few seconds, but then the temperature around the wedding tackle went from warm to hot to raging inferno, and I remember only too well pelting down the stairs three at a time from my bedroom to the bathroom, where it took several minutes of desperate and painful scrubbing with cold water and lathers of soap before the crown jewels had quit steaming and got back to anything like a normal body temperature. Nope, once was enough and never to be repeated, but I have often wondered since why the heck we thought that aromatic testicles would be a turn-on and make us more attractive to the opposite sex in the first place. Another one of life's mysteries. But back to the patchouli oil…

Subsequent to Dougie and I visiting the Robin Hood wearing the stuff for the first time, it was jokingly suggested by the bar staff that they knew when we were leaving Highclere because of the strong patchouli aroma in the air, even though our house was a half mile away. Obviously on this occasion, Olga had seen me parking the bike and poured my drink on that pretext, although I had to admit the patchouli oil was a high octane smelly, so who knows? I chuckled at the now familiar joke; 'Yeah right,' I held up my glass in a toast. 'The first one always goes down the best.'

It was still early, and we were able to chat for a minute or two with only a few interruptions as several patrons came and went. It would be its normal bustling self soon enough, especially as this was the free spaghetti night.

'Just going to clear a table, back in a second,' Olga said and headed off to the restaurant. On her return and having deposited the few dirty plates and the cutlery she had collected, Olga sidled up to me and in a conspiratorial tone informed me: 'There are three gorgeous girls in the restaurant who saw you come in; they said they love the way you walk and would like to buy you a drink.'

'Really?'

'Yes really, and they paid me already... another Dirty Bird and ginger?'

'What else?' I drained my glass and handed it over. The evening ahead had suddenly started to take on a new look, and with Dougie arriving at any time, we could be on to a winner. Just who would take on girl number three was a small problem that would resolve itself in due course, I reckoned; it wouldn't be my concern anyway because I was here first and that meant first choice, so I had better check them out. But first things first, they could be three also-rans from Crufts for all I knew, and knowing Olga, her description could have been a deliberate exaggeration.

'Right then, I shall go and introduce myself and say thanks.' I picked up my drink, winked at Olga and made my way out to the restaurant. I put on my best super cool expression and adjusted my walk – the one the girls had admired so much on my arrival – and turned the corner into the restaurant area.

I stopped dead in my tracks.

It was the point of no return because they had seen me enter and it would have looked cowardly and embarrassingly bad if I had turned on my heels and retreated, which is what I would dearly loved to have done. *They*, the three 'gorgeous girls' in question, were three male hairdressers who I had seen many times at parties and other locations and who now sat smiling and waving at me. One of the trio I knew as Philip, and although I had never been introduced to him, he was a regular at such places as Elbow Beach staff club. Forcing a smile in return I strolled as casually as possible over to their table, and dropping my voice several octaves, said thanks for the drink, expressed my hope that they were all well and hadn't it been a very nice day; then hurriedly made my excuses before they had chance to ask me to join them, and returned swiftly to the bar. I did not actually back out, but that was my inclination.

When I got back, Olga was beside herself with laughter and holding her sides, such was her delight having unobtrusively witnessed what had happened.

Yep, I should have guessed; she had set me up good and proper and I had to admit on reflection that it was very funny. It didn't matter what I said to her about keeping it quiet, I knew that the story would be circulated throughout the Hood that night, and I would just have to take all the resultant stick that would come my way.

'Did they actually say they loved the way I walk?' I asked Olga once her mirth had subsided and I had regained my composure.

'Oh yeah, they really did,' and off she went again laughing so much the tears rolled down her leg.

At least that's what I later told everybody.

Having waited for Dougie's arrival, we sat down to eat, although not before Olga had recounted the story to him of my embarrassing experience earlier – something she repeated to pretty much the entire clientele at the Robin Hood that evening. The free weekly spaghetti Bolognese (and crusty bread) evening was as good as it was substantial, the thinking behind it presumably that diners would stay for the evening and spend more on drinks, which was pretty much the case, but equally I reckoned, because Tinny, Jack and Richard were always looking for ways to please their customers.

The usual crowd were there including the other two members of our small squad, Terry and Rob, who had arrived as our food was served, and closely followed by the *Dazzlers*, completing the Magnificent Seven line-up.

Sometime later we had decided to move on for a change of scene to the Front Street bar the Rum Runners, and were just about to leave when Richard Floyd breezed in and called Dougie and I over. He had just arrived back from the airport, having been to New York for a few days, and his uncharacteristic stern expression indicated something was amiss.

'One of my CID friends was on duty at the airport and he took me to one side,' he told us. 'He obviously knows you, because he named you both and he knew we were friends.' Dougie and I stayed silent. What was coming? 'According to him there has been a tip off, and there is going to be a raid on your place, Highclere. They will be looking for drugs.'

What? We were utterly amazed and just stood with our mouths open for a few seconds taking it in. It was crazy, we did not have anything to do with drugs… well alright we indulged in a bit of *home grown* occasionally… and perhaps we had been known to pop a few *Black Beauties* when the need arose and we needed to keep alert and lively when there were two parties that were occurring on the same night, both of which needing our attendance. Then there was the *Acapulco gold,* and on one occasion some *Moroccan hash* that we had been offered at a friend's house and inhaled through water in an improvised cow horn, which we were told enhanced the effect, and boy it did! But this was all minor league, and besides we never, *never,* kept any of these substances at the house if we could help it. We knew that if ex-patriot workers were found guilty of drug usage on a large scale, they would lose their jobs and be expelled from the island. Bermudians facing the same charge could, and often would, receive a prison sentence we were told. Then we remembered… an excited Graham had arrived home the previous day to tell us that he had been offered a quantity of *Columbian Red,* a well thought of South American type of marijuana. He would not mention a name, but Graham told us that the guy was leaving Bermuda and did not want to risk taking the goods out with him, so had offered it at a 'knock down' price of twenty dollars. We asked him how much he had, and Graham had shown it to us.

'Bloody hell,' Dougie had raved. 'There's enough there to get the whole neighbourhood stoned. And there was. It was indeed a sizeable amount and a bargain at twenty dollars as the seller had claimed.

Jeez, where was Graham? He hadn't arrived at the Robin Hood, and perhaps he was off somewhere else that evening. Hell, if he had it in his apartment and we were raided, all of us could be implicated, but worse still, it was a cast iron certainty that Graham would be for the chop. 'When are they making this raid?' Dougie asked Richard who had been listening to all this.

'My contact didn't know, just sometime soon,' he shrugged.

'Can I use your phone?' I asked Richard, and he ushered me through the bar into a back room that served as an office. Please let Graham be in, I silently prayed as I dialled our home number which luckily would also register in the apartment. After three or four rings, which seemed to take an eternity, it was answered. It was Graham's voice. Hallelujah! I told him to just listen, not to ask questions, and I related quickly but succinctly as possible what Richard had told us. 'You need to get rid of it and off the premises,' I told him. 'Do it now because we have no idea when the raid is happening.' And I put the phone down, feeling mightily relieved, but still puzzled why the police had us tagged as drug dealers or even big-time users.

We discovered later that Graham had flushed the whole lot down the toilet and left no traces of the grass in his apartment. And being a very thorough bloke, he even went to the lengths of laundering his clothes. Fortunately, or perhaps under the circumstances unfortunately, there never was a raid, and although Richard always maintained that what he told us was true, and we assured Graham that it was our genuine belief that we would be turned over by the cops, he never believed the story, convinced that it was just another Dougie and Colin piss-take.

FIFTY

About a year after that event, one, or all of the partners, had got wind of an international competition that was being arranged in New York – one of the first internationals between the USA and Great Britain – and through George Harris's effort, they yet again came up trumps and had somehow managed to have Bermuda included in the fixture. It was now to be billed as USA v Great Britain v Bermuda.

What a coupe.

Those who wished to be included on the trip were asked to give their names along with the necessary sum required for the five-day event. The flight over was included and the only other requirement was that we pay to have new royal blue blazers made, that would display the *Robin Hood Bermuda* embroidered badge on the top pocket. In addition, Richard had the idea of sponsoring one of the British players – a young very promising Welshman – who the Robin Hood would fly to New York and install in the hotel with the rest of us where the tournament was to be staged.

It was an exciting time for those who expressed an interest in attending this event, a piece of darting history in fact. We were going to be a knockout in the Big Apple, if not for our darts prowess, then for our cool, tailored blazered image (we thought). The English and Bermudian accents would certainly help too.

On our arrival at John F Kennedy Airport, we split into groups and hailed taxis to take us to the Royal Manhattan Hotel. Richard Pedro, Jack and I happened to be at the front of the queue, and as we were loading our stuff into the trunk, Jack whispered, 'Let me do the talking. I know these guys and if he thinks we don't know our way around, he will take us on the long route and charge us more.' So we did as he suggested and kept schtum.

Let's just say that our driver was no mug and had sussed us out right from the start, and more particularly, had sussed out Jack, because we arrived at the hotel an hour and twenty minutes later only to find that everyone else had arrived before us – some by as much as thirty minutes and all, it transpired, had been charged less. Richard P and I decided to keep quiet about Jack's 'knowledge' of New York cab drivers, and simply paid up and looked big. Jack's only comment was a mumbled remark about the snarled-up traffic, as he made his irritable way to the hotel check-in desk.

For some reason that now escapes me, Colin Marshall and I were the only two from Highclere who undertook the trip. The venue was to be on the lower ground floor of The Royal Manhattan Hotel, where we were staying; the space having been converted into a tournament room that contained over twenty individual dart boards. There was a giant electronic board – a forerunner of the same board that was later used at tournaments in the UK – that had been set up on a raised area in preparation for the final crunch match, and the anticipated capacity audience.

Twelve of us had booked rooms in the hotel, and after inspecting our accommodation, we decided to get down to the nitty gritty of what our visit was really all about and explore the surrounding area, and for some of us, specifically where to find the world-famous Maxwell's Plum singles bar. Richard Pedro and I were sharing a room, and most of the other members of our party were doing likewise in order to mitigate the cost.

Richard Floyd and Jack had booked themselves suites (of course) and one other member who had splashed out, had invited us all over once we had unpacked and got ourselves settled. The booze was already flowing when we arrived, and the air was heavy with the distinctive aroma of certain herbal substances. One of our number who shall remain incognito, had arranged to meet up with a friend when we arrived, and take delivery of some Vietnamese plant life which he had been warned was quite powerful. This was borne out by the fact that another of our group had to be forcibly restrained from leaping out of the window, assuring us earnestly that he had miraculously obtained the power of flight. Our reasoning in holding him back was that it would not be a good start to our visit and might attract some very bad publicity for Robin Hood and Bermuda. The suite was on the fifteenth floor.

The tournament began the morning following our arrival, and after a typical American breakfast at a nearby diner, we returned to the hotel to find out who each of us had drawn in the first-round matches. It really didn't matter of course because all the competing players from the US and UK were area and regional champions or full internationals. We were going to be up against it, whichever way it was looked at, and apart from our star player and Robin Hood team captain, Ian Crawford, we all expected to be taking early showers, or more accurately early trips to the bar. The plus side was that we could get a welcome meal at one of New York's numerous eating establishments and an early appearance at the iconic, Maxwell's Plum.

Being run by the Americans the tournament was a glitzy and elaborate affair, with TV cameras, traders selling darting accessories and other goods, and over made-up ladies who, we suspected, usually plied their trade on the streets above, but tempted with the prospect of lucrative pickings had infiltrated the packed auditorium. There was also a flamboyant cowboy-like character working the crowd, complete with massive Stetson and a six-gun belt and holster, except that instead of a Colt 45, the holster was full of a suspicious looking substance, which he openly dispensed to customers with a silver spoon. It was all so surreal – like being in one of the more colourful Hollywood B movies and a real eye opener for us Brits and Bermies, that was for sure.

The individual matches would be best out of three games of 501, and in those days, it was required that you start, as well as finish on a double. But surprisingly and against all the odds, three of us managed to claw our way through to the second round. Ian was no great surprise, but for myself and one of the others it was a matter of almost total disbelief, particularly in my case because I was playing an area champion from somewhere in the south-west of England. But we did have a secret weapon.

Earlier, with breakfast over, we quickly called a meeting of the Bermuda team and had agreed that those not playing, or who had already completed their games, should congregate around a team member who was engaged in a match and – not to put too fine a point on it – barrack the hell out of his opponent. In my opening game I had barely found my starting double when my Brit opponent checked out on a double sixteen; it looked like being a very one-sided affair, if not a humiliating slaughter. Then several of my teammates arrived. To say they engaged in barracking in no way describes the treatment they inflicted on my rival, who was jeered, taunted and abused in no uncertain terms by the Bermudian contingent, which had pretty much swelled to a full complement during the second and third legs of the game. And it worked, because after narrowly winning the second leg, I went into the third backed by my colleagues, and with my opponent almost a slobbering wreck, I checked out well ahead with that darter's dream finish, a double top.

I honestly felt embarrassed and a little sorry for the Englishman as he gave my hand a perfunctory shake, a mumbled word of congratulation before hurrying off in the direction of the bar – or was it the roof? With three of our number through to the next round, it had been a very good morning for team Bermuda. But needless to say, our victory celebrations were short lived, with two of us being summarily dismissed in our second leg matches that afternoon. But at least we had the satisfaction of seeing our colleague Ian battle his way through to the following day's third round draw.

As I had been eliminated from the competition early in the afternoon by two straight legs, I decided to have a couple of hours' recuperation in my room with the aid of a bottle of Cockspur that had travelled with me in my flight bag from Bermuda. There are two things that stand out for me from that afternoon gazing out on the Manhattan skyline from our tenth storey room: the unbroken serpentine procession of yellow in the streets below as the iconic New York taxis went about their business, and the continuous sound of traffic horns and wail of police or ambulance sirens, some near, some distant, but ever present. I woke up several times that night, and those same sounds were still audible ten storeys below.

Deciding to have a very early awakener with a black coffee laced with you know what, the day's events suddenly called up a memory from two years before when I was living in the small fishing village of Polperro in Cornwall, also concerning the game of darts and coincidentally, some Americans. I related the following tale to my roommate Richard P.

Memories of the Polperro summer of '72 were of laughter, long hot days with party-filled nights and Newcastle Brown Ale in the quayside Blue Peter pub, which was the establishment of choice for all of us casual summer workers that year. Occasionally we would wander a few yards into the village and partake of a pint or two at the Three Pilchards or Noughts and Crosses establishments just to be even handed and sociable.

The kitchens to the busy restaurant where I worked occupied the basement area, with our only ventilation, a long single hung window opening out at pavement level louvre style. With no dumbwaiter lift installed, our mini-skirted waitresses had to be super fit as they continuously ran up and down stairs with customers' orders and it was by extreme good fortune that my work station was directly under the said stairs. Do I need to draw a picture here?

There were many prearranged coach parties arriving throughout the week and in fact they were the mainstay of our lunch time trade. My bosses and the owners of the Saxon Bridge were Mr and Mrs Antony, not their real surname, but it made life easier for all those who could not pronounce Antoniewicz, or some such handle that Mr Antony – a Polish national – possessed.

Mr Antony had taken refuge in the UK after the Second World War to escape the Russians, and he would often regale me with stories from his wartime exploits and the often-grisly accounts of the Nazi occupation, including the notorious Katyn Forest massacre. He was as tight as a duck's chuff, and that, as we all know, is water tight, and he had the worst case of halitosis I have ever encountered, which I reckoned would have been able to stop a charging rhino in its tracks. Consequently, when having a conversation with Mr Antony, it was advisable to stand well clear to avoid the blast of fetid air that was directed in your direction.

Although there was an obligation on the owner's part to feed the staff in between each shift, there were strict guidelines laid down on the type and quantity of grub that we were allowed. For example, no smoked salmon, but tinned tuna was okay if you wanted fish and the tin was already opened, and lamb chops were a no-no, but ham was alright, as long as it was sliced thin enough to see through it. The only exception to this rule was, if after a lunch time session there were portions not sold, we were regarded as garbage disposal units and could have our pick. It was my good fortune that after the lunch hour rush, Mr Antony and his missus would retire to their living quarters on the top floor for their afternoon nap and leave me in charge. During this period I would change the setting on the ham slicer from wafer thin to doorstep thick and along with a mountain of crispy hand-cut chips and three or four fried eggs, I would tuck into my idea of heaven, always mindful to adjust the slicer to its original setting. All of which has nothing whatever to do with darts but is simply an introduction to an incident involving a game played at the Noughts and Crosses public house one afternoon.

After one particularly busy lunch time session when two pre-booked coach parties had descend on us, and having cleared the kitchen in preparation for our evening service, I decided that I badly needed a pint. Leaving my colleague Wendy in charge to serve any cream tea devotees who might happen to drop by and telling her where I would be if needed, I popped out to the pub just around the corner from the restaurant. It was a rarity to have customers after the restaurant's lunch session, because there was a plethora of quaint cafés and tea rooms in the village for those who liked to have their cream teas served in more olde world surroundings.

On the way I called in to collect my mate David who, along with his wife Kay, ran a small Aladdin's Cave of a shop called *Stuff* that sold everything from psychedelic posters and joss sticks – very much in vogue at that time – to Polish enamelware and handmade wooden toys. We were enjoying a game of darts, when we became conscious of an American family watching us avidly with the father explaining to his wife and teenage daughter the scoring procedure and the rules of the game, all in a typical loud, all-knowing American way. But it was also obvious that he didn't have a clue what he was talking about.

David and I decided after a brief whispered discussion, that the next game would be somewhat different, and we began to chalk up complex and obscure mathematical symbols and equations on the blackboard. We didn't understand a thing about the stuff we were putting up, but on the face of it our game of five-oh-one was becoming Einstein's Theory of Relativity.

Luckily the Yank wasn't a mathematician or scientist and the gentleman struggled more and more to 'explain' what was going on to his attentive family, but he was not about to lose face with them and admit that he didn't have a clue what these two mad Limeys were about. You had to admire his stamina and the sheer balls of the man.

At the conclusion of our best-of-three and after we had erased the algebraic nonsense from the blackboard we asked him, as an obvious connoisseur of the game, if he would like to join us. But looking at his watch pointedly and on the pretext of having to be somewhere else, he ushered his family hurriedly from the bar, leaving the two of us and a spluttering landlord rolling around the saloon bar with laughter.

Now almost two years later in New York, having tucked into a substantial dinner (we found that substantial was a word that always described helpings of food in America, whether it be breakfast, lunch, dinner or just in between snacks) and feeling good and not having to worry about the mundane task of throwing arrows the next day, three of us piled into a waiting cab, and gave the instruction: 'Take us to Maxwell's Plum.'

'The short way,' Richard P added.

'And step on it,' Colin M chipped in – a bit unwisely I thought. It doesn't do to piss off a New York cab driver.

We had really gone to town on the way we looked, with all of us sporting tailored blazers and cream slacks, and with those colourful embroidered *Robin Hood Darts Team, Bermuda* badges sewn on the breast pocket. If we didn't score tonight, then I was joining a monastery… make that a nunnery.

The whole darts thing, if I'm honest, was merely a side show for us, with the main feature being able to let down our in-vogue long hair, and have a few days to let rip in the Big Apple. But in fairness, although our prowess with the arrows left a lot to be desired compared with the professionals, it had provided us with some cool jackets and an excuse to visit, what was to us, one of the hottest spots in Manhattan. The bonus was that we actually won a few games – well three to be precise – even if that was due more to our barracking and intimidation techniques, than skill. And our mate Ian was still in there chucking darts, bless him.

The atmosphere at Maxwell's Plum was electric, not to mention noisy, and a quick appraisal gave me the impression that the mix was

60:40 of women to men; very much favourable odds for us. The focal point was a huge four-sided bar in the centre of the enormous room, and overlooked at the rear by the famous restaurant set above the whole boisterous scene. There you could indulge yourself in anything from a cheeseburger to a thirty-ounce steak, or lobster and truffles. Wow. The place was legendary.

We all split up once we got in, with Richard and I bulldozing our way to a section of the bar where we had spotted two likely ladies – one blonde, one brunette. The last we saw of Colin Marshall was him making his way towards the restaurant level.

'Which one do you want?' I yelled at Richard.

'The brunette,' he yelled back.

That suited me – blondie looked good. The noise of vigorous conversation between several hundred people was deafening, so having sidled over to our targets and raising my voice, making sure that the blazer and Bermuda darts badge were centre stage, I bawled at blondie, 'Hi, I'm Colin, can I buy you a drink?' She looked me up and down, but before she could have the chance to answer and blow me out, I added: 'Please don't say no and ruin my evening.' That usually worked, and she laughed (always a good sign) before replying.

'Thank you; I'm drinking white wine.' Whatever turns you on I thought and went about the anticipated difficult task of trying to attract the attention of a barman, but which, I was delighted to note, was almost immediate. I ordered the concoction and my own Budweiser; we clinked glasses (this being the era when beer drinkers still drank out of glasses, not straight from the bottle), said cheers, and now getting a close up and uninterrupted view of my new companion, I was giving myself a mental pat on the back for my impeccable taste regarding this lady.

Normal conversation was of course impossible, so putting my mouth to her ear – getting off at the same time on the peachy smell of her hair and perfume, which could have been anything from Old Spice to toffee apple for all I knew, but very nice nonetheless – I shouted: 'What's your name? Mine's Colin.'

'I know,' she yelled back into my ear hole. 'You told me already.'

Did I detect an exotic accent here?

'My name is Inez,' she informed me.

I was right... Mexican? South American? Perhaps Cuban? Bloody 'ell, this was a first. Another whiff of her scent and I persevered: 'Where are you from, Inez?' already imagining a holiday involving ice cold mojitos and mariachi bands, I quickly decided to risk a guess in the hope of dazzling her with my worldly knowledge, by hazarding... 'Mey-hico City?'

She looked at me quizzically as if to say *are you taking the piss mate*, before replying,

'Don't be silly, I'm from Birkenshaw near Leeds. Do you know it?' She had obviously sussed out my English accent and thought I might be familiar with the place; then after absorbing that surprising piece of information, we both laughed at the absurdity of it all.

It transpired that Inez and her friend Patricia were both ex-pats working in New York as secretaries, and having relaxed in each other's company over the next couple of hours in Maxwell's, we arranged to meet the next day at the apartment block where they, and as it happened many other non-American girls all working in the Big Apple, lived.

Calling for them at their apartment block was an experience. The place was exclusively for foreign female secretarial workers, and as such was an obvious target for strange men with grubby raincoats and perverts with staring eyes... oh, and us of course. The foyer was as far as you got, because there you were stopped by serious looking men wearing uniforms and tell-tale bulges under the arms. They were all big blokes and looked as if they had forgotten to take the coat hangers out of their jackets. All understandable I guess, and in addition, only on confirmation by internal phone that you were expected, were you allowed to wait in the lobby for your dates to emerge from one of the banks of elevators. No visitors ever got as far as the stairs or lifts we were told. This was a million miles from the nurses' home in Reading, where Jim, Ray and I had been regular visitors, but this was an unfortunate necessity in New York City.

What followed was a very pleasant couple of days doing the

sights, which of course included a trip to the viewing platform atop the Empire State building, which was after many years, then only the second highest structure in New York. The twin towers of the new World Trade Centre were now a joint number one, and although the construction was completed externally, work was still continuing on the inside and they were therefore still not open to visitors.

We had such a good time with our hostesses that we felt we should invite them to visit us in Bermuda at some future time in order for us to return the compliment, which we duly did, and was immediately and gratefully accepted.

The last full day of our visit was taken up with the final of the tournament and a special match that was organised to pit a US team member to be nominated by them, against our own. And again, all this was instigated by Richard of the Robin Hood. One thousand dollars was suggested with the game to be a marathon ten thousand and one straight off, and of course, finishing on a double. We had a whip round for the one-grand stake, and being somewhat short of the required sum, the Robin Hood made up the shortfall. The darts displayed was breathtaking as was the result for us, with the Bermudian-backed Welshman losing in a close fought match. Never mind, it was a great way to finish our few days in the city that never sleeps.

Four of us had already decided on our final night being spent at one of the nearby Steak and Brew establishments, where we indulged – correction, over indulged – in another enormous meal that consisted of a twenty-ounce steak, lobster tails and an asteroid sized baked potato. In addition, there were free, all-you-can-eat salad and fruit bars that gave the appearance of a windfall in the Amazonian rainforest. And as if that wasn't enough, another table groaning under the weight of just about every sort of bread and pastry that bakers could devise. Later whilst we were wondering where the hell we had put all that food and were relaxing with yet another bottle of some wine with an unpronounceable name, to our complete amazement one of our companions fished out a stubby object from a pack of small cigars and lit up. The amazement wasn't that he was smoking, which was permitted in restaurants in those far off days, but that he announced it was the last of the Vietnamese grass that he had purchased at the beginning of our trip. It was a heavily disguised joint. 'Don't worry,' he assured us. 'They won't know it's me. Anyone want a toke?'

No we didn't, thank you very much. It was one thing to have a puff in the privacy of your hotel room, but quite another in a busy restaurant, and after some very anxious moments with the waiters noticeably sniffing the air as they orbited the tables – in ever decreasing circles, we noted in panic – I for one, was glad to get outside and onto the sidewalk (did you get that? sidewalk) without having my collar felt by some beefy New York cop.

How we got away with that one, I will never know.

With only one and a half hours' flying time to NY, it was a popular destination and there were more trips. It was a strange thing but because of the diminutive size of Bermuda that at times invoked a feeling of claustrophobia, it was always good to get away for a break. But such was the island's magnetism and seductive allure, it was always good, even after a short weekend away, to return to *de Rock*, and home.

FIFTY-ONE

We were living at Look Over on Harbour Road; a pretty three-bedroom single storey cottage dressed up in cream and powder blue paintwork, all under another ever-present white Bermuda stepped roof. The approach was by way of a sloping path and steps from the road up to a terrace that ran most of the length of the house, and looked out over the Great Sound and the city of Hamilton on the opposite shore.

It was meant to be a very brief tenancy and a stop-gap measure. Having left Highclere due to its unexpected sale, and because we had not been given notice as per our agreement with the agent, he had been persuaded by us to give us Look Over until that too was sold. Predictably it was yet another of the properties on his books. We knew from day one of our occupancy that Highclere had been on the market, but because we had never experienced any interested parties who had gone to view the house, as far as we knew at least, we had slipped into a happy state of complacent reverie. So the sudden announcement that a buyer wished to take possession, shocked us back to reality.

We reminded the agent that there had been a verbal agreement of one month's notice in the event of a sale, but as there had been nothing in writing he insisted that as his client wanted almost immediate possession, we were required to vacate by the following weekend. But we weren't having any of that. We demanded that he find us another property before we would consider moving, and after some heated words and what amounted to a stand-off, it was him who blinked first and came up with Look Over. But puffed up with our successful negotiating skills and realising that we had him by his treacherous gonads, we further demanded that he give it to us rent free for a month and thereafter – if there was a thereafter – at a reduced rent in recognition that the new property had only three bedrooms as opposed to the five, including Graham's garden apartment, at Highclere.

Seeing his fat sales commission beginning to sail slowly down shit creek into the sunset, he reluctantly and angrily agreed to our demands. I thought his behaviour of kicking our overstuffed foot-stool across the room and throwing his briefcase down at Dougie's feet was a trifle dramatic and we told him so. It didn't help that Dougie told him: 'Keep your bleeding hair on', because that is not something you say to someone who is bald as a snooker ball. It was as good a deal as we were going to get, and that weekend we packed up our things and our share of the extensive bar, and made tracks for Harbour Road in Paget.

We had scored a victory, but soon realised that if we were unable to find another suitable property at an affordable rent, preferably within thirty days, then it would be a pyrrhic one. Even with the additional elements that Colin M had already found himself a bachelor pad elsewhere and moved on, and Steve, who had only been lodging with us until he sorted out an apartment of his own, also managing to get himself fixed up, it still left four of us having to share a three bedroom house.

We got by initially with Robbo sleeping on the sofa, which he seemed content with, as were the rest of us. But the already worse-for-wear sofa had lodged a strong complaint about the excessive use by busting a spring, so some bright spark suggested that we have a darts competition to decide who it was that should move out. I had no worries about this, after all I was the only one who played league darts every week for the Robin Hood first team, and an international to boot; also, I knew that Dougie was a mean player in his own right and a star of the second team, but the other two were rank amateurs. But in accepting the challenge, I really should have known better.

We decided to play to 1001, beginning and finishing on a double, with the last person to check out being the, soon to be homeless, loser. I have no wish to relive that disastrous and embarrassing afternoon, but suffice it to say I was crap and simply could not throw a double finish to save my life, with the result that I was facing eviction and the prospect of looking for somewhere to live… on my own. Whether my poor form was due to the glut of Cockspur the night before coupled with a few beers and a large coffee laced with something stronger after breakfast that day, I really couldn't say, but I doubt it, because those things usually enhanced my technique, and besides, the others had easily consumed as much as me. I had visions of a homeless future that entailed a cardboard bed, a cocoa tin for loose change on the pavement, and a scruffy lurcher dog on a piece of string, all running alarmingly through my head. More importantly – much more importantly – I would have to separate from my good mate and brother, Dougie. We had formed a solid and genuine bond in the time we had known each other, and built up a partnership in crime that seemed – for some reason – to be the talk of The Robin Hood. It appeared that my name was never mentioned in that hallowed hall of alcoholic joy unless paired with Dougie's and vice versa – we were the *Thelma & Louise* male equivalents. So I did the only thing any decent sporting man would do under the circumstances. I told them all to stuff it and that there was no way that yours truly was moving out on the strength of a stupid game of darts; after all wasn't *I* the original member of our little group? And hadn't *I* been the one to invite each of them to share the house at Highclere? *I* was de man! 'No sorry,' I told them. 'I'm staying put'.

As it happened it all turned out rather well. Robbo confirmed again that he really didn't mind the present sleeping arrangements (we got the impression that there was something in his past that predisposed him to slumming it on beat-up sofas), after all it was only for a month or so, and in any case, he told us, he thought that he knew where another housemate was required. Dougie also told me in confidence that had I moved out, he would have left with me so that we could hunt for a suitable property for the two of us. That's nice I thought, but in all honesty, I would have done the same had the situation been reversed.

It so happened that Robbo had heard that our Scottish friend 'Mad' Matt Taylor and a guy called David Arkle had moved into a house called All Cedar, just two doors away from us, and they were needing a third person to help spread the cost of the rent. This was the whisper that Robbo had heard which turned out to be accurate, and as he knew the guys, it sounded like the perfect solution. Matt was well known to all of us and his antics alone would fill a book – a very thick book at that – hence the moniker, 'Mad'. David, we had also met, but he was, sadly for him, only on a short-term contract, but being employed at the same company as Matt, he had found the perfect partner to make the very most of his time in Bermuda… in truth he probably never knew what had hit him.

And so our housing arrangements were settled – for the time being at least – with Robbo agreeing to make the move in a week or so, and giving the three of us and Robbo some space. It was the perfect result.

That Sunday, Adrian had emerged from his sofa and was busy in the kitchen (if you can call staring at a tinned Fray Bentos steak and kidney pie heating up in the oven, busy) preparing lunch for himself.

'What are you doing, Robbo?' Dougie asked.

'Taking the fucking dog for a walk,' he shot back. He could be so cutting could Adrian.

Obviously, Robbo had hitherto stashed his pie in some place beyond our reach, but as Dougie and I were feeling a bit peckish ourselves, and knowing that Mother Hubbard's cupboard – aka our fridge – was bare of food, we asked him if we could share his scratch meal.

'Sod off,' he told us, 'this is my breakfast and lunch. There's bugger all left in the fridge thanks to you gannets.'

'We're growing lads,' Dougie told him, but Adrian was adamant that he wasn't sharing his pie with anyone and proceeded to carefully remove the item from the oven and place the whole thing, still in its tin, on a plate. Then having carefully removed the hot lid, like a petulant child, he hugged the plate to his chest and retreated to the false safety of the terrace. He was sitting on the coping when we joined him, one of us either side and with forks poised.

'Oh, tits alive,' protested Robbo using his usual means of protest; but he knew he was always going to be on the losing side, and giving in to the inevitable, he reluctantly allowed us to dig in to his brunch. Dougie was right; we were growing lads and it was probably with some relief for Adrian that he was due to give up his sofa and move a hundred yards down the road to All Cedar.

Between Look Over and All Cedar was a cottage occupied by Anne, an attractive staff nurse who worked at Hamilton's King Edward VII Hospital. She was about my age, I discovered, and not to put too fine a point on it, was sex on legs. It was the second Saturday after our move to Look Over and Graham, having taken an instant interest in Anne, was not slow in declaring to his house-mates that he would be the first one to 'get in there' as he put it, and then rather unwisely as it turned out, bet ten dollars on that happening. The following morning all four of us were lounging on our front terrace after a hearty Chicken Coop breakfast and admiring the now familiar view across the Great Sound. This was made extra special with some dewy cans of cold beer clutched in our fists and we were in a serene state of mind.

Suddenly Graham stood up, adjusted his pants and confidently declared that he was going to call on our neighbour Anne with a view to chatting the lady up and making a date. He downed the last dregs of his Amstel and was about to leave, when I asked him if he wouldn't mind asking Anne if I had left my wallet at her place because I couldn't find it anywhere, and assumed that it had dropped out of my pocket when I had put my strides back on. There was a beat or two, as they say in acting circles, when Graham was frozen in tableau mid stride. He then slowly lowered himself back into his chair and turned to me with his mouth open as if undecided what to say.

'Would you mind?' I asked again.

'You didn't?…' he began.

'Yes,' I confirmed, after taking a long swig of beer.

'I mean, you couldn't have…?'

'S'right.'

'You bugger,' he managed; and in fairness he maybe had a point.

'But before you go,' I added, and held out my hand. 'Ten dollars I think you said.'

'You bugger,' he repeated, with slightly more venom this time. Then after fishing around for his wallet he smacked a ten-dollar bill in my hand, followed by a few seconds of silence. Then Dougie gave out one of his great barks of laughter prompting the stirrings of a giggle from me, and Graham to his great credit, joined in and we all fell about in hysterics.

'But I only made the bet yesterday morning,' Graham protested.

That was true, but had Graham not thrown down the challenge the day before, perhaps things would have been different, although thinking back and remembering the lovely lady in question, perhaps not. I was only surprised that Dougie had not beaten both of us to it.

For the brief time we were in Harbour Road, Anne and I saw each other on only one other occasion but our drifting apart coincided with the lads' departure from Look Over, and the fact that Anne and the Look Over three (as we had become), moved in completely different circles. I was told years later that she had married a doctor. She was quite a catch and a lovely girl, and Graham never did call on Anne to ask for a date, or so he informed us.

It was about this time that two other Bermudian characters came into our lives: Ricky Corriea and Robert Henderson.

It was a normal weekend except for the fact that Dougie and I had arrived at the beach early and way ahead of the rest of our mixed-sex group of friends. Having missed a full-sized breakfast at the Coop, we planned to break our usual routine by cutting our time at the beach and driving off in search of lunch somewhere and then meet the rest of the gang at Flamingo Beach as per our normal Sunday schedule. But because it would just be the two of us, we decided to hit Warwick Long Bay beach for a change.

Later, Dougie had wandered off to do a bit of philandering with a couple of bikini-clad ladies he had spotted further along the beach, and I was in a world of my own, gazing out to sea with the water gently lapping over my feet. As was my custom, I was taking it all in and thanking the Gods of Roofing for the good fortune in giving me the opportunity to live in that paradise on earth.

I was vaguely aware of Dougie and the two beach beauties wandering back towards me, but I was too involved in my meditation to take much notice, even though I half registered that he appeared to be trying to attract my attention. I took a long deep sigh, and turned back to see where Dougie and his glamorous companions had got to, but my good friend was making his way back towards me, leaving the two lovelies to continue on, but who, I noticed, were occasionally looking over their shoulders at the two of us in a captivating sort of way as if to say: come and get us.

'Why didn't you come over?' Dougie admonished me. 'We could have been in there.'

'You reckon?'

'Definitely, the one in the red bikini said she thought you had a nice arse.'

'Why would a woman admire a man's arse?' I queried 'Do *you* think I've got a nice arse, Douglas?'

'I try not to think about your arse.'

'Makes sense,' I said, 'let's go eat.'

As we were mounting the Suzuki in the beach car park and preparing to move off, two familiar faces arrived on their own two-wheeled machines. Familiar faces, but only in the sense that we had seen them a number of times at the beach together, and often in the bars around town, and inevitably Elbow Beach staff club. We had never spoken, but that day for some reason, they engaged us in conversation and before we roared off to find food, we had exchanged names and agreed to meet at Flamingo Beach where we later introduced them to the rest of our motley crew, thereby inducting them into our exclusive little clique. Rick was to become a regular, and often tagged along with us on our nightly jaunts, but Rob seemed to move in slightly different circles involving his Bermudian buddies.

There was a band playing country music that afternoon, I recall, which is okay I guess as long as you like listening to songs about beat up trucks, two-timing women and fucking hound dogs called Blue.

FIFTY-TWO

It was not long after we had settled into Look Over that Dougie left on a trip to experience the Trinidad and Tobago Carnival with one of his many lady friends, Liz Winter – the nurse who had thrown the Christmas Day dinner party where Dougie and I had first met, and had entertained me one lunchtime with her experience concerning gas gangrene.

He was gone for a week, and naturally on his return, Graham and I wanted to hear all about that famous event, thought by many to be second only to the Rio Carnival as the most spectacular in the world. He recounted the whole experience, which it transpired had been slightly tarnished by the fact that he had picked up some local bug for which he had been prescribed antibiotics by a local doctor. But Dougie being Dougie, having felt okay after a couple of days, didn't bother taking the rest of his pills.

We did not understand antibiotics and their specific purpose back in those seventies' days, so Doug brought the leftovers back to Bermuda with him on the off chance that he might have need of them again one day. But they don't work like that of course and are designed to be taken as a complete and unbroken course over the period of a week or so. Even so, when our new friend Ricky Correia was visiting one evening prior to our nightly pilgrimage to the Robin Hood, where we would make dollar offerings to the God of Rum, he saw the said capsules, exotic yellow and green things in a blister pack, sitting in a dish on the kitchen table, and being a nosy bugger, he asked what they were. Dougie immediately latched on to this, and he informed Rick conspiratorially that they were the drug commonly known as speed, that he had picked up when in Port of Spain. As if they would come ready packed in plastic, I remember thinking. But that obviously did not occur to Ricky at the time.

Ricky's eyes lit up and asked if he could try one, but Doug shook his head and with a serious look told him no, they had cost him, and anyway he had only been able to buy enough for his own use. As we suspected would be the case, Rick wouldn't let it go, and it was only after he was reduced to pleading that Dougie appeared to relent and gave up one precious capsule. The immediate effect was slight, but noticeable, with Ricky starting to bounce around like a rubber ball. And it got worse. At the Robin Hood later, he sounded like a drunken commentator at a football match and we could not stop his endless inane chatter, until Richard Floyd appeared and tossing us the keys to the storeroom, asked Dougie and I if we would go fetch a fresh keg of beer for the bar. Something we had done in the past.

'I'll get it,' volunteered Ricky enthusiastically and with great gusto grabbed the keys and rushed off to the storeroom.

'He'll never manage one of those on his own,' I said. But I was wrong. Ricky appeared on the trot, albeit on bowed legs, all five foot three inches of him, lugging a full keg of best lager on his shoulder and grinning from ear to ear.

'Who's going to tell him?' Doug asked after Ricky had stumbled past and disappeared into the bar like a turbo-charged gremlin.

'Not me,' I said. 'Best let him enjoy himself.' Dougie nodded sagely.

It was the first time I had seen the placebo effect in action, and I was impressed.

It was during our time in Look Over that I witnessed what turned out to be a little piece of history. Work was a bit slack, and my boss suggested I take a week of my annual leave, and as I had no plans for trips later in the year, I readily agreed. It was the first Monday morning of my unplanned vacation; Graham and Dougie had left for work and having the house to myself I decided to have a lazy morning before riding into Hamilton for a lunch at The Rum Runners and catch up with my old mate and ex-Highclere housemate Steve, who was still resident chef there. Then perhaps, if I felt like it, take a ride out to St George's which I had not visited for some time.

As usual I retired to the front terrace to enjoy my second mug of tea and a toasted ham and cheese sandwich with Branston pickle – one of my favourite snacks – and catch the arrival of the cruise ship, *Sea Venture*, across the water in Hamilton.

The Sea Venture was a cruise ship, operated and owned by Flagship Cruises that during the summer season did a weekly crossing from New York. She arrived Monday morning and departed three days later on Thursday morning, always to great fanfare. A jazz band would be playing up a storm on deck as she slowly pulled away from the quay amid much cheering and waving from the typically vocal American passengers. The ship was named after Sir George Somers' vessel, which in 1609 on its way to relieve the colonists in Jamestown Virginia, foundered in a hurricane off the, then relatively unexplored, island of Bermuda – or Isle of Devils as it was inexplicably then referred to. None of the crew were lost, and after ten months they were able to refloat *Sea Venture* along with two smaller craft they had built from the indigenous Bermuda cedar during their time on the island, and carry on to the New World. It is said that Shakespeare received his inspiration for his play *The Tempest*, based on Somers' experiences. Sir George duly claimed the islands for the crown, and although they were renamed after the original discoverer, the Spaniard Juan de Bermudez, they are also known as Somers Isles after Sir George, who you could say simply rediscovered them. This new *Sea Venture*, therefore, was a weekly reminder of Bermuda's origins.

I was interested to learn much later, that *Sea Venture* was preceded by the ship, *Queen of Bermuda*, which also undertook the New York–Bermuda run, and in the early fifties had on board as one of the service crew, one Thomas Hicks, who worked as a cabin boy and later as waiter. Very soon after his seagoing career had ended, Thomas rose to national and international fame as Tommy Steele.

Sea Venture arrived, as she always did right on time, and in those days before the new generation of giant cruise ships, she was an impressive sight cutting sedately through the calm waters into port under the warm Bermuda sun and docking alongside Front Street. As I sat there at peace with the world, idly pulling fluff from my navel with the tea bag squeezer and planning my week ahead, it occurred to me that I might like a third mug of tea, and being adventurous and feeling rather devilish, make myself another toasted sandwich. But before that, an extended shower and a change of clothing from the tatty tie-dyed tee shirt and faded Levi cut-offs I had thrown on.

It must have been not much more than one hour since the arrival of *Sea Venture*, that, as I was brushing the crumbs from the second sandwich off my fresh Tom & Jerry tee shirt, and lighting up my first Kool of the day, it appeared that the ship was moving away from the quay. Surely not? I put down the month old and heavily thumbed copy of Penthouse I had been reading and stared across the water in disbelief, and yes, slowly but unquestionably, the *Sea Venture* was edging away from its mooring. She was leaving for goodness' sake, and I watched fascinated as she manoeuvred into position and headed back out to sea, wondering just what the possible reasons could be for her rapid and unscheduled departure.

Because we did not possess such dubious luxuries as televisions at Look Over, I was at a loss to even guess the reason for the ship's hurried departure, but figured that I would find out more when I got to Hamilton. But being a hygienic boy, I gave my gnashers a quick brush, swept a brush – a different one – through my mop of hair, locked the front door and pelted down to where my shiny Suzuki was parked. Then a thought occurred to me, and rushing back up to the house and stripping off my tee shirt as I went, I selected a fresh Fred Perry polo from my depleted drawer – making a mental note to pay an overdue visit to the Quicky Licky – and skedaddled back down to my bike. The reason for the shirt change, you see, was that on the one occasion I had worn the Tom & Jerry tee shirt in town, I had been pulled to one side by one of the boys in blue and 'advised' in all seriousness, to go home and change it. Hard to believe now, but Bermuda was a place that expected and indeed demanded certain standards with regard to dress, such as no swimwear and other 'unacceptable clothing' to be worn in town, and definitely not in the many retail establishments. It was strictly ties and jackets for men when eating out at night – that sort of thing. So the fact that my shirt showed an inebriated Tom cat holding a cocktail glass with bubbles signifying drunkenness popping out of his head, above the slogan 'Happiness is a Tight Pussy', it did not endear me to the authorities.

The town was full of news about the cruise ship's departure when I arrived twenty minutes later. It appeared that the famous Cunard ship *QE2* had lost all power en route from New York to the Caribbean, and a distress call had been put out to ships in the area. The fact that she was not that long out of New York and Bermuda is relatively close to mainland United States, meant that *Sea Venture*, just two hundred miles away, was almost certainly the closest vessel to hand. With the maritime law of salvage, it also meant that it was potentially a very lucrative action. What followed was worldwide news, because passengers were transferred from the Cunard ship to the *Sea Venture* and were brought back to Bermuda for repatriation. Ocean-going tugs brought the stricken *QE2* to anchor in the Great Sound, where it waited for the necessary parts to be shipped out along with the engineers to make the vessel seaworthy once more.

A newsworthy and momentous event, and I felt lucky to have been a small part of it.

FIFTY-THREE

Bermuda was one long series of adventures, parties and larks, some questionable and many bordering on the tasteless, but mostly harmless fun interrupted only by the daily disruption of work. Everything was light-hearted and carefree, and the overriding memory for me of those times is of days and nights filled with camaraderie and laughter. Lots and lots of laughter. It was not surprising therefore that we rarely sat down with each other and talked of serious matters or our lives before Bermuda. What we saw was what we got with the many characters within our own growing circle of friends and acquaintances. So on this particular Sunday with Graham having got lucky the night before with a rather athletic and toned young lady who once again turned out to be a nurse – a fact that he had been delighted to phone and inform us of at the outrageous time of 8am, which included giving us the details of the breakfast he had just been served in bed – it was just Dougie and me at Look Over.

The night before had been a fairly typical one; we had started at the Hood before moving on to other ports of call and then attending two parties – one in Warwick near the South Shore, and another at Spanish Point after which we had finished up arriving home at some ungodly hour. Time didn't matter of course, we rarely looked at our watches, and the only thing we were aware of was getting back to Look Over sometime just before dawn. We had an uncharacteristic full English breakfast at home (instead of at our favourite five starred establishment, the Chicken Coop) which had the effect of clearing out the Look Over fridge entirely of food, and then having lounged about on the terrace for an hour or so, we discussed what we would do for the rest of the day. These were the days when all supermarkets closed on Sundays, so food shopping was out of the question, even if we had been bothered. We had nothing planned; no beach that day we had decided and no treating ourselves to a long leisurely meal at one of the many establishments that offered the famous Bermuda Sunday brunch. We seemed both to be in a strange pensive mood and, oh sure, we would slope off into Hamilton for some refreshment later that evening, but perhaps an afternoon playing some new music recently purchased at Sounds Plus on my Sony twin deck, with some serious down-time and conversation in the sun thrown in. Then for some inexplicable reason Doug suggested we grab a six pack – beer being the only items left in the depleted fridge – and climb up onto the roof to cool out. The roof?… well why not, I thought, it was as good as anything, even though it would be, for me, a case of busman's holiday. I was always up for something different and to be honest, nothing Dougie ever suggested surprised me. So after clambering up the side of the boundary wall and heaving ourselves onto the low eaves, we carefully made our way to the ridge where we made ourselves as comfortable as possible against the chimney breast. We sat there for several minutes taking in the stunning view across the Great Sound, interrupted only by the sounds of two fizzy twangs as we pulled the rings on our beer cans. It was another warm spring day with a cornflower blue sky and the odd passing woolly cloudlet hazily reflected in the blue-green waters of Hamilton Harbour. Pleasure boats criss-crossed each other's frothy wakes, and on the opposite shore were the upmarket retail establishments of Hamilton's Front Street, the coral-coloured walls under the gleaming white roof of the Royal Bermuda Yacht Club, and the impressive lines of the Princess Hotel standing proudly at the western edge of town.

It was one of those moments when talking was uncalled for and one that deserved the respect and awed silence that we were displaying. It was an unusual situation for us. Not the beer of course and not even the roof thing for me, but there was something else: the fact that both of us coincidentally seemed to be in contemplative and serious moods. This was new territory. Even when we were lazing around the house, there was always the banter, the lewd jokes or shared experiences with the lads and tales of past exploits, and of course the continuous music of the Moody Blues, Steely Dan, The Sweet, Thin Lizzy and the many other favourites we all shared. The two of us on the roof was a new experience right enough and perhaps perched high above the world surrounded by that amazing panorama, it brought out the more serious side of our personalities.

In our relatively short time together, we had formed a close attachment, but Bermuda was all about going through the motions regarding the necessary weekday work pattern and then spending evenings and weekends embracing life to the full, squeezing every last drop out of every single minute, and avoiding anything that resembled serious conversation or displaying deep-seated feelings to each other. Heaven forbid, there was no time for that.

That had been the pattern of our lives, but for some strange reason that Sunday was somehow different. As we took in the impressive view of Bermuda's capital, and the coastline that stretched from Hamilton down toward Spanish Point, and beyond across the sound to Somerset and Sandys Parish, we began to relate stories of our past lives and our pre-Bermuda days in England. Dougie told me of his early life in his home town of Bedford; his apprenticeship as a printer and subsequent job with The Metal Box Company, before seeing the job advertisement in the Daily Mail that would ultimately bring him to Bermuda. In between swigs of beer, I learned of his mates back home and his many adventures including a road trip across Europe. He told me about past loves – or at least Dougie's loose interpretation of past love – and some of his plans and thoughts for the future. I discovered for the first time that he had a sister, his only sibling, who he constantly referred to as his 'stupid' sister. Whether they had a strained relationship or it was just his idea of a term of endearment, I never found out, but it became apparent they were not close.

For my part I recounted my early life in Reading as an only child, and my own experiences leading up to my journey of discovery to those beautiful islands. Then for the first time since arriving, I opened up about my disastrous marriage that had finished almost before it had begun back in 1968. Having married at the age of twenty, I found myself alone just eighteen months later. Alone but the father of a six-month-old baby daughter who had been taken from me before I could start to really embrace the joys of fatherhood. A daughter who was at the time of my relating the story, six years old. It became a flood waiting to be released and I found myself offloading to my friend in a pouring out of previously withheld memories. Dougie listened in silence as I told him of my humiliation, and deep hurt that the separation had caused me, then when I had finished, I felt a strange sense of relief that I had at last been able to share my thoughts and feelings with a trusted friend.

There was a lengthy pause as Dougie took it all in. 'So do you keep in touch?' He wanted to know.

The guilt that I had always kept to myself and well hidden under the veneer of a Jack the Lad exterior with not a care in the world, suddenly came rushing to the surface but I told him honestly that, no, I did not keep in touch, and explained why not. He showed no surprise or shock, but simply nodded in acknowledgement. I had told him in my outpouring that it had been made quite clear to me by my wife's family, that whatever the rights and wrongs of the situation – and there was absolutely no doubt that my wife had coldly and cruelly walked out on our marriage in favour of a new man in her life – that when you got right down to it, blood is thicker than water and moreover the only consideration then was for the welfare of our little girl. A sentiment I could hardly disagree with. But being left with the distinct impression that I was no longer considered a part of the family it left me in an unpleasant limbo and, with all my old pals having moved away or themselves becoming married and settled into new lives, also very lonely.

Then having by chance met two guys in the form of Ray and Jim, who had turned out to be life savers at that dark period, I had started slowly to resurface into something resembling normality. My own parents were themselves hovering around sixty years of age when all this had erupted in my life, and I also somehow felt responsible for their sorrow and anger at what had happened. It was an extra burden that I had been carrying. The culmination of all this led me to relocate to Cornwall as a means of distancing myself from the memory of it all. It was, I conceded, a stupid and spiritless action, and the right thing would have been to stand my ground and do everything I could to ensure my young daughter grew up knowing who her father was. It would not have been easy and perhaps an impossible task given the hostile attitude towards me, but I had taken the simplest route and I had later come to realise that I would probably go through the rest of my life regretting my actions.

It was a liberating morning for me, and I felt a strange sense of relief that I had been able to share my feelings with someone who I knew would not be judgemental. I still retained the sense of guilt I felt in the way I had responded to my situation, and the degradation, and sense of betrayal I had experienced six years previously was still a slowly healing wound. Perhaps one day, I thought, I would tell him about Stevie and an equally raw sense of guilt I felt towards her and what amounted in my mind to desertion in her hour of greatest need. But not that day; I had done enough unburdening. It was exhausting. I sighed deeply. Bloody hell I was a pathetic embodiment of guilt and regret.

There was silence for a minute or two, then Dougie asked: 'When did you know your wife was having an affair?'

I thought about it, then said: 'I was having a nice soak one day, when she opened the door, plugged in the hair dryer and threw it in the bath.'

There was a brief look of horror on my friend's face before he realised I was joking, then we both threw back our heads and laughed out loud. Always finish a serious discussion with a good laugh, I told him, and that was that.

One way and another it was quite an eventful day, because later that afternoon we had front row seats as Matt who, completely and comprehensively hammered, had climbed on to his own roof at All Cedar and was raucously singing a selection of Rabbie Burns songs. We were treated to such rollicking crowd pleasers as 'A Man's A Man For A' That' and 'A Pint O Wine'. We fully expected that Matt's neighbours opposite would be raising hell, but having experienced the result of complaining about noise, the two ladies were nowhere in sight. True, the music volume had been turned down by Matt and his buddies in a previous encounter, but we were told the price of that was a verbal ear bashing. At least that's what we were informed by one of Matt's housemates.

Matt, we later learned, was a bit emotional that day because it was his dad's birthday, so he did what anyone would do – got pissed, climbed up to the roof, and started singing Scottish songs.

Makes sense to me.

FIFTY-FOUR

One typical busy Friday evening, Dougie and I were in the Robin Hood as usual and playing paddle tennis on the newly installed machine just inside the front entrance. This was the zenith of technological progress and sophistication in 1974.

We suddenly became aware that we were being watched, and half turning we saw two young ladies – obviously American from their loud heavily accented comments – gazing with apparent interest at what we were up to. We said hi, and returned to our match; there was a large Cockspur and ginger riding on the result. There were some oohs and aahs as one or other of us won or lost a point, and knowing that we had an appreciative audience, we began to really turn it on and go all out for that winning shot. Our own responses to winning or losing points, was somewhat more basic than ooh or aah, and the air became quite blue in parts. At the completion of the game, we paused to engage the two young women in conversation and get a good look at them. They were maybe early twenties; one was tall and slim with a good figure and nice legs. Her face didn't quite match her other attributes, but you know what they say about pokers and mantelpieces. Her companion could be best described as lacking, and had obviously been a late-comer in the queue that doled out allure... I am being kind here. But the poor love's biggest curse was her face; it was pimple city. I didn't have to ask Dougie what he thought, and still smiling at the mismatched pair of girls, I side mouthed to my mate: 'Best out of three?' Affirmative, conveyed the slight nod that came back.

'Okay, girls,' said Doug, 'stick around; we've got a game to play here.' They giggled like two school girls, and snuggled in closer as we began our crucial first game with the messages they were giving out shining through loud and clear. Horizontal tango was definitely on the agenda that night. The question was, with who, by whom?… or should that be, with whom by who? Whatever.

When the score stood at one each, things got really serious, with much grunting, cursing and even the mock threat of physical violence, but surprisingly, I managed to pull something extra out of the bag at the last minute. I held my fist up in triumph (we had done this once before, and I had come a poor second). Dougie slammed his fist down on the machine, buggering the darn thing up in the process, and requiring a technician to come out and fix it, as it turned out. But we shook hands; it had been a hard fought but fair result, and we all retired to the bar for a well-deserved drink.

The rest of it is history as they say. Leggy girl number one came back to Look Over, following me shakily on her hired moped, and Dougie stayed in the Robin Hood with American girl number two. I had no expectation whatsoever that he would return home other than alone – he had his standards. He told me later that her name was Netta, but he had nicknamed her Etna on account of the eruptions on her face.

Unnecessarily cruel I reckoned. It didn't stop me laughing and nearly choking on my morning tea though.

I had heard my housemate's noisy return sometime after one in the morning, it was obvious he was still a bit peeved and there was no effort to close his bedroom door quietly, but come the morning we both timidly emerged hungover and slack eyed for that first welcome hot drink of the day – coffee for him, good old English breakfast tea for me.

'How'd it go?' he asked me, as we settled down on the front terrace, obviously alluding to my companion the night before.

'Bloody murder,' I told him honestly. 'She was like an out-of-control clockwork toy; she just wouldn't stop moving around.'

'Sounds good to me; what's wrong with that?'

'No really, I reckon she must have learned about sex on a big dipper; it was like riding a rodeo bull on speed.'

'Well, it saved you the hard work, what's the problem?' he asked.

'You like to pace yourself don't you… I mean, well you know, you don't want to… you know what I'm saying.' Adding: 'I had to throw her out in the end.'

Dougie looked aghast, 'You what? Why didn't you send her in to me?'

'Didn't want her to leave disappointed,' I chuckled.

I didn't remind him of the times when it was me who had been left with the plain Jane.

David Arkle had in a short time, immersed himself in the ex-pat lifestyle, and he became a regular at The Robin Hood and Rum Runners amongst other establishments, and if there was a party to be had, and there always was, you would find him there. In addition, he was a handsome bloke damn it, and the ladies loved him. So when we learned through Matt and Robbo – now ensconced at All Cedar – that Dave had a girlfriend arriving for a holiday, Dougie and I were anxious to check her out. We were also amused at the thought of her staying in the same house as Matt. Robbo had already caught Matt spying on him through the bedroom window one afternoon as he was 'entertaining' a young lady hotel receptionist. He told us that as he happened to look up after a particularly athletic session, he saw just the top of Matt's head and a pair of eyes peering over the window sill. How long he had been doing his impression of Peeping Tom, Matt never let on, but in any event, Dave and his girlfriend had better be careful we thought.

We never did get introduced, but an almost daily ritual after work for Dougie and me was to ride slowly past All Cedar, trying to cop a look at the lady who, we were reliably informed, sunbathed topless on the terrace. We must have made it pretty obvious I suppose because Dave informed us that his lady had reported 'two weirdos' repeatedly riding up and down standing up on their motorcycle footrests like a poor man's display team and staring at the house. He just laughed… and we still didn't get an intro.

It has to be borne in mind that Dave was probably the most sober of all of us, and although enjoying a bevy or two, he never seemed to be anything other than calm, relaxed and totally together. So when we were told that on one occasion, he was so bladdered that he sensibly decided to walk back to All Cedar from the party he had attended, it took us by surprise. The thing was, as a relative newcomer on the island, he had absolutely no idea how to find his way back home, and instead of approaching one of us for a lift, he quietly left at some point to make the journey alone. Getting back from Hamilton which he had negotiated on numerous occasions, no problem, but from a party somewhere out in the sticks, well that was a different proposition.

He was found wandering somewhere on the North Shore in the early hours by a police patrol car and the officers had offered to take Dave home. Problem was, he could not remember the name of his house; only that it was by the water and he shared it with *a funny Scottish person* and another chap who kept saying 'tits alive'. Hardly a detailed description, but somehow, through trial and error, and much searching, by some miracle they delivered Dave safely at the door of All Cedar. This was how it was told to us; from fragments that David could remember, and second or third-hand from one of the cops involved, who we happened to know. On hearing the whole story, nobody laughed louder than David himself, who could see the funny side of events. And although we never voiced it, Dougie and I reckoned that the cops knew exactly where Mad Matt and Robbo lived.

Dave regretted having to leave Bermuda after such a short time – he had only been on a six-month contract, and even that had been cut short we learned – and the social life there seemed to suit him to a tee. We were all sharing a farewell drink or two on his last evening, and he made the observation that to sum up Bermuda, he would say that it was: 'All the right people in the right place at the right time.' I thought about that and told him. 'It's even deeper than that, because I would go further and say: 'It is all the right people, in *exactly* the right place, at *precisely* the right time.' To be young and living in Bermuda in the glitzy seventies, was as near to perfection as you could get in my book.

FIFTY-FIVE

I have said it before: there was hardly a weekend when there was not a party in progress somewhere on the island, indeed there were times when we would be confronted with a choice of gatherings to attend. Not that this ever bothered us, because in the name of fair mindedness and equity, we always made an effort to donate the pleasure of our company to each one of the party-givers, however many of them there happened to be and regardless of location. It was tough, but we managed very well.

Admittedly, in what passed as the winter months things did slacken off slightly; largely due to the fact that unlike the conditions that prevailed most of the year, the cooler evenings sometimes excluded the use of outside areas. But this was largely offset by a protracted Christmas period where, if anything, the numbers of parties increased during the two-week festive period leading up to the big day. Likewise New Year and any other excuse that could be found to get down and dirty. So to encounter a weekend during the spring when there appeared to be not one single party scheduled, was as rare as Viv Tierney saying 'My round' and meaning it. But that's exactly what happened in early 1974.

Well, not strictly true because we had heard through the extensive Robin Hood grapevine that there was in fact a private invitation-only party over in Flatts Village, moreover at a house where there had been a big bash the previous summer. Although Dougie and I had not met back then, he must have also attended that party because we both remembered the location and feeling put out and rather let down by the occupants of the property, we decided that the 'invitation only' status was either a misunderstanding or an unforgivable oversight, and on the off-chance that it was indeed a private bash, then this could not in all conscience be allowed to set a precedent, and naturally we decided to put in an appearance.

Having armed ourselves with the usual large bottle of preferred spirit or packs of beer per person, Dougie, Ricky, Graham, Rob, Terry and I rode out convoy style to Smith's Parish. Terry, it has to be noted, was car-less and riding pillion on Rob's machine.

Terry's Mini Clubman was at home a little worse for wear, having collided with the airport bus a few days earlier. He had phoned us on the evening of the accident and in his words told us: 'Sorry chaps, I've been unavoidably detained because I've broken the airport bus.' The bus, it appears, had a fibreglass body, and was split along the complete length of one side.

Oops with a big 'O'.

It had been several months and many parties since the last shindig at the Flatts house, but eventually after a few wrong turns, we found the property set back off the road and sure enough on inspection, we found the doors locked and the windows heavily curtained. But there was clearly a gathering inside judging by the energetic music we could just detect reverberating through the walls, and it was clear that with the windows and doors closed off to us, here was a property that must enjoy the advantages of air conditioning. Not a common feature of rented properties in those days, even in a sub-tropical climate like Bermuda's.

So it was obvious that security measures had been employed in order to keep out the riff raff, which they quite rightly assumed may converge on them at some point if certain people got to hear about their cosy little shindig. And they were right – we had. Almost total security as it turned out, but as we quietly made our way around the house to try to find a way in, we struck lucky on the second circuit, locating a two-inch gap in the French windows that led to the rear garden. This was either an omission on someone's part, or they had been opened slightly by one of the guests to let in some air. Either way, it was the break we had been relying on.

We could not see into the room because, as elsewhere, the drapes had been closed, but the murmur of conversation and the oily sound of Barry White clearly came to us as we prepared to make our presence known. We might as well be bold about it, we thought, and as Dougie and Rick quickly opened the two sliding doors wide, I parted the curtains to encounter a long sofa with its back to the window and containing several people. But what was a sofa to us? We laughed at sofas. Ha-ha we went, and in single file we climbed over the back of the piece of furniture (light green and brown with a delicate stripe) separating the seated individuals in the process, and before anyone could speak such was their surprise, Dougie, brandishing his bottle of Cockspur, enquired in an authoritative manner: 'Where's the bar then?'

'This is a private party,' one of the obvious hosts who had come forward, informed us angrily as he squared up to Dougie.

Ignoring this fact, of which we were of course already aware, I repeated the question: 'No seriously, where's the bar?' brandishing my own bottle of rum in the process.

Host number one quickly switched his attention to me and was joined by host number two who seemed rather shaken and emphasising the word *private*, repeated his colleague's entreaty only to be met with Terry chipping in: 'Down the corridor by the front door – same as last time is it?' And we six processed from the sofa, ignoring our two would-be assailants, strode across the room towards where we were sure the bar would be; encountering on the way, a mixed reaction from the twenty-odd guests, which ranged from shock to ill-concealed amusement.

Host number three – for there were three hotel worker guys who shared the house – gave a half-hearted, 'but this is a… you can't just …' but got no further, except to mutter resignedly as we brushed past him: 'Oh sod it.' We were in, and there would be no more resistance. But just to smooth the waters so to speak, we made sure our presence was felt in a positive way and having poured ourselves drinks and clinked glasses in celebration of our victory, we mingled with the guests as if this was just another normal open party, before putting phase two of the operation into play.

Before leaving the Robin Hood, we had briefed a number of people there what our intentions were, gave rough directions how to find the house, and told them to give us one hour before converging on the property where, with a bit of luck and a following wind, they would find the place wide open and welcoming. It hadn't been a walkover – well it had, because we had walked over the soft furnishings – but everything went according to plan in the end and having socialised for a half hour or so and checking my watch, I sidled off to the bar as inconspicuously as possible which was as stated, adjacent to the front door, turned the key, checked for bolts and rejoined the party. As anticipated, the regular crowd, easily over one hundred, and probably having encountered a few dead ends on the way as we had, arrived piecemeal at the party over the following hour or so. With very good grace we thought, given the circumstances, the hoard was accepted with just a few shrugs and a bit of eye rolling by the three hosts. It was a matter of Hobson's choice.

One surprise arrival was my ex-Little Arches housemate, Trish Charters, who I had not encountered for some time. We greeted each other like old friends, which of course we were, after which Ricky approached me to enquire who the 'hot chick' was. I told him about her; then introduced him to Trish and left them to it. It wasn't exactly what you would call a perfect match and apart from Trish's cut-glass accent, you would not find two people so physically dissimilar, with Rick's five feet three inches looking up into the face of Trish, a good six inches above him. It was obvious to me that although she agreed to a dance with Ricky and was perfectly polite to him, any advances from Rick would be politely diverted. She had told me during our chat that with her traumatic experience the year before, men were temporarily off the menu. But Rick was not perturbed by her coolness and waded in, bless him.

Later, with the party still in full swing, Trish approached me to say she was leaving and hoped that we would bump into each other again. We chatted some more about our respective adventures, and she assured me that she was once more, enjoying life to the full. As she was saying her final goodbye, Ricky suddenly appeared and with his best hang-dog expression said that he also really wanted to leave, but as the rest of our little band were still giving it large and probably would continue to do so for some considerable time – including Graham who had given Ricky a lift to the party – he asked Trish if he could trouble her for a ride home on the back of her moped. Trish being Trish, told him ok, and I will never forget the sight of them puttering off down the drive; tall Trish in front, with the diminutive figure of Rick at the rear, holding on to Trish like an amorous limpet.

I did not see Trish again and assumed she had left Bermuda for the States, where she had often expressed a wish to visit and possibly settle, but Rick told us the next day that she had dropped him off later that night, having fended off his request for a date, patted him fondly on the head, and ridden off – his own words. Good old Ricky. He was a great sport and on reflection, even he could see the funny side of it. For our part, we thought it was hilarious.

As far as we knew, there were never any more private raves after that.

The word had spread.

FIFTY-SIX

As expected, the axe came down soon after our rent-free month at Look Over expired, and we were told by phone to vacate the house at the earliest time. This was after one failed attempt on the agent's part to get an acknowledgement from us when Dougie, who answered the telephone and recognising the voice, had said, 'Solly long number,' and put the phone down. Officially we should have begun paying rent immediately after that first four weeks, but we didn't bother and unbelievably nothing more was said. So in fact it transpired that we had almost six weeks rent free, which was just fine with us and fair-do's, after our treatment at Highclere.

Our Bermudian friend Ricky Correia had for some time expressed his keenness to find a place we could all share together; what the hell, we weren't proud, and if we could find a suitable place and there was a spare room, it might be fun to have Rick around. And it was obvious that although he often referred to us as *those Limey bastards*, he seemed to be intrigued by our eccentric ways and irrepressible approach to life. But what we did not know was that Rick had been actively looking for suitable property for some time, and during those last days at Look Over, he greeted us excitedly one night in the bar and announced that he had found a house to rent at Mount Hill, Pembroke, not far from the Hamilton city centre and minutes from the Robin Hood. It was a four-bedroom house with a garage and with the rent set at four hundred dollars per month, it was a steal, according to Rick. As an added bonus, we found ourselves in the novel situation that the place was not on the bloody market for once.

There was a potential problem however, because Mount Hill was almost exclusively populated by black Bermudians and had a bit of a reputation according to Ricky; although in fairness, we could never quite pin down what that reputation was. Being a black area was not a problem for us of course, only that we wondered how four white boys would be greeted as neighbours. Rick had organised a viewing for us and acquired a key, but it was more than a bit ominous that the agent (not our real-estate friend from the immediate past, thank goodness) was not interested in meeting us on site and was happy to let us get on with it. But nobody else seemed to be bothered by that, and with Graham also up for the move, we all made our way to the property in convoy one Saturday morning.

We liked the house and the location seemed ok. It was a pleasant enough area as far as we could see, with the house at the top of Mount Hill occupying an elevated position above the city, although unfortunately not with a view to speak of, and as Rick had stressed to us on several occasions, the rent was reasonable. There was even the sound of some fancy flute music emanating from a house opposite which lent a certain charm to the scene, and just around the corner under a large tree, was a makeshift desk and a rickety chair, upon which sat a guy studying what appeared to be a ledger. He was, we soon found out, the local dealer in 'home grown' – Bermuda's equivalent of ganja or hash. What could go wrong? But a remark made by Graham and answered by me, more as a joke than a serious observation at the time, proved to be somewhat prophetic.

'What do you think our new neighbours will say when they see us moving in?' he asked facetiously.

'There goes the neighbourhood,' I joked.

Then after only two days in residence, we were burgled. My beloved Sony hi-fi system was taken as was most of Rick's electronics, but our record/cassette collections were untouched. It was strange because no damage had been done, and even the front door was unmarked. Whoever had entered had simply picked the lock – which in truth, could have been cracked by a six-year-old. No drawers had been turned out and apart from the few expensive items mentioned, nothing of great note had gone... even my Canon camera, clearly visible on my bedside cabinet, had been ignored. But Dougie and Graham had noticed there was a personal almost valueless item taken from each of their rooms. It was puzzling and annoying in equal measure.

More than just a burglary, it had the distinct smell of the delivery of some sort of message from the Mount Hill denizens. What that message was, however, we were unsure of. Ricky advanced the idea that it was simply to give us new white boys notice that we were unwelcome additions to the neighbourhood, although that seemed to be a little far-fetched. But that said, neither Graham, Dougie or I had any better suggestions, and if indeed we were not welcome – what then? As it turned out, we learned several days later that Ricky had pretty much hit the nail on the head.

The four of us held a hastily called conference in the Rum Runners that evening; a practical move because finding a quietish corner in the Robin Hood was next to impossible. I was fuming, as was Ricky. Graham was merely thoughtful and although Dougie had lost virtually nothing in the robbery, he was spitting blood. But we all agreed that this had been no normal theft, and our reaction to it might make the difference between a relatively peaceful existence in Mount Hill, or more misery in the future. We unanimously decided therefore that the police would not be contacted for the time being. We came to the decision that we would, initially at least, adopt a softly-softly approach, but at the same time make it clear that we would not tolerate this kind of behaviour; something of a tightrope walking exercise, and exactly how we would go about it presented a problem for which we temporarily had no answer.

After much pondering, drinking, scratching of heads and more drinking, our best – and only – idea was that we would compose a suitable poster sized message, and ask to have it installed in the Mount Hill local shop window. Our new neighbourhood shop, it must be made clear, could be better described as a shack – not so much a supermarket, more a hyperhovel – that served the Mount Hillians. The message had to be carefully thought out and even then, would the owner accept our advertisement, we wondered.

The restorative and medicinal properties of Cockspur rum are truly amazing, and back at the house – a house without music of course – we had after a couple of hours, and with the assistance of that sublime Barbadian spirit, drafted a message that we felt struck the right balance and conveyed a suitable non-confrontational message. Ricky was the only one who disagreed and protested that it was far too feeble and he likened it to knocking on a neighbour's door and asking for our ball back. But he was overruled and with the shop keeper's surprising but welcomed consent, it was stuck on the outside wall of the shack the following morning. It was Wednesday.

The gist of our posting was this: to inform the residents that we had been burgled on Tuesday (as if the inhabitants didn't already know), and to list the items taken. Further: to stress that we were disappointed because we had been looking forward to a long stay in the area and were anxious to fit in and become part of the community. And finally: expressing the wish that our property be returned to us at the earliest time, after which no more would be said and no action taken. We each signed it to give it a more personal, albeit united touch.

We arrived home from work the following day, hoping against hope that there would have been some sort of response to our poster, but there was nothing, leaving us disheartened and somewhat depressed. Our first reaction was anger and a strong temptation to report the burglary to the authorities and to hell with it. But a more cautious and prudent approach was suggested by Graham, who quite rightly pointed out that it had been just ten hours since our overture had been made. But, as Rick pointed out to Graham, he – Graham – had not had anything of real value nicked. Nevertheless, the rest of us calmed down and agreed to wait a little longer. To be honest, Rick and I had already reconciled ourselves to the fact that our precious possessions were gone for good. We were an uncharacteristically sombre bunch who filtered off to our places of work the following morning, and what followed for me was one of the longest working days I had experienced in Bermuda. It wasn't just the loss of my expensive sound system, but the fact that we had committed to live in an area where we were clearly regarded as undesirables and definitely not welcome.

Dougie and I arrived home from work at the same time, and were greeted by two grim looking housemates. 'Ok, hit us with the bad news,' Dougie said as we climbed the steps to the front door. 'What's bloody happened now?'

'We've been broken into again,' a distressed looking Ricky informed us. 'You had better come and look.' Oh God, what were we going to find? Then as we entered the house, Ricky and Graham could no longer contain themselves and gesturing towards the living room dramatically as if introducing the star of the show, they broke into uncontrolled laughter – there in its usual place was my Sony cassette deck.

'And that's not all,' Ricky enthused. 'All my stuff is back too.' We could not believe it, and our incredulity was even more enhanced when Dougie found his cheap cigarette lighter back in place by the side of his bed.

'They even brought back my hair brush,' Graham beamed. Those were the two insignificant personal items that had been taken from the boys.

'When you said we had been broken into...' Dougie began.

'I wasn't lying,' Ricky chortled. 'The bastards picked the lock to get in again.'

It had been a message, as Ricky had suggested right from the start, but what that message had signified, none of us could ever get our heads around. What mattered was that our measured reaction had obviously been the correct one thanks to a bit of intelligent thinking, and there was a collective feeling that a large dark cloud had been lifted from us. It was still only Thursday, and the busy weekend Dougie and I had planned now took on a rosier aspect with much to look forward to. It was going to be a good couple of days.

From that moment on, we were greeted with friendly nods and even the glimmer of a smile from time to time, from our fellow residents, and there was a distinct feeling that we had passed the test and been accepted into the community. And the flute player in the house opposite continued to provide sweet music, which we saw as a sign of much better days ahead at Mount Hill.

FIFTY-SEVEN

We had moved house for the second time in six weeks, which for most people would be a major hassle. Even without those extra annoying hitches, like burglary, it is something that can be very disruptive and takes time to ease into. Not so with the four of us who considered it almost routine. For a start we did not have the encumbrance of furniture to shift from place to place, nor any of the other necessities of life like kitchen equipment, bedding and garden tools. Carisbrook, like our previous places of residence, came complete with a full complement of everything needed for our comfort and well-being; although the garden equipment was superfluous to needs because we had planned to not bother. Besides, we had a full weekend already set out and nothing would detract from that – particularly as our property had been returned and we felt secure again.

I was paying in my wage check as usual at the bank, and as always had made for Linda Jansen's window. The previous week, we had learned that Linda was throwing a party and the usual rave crowd would obviously be there – of course. Formal invitations were almost unheard of because the whole concept of throwing a party at that time was to cram as many people as possible into your place of residence and just let rip. Invitations were pointless anyway because a party only had to be mentioned at the Robin Hood and half the ex-patriot population and a plane load of ravers from Toronto or New York would simply turn up. At least that's the way it seemed. Gatecrashing was a term that had little meaning in Bermuda. There was one notable exception of course at the 'private' Flatts Village shindig where we didn't so much gatecrash as lay siege to, invade, and overrun the place. It was a slap on the wrist and had been a message to never close your door on the dedicated army of partygoers again.

Being the only one at Linda's window that Friday, we had a chat about the following evening's entertainment, and she asked if I intended taking a partner. This took me by surprise, as one of the primary reasons for attending a rave was to get off with a member of the opposite sex and if luck was in, get to serve a young lady her breakfast the following morning. So the answer to Linda's question was an emphatic, but questioning: 'No. Why?'

'It's just that Tina is at a loose end and needs some cheering up,' she told me, motioning to one of her colleagues a few positions along. 'She's got a bastard of a husband who's out every night getting drunk and picking up anything in a skirt,' Linda went on. 'She needs to have a good evening out and I've invited her to my party, but she is too insecure to go on her own and I thought...'

I knew Tina, who had been introduced to me by Linda at the bank months before, but only in passing and I knew nothing about her or her situation. She appeared to be in her mid to late twenties and had always struck me as a sad person, and although pleasant, on the odd occasion I had to find an alternative teller when Linda's position was busy, she came over as a lonely and shy girl. Now in view of what Linda had just told me, it explained the reason why.

'Sure,' I said. 'Why not.' This obviously pleased my friend who probably thought she would have to use more persuasion, and I moved over to wait behind a customer whom Tina was serving. Although I would have guessed that Tina was probably not my type, or the sort of person I would have picked out from the crowd, I was secretly chuffed that Linda had thought of me as the one to take her friend out of herself and give her a fun-filled evening. Besides, she wasn't bad looking by anyone's standards. There was of course the probability that I would not be to Tina's taste.

'Hi, Tina. Look, Linda is throwing a party tomorrow night and I wonder if you would come with me?' I blurted out as I reached her section. She seemed taken back, so I hurried on … 'I know you don't know me that well, but to be honest I am at a bit of a loose end, and would appreciate your company,' I lied whitely. There was hesitation as Tina took in what I had said, then:

'I can't… I'm married, you know.'

'Yes, I do know, but Linda said that…' I stopped myself from saying… *he's a sleaze bag and is on the shag every night*, because that, I realised, was an avenue it would be unwise to venture down at that point.

'…you are also at a loose end yourself but didn't want to go on your own,' I improvised

'I really appreciate it but…' I was losing her and I now saw it as a challenge to get this sad girl out of the house for just one night, and with the help of my friends, bring a smile back to her face.

'Is it this?' I said, stroking my beard. 'I mean, I scrub up quite well once I have chipped off the dirt, or perhaps you don't like the way I dress… but the alternative is much worse, they tell me…' I was rambling.

'No, no nothing like that.' And she looked anxiously over my shoulder at the small queue that had begun to form behind me. Then dejectedly she said, 'I just can't, but thanks for offering. It would have been nice.' And that was that. Whether she was just being polite and letting me down gently, or genuinely felt that it would be the wrong thing for her to do, I never really knew, but my overriding regret I can honestly say, was not to have had the opportunity to give Tina at least one enjoyable night out, in what was obviously a very cheerless life.

I saw Tina on several more occasions at the bank, but the subject never arose again when at odd times I found myself at her position. Then suddenly after a short time, she was gone. Back to the UK Linda told me, but under what circumstances I never found out.

Apart from the trio of bastards known to us as the insurers, who were once again present at Linda's bash the following night, there was a great crowd of people present. The only difference this time, it was Richard and me doing the smirking, and the three of them looking slightly uncomfortable. They must have had a good idea one or both of us were responsible for their sudden call of nature at the Highclere Valentine's bash.

We learned later that early the following morning, a dog walker had discovered a sleeping partygoer under a hedge adjacent to Linda's property, and on being awakened by the wet nose of a German shepherd, he went completely ballistic and punched the poor hound on the nose. I hoped that it was nobody we knew – we were all animal lovers.

People make for successful gatherings, simple and pure, and at the danger of being multi-repetitious, the ex-pat singles crowd were out to have the time of their lives, making every minute count, never quite knowing how long their sojourn in Bermuda would be. The close friendships I had formed with Penny, Jane and Sandra – the three *Dazzlers* – and my bosom mates Terry, Rob and the extraverted and gregarious Dougie, were the cherries perched on top of the already rich and delicious Bermuda cake. Like me they had an insatiable appetite for life and we all lived it as if there would be no tomorrow, which was always a possibility as far as Bermuda was concerned.

It was a bit of a damp squib all round for me that weekend as far as female company was concerned, although I was happy just to have had my music centre returned and was high on the knowledge that our future at Carisbrook seemed to be assured. But that didn't stop me chancing my arm at Flamingo Beach on the Sunday, following our routine afternoon frolics at Horseshoe Bay.

I had deduced – with my extensive knowledge of English dialects – what I believed to be a Berkshire accent emanating from a table where four pretty and giggly ladies were having a good time. Berkshire is my home county, so having sidled over, I asked them: 'Are you lovely ladies from anywhere near my home town of Reading by any chance?'

They all stopped giggling and looked up at me nonplussed, before one of them replied: 'Close. We're from Basingstoke.' Close yes, but not even the same county, but I didn't say that, instead…

…'Ah yes, famous for railway sidings and hookers.'

It has to be borne in mind that I was into my fifth or sixth beer by that time, and my usual bonhomie and judgement had long since deserted me. I was confident that my remark had been a successful opener, because one of their number, smiling seductively, rose to her feet, and gently taking my beer from me, passed it over her lips before tipping the contents of the bottle over my head. It was obvious that she had taken offence to what I had intended as a light-hearted and innocuous remark… about railways… and had shown her displeasure accordingly.

There were a few seconds of silence as my watching friends took this all in, then Rob said with a serious expression, 'I suppose that means a shag is out of the question,' and threw back his head and laughed, seriously dazzling several people who were not wearing shades. Terry gave one of his silent laughs which was more of a wide angled grin, but nevertheless gave rise to a slight bounce in his Afro as he enjoyed the moment, and Dougie let go with one of his loud guffaws.

For my part I didn't find it funny.

Not fucking funny at all!

FIFTY-EIGHT

Bermuda was a super prosperous place. There was no depression poverty and unlike her Caribbean cousins a thousand or more miles to the south, where deprivation and hardship could still be part of the national life, Bermuda's residents enjoyed an exceptional standard of living. As in any society there were poorer elements within the community, but overall, the island was a beacon of affluence with a per capita income that matched the world's richest nations. A huge bonus for us ex-pats, who were familiar with the British swingeing tax system, was that there was no income tax. Couple all of this with Bermuda's sub-tropical climate, world class beaches and stunning topography and there was a good deal of justification in referring to it as an earthly paradise. But even within this environment, there was still an area in Bermuda that was regarded as extra exclusive and was populated, it was said, by the super-rich. Tucker's Town in St George's Parish.

Although residents are free to travel through the area as they are in any other parish on the island, there was an understanding that unless there was a specific reason to visit, then it was 'preferred' that you stayed away, and back then there was a board on Tucker's Town Road signifying that fact. It hadn't stopped me visiting on one or two occasions to take in the expensive houses and the charming bays with their pristine secluded beaches, and it has to be said that I was never stopped or taken to task by anyone. So when Nobby and I were sent there on a job, I was looking forward very much to several days' work in that quietly exclusive community. It should be borne in mind that many of the top tier of properties in Bermuda, costing mega bucks, belonged to non-Bermudians who were also mostly non-residents. There is a system that excludes properties up to a certain level of value from being purchased by non-Bermudians, thereby assuring that the more 'affordable' housing is reserved for islanders. By definition, therefore, the more exclusive homes are owned by the very wealthy… that's not to say that there are no wealthy Bermudians living in impressive homes across the island including Tucker's Town – quite the contrary.

The house in question that day stood towards the end of Tucker's Town and belonged to a very rich West German industrialist; a visit from him, we were told, was a rare occurrence. It stood on a mini promontory surrounded by beautiful gardens containing masses of the striking Iris-like Bermudiana and red Chinese hibiscus. There was an impressive timber pergola of slightly oriental design, stretching the length of the garden to the edge of a low-level bluff, and terminating in a large circular paved viewing and al fresco dining area; the whole length and circumference of it adorned with a Petrea vine that sported a breathtaking display of cascading purple flowers.

The garden's perimeter was bordered by a splendid two-toned red and orange lantana, with a backing of multi-coloured oleander, the whole of which enclosed several lawned areas that had been mown to within an inch of their lives. There was a covered veranda running the full width of the rear of the house under which were several life-size statues with planters of various coloured small flowers arranged at their feet – which reminded me of pictures I had seen of Roman villas. Although no gardener was in evidence that day, it was obvious that the property's absent owner had ensured that his grounds were kept in immaculate order.

I was no horticulturist by any stretch of the imagination, but I had acquired, through curiosity, a basic knowledge of the beautiful Bermuda flora, often making a nuisance of myself with neighbouring gardeners asking what this or that plant was, such as that occasion the previous year when I had admired the stunning Royal poinciana in Woodbourne Avenue. But Nobby also seemed to have a good deal of experience in those matters and had filled in the blank spots for me and added to my fund of knowledge that day in Tucker's Town. It was a beautiful garden by anyone's standards and obviously kept in superb condition during the owner's long absences.

We had an exploratory nose around the rest of the grounds noting the abundance of land-crab burrows amongst the flower beds and borders. These creatures were quite a common sight and whilst often making themselves comfortable accommodation in gardens, they would return to the sea during the mating season. You would often encounter them hurriedly crossing roads, with many losing the race to get to the opposite side and being sent to that rock pool in the sky by passing vehicles that were often infringing the twenty mile an hour speed limit. Mad bastards!

To complete the surveillance, we took sneaky peeks through the windows taking in the sumptuous décor, fine antiques, and what we judged to be original paintings adorning the walls. Although our view was limited, we could make out expensive looking Eastern rugs on the flag-stoned floor, and what looked like silver ornaments in a massive glass case. My God, I thought, I hope they have a first-class security system, and jumped back from the un-shuttered window at the thought.

The work we were involved in was replacing damaged tiles and re-grouting the whole of the drained-down swimming pool, and was a part of my contract that stated in the absence of my roofing work I would be obliged to undertake whatever other work was required within the company's remit.

We set up the ubiquitous transistor radio on the edge of the pool – a necessity according to my working partner, Nobby – unpacked our tools and materials and set to work in the time-honoured leisurely Bermuda way. The empty pool was a sun trap and with the hot sun reflecting off the tiled lining, it was extremely uncomfortable as the day progressed, and made for even slower going than usual. But the location more than made up for it and we had frequent water breaks to avoid the very real danger of dehydration, each time taking in the views across the small adjacent beach and the impressive properties beyond.

We chatted to each other about our lives as we worked and Nobby was, as always, interested to learn about my life in England, and Cornwall in particular. Nobby had been seconded to me on my second roofing job, and because we worked and got on well together, he became my default work partner on certain projects, particularly whenever a roofing contract came along. We had become good friends, and on one occasion, I had been taken to Nobby's home to meet his wife – a rare honour for me.

It occurred to me that day, that although we had worked together on a number of occasions, he was only known to me as Nobby. So I asked him: 'What's your first name, Nobby? I assume your family name is Clark.'

'Clark?' he frowned. 'Why Clark?'

'Well, you know – Nobby Clark.' Still more puzzlement. 'As in Chalky White?… Dusty Miller?' No reaction. I shrugged and held my hands out palm up. 'It's obviously a purely British thing, so why do they call you Nobby then?'

Nobby stood up and with a grin, loosened his belt and slowly lowered his jeans.

'Fucking hell, man… put that away before you have somebody's eye out,' I spluttered. And that was that. I was too gobsmacked to find out his real name and to this day I only remember him as Nobby. But the image is indelibly printed on my brain.

The memory of that day in Tucker's Town is a particularly pleasant and yet strangely poignant one for me, which has nothing whatever to do with Nobby's todger. The image of the wonderful garden within the peaceful ambience of that corner of Bermuda, and looking out over a deserted beach below, where brightly coloured parrot fish cavorted in the gentle surf, are all forever readily retrievable in full colour inside my head.

Sitting on the parapet wall surrounding the pool during our lunch break, taking all that in and listening to the sound of Dobie Gray singing 'Drift Away' issuing from the radio, it became one of those perfect moments and snapshots in time that has stayed with me throughout my life.

When old songs are played and there is sometimes that magical bitter-sweet emotion of sadness combined with the sheer joy of times past, and whenever I hear that song, delivered of course by Dobie Gray – no substitutes accepted – I am instantly transported back almost five decades to that perfect day in beautiful surroundings, overlooking the ocean, that special Tucker's Town feeling enveloping me once again.

FIFTY-NINE

It was Friday morning. I had been working on the roof of the new Royal Gazette building in Par-La-Ville Road, Hamilton, and we were looking forward to completion later that day. My boss had turned up with the site foreman, and we went over the roof together where I pointed out two or three small problems that needed some minor carpentry work carried out by the builders. We saw that David, our superintendent, had turned up with some extra materials I had requested, and with our inspection completed I accompanied my boss and the building foreman back down to ground level. David had begun to offload the extra rolls of the neoprene latex sheet that was used as the roof covering, and he and I were beckoned over to the interior of the building by our boss to brief us on our next job the following Monday.

The inside walls of the new construction were being sprayed with a substance that gave off clouds of white choking dust-like particles, making it impossible to conduct our business, and we soon decided to retreat to the fresh air. We were told that it was a form of asbestos fireproofing, which at the time meant nothing to us. But it was only a short time later that the toxicity of blue asbestos was brought to light and banned in any future construction work. The use internationally of the material up until that point had been on a massive scale, and I have often wondered if asbestos was indeed the substance used that day, or some other material. Knowing that the deadly effects of asbestos on the body, even in minute amounts, can be delayed for many years after exposure, I can only hope that I was misinformed.

The following morning I had dragged myself out of bed, joining the others in the kitchen where there was a conglomeration of yawns, farts, smokers' coughs, and a scratching of balls… just the usual Saturday morning really. There was a God-awful taste in my mouth, and the first thing I did was to go to the fridge and select a can of grape juice.

'Jeez,' I exclaimed after downing the contents, 'I must have used someone else's toothpaste last night, I've got a mouth like a galley slave's loin cloth, it was bloody rank.' The night before, of course, had involved Elbow Beach staff club, but then as an add-on, we had been invited back to someone's pad for a 'nightcap' or two. Hence our zombie-like appearances as we all shuffled around in slow motion, making tea or coffee, and sliding bread under the grill.

Dougie had taken himself off to the bathroom for a shower, and on his return he was holding up a familiar looking item.

'This what you cleaned your teeth with?' Dougie tossed a tube of something onto the work counter. 'It was with your toothbrush,' he said.

What!

No wonder my mouth felt as if something had died there – it was a tube of haemorrhoid cream. 'Alright, which one of you switched my stuff for this?' I waved the offending article in the air, but all I got were shrugs from the innocent looking cherubs in front of me. As far as I knew, none of my fellow Carisbrook occupants suffered with piles, so it followed that some bugger had purposely bought the stuff to play a wheeze on yours truly.

'Well at least your teeth will be dingleberry free,' Rick chortled, barely able to contain himself.

'Handy if you get a case of the Chalfonts,' Dougie added.

'Chalfonts?' Rick stopped his chuckling and looked puzzled.

'Chalfont St Giles,' we hollered in unison.

'It's rhyming slang,' Graham prompted, then a moment's continued puzzlement from Ricky before the penny dropped.

'Ahh, right… but what the fuck's a Chalfont St Giles?' So we told him. 'You fucking Limeys,' he grinned.

I never did know for sure who swopped my toothpaste, and nobody ever admitted it. I have my suspicions though.

Oh yes, I have my suspicions.

SIXTY

Whilst there seemed always to be something going on, and at least a surprise or two that consistently seemed to occur as we had made our way from one watering hole to another, Dougie of course had to go one better by packing in several dramatic incidents in just one night.

He had met a very attractive lady one night at the Elbow Beach staff club, and a date had been arranged for the following Friday night. He had intended wining and dining her at one of the more salubrious eating establishments – probably The Chicken Coop or DeGraffe's – and had arrived at the nurse's quarters in Hamilton on Friday evening at the appointed time… yes, the lady was a nurse. What was it with us and nurses? But because Dougie had forgotten her name by the time he recounted the story to me, what she was called will forever remain a mystery. Although in the unlikely event that she happens to read this, perhaps she would be kind enough to make herself known to me, and I will forward on Dougie's present whereabouts, should a claim for compensation be considered.

Anyway, the nurses' quarters were policed by a fearsome woman known as The Matron, who was very protective of her young ladies and made it known to any man daring to arrive at her establishment, they were not approved of. Even Prince Charles would have been sent away with a flea in one of his impressive ears. There were no exceptions by all accounts and so if this was her view of all men and particularly so with respectable, butter-wouldn't-melt-in-the-mouth individuals like Mad Matt or Robbo, it was pretty plain. that had she owned Rottweilers, they would have been instantly released at the sight of Dougie. Nevertheless, having braved the Gorgon's stare, he duly collected his date who, according to Dougie, looked ravishing in a black fitted top over a stylish white ankle length gypsy skirt.

Having made herself comfortable sitting side saddle on Dougie's trusty bike (a necessity due to the long garment) he opened up the throttle and was no more than twenty feet into the journey, when a cry of distress issued from the lips of his passenger and the bike came to a sudden and shuddering halt. Looking back in alarm, he saw two things in close order: a shapely pair of naked sun-tanned legs with no skirt, and the said garment firmly snagged in the chain sprocket of his bike. The skirt had been ripped completely off. The now half-naked girl jumped off the bike in some distress as can be imagined, and without a word – no not true, I believe there must have been at least one word and it wouldn't have been gosh – she sprinted back to the nurses' quarters.

There was absolutely no way Dougie was going to follow her and face The Matron again who would now have had her suspicions confirmed that he was a rampant sex maniac.

Not three minutes had passed since the delightful young lady had left fully dressed and had then rushed back in anguish, stripped to her undies. What conclusion would anybody have come to? It took some time, but eventually the remnants of the skirt were removed from the chain, leaving Dougie covered in oil and grease. But hey, it was Friday night and there was no way on God's earth that Dougie's evening was going to be wasted… unlike the skirt. So having returned home to an empty Carisbrook – we were probably all out at Elbow Beach by that time – he washed and changed and decided to kick the night off again with a few bevvies at the Hood. Now there was a change. It was still relatively early as far as partygoing was concerned, nothing began in earnest until midnight at least or until the bars closed at 1am, and so after one or two drinks, Dougie decided to try his luck at the popular 2001 nightclub on nearby Bermudiana Road.

The entrance was at street level from where there was a flight of plush carpeted stairs to the night club proper on the floor above – and remember, as with all such establishments, a jacket and tie was mandatory in order to gain entry. Plus, an entrance fee of course.

In case you have forgotten from an earlier description, it was a large room complete with revolving mirror balls and dramatic lighting. A bar was positioned half way down the left-hand side as you entered and took up one half of that side of the room. On the right about midway was the disc jockey's station equipped with the paraphernalia that, well, disc jockeys use. Tables and lounge-type furniture were dotted around and there was a rectangular area for dancing in the centre of the room. It was a very stylish set up and the sound system was fantastic. Perfect unless you wanted to have a quiet chat with your friends.

It didn't take long for my friend to come up trumps and with the aid of several strong cocktails and some silly dancing thrown in, he persuaded a downy thighed young nymph, as Dougie always put it, to accompany him back to Carisbrook where he knew they would have the house to themselves. Unfortunately, with perhaps half a bottle of Barbados rum swilling around inside him by this time, he missed his footing at the top of the stairs and rolled arse over apex to the bottom, losing the heel from one of his platform shoes in the process. Luckily the carpeting saved him from any serious injury, but the hitherto smooth-talking Douglas, looking decidedly uncool, limped along with one heel missing and swearing like a drunken sailor. He never did discover what became of his newfound date. She had disappeared completely.

But hey, once more… it was Friday night…

…So alone again, Dougie returned to the house where he performed a hasty repair on the wounded shoe, unbelievably with the aid of a hammer and a two-inch nail. For some reason he did not enjoy the luxury of several pairs of shoes to choose from: plenty of pants and a multitude of shirts, but not that well-endowed in the shoe department. But a quick paint job had always been the cheaper solution. It had been an eventful if slightly less than successful evening so far and it was getting late, but there was still a party to go to.

It was after 2am when Dougie eventually presented himself at the party, one foot clicking as he walked, and sounding like a one legged Fred Astaire, courtesy of the pointy head of a nail. The pickings were somewhat thin on the ground he later told us, with most people having partnered off or were slumped across chairs and sofas looking the worse for wear. It was still packed, but that was largely due to the weather having turned nasty and had everyone retreating inside as the rain began to bucket down. One particular girl caught Dougie's eye that seemed to be alone and was sitting quietly on a chair in the corner of the room. The reason for her solitude and glum countenance, it turned out, was that her escort for the evening had sloped off with another female and left the poor girl stranded.

Excellent.

The lady was, according to Dougie, of the weightier kind, and after a few dances, probably inflicting collateral damage to the floor with the lethal shoe, it didn't take long for him to dispense with the niceties and suggest that she accompany him back to Carisbrook, ostensibly for coffee before he took her home, which was readily accepted along with all that the invitation suggested. The shower of rain had become a deluge and steering the bike in the rain, hampered also by the weight of his pillion passenger, was a hazardous journey, but with a lot of luck and Dougie's determination to turn a disastrous evening into a moderately enjoyable one, they eventually made it back to Mount Hill and home.

Where the rest of us went that night after Elbow Beach, I can only guess, but was almost certainly another party. The house was still empty when Douglas and partner arrived, and none of us witnessed what happened next. His companion retired to the bathroom to do what young sopping wet ladies do, and Dougie went to his bedroom, stripping off his drenched clothes as he went, piling them on the floor at the foot of his bed. Everything then became a bit hazy according to Doug, because he remembered crashing on the bed, followed by a very drunk young lady entering the room, tripping dramatically on his sodden clothes and taking a flying leap, bouncing off him and coming to rest yin-yang style beside Dougie. After that it all went blank, which if Dougie was telling the truth, was probably a blessing.

Perhaps it was the body's way of saving Dougie from further trauma because the next thing he remembers was waking up with the overriding thought that he hoped none of his housemates had seen his less than nubile companion. He was wrong of course, because on arriving home just before dawn, I barged into Dougie's room to see if he had arrived back, and took in the whole indelicate scene. I really should have taken some photos because it was a study in still life – my blundering in had not stirred them. But I couldn't do that to my best mate. I wasn't that cruel. Still…

Amazingly the whole episode was played out again almost to the letter some months later. At breakfast one Sunday morning one of the boys asked who had bought the new denim shower curtain, which on inspection was a huge pair of jeans hanging over the shower rail to dry. It had been another rainy night, and after creeping along the corridor to Dougie's room, the door was carefully and quietly opened to reveal him and another sizeable lady sound asleep and nose to tail… as it were.

'Hell,' Rickie had whispered. 'It must be like having your face eaten by a giant pumpkin.' And on that note the door was gently closed and they were left to sleep it off. Dougie was constantly reminded about both incidents and he had to endure the jibes and innuendos for a long time after that. In fact, he still does.

I suppose it didn't help that after the second occasion, he was presented with a tin of Chum, purchased from our neighbourhood shack, for Dog of the Year 1974.

SIXTY-ONE

We had recently entertained Inez and Pat, the two English secretaries Richard and I had met in New York, and they had spent a week in Bermuda; Inez staying with me at Carisbrook, and Pat at Richard's mother's house, where he still lived in Spanish Point. They also arrived with another of the secretaries living and working in the Big Apple: Annabel, a New Zealander. Naturally Dougie and I re-christened her Kiwi.

The girls enjoyed their time on *de Rock*, and girls being girls, on most days when we were fulfilling our work commitment, they would meet up to shop in Hamilton, then ride off to the beach on their rented Mobylettes, or explore the island, visiting the 'must see' locations that Richard, Dougie and I had recommended to them. Then each evening we would take them to a variety of bars and restaurants, and on one occasion, Dougie and I took the girls to one of the legendary parties that was being thrown in Paget, not far from town.

It was at this party that we bumped into our erstwhile housemate Robbo, and noting that his tongue was hanging below his chin when he saw Inez, I obviously felt obliged to introduce him to her. 'Tits alive,' he confided to me later, 'you can sure pick 'em.'

We had all heard of the visit to Bermuda by Muhammad Ali a short while before, and later at the party I had mentioned it to Robbo and asked if he had met the man in his capacity as sports writer for the Royal Gazette.

'Oh yeah, I actually got an exclusive interview with him,' he told me enthusiastically.

'You never told us. How the hell did you manage that?' I asked.

'I went to the press conference, and I was just about the only white face there', he said, so Ali pointed at me and called me up onto the platform.' Adrian paused, as if the memory was causing a problem for him. He went on to tell me that Ali asked him where he worked, then pointing to several black members of the press who were present, he asked each in turn: 'Could you do his job?' Of course, each of them replied in the affirmative, much to Robbo's embarrassment. Ali had set him up to make the point that a black man should be doing Adrian's job. Robbo felt totally humiliated, he told me.

The next morning Robbo received a call from Ali's manager asking him if he would like an exclusive interview with the great man. Would he, by God? He would just have to put the previous day's debacle behind him, and a time was arranged for later that day in the Hamilton Princess Hotel where Ali was staying. Ali was all sweetness and light, and apologised profusely for the press conference incident, telling Robbo that it was the sort of thing that was expected of him, and was all part of his Muslim persona. The exclusive interview was his way of apologising to Robbo and making amends.

Staying with my old mate in England nearly half a century later, Adrian told me that the interview was still the pinnacle of his career, such was the impact the iconic boxer had on him.

The high point of Inez and Pat's visit, they told me, was when we took them for the famous Sunday brunch at the Henry VIII pub on the South Shore. It was our aim to give them a memorable time and for them to return home to New York overflowing with great memories of Bermuda, and of course, the guys who had entertained them. Our week in NYC several weeks earlier had been a blast which in no small measure was due to Inez and Pat's very welcome company. So it was the very least we could do in return.

Ricky had reason to fly to New York after the girls had left Bermuda and naturally, he looked them up during his visit. He had also met two more of the British secretaries through Inez, who were staying in the same apartment block in Manhattan that Richard and I had visited on our first evening out with Inez and Pat. At Rick's suggestion, his two new acquaintances had also flown to Bermuda a few weeks later – although neither had stayed at Carisbrook.

It was Friday April 12th 1974, and I have a very special reason to remember that date. Dougie, Rick and I arrived at Elbow Beach staff club, faithful as always to our Friday night schedule, and because we always arrived fairly late in the evening having propped up other bars for a couple of hours or eaten out at one of the many establishments in Hamilton in order to limber up for the weekend ahead, the place was full. Terry and Rob plus all of the other regulars were already present and there was the customary party atmosphere. I remembered that some years earlier there was a television pop programme in the UK whose introductory line was: 'The Weekend Starts Here'. Which summed up perfectly how we felt about Elbow Beach staff club on a Friday night.

We did a bit of mingling, interspersed with some dancing and our fair share of helping out the rum distillers in Barbados and Bermuda. Then as I chatted with Rick about the attributes of a particularly well-endowed redhead he had been dancing with – most of the time with his head wedged between her boobs – I spotted a blonde across the room who had her back to me and was talking to a group of people.

'Bloody hell' I exclaimed to Rick. 'What's she doing here?'

Looking in the direction of my nod, Rick took a moment to check it out, then smiled and said: 'Ahh, you think that's Inez right?'

'It is Inez… isn't it?'

'Course not man, she's back in New York.

'That's what I thought but…'

Rick cut me short. 'Only one reason she could have come back right?' he said, reading my thoughts, and he sniggered. 'I know where you're coming from, man. Same hair, and you're right; from the back she does look like Inez?'

'Same figure. And great legs,' I enthused.

'No, man, that's not her.' He paused for effect. 'But I do know who it is.'

I took my eyes off the blonde and looked at Rick. 'Who?'

'My hairdresser, Janet.'

'You've got a hairdresser?'

He looked at me in disbelief. 'I know it's an alien concept for you and Dougie, but some of us actually care about the way we look,' he chided me. 'Want me to introduce you?'

'Bloody right I do,' I told him, because Rick's hairdresser had now turned and was scanning the room so that I could clearly see her features for the first time, and I felt myself looking at a stunningly attractive woman.

'Oh, but I gotta tell you,' Rick warned me. 'The good-looking guy next to her… that's her husband, Robert. He's also a hairdresser.'

I didn't care. I just nodded my head dumbly and let Rick lead me over to the small group where he made introductions. Robert returned the compliment by introducing us to their small group of friends, but I never took in their details because Janet was no less stunning close up and I was totally enthralled. There were many beautiful women in Bermuda at that time, and it had been the mission of our little group to meet as many of them as possible; but sometimes there is an added inescapable something extra that makes one stand out. It cannot be explained or defined, and is picked up perhaps by just one individual whose radar is activated by that invisible quality. This was one such moment. It had been Janet's birthday the previous Tuesday it transpired, and they were celebrating it belatedly at Elbow Beach, which as it turned out, was not a venue they often took in and which explained why their faces were not familiar to me.

Singles and married couples were two distinct groups of people in Bermuda's ex-pat community, often having their own respective haunts, but with attached couples mostly confining themselves to the company of other married friends at private dinner parties and suchlike, and which explained why I had most certainly never seen Janet and Robert at the staff club or elsewhere for that matter – I definitely would have remembered. We chatted and I considered asking Janet for a dance, but quickly dismissed the idea as being far too forward on the strength of such a brief association, and with her husband present. But with the Stylistics music wafting across the room, it would definitely have been a: *You Make Me Feel Brand New* moment.

Dougie and the lads joined us in due course, we all got to know each other, and I asked Robert what they were doing the following evening, so when he told me they had nothing planned, I eagerly gave him details about the party at All Cedar, on Harbour Road.

After they left, Dougie elbowed me in the ribs… 'Eh, eh… I saw the way you were looking at her… eh!' And he elbowed me again. He was right. What the heck was wrong with me? It was months later when Janet confessed that she had in fact seen me before I spotted her that night and had been playing a silly game with Robert identifying men and women in the room who had caught their eyes, and she had pointed me out. It apparently surprised Robert because Janet had always shown a dislike of beards, and there I was, long haired and bearded. Her unexpected pick of the pops.

SIXTY-TWO

Not long after Dougie, Graham and I had left Look Over for pastures new in the shape of Mount Hill and Carisbrook, our erstwhile neighbours at All Cedar announced they were having a rave and Adrian had asked us to spread the word via the Robin Hood and other drinking establishments that we frequented. No problem there; you only had to mention it in the bar of the Hood and like locusts swarming over a farmer's crops, the hordes would arrive from the four corners of Bermuda. Not that they needed our assistance because between Matt, Adrian and their recent acquisition, Neil Morgan, who had taken Dave Arkle's place, and was known exclusively as *Irish* for obvious reasons, they covered more ground than any of us in their nightly assault on the bars and clubs of Hamilton.

All Cedar was not a large property, just your average size for a three-bedroom, one-bathroom small family house, but most importantly with enough outside space to accommodate a fairly large bash. At least that's what they thought. They had assumed – wrongly as it turned out – that as a relatively newly occupied property and this being their first party, a fair bit of vocal publicity was needed. Big mistake! For some reason this particular party seemed to catch the attention of not only the usual bunch, but many people that were not regular attendees. Could it have been its location overlooking The Great Sound and close to Hamilton? Doubtful, and in my opinion, it was almost certainly because of the reputation of the occupants whose exploits were already becoming legendary, almost always for dubious reasons.

As the house filled up on the keenly anticipated night and overflowed into the rear garden, the only space remaining after a short time was the small front terrace, and it was at this stage that many would-be party goers – we learned later – had no choice but to go home or back to whatever bars they had come from. The house and grounds were jam packed and for some this was just too much, and many of the ravers, although not all, drew the line at having to party in Harbour Road itself. It was impossible to calculate just how many were there, but it was a heck of a lot and without the aid of alcoholic nerve tonics, it would have been unbearable for the rest of us. As it was, I had barely noticed the overcrowding.

The lounge area was just a mass of couples dancing and smooching to the sounds of Gladys Knight, The O'Jays, Eddie Kendricks and such like, and we all seemed unaware of a strange indefinable change in the topography of the room. For my part I had a hazy image of most of the dancers, including ourselves, cramming into one portion of the room, and in my rum induced state, not quite being able to understand why. But we saw out the evening and somehow found our way back to Mount Hill in the early hours, only to be rudely awakened, by the urgent ringing of the phone. Both Dougie and I dragged ourselves out of bed – not the same one I hasten to add, neither of us was that far gone – and arrived at the phone together. I answered it. It was Robbo, one of the All Cedar rapscallions and our erstwhile housemate.

'Who is it?' asked a sleepy Douglas.

'Robbo,' I mouthed.

'Oh man, you should see the state of our floor,' Robbo spluttered.

'Does he know what bloody time it is?' was Dougie's grumpy concern.

'Why what's wrong with your floor, and by the way, do you know what time it is?' I said echoing Dougie's sentiment.

'Yeah it's, hold on… seven minutes past eight.'

'I know that you dick, I'm just saying…'

'It's our floor,' he repeated.

I sighed. 'So you said. What's wrong with it?'

'It's bloody collapsed.'

'Their floor's collapsed,' I side mouthed to Dougie who was standing next to me.

Dougie yawned and stretched, 'Far out.'

'We knew something was wrong last night,' I told Robbo. 'Just couldn't figure out what.'

'I know,' he went on, 'That's why we all kept sliding down to one end of the room… it's wet too, it looks like it's collapsed into the water tank.'

'So what does Matt have to say about it?' I was chuckling, so was Dougie, who had his head cocked listening in. We couldn't help it.

'I can't wake the bugger up, that's why I'm ringing you guys. What do you think we should do?'

'Just a minute,' I said. 'Let me consult my learned colleague.'

I held out my hand holding the phone so that Robbo could hear both Dougie and me as I repeated what Robbo had said and that our advice was needed. 'That's a bleeding laugh,' was Dougie's first offering and we both found it difficult to contain our mirth at our pal's misfortune. But there was silence on the other end. Then following a brief discussion with the phone cupped in my hand, and having agreed on the course of action the residents of All Cedar should take, I put the phone back to my ear.

'Right, this is what you do… nothing,' I told him.

'What…!'

'No listen. If you report this to the landlord, he will soon find out from the neighbours that you had a party with a couple of million people, and you will get charged for the repairs, which let's face it, will be in the hundreds if not the thousands of dollars… hold on, Dougie's saying something…'

'And they will probably also get kicked out,' Dougie shouted at the phone.

'Dougie says that you will also probably get kicked out.'

'Yes, I heard, but...'

'Then,' I cut him off, 'leave it for a couple of weeks at least before you report it, and when you do, really lay it on thick and bollock the landlord for renting out a sub-standard property. Tell him one of you almost broke a leg or something like that.'

'You reckon.'

'Definitely... hold on, Dougie's saying something else.'

'Tell him they should push for a reduction in rent or a month free.'

'Dougie say's push for a reduction in rent or a month rent free.'

There was a lengthy silence. 'Um, you think that might work?'

'We do – definitely.' Another moment's silence, then...

'Can't see us getting away with that... gotta go, Matt and Irish are here...' and he hung up.

'That's our good deed for the day,' I told Doug as I hung up the phone.

'Yep, nice to help our friends. I reckon we are two responsible, upstanding citizens and a credit to the community.' He smacked his lips. 'Let's go get some breakfast.'

'Chicken Coop?'

'Where else?'

We learned later that the All Cedar boys had reported it that same day, and although they sweated on the comeback, it must have never got back to the landlord about the party, and a new floor was installed with no financial penalty for the boys. Lucky or what.

The next time we ran into Janet and Robert, they told us that they had turned up at the party, but it proved impossible to even get through the front door, such was the crush, and they returned to town disappointed.

But not as disappointed as me, I wanted to say.

SIXTY-THREE

I had not returned home after a bash the previous night, and I had stayed over with a past female acquaintance that I had run into at the party. I had not seen her for a while, so felt that we should do some catching up – mostly to do with discussing the cold war, the pound-dollar exchange rate, and the obscene price of yellowfin tuna.

There was an amusing incident at the party when Mac Eddey, a great character who we had met at a previous party at a house he shared with several other guys, had gone missing. Somebody had noticed his long absence, and he seemed to have disappeared, which was a bit of a concern because when last seen he was as pissed as a pudding. He was not in the garden, which was a regular spot for those who had imbibed a little too much alcohol, to usually end up in a flower bed or amongst shrubbery – dispensing fragments of carrot and the odd tomato skin amongst the flora. Then someone found the shirt that Mac had been wearing, halfway up the stairs; then his shoes at the top, followed at regular intervals by his slacks, then his underpants and finally a single sock immediately outside the bathroom door. We found Mac, safe but snoring loudly, slumped on the toilet seat wearing nothing but the remaining sock. He has vehemently denied this ever happened and has maintained that position down the years. But those of us who witnessed it have never forgotten that image. I mean, who wears pink striped socks?

It was yet another occasion when it was unfortunate nobody had a camera to hand.

That Sunday we had promised our housemate Ricky that we would prepare a typical English Sunday lunch for him. Having been presented with a complete leg of pork by Steve Croucher, which we were told had been legitimately acquired and was surplus to needs at the Rum Runners where he worked. It seemed the ideal opportunity to give Rick a taste of old England. He had driven us mad with his request for some British grub for some time, never having had the full Sunday experience, so we agreed to push the boat out in style for him, even though it meant foregoing our regular Horseshoe Bay gathering. But with a bit of luck, we reasoned, we could still eat, clean up the kitchen (a job we had earmarked for Rick anyway, having told him that it was also traditional in England for the guests to wash the dishes) and still get to Flamingo Beach for the weekly late afternoon musical bash.

In spite of the prospect of a huge Sunday lunch, Dougie and I had already agreed the day before that we would be breakfasting at the Chicken Coop as usual. It has to be repeated that our appetites in those days were enormous, although Dougie's was on a different level entirely and I suppose his could be better described as epic. I hoped, as I kicked my bike on to the stand in the Carisbrook drive, that he had not already left in the belief that realising I had spent the night elsewhere, I would be making a day of it. I should have called him before I left my lady friend's apartment, I belatedly realised, but I hadn't and there were no mobile phones in 1974.

I needn't have worried because Dougie had surfaced and was lying on the sofa wearing my velvet barrow boy cap that he seemed to covet, and with his eyes closed. He had a thing about my favourite cream velvet item of headwear. There was a mug of tea on the floor beside him and he was wearing my cans, listening to an album on the stereo. I had installed my state-of-the-art Sony twin tape deck piece of kit in the living room, as I had in the past, so the boys could share it if they wished. But Dougie was the only one of the four of us at that point who never bothered to purchase a sound system of his own, and so made full use of mine. Ricky owned his own record / tape / radio receiver / stereo system / TV installed in his bedroom that had everything except Tony Blackburn and Pans People. And Graham had recently invested in a new Teac stereo tape deck with upgraded speakers, and had been driving us nuts by continuously playing his latest acquisition – the album *Tupelo Honey* by Van Morrison. It wasn't a new release, but Graham had just discovered Mr Morrison and had been generously sharing his experience with the rest of us, and finding to our dismay that his closed bedroom door was no match for Van's vocal excellence.

Graham had arrived home from wherever he had spent the previous night and had yet to put in an appearance, and with Rick's bike also parked outside, it appeared our Bermudian buddy was having a similar lie in. There was a blissful look on Dougie's face and because my stereo deck did not have the automatic cut-off that many units had when headphones are attached, I could hear exactly what was playing. It was one of his favourite tracks and also one of mine; a piece called 'Procession' from the Moody Blues album, *Every Good Boy Deserves Favour*. It's a strange, intriguing piece of music, with some bizarre effects, many produced by Mike Pinder's famous Mellotron, including sitars, some plinky kind of ancient keyboard like a spinet or harpsichord, and a deep throated church organ. In short, it's weird, and therein explains why Dougie and I enjoyed it so much. There is a point at the end of the track where it morphs brilliantly into 'The Story in Your Eyes', and it was just coming up to this point when I decided Dougie needed waking up. So making sure he was unaware of my presence by stealthily inching over to the tape deck, I twisted the volume control to maximum.

I don't believe I have ever witnessed a human rise in the air unassisted from a prone position before or since, and it could well have passed as the inspiration for the Harrier vertical take-off aircraft that followed years later. It was quite a sight with Dougie, eyes bulging, ripping off the cans, and hurling them with an impressive number of quality expletives in my direction.

'Sorry,' (I lied) 'I thought I was turning the volume down (I lied again). You coming to the Coop or what?'

'What?… eh? I can't hear a fucking thing. I think my eardrums have exploded.' Then after a lengthy pause with Dougie frantically poking his fingers in and out of his assaulted hearing tackle, asked: 'So, are we going to the Coop or what?'

'Er, yeah, but we had better get that pork in the oven first,' I suddenly remembered. 'It's a big old joint and will take some roasting.'

'Shit I nearly forgot,' Dougie admitted, and we hurried into the kitchen and bustled around with various pots and pans and began cutting the massive leg down to size. We eventually manhandled it into the oven which was set on a low temperature. 'Hold on, what about the roast potatoes,' he remembered as we made for the door.

'They'll be like bleeding golf balls if we put them in now.'

'Oh yeah…' And with that, we left the house, making sure to lock the front door, hoping that our two slumbering housemates had remembered where they had put their keys, and sped off to the Chicken Coop on the Suzuki. It has to be mentioned that the front door lock had been upgraded since our burglary experience, needing to be unlocked from inside as well as out, and knowing how lax we all were with keys… ah well, they could cope. There was always the back door.

We had our usual large breakfasts, a bit of most things on the menu for me, and because Dougie said he fancied something a bit different, he ordered six eggs on six slices of toast. 'With double home fries on the side,' he called after the waitress. We were relaxing and belching contentedly over our second mug of tea, discussing serious worldly matters such as how much rum did we think we managed to get through in one week? Well, we figured, taking into account the bottle we each always took to parties and made absolutely sure we always drank whilst there, plus our home consumption – which was marginal on account of the fact we were rarely home – my reckoning came to at least five bottles apiece. Dougie shrugged and said he didn't know, but that it must be: 'A shit load.'

There were also more weighty subjects up for discussion, like the book on Charles Manson that Doug had recently bought and was fascinated by. We both found it hard to comprehend that people like Manson could have so much power and influence over people. Dougie was not an avid reader, he had told me, having possessed just one book in the past, which was green he remembered, and had been useful when a leg on his coffee table needed bolstering.

We discussed the relative merits and attributes of the various ladies we knew, swapping details of some of the weeks' encounters and giving our opinions on the prospects for an eventful weekend ahead, even though we still had the current Sunday to get through.

'Better get back to that roast,' Dougie sighed resignedly.

I knew how he was feeling. 'Wish we hadn't offered to do it now.'

'Me too,' he said. 'But we'll make Ricky wish he'd never asked.'

I laughed. We had discussed just how much Rick could actually eat, after he had boasted to us that his appetite was equally as massive as ours and he could match us Limeys mouthful for mouthful.

We would see. We drained our mugs, stubbed out our Kools, and left the Coop.

Ricky had finally surfaced by the time we returned to the house. The first thing Dougie did was to hurry to the kitchen to inspect the pork, which having been in a low oven for only ninety minutes or so, had a good deal of roasting yet to do – which was fine as we did not intend eating for at least a couple or so more hours, giving our breakfast time to digest.

'You peel the spuds and I'll get the Yorkshire mix done when I've had a shower,' I told Doug, and took myself off to the bathroom as he crammed the massive pork joint, now cocooned in a coat of tin foil, back in the oven having increased the temperature. Graham had also surfaced, Rick informed us, and had already left the house to do whatever it was that he had arranged for his Sunday. This came as no surprise as he would often be playing football at some point over the weekend, or doing a spot of fishing with his mates; Graham and his weekend social life was a bit of a closed book to us. He would get very agitated with us when we teased him about how he never seemed to catch any fish for dinner, justifiably I suppose, because we were world class micky takers. We would sometimes catch a glimpse of him if he came back to shower and change before zooming off again to whatever other activity he was involved in, and like the rest of us, he would sometimes stay out overnight. It had been known for the house to be totally empty from Saturday afternoon through to Sunday evening, on the occasions when we had all found alternative accommodation for the night. But we preferred our own beds given the choice, because laziness dictated, and we agreed that it was much better to bring a companion back to the house whenever possible.

We all shared responsibilities at Carisbrook, but there was no obligation on any of our parts to necessarily spend our free time together. We were all able to lead separate lives if we so wished and although Doug and I tended to stick together most of the time, we too temporarily did our own thing when lovely young maids, who were prepared to tolerate us, put in an appearance.

Much later, we were enjoying some pre-luncheon beer when Ricky declared: 'I'm starving man, when the hell are we eating?' It was the third time he had asked the same question, having foregone breakfast by way of training for his promised typical English Sunday lunch.

I began to refill our beer glasses. 'Well have this and then it should be ready,' Doug told him, looking at his watch.

'I don't need any more beer,' Rick said, covering his glass with his hand.

'Yes you do. You wanted a typical English Sunday lunch and beer is a part of it.' I brushed his hand away, and poured the Amstel.

'We should have got some wine in,' he complained.

'We don't have wine with Sunday lunch in England,' Doug chipped in, and of course, in those days we didn't… at least not the working classes, which straining the imagination to its fullest extent, I guess we were part of.

If we were not entertaining, it was common practice for us to eat at the breakfast bar, aka one of the kitchen worktops, and that's what we were doing on this occasion, with Dougie and me sitting together on one side, opposite Ricky on the other. We had already dished up before calling for Ricky to come and *greeze*, and the look on his face as he hoisted himself up on the stool, was a treat to behold. Rick, all five foot three of him, momentarily disappeared behind his dinner plate stacked high with food and dominated by a pile of mashed potato of Himalayan proportions. It was lucky that within the kitchen's inventory were some super-size platters with the circumference of small dustbin lids – but only three. One had a nasty crack across the full length of its surface, which we gave to Rick. He was never going to notice it with the amount he had been served.

Rick peered around the mound of potatoes and with an astonished expression uttered, 'White mountain!' then disappeared again behind the spuds.

'Gravy?' Dougie enquired, and without waiting for an answer, poured a half pint of the stuff over the whole of Rick's plate, steaming up Rick's glasses in the process and which, along with his look of astonishment, gave him the appearance of a cartoon mole. We did not have the luxury of owning a gravy boat, but even if we had, it would have been nowhere large enough to take the amount of onion gravy we had made up and decanted into a large pottery jug that had hitherto held our unimpressive collection of utensils.

'And what are these things?' asked Rick, prodding his two huge Yorkshire puddings that accommodated a pile of roast potatoes.

'Yorkshire pud, now get it down your neck before it goes cold,' he was told.

In spite of our substantial breakfasts, Dougie and I set to with a vengeance, and having cleared our plates fifteen minutes later, we could not help smiling at the efforts of our housemate who had barely got through half the meal, and was mopping his brow furiously.

'How is it, Rick?' I asked.

'I'm done in man. Are you telling me this is what you eat in England… every Sunday?'

'Yep,' I confirmed. 'Another beer?' And before Rick could reply, Dougie interrupted. 'Custard with your apple tart?' and he produced a large tray from the oven holding an XXL sized pudding.

Rick's eyes goggled. 'You have got to be fucking joking,' he squeaked, as he staggered to his feet. 'I'm going for a lie down.' And he rolled out of the kitchen like a sailor coming ashore after a month at sea, and made his way to his bedroom where he stayed for the rest of the afternoon.

SIXTY-FOUR

Embarrassment is a funny thing. That's to say, what may be highly embarrassing circumstances for one person, could just as easily be a non-event, or simply mildly amusing to another. I suppose it all boils down to how self-confident you are and whether or not you give a monkey's about what others think. We are all different and whilst some people, like my erstwhile shy friends from my early days in Bermuda, accountant Ian and Canadian carpenter Dez are highly sensitive, others like Dougie really didn't give a toss one way or the other.

Men seem to be more prone to denial than women. If a bloke trips over in the street, he will immediately leap to his feet and carry on as if nothing has happened, whistling nonchalantly as he goes, even if he is in agonising pain and has two ends of a femur poking through his leg. It's because we men – apart from the obvious macho thing – hate to look like prize plonkers and show our embarrassment to the world. That's also the reason why we never ask for directions by the way, and explains why Moses took forty years to get out of the desert.

My one brief embarrassing moment when the barrack roof had been set alight the year before at the US military quarters at Kindley Field, had been nipped in the bud by the fire chief who, instead of giving me a rocket, had congratulated me on providing him and his team with a real live blaze that had taken them away from the tedium of constant drills and simulations. My embarrassment had performed a 180 degree turnaround and been transformed into feelings of pride and accomplishment.

But a cringe-inducing incident was about to happen one Sunday at Horseshoe Beach.

Several of us had indulged ourselves in some Mexican food the night before, and although I was not a lover of that country's cuisine because I knew from experience that the combination of ingredients would have an explosive effect on my system, it was a case of having a rare craving for a plate of chicken burritos. Beans in their various forms affect most people, but with me not at all – at least not unless they combine with certain other items, then watch out. As usual, I had ordered a larger than normal serving, and the combination of refried beans, hot chilli and lashings of sour cream and guacamole, had during the following morning developed from a suspicious rumble to a potential toxic discharge. I really should have known better.

There were a dozen or so of us at the beach that afternoon, and I had left the group on several occasions, ostensibly to take a refreshing dip, but in fact to make pretty green bubbles in the surf, well away from other bathers. Then I made a fatal error because, having had the feeling that another nuclear fart was on the way, instead of plunging into the water to let one go, I strolled over to a deserted piece of beach as casually as I dared, where there was no one in range to succumb to my version of a chemical weapon. As an aid to quick dispersal of said gases, there was a pleasant breeze blowing that afternoon and I was confident that as long as my look of extreme satisfaction as I offloaded didn't give the game away, I was quite safe.

Then three things happened in quick succession. I let go with what could be best described as an SBF – silent but fatal – trump, such was the pestilential aroma emanating from me. This was immediately followed by a sudden and complete drop in the steady breeze that up until then had been an ever-present weather feature; and thirdly, as if to order, Gaynor, one of our female companions, decided to skip over for a chat. I was tempted to wave my hands about in a forlorn attempt to disperse the almost visible cloud that hung off me like a dead tramp's vest, but that would have been pointless. All I could do was pray that the breeze would return with full force – and quickly. But of course, it didn't. Smelly farts are like faithful Labradors… you try to move away from them but they stick close.

'Phwoar! What's that pong?' I said, trying to bluff my way out of it as Gaynor approached. But she was having none of that old rubbish and she stopped dead with a look of extreme distaste, barely a yard from me. Then taking two exaggerated steps backwards – yes, she actually backed away from me – and waving her hand in front of her nose, she about turned, skirted around me and ran into the sea as if to cleanse herself of the noisome odour. The Gods were having a right old laugh that afternoon, because for the rest of that day and beyond, Gaynor pointedly avoided me, waving a hand back and forth in front of her face if I got near to her, as if to disperse a rotten smell, which of course was her way of rubbing my nose in it… so to speak. Of course her actions aroused the curiosity of the rest of the gang, and she took great pleasure in giving them the fetid details of my rebel innards.

Mare!

But I had to be thankful for small mercies, I suppose, and putting it into perspective I could have made things infinitely worse by following-through in my Hawaiian shorts, which *really* would have been what you call an embarrassing moment.

The incident at Horseshoe had got me thinking, and I made a mental note to suggest that we have a session at the house of *What Was Your Most Embarrassing Moment?* over drinks with the boys one night before descending on the Robin Hood. I reckoned there would be some amusing tales to tell. For my part, I could think of two or three from my past that would raise a grin or two.

When I was very young, running round the junior school playground in my baggy grey flannel short trousers with socks around my ankles, and the almost obligatory collection of grazes on my knees and elbows, I lost a pocket. That's right, a pocket.

My mum was about to throw out an old blazer of my dad's. It was a burgundy colour and a garment that I do not recall him ever wearing or would even think of wearing come to that. He was definitely a grey herringbone sort of bloke. Anyway, this particular jacket had patch pockets and I immediately saw the potential so I asked if I could remove one. This I saw as a very cool pouch for carrying around all my important stuff like conkers, a magnet, cigarette cards and a pen knife. Yep, a pen knife. Knife crime was unheard of back in the fifties unless you happened to live in downtown Chicago or London's East End. Kids could be trusted to use them properly for sharpening pencils, peeling apples and carving bits of wood – not people's faces. Every schoolboy owned one and what is more, with the full consent of our parents.

Then during one playtime period, the string securing my spiffing new pouch to my snake-buckled elasticated belt must have broken, because as we were all lining up ready to go back into class, a teacher, Miss Threapleton by name, held up a familiar object and asked the whole assembly (bless her) if anyone had lost a pocket. Reluctantly, with lowered head and smouldering cheeks, I stepped out of line and on skinny legs retrieved my prize possession accompanied by the laughter and jeers of a hundred school chums and, horror of horrors, a gang of sniggering teachers. Even at eight years old I fancied Miss Threapleton like mad and without knowing what I was supposed to do with a woman I was in love with, or what part of me I would do it with, I had nevertheless made up my mind I would marry Miss T one day. But then making our way back to the classroom with my face still glowing and the school's laughter still ringing in my ears, I decided that she had blown it for good with me, and I decided to rethink my marriage plans.

Another more recent incident transpired two years before I left England and involved my girlfriend at the time, the lovely Stevie. Back in the late sixties in the UK, when landlords were all powerful and tenants had little or no rights at all, Stevie had rented a bedsit in a rambling Victorian townhouse in what had once been a salubrious part of Reading. She had qualified as an SRN but having taken exception to some of the practices within the profession at that time, had decided to leave the NHS and enrolled with a local upmarket nursing agency.

One of the rules of the house where her flat was situated, was strictly no overnight stays, which of course most of the younger tenants often chose to ignore, including the two of us. Early one morning there was a sharp rap on the door and a voice, easily identifiable as the battle-axe landlady, demanded entry. I shot out of bed, grabbed my clothes but with nowhere to exit – because the bedsit was on the third floor and hanging out of the window was definitely not an option – I squeezed myself into the only available hiding place; a tiny cupboard with a stout door. Crouching into a ball and clutching my clothes, I could hear muffled voices as the crone was admitted, but although I had my ear pressed to the woodwork (I had no choice given the confined space) I was unable to make out what was being said and I definitely detected a male voice mixed in there somewhere. Then without warning the door was flung open and glaring down at me there she was in all her mythological glory – mythological in the sense, half woman half beast – and with forced jollity the only thing I could do was to smile and wish her a 'good morning,' as if this was the most natural thing in the world.

But then after taking in the pathetic piece of humanity for several seconds, she hissed in a measured tone: 'Out of the way, I need to read the meter.' I hadn't noticed that in fact this was the meter cupboard and I had been wedged tight between it and the door. It was a difficult task, but having cleared a space by heaving myself into a contortionist's stance, I eventually managed it. I was definitely not going to extract myself from that version of Calcutta's black hole and expose myself in full daylight. Then having completed her task, she closed the door on my naked form, leaving me in total darkness once again still clutching my bundle... stop sniggering, you know what I mean.

Hypocritically, the male voice I had heard turned out to be the landlady's toyboy live-in lover. One rule for the tenants and one rule for the landlady it seemed, because with Romeo present, Stevie had been summoned to endure a dressing down later that day, and having done so, was given a 'final warning' on pain of eviction. It was all cringingly embarrassing at the time for sure, but a story I have dined out on many times since.

As a footnote, Stevie had decided that she would be better off elsewhere, and without notice and having paid her rent in full to avoid any repercussions, she temporarily moved back with her parents while she searched for suitable alternative accommodation. But revenge is sweet and unbeknown to Stevie at the time, with the help of a work colleague and a firm's van, I collected Stevie's belongings as arranged, and making sure the landlady was nowhere in the vicinity, also removed the door to Stevie's erstwhile bedsit and manhandled it into our vehicle. Stevie's things were delivered to her as promised, and the bedsit door was last spotted in the Thames passing under Marlow Bridge.

We never did get that 'What Was Your Most Embarrassing Moment?' evening in, but if we had, Dougie would probably have quoted an incident that had happened in the recent past when coming home very late one night and extremely bladdered, he drove into the garage and immediately became disorientated and unable to find his way out, even though it was your regular sized lean-to affair. It caused much hilarity when he told us later that morning, but the laugh would be on me some weeks in the future, when I was to have a similar experience in a 'magic forest'.

SIXTY-FIVE

It is no exaggeration to say that for me, there was not one weekend during the whole of my time in Bermuda that was not memorable. Perhaps it was something that occurred during a Friday night Elbow Beach session or at one of the interminable parties. Perhaps on the water and camping out on one of the small islands; an excellent evening of entertainment at the Forty Thieves, or a weekend spent in New York. And more often than not, the company of a pretty lady. Often a combination of several of those things.

It was shaping up to be a busy weekend – busier than the normal busy weekend that is. Friday night was going to be the usual Robin Hood gathering before going on to our habitual Elbow Beach super soirée; followed by a party given by someone we had never heard of, at a house we had not been to, but one that offered a Chinese supper as well as the usual party capers, we had been reliably informed. A free greeze and a rave; this was our sort of shindig. This may or may not mean breakfast on the way home at our restaurant extraordinaire, depending on the time and the quantity of the Chinese nosh, but almost certainly a breakfast of some sort would be called for. We needed our sustenance. Then it would be home for a couple of hours of welcome shut-eye followed by an also much-needed shower, and then having sorted out smart shirts and strides, make our way to a friend's wedding reception. Following the reception, the party that night was being held at a house off Middle Road in Devonshire, where we knew there was a large swimming pool – so a lot of potential there – then once again an early breakfast / late supper, before home and bed.

On to Sunday where we would meet up with the usual gang of friends at Horseshoe Bay at lunch time, having stopped off at the infamous Roach Coach for some liquid refreshment to take with us, and an afternoon arsing about on the beach and showing off our Frisbee prowess, interspersed with swimming and an undoubted much-needed cooling off in the inviting waters. And hopefully for me, the presence of Janet, who I just could not get out of my mind. At the very least, there would be the usual fooling around with some of the ever-present contingent of beach lovelies. Then on to Flamingo Beach where there was always live music on a late Sunday afternoon, where we would sink a few beers before returning home for a rest before another evening at our favourite watering hole.

Yes, it was looking to be a busy and eventful couple of days.

The Friday night went as expected with the normal letting down of hair after a busy week's work, at Elbow Beach, and the joyous prospect of a lively weekend ahead, with the bonus event of a late-night Friday party with grub. It was a lively affair; the drink flowed, the music was fairly sedate for a change, lending itself to a lot of smoochy dancing with some of Dougie's 'downy thighed nymphs' in attendance. The party was slightly unusual in that proper food was on offer, not just the usual assorted nibbles. A buffet supper of Chinese food was laid out on a trestle table that was constantly being replenished from the kitchen. It was almost a losing battle because no sooner had another dish appeared than the locust shape-shifters posing as human guests, made it disappear faster than a choir boy's pants in a priest's confessional. There were a few fresh faces present including a bloke about our age that Dougie and I had taken great schoolboy delight in learning was a native of Norfolk. This presented us with a great chance to try out our Norfolk accents, or at least our interpretation of that brogue.

His name was Barry and it transpired that he was a resident of the city of Norwich, but strangely seemed to have very little or no trace of a Norfolk accent much to our disappointment. But as we chatted to him, we mercilessly began to yank his chain with our own renditions of the dialect.

'Ar ya roit baw?' enquired Dougie as we approached Barry.

There was a look of disquiet on Barry's face. 'I'm very well thank you,' which prompted stifled giggles from us.

'Where yew frum then baw?' Dougie knew perfectly well where he came from.

'Oi rekun he's 'merican,' I hazarded.

''Merican?... You know how t'ride hoss?' Dougie was milking it.

There was more consternation; are they taking the piss Barry must have been thinking, then cautiously... 'I'm from Norwich. What about you?' We ignored the question and ploughed on.

'Narch, where's that at?' Then before he could respond to my question...

'Jus den rud,' Dougie happily informed me.

Barry was now eyeing us menacingly. There was an ominous silence; our Norfolk friend was looking totally jarred off with our mickey taking and he just stood there, one hand on hip, the other toting a full beer bottle, staring at the two morons in front of him.

But Dougie was determined to keep it up and challenged him: 'Wus up then?'

Then quite calmly under the circumstances Barry leant forward and said: 'Why don't you two bugger off and annoy someone else.' We were being dismissed albeit now with a slightly amused look on Barry's face in spite of himself. Nevertheless, we thought we would leave in the manner in which we had arrived.

'No need t'be horsetile,' I cut in as we turned away to get refills at the bar.

'Horsetile?' Dougie's turn to look puzzled as we walked away.

'It's jes a eggspreshun.'

'I dona wot yhoore talken 'bout baw.'

'Me nether,' I confessed, then we dissolved into childish laughter again, which continued through the egg noodles and chicken gong bao, much to the detriment of our shirts that were newly washed and clean on that evening.

After a couple of hours' sleep and a late breakfast at the Coop (it was after 10am, so very late for us) we decided that it would be rude of us if we did not drop by the Hood for a pre-lunchtime drink before going back home to change for the wedding reception. The function was informal in the sense that it was not a sit down do, and was held as we expected, outside in the extensive gardens. It was a pleasing way to spend the afternoon. There was a huge spread and the bar was free, with guests helping themselves. All very civilized. We were elated to see that there was no shortage of our favourite Cockspur rum, and even a couple of bottles of the delightful Goslings Black Seal. Then after wishing the happy couple maritial bliss; the best of British luck, and Dougie elbowing the groom playfully as he confided: 'she's a great shag,' we set about circulating with the many familiar faces present on a pre-planned course to the massive table of goodies. It had been three hours since breakfast.

We had managed to put away a bottle and a half of our favoured tipples in total, when I looked at my watch and noticed in a somewhat blurred fashion, that it was time to make a move and get back home for a shower and a rest before embarking on our evening's activities, which would culminate with that night's thrash at the Devonshire house. But Dougie was not ready to leave. There was a half bottle of rum that we had started and still required finishing and he was nothing if not mindful of avoiding leftovers. 'But how are you going to get back to Carisbrook?' I asked him. Although according to Dougie later, what I actually said was: 'sowar yooo gwinta geba toooo Carsbroo?'

'Don't worry about that,' he said. 'There'll be someone who will take me'... No fair's fair, it was: 'dun rowee bat tat dheeere, illbysumwun hooo'll tek hic me.' This exchange was overheard and confirmed to us later by a highly amused couple of friends.

After one failed attempt, I managed to jump a little shakily on to my devoted Suzuki and ride off; not so much with a roar but more of a throaty shriek, or was that from me? I really don't recall.

I had been home for an hour or so, having had a long and refreshing soak under a tepid shower and was relaxing with the latest copy of *Playboy*, listening to some Grand Funk Railroad who were loudly proclaiming – in case I was in any doubt – that *We're An American Band*, when Dougie crashed in. His language was a dark shade of blue with an impressive number of new words whose meanings were nevertheless crystal clear, and he had dirt and a collection of scratches to his face. His hair was reminiscent of a yak's arse; his shirt was torn; there was a long tapering rip in one leg of his strides, and he carried a blue shoe in one hand (blue was the colour that weekend). I stared at him for a moment in amazement. 'What the hell happened to you?'

'I need a drink,' he growled, 'and a shower, in that order.' He hobbled over to what passed for our drinks cabinet and poured himself a stiff whatever it was that came first to hand. Then he threw himself down on the sofa. Another drink was almost certainly what he didn't need, but I wasn't going to tell him that and push my luck. Who was I to talk? He'll tell me when he has calmed down, I thought. He did, and it went like this:

Having polished off the last of the bottle we had started earlier at the wedding reception, he looked around for who might give him a lift back to Carisbrook. Dougie had been talking to the lovely Angela shortly before and she had told him that she would be staying on and if he needed to leave, then he was welcome to borrow her Vespa scooter. There certainly would not have been any shortage of lift offers for Angela if needed later that was for sure. So not having found anyone who was leaving at that precise time, in the direction of Hamilton or Mount Hill, Dougie took Angela up on the offer. There was a moderately long driveway to the house but it was only after a few yards that Dougie managed to twist the accelerator a bit too mightily and bouncing off the boundary wall at speed, landed in a tangle in the gravel. The result was a scraped and scratched and thoroughly pissed off Dougie, and a Vespa with the handlebars now facing back the way they had come. The steering stem had snapped.

'Bloody hell, what did Angela say…? Oops?' I hazarded. I couldn't help the slight attempt at humour. Dougie, although dishevelled, was obviously not seriously hurt, just injured pride.

'She wasn't pleased is the best way I can describe it,' he said. 'I told her I would get it fixed. Holy shit, it's going to cost me an arm and a leg.'

'And you didn't even get out of the drive,' I ribbed him. 'But it could have been worse.'

'Oh really, how?'

'Well, it could have been me.'

'Yeah, very funny. I need a shower.' And he hobble-stomped off to the bathroom.

One thing about Dougie is that he's resilient and one of life's eternal optimists, because less than an hour later looking more like his usual self with a change of clothes and his scratches hardly noticeable after some gentle lathering, he bounced into the lounge.

'So what's the plan?

'No plan,' I said. 'Take it easy for a while if you like, then we'll meet the others at the Hood.'

'I'm ready now, let's go,' he enthused. Dougie was bloody amazing.

Then I remembered. Terry's mini cooper was back on the road. 'Terry said he would pick us up in his motor if we wanted. I'll give him a call.' I didn't really feel up to taking the bike out again if I didn't have to, and after Dougie's near-death experience, I didn't want the accident-prone git sitting behind me on the Suzuki that night, thank you very much.

'Sounds good to me; you can be a bit of a mad bastard on that bike,' and he laughed that rumbling Dougie laugh. Angela's injured bike and the impending repair bill was very firmly filed away in one of the hidden recesses of Dougie's mind – at least for the time being.

As it happened, we had to wait another hour for Terry to arrive, accompanied by Rob who he had collected at Deepdene Manor where he worked. Rick had arrived back at the house in that time and having got himself ready for the evening, asked if he could tag along with us. It was a squeeze at the best of times with four of us in that small car, but what the hell, Rick was not the biggest of guys and so he was shoehorned into the back between Dougie and me. It was a short drive to the Robin Hood from Mount Hill, but that evening's party was way out in Southampton, so the idea of Terry driving us was an attractive one. The term 'way out' is of course a relative one and in terms of Bermuda, it meant we had to cover mileage that didn't even get into double figures. For me as usual, with a couple of hours rest after a session, I felt as right as ninepence and raring to go, and Dougie's recent experience featuring the argument with an innocent wall, along with the excessive booze, also seemed to have been put behind him. To a casual observer we were both as sober as proverbial judges, but that was the advantage of having youthful metabolisms.

Where did those days go?

It was a particularly jolly evening at the Hood, with an even more packed house than usual, and so it was approaching midnight when we decided to move on – along with half the pub it seemed and we became part of a mixed convoy of cars and two-wheeled conveyances. We had whipped up our party enthusiasm at the bar to such an extent that we arrived at the brightly lit house on Middle Road, not far from the Port Royal Golf Club, and hit the ground running. Dougie was in his *bumping* mood and jumped straight in with a couple of girls who were dancing by the pool. They were either unaware of Dougie's reputation on the dance floor, or were two attractive masochists.

I knew that Janet and Robert would be there and hoped that I would be able to manage to get a dance or two with Janet without making it too obvious how I was beginning to feel about this lovely woman. The sound of Bachman Turner Overdrive and 'Taking Care of Business' was currently blasting out, and which under normal circumstances would have had me leaping around the dance floor like a demon, but perhaps a bit of the Roberta Flack or Olivia Newton-

John and other smooch-friendly music would be more appropriate before I asked Janet for a dance. Reflecting back years later, Janet and I later adopted Olivia's 1974 song '*I* Honestly Love You' as our personal anthem, which I know will prompt much sticking of forefingers down throats and mock gaggings.

As it turned out, I was being over cautious and although we did manage a good deal of time together that evening, with Robert chatting to acquaintances on and off, it was Dougie that targeted Janet each time a bump number was played, and he spent more time with her than I did.

I had no idea what could possibly develop between me and Janet. She was married to a thoroughly nice bloke and although I knew instinctively that there was a mutual attraction between us, I could not see any future beyond the next party or a chance meeting in a bar or restaurant. To cover up my excessive interest I forced myself to do my fair share of circulating and dancing with several of the mini-skirted and hot-panted partygoers in the customary manner. All that talent, and I only had eyes for the blonde stunner who was already permanently attached. What was wrong with me? I asked myself for the hundredth time.

Later, the song that was being played was 'The Streak' and I looked for Dougie in the crowd, half expecting him to take his cue from the music, strip off, run a full circuit of the pool and jump in yelling 'Geronimo!' I located him still fully clothed, but wearing a policeman's helmet; where the hell did he get that from? I had not been aware that the Old Bill had put in an appearance, but there was my mate bumping away as if his life depended on it to the Ray Stevens song. It was not even a dance number of any description in my book, but then Dougie could bump to anything – even The National Anthem, if pushed.

Then I saw an irate looking man in uniform making his way through the throng towards Dougie. Oh no, the cop was destined for the pool, I just knew it. Once he managed to catch up with Dougie it was a dead cert that they would both end up very wet.

I knew how Dougie's mind worked, especially with the aid of Cockspur rum. But no, I was wrong, instead as the cop was about to grab Dougie, it was the lawman's helmet that ended up doing the breaststroke as it was tossed high in the air and landed with an unlawful splash in the deep end. Everyone was in hysterics and the vexed policeman shook his head in disbelief as he attempted to extricate his pointy headwear from the water which was already being used in a mock game of water polo. Then excitement over with the cop eventually retrieving his headgear, everyone returned to the important business of having a bloody good time, and with a sad expression of acceptance, a meek looking plod shook his saturated helmet (steady on, you know what I'm saying) and headed for the gate as unobtrusively as possible.

We never did find out why he had been there in the first place, and he probably shouldn't have been, which would account for his diffident behaviour. Whatever; it had obviously been a very short and not very sweet experience for him.

We piled back into Terry's car about 4am with poor Rick wedged tight between Rob and me in the back. Dougie had made it very clear that he was not going to be crammed into the back on the return leg home.

'You know what, Rick, I never realised it before, but you are a very attractive man,' I told him earnestly.

Rick stared at me disbelievingly with a half-smile on his face as if to say, *This is a joke right?* then swivelled his head sharply at the sound of Rob's voice.

'That's right, and what's that aftershave you're wearing? It's driving me crazy,' and we both leapt on Rick.

'You crazy Limey bastards,' he screamed as he disentangled himself. 'I should have known better than to get a lift with you guys.' Everyone in the Mini was laughing except the unfortunate Rick Correia. We always managed to throw him a curveball at some point, but he never took offence for long, and this time he followed up with one of his own: 'Besides,' he said, 'Terry and me are engaged – tell 'em Terry.'

'That's right, he's my bitch, keep your hands off.'

Now we were all laughing.

'Are we stopping at the Chicken Coop?' Dougie asked. 'I could eat a bleeding donkey.'

'That's what they usually put in the sausages at the Coop,' Rob contributed, wearing his chef's hat.

'I don't fancy it,' added Terry. I just want to contemplate on a cocoa then hit the sack; it's been a long day and night.'

'Not as long as ours… that right, Colin? And since when did you drink cocoa?' Dougie added.

'Since Mr Correia and me got together.'

'Come on you guys. Tell them Colin, we always stop at the Coop.' Dougie was starting to sound desperate.

'I know,' I said, 'but I filled up at the party. That was a good spread tonight; and I'm knackered too.'

A note of what bordered on panic crept into Dougie's voice. 'So did I, but that wasn't proper grub. I'm starving. What about you, Rick?'

'Nah, I'm pooped, man.' Ricky was also being uncooperative.

'You bastards.' And then as if he had regressed twenty years and was once again a small boy who could not get his own way, Dougie whined: 'But I wanna stop for some breakfast… go on Terry, pleeease.' If he had been able to stamp his foot in frustration, he would have, although that would have been an unwise move in Terry's Mini.

Unmoved by the tantrum, Terry drove on as Dougie swore and cursed at us throughout the rest of the ride. 'I'm gonna get my own back on you lot,' he promised as we drew up outside Carisbrook. 'You just wait.' And he flounced off to the house ahead of us, still muttering under his breath.

'You guys fancy a nightcap with us?' I asked Terry and Rob. They looked at each other in silence for a second or two as if deciding on some far-reaching issue, then:

'Yeah, go on then,' said Rob.

'The cocoa will still be there when I get home, so let's live it up,' added Terry. To be honest, I did not recall any of us at any time, day or night, ever refusing the prospect of another drink, so their acceptance was purely routine.

Dougie was obviously in the kitchen when we got inside, evidenced by the loud clattering of pots and pans along with muffled curses from that direction. What was he doing?

'Okay what's your pleasure?' Rick had elected to be barman and began to administer drinks. We had just made ourselves comfortable having selected *Tubular Bells* as the album of choice, when Dougie rushed into the room carrying a part empty box of eggs. Then still in his sulky schoolboy mode, he held them up and shouted at us: 'Eight eggs see... and I'm having 'em all,' adding as an afterthought: 'And you're not having any... bastards,' before galumphing off back to the kitchen. This struck us as the funniest thing we had ever witnessed, and illustrated it by laughing uproariously and triggering yet more shouts and swearing from the kitchen. The last we heard from Dougie that night was just before he went into his bedroom and, giving out a last mighty heartfelt 'Bastards!', he slammed his door in a final show of displeasure.

And that was just Saturday. What did Sunday have in store for us?

SIXTY-SIX

In spite of having necked a plateful of omelette, which had started out as scrambled egg, just four hours before, Dougie was still up for a breakfast at the Coop, albeit one of a moderate size by his standards. He seemed to have forgotten already the melodrama a few short hours previous. Then it was on to Horseshoe Bay via a stop at the familiar and infamous Roach Coach, where I had made the mistake of indulging in one of their shit-through-the-eye-of-a-needle burgers the year before, and purchased several cans of soda to take to the beach. I still hadn't eaten from there since, nor would I be at any time in the future. Canned items were pretty safe, especially as we always washed them thoroughly with sea water before burying them in the sand to keep cool before another wash then consumption during the afternoon. Purchasing them from the Coach had become the regular practice. But perhaps unbelievably, there was no alcohol. For some reason, we never took beer or any other booze to the beach and it became the accepted norm – probably because invariably we would have already absorbed several quarts of the stuff over the previous thirty-six hours and wisely deciding that we would give our livers a brief vacation. But whatever the reason it wasn't a bad decision looking back. But it didn't prevent us from sinking several beers later at Flamingo Beach, which was always sandwiched between our afternoon at the beach and our evening exploits.

Terry and Rob arrived shortly after us at the beach; poor old Rob having had to prep lunches at the hotel before he could knock off. Then others arrived during the afternoon and it was not hard to see why Horseshoe was a regular haunt for many of the ex-pats. It was not uncommon for us to have a dozen or so in our little clique. We talked and laughed a lot during those Sunday afternoons; laughter was the one commodity that filled our non-working time in great abundance, and is forever present when reminiscing our early- to mid-seventies days in those beautiful islands. Frisbee was a popular beach game and we would throw ourselves around with great abandon to show off our prowess with the plastic disc, and even though I say it myself, we had become expert in the art; especially if there were leggy beach beauties nearby whom we were trying to impress. Rick would often be borne out to sea, carried over our heads on a Li-lo and ceremoniously dumped to great applause, but don't ask me why, it was just part of the routine. And there were often competitions to see who could stay upright the longest, carrying young ladies on our shoulders and doing our damnedest to topple the competition. It was during one of these escapades, that a silver dolphin-head torque bracelet I wore, was torn off in the fracas, never to be seen again. On another Sunday yet to come, I would lose a silver and garnet ring that Stevie had given me. All because of our silly games.

If we had a bored moment, one of us would dash out of the surf yelling 'SHARK' at the top of our voice and take bets on which American tourist would be last one out. The only sharks that might conceivably be close inshore were small nurse sharks and pretty harmless. But the Yanks didn't know that. All of these juvenile activities carried out by twenty-something adults, but harmless, hilarious and uncomplicated fun. The sand at Horseshoe, like other beaches, has of course that blushing pink hue that was synonymous with Bermuda, and crystal-clear waters where brilliantly coloured parrot fish were a common sight – often nosing you gently out of sheer curiosity, or cavorting playfully with each other. It was as close to paradise as you could ever get.

But then I might have mentioned that already.

Sunday had been standard issue up to that point, then at about what we British term as teatime, it was down the road to Flamingo Beach for a few beers as a precursor to the evening's entertainment; more chat with friends, and the added enjoyment of some live music, which that afternoon turned out to be a jazz band. Modern jazz is my least favourite of musical genres, I have to say. It has always sounded to me like a collection of diverse instruments all competing to change a basic melody into something that barely resembles the original, and sometimes in the most bizarre way. But that's me, and to be honest, it was perfectly suitable as wallpaper to the important part of the afternoon that was all about meeting up with more friends and enjoying the late afternoon Bermuda sun.

The speed limit on the island was 20 mph, and a mere 15 mph in town as I previously explained, and with its sub-tropical climate, most of us got around by some sort of motorised two-wheeled means; in my case the sporty Suzuki trail bike that had replaced my ignominious, red and white Honda moped but which, in fairness, had been honest and trustworthy whilst in my care. As usual, I had ridden the Suzuki to the beach with Doug as passenger, and having spent an hour or so at the beach bar with the rest of our gang, Dougie and I decided that it was time to return home for some much-needed grub and a freshen up in preparation for the coming evening. We had perhaps downed two beers... well alright, maybe four... at the most, and as we never took alcohol to Horseshoe, we were definitely not feeling the worse for wear. A little weary perhaps having had a strenuous Friday and Saturday with only a little sleep between events, but that was nothing unusual and just about par for the course, so what happened next was certainly not because of being unduly under the influence, but more an error of judgement.

The 'standard' Sunday was about to become a memorable one.

As I kicked the bike over and Dougie had clambered aboard, I revved the engine – as blokes with motorcycles do – and simultaneously, but inadvertently, slipped the clutch with far too much vigour. The front end shot skyward, then with me goggle-eyed and wondering what had happened, and my pillion passenger screaming in my ear, we executed the perfect wheelie as we tore down the drive. The spectacle brought the patrons to their feet, whooping, whistling and applauding our brilliant skills. Little did they know. It was a manoeuvre I never thought possible with a pillion passenger and certainly not one that I would have attempted through choice, and most *definitely* not one that I could ever believe would end happily. But it did, and we kept on going like professionals. Luckily the cheering crowd could not see the terror on our faces and hear the stream of expletives that issued from our mouths as we miraculously sped one-wheeled away from the bar.

Once we were out of sight we reverted to two-wheels with a bump, and having made South Road, I stopped the bike to take a breath. 'Jesus, man, what happened?' asked Dougie.

'Buggered if I know, but have you ever seen a wheelie like that?' I enthused.

'No and I don't want to see another one you mad bastard.' It was only then that I had to admit to my friend that it was utterly and comprehensively unintentional, and was merely the result of a cock-up on my part.

'Well I won't tell anyone if you don't,' he said. 'They think we're bloody heroes.' He was right, we were, and in spite of our terror a minute before, we both broke out in broad grins, before setting off for home and a change of underwear. This time a little more sedately.

I am told that ageing Bermudians who were present that day, still relate the story to their grandchildren... the wheelie, not the underwear or the screaming pillion passenger.

We kept those details to ourselves.

SIXTY-SEVEN

A tradition had been established at Carisbrook that after dinner on a Friday evening, taken either at home or at one of our favourite eateries, we would relax at the house for an hour or so before setting out for our evening's entertainment, listening to some crazy Cheech and Chong tapes or a selection of music catering to our eclectic tastes, and amusing ourselves in a card session playing the game called Crazy Eights. Without going into the intricacies of the game, of which there are very few it has to be said, the bottom line is that when one player manages to get rid of all his cards, the others have to total up what is left in their hands, and having set a cut-off point of say, five hundred, the player with the lowest total at the end of the session is the overall winner. There are three master cards, one of which is the deuce which, when laid, requires the next player to pick up two cards unless he himself can produce a deuce. Therefore, if three players lay down a two and the fourth player cannot follow suit, then he has to pick up two plus two, plus two – six cards to add to what he already holds. If one of the other players then manages to go out by laying his last card, the poor devil that picked up six is left with a mitt full. There are two other master cards that require missing a go and changing the suit, but that's immaterial to the story.

There was always the usual banter between the players, sometimes involving just Dougie, Graham, Rick and me, but on numerous occasions, included Terry and Rob. More often than not, with a bit of creative play – aka cheating – we were able to catch Rick with a fist full of cards and a massive total, at which point he would storm off to his room muttering his usual impressive collection of expletives which always contained the familiar accusation of 'Limey bastards.' He would make a big play of slamming his door shut and seconds later turn his stereo player to full volume with hopefully something to our musical taste. It was a regular feature of those card schools, but it never failed to raise hoots of laughter from the rest of us. Then later, after having prepared ourselves for the evening, one of us would knock on Rick's door and shout above the music that we were ready to go, at which point he would appear with a big smile on his face as if nothing had happened and fall in with us as we left the house.

We had on numerous occasions run into Janet and Robert at various locations – sometimes by accident and others by design. Always by my design that is, because through devious means I would sometimes be able to discover what their plans were and make sure that I, and often the rest of the gang, would show up. There were also occasions when seemingly innocent, I made sure Robert knew where the big party was on a Saturday night and hoped that he and Janet would turn up. I could not see any future in these actions, but on the other hand I could not get Janet out of my head.

There was one such instance when purely by chance as it happened, Janet and her Bermudian work colleague Jeannie, were at Horseshoe Beach one Sunday afternoon. Robert, it transpired, was a cycling fanatic, and was off with his pals somewhere on the island working the pedals. Rick had already confided to us that Jeannie, a very attractive Bermudian, who he had met during his regular hairdressing forays into the salon where she and Janet worked, was much to his fancy and he had tried several times to persuade her to go out with him, always without success. I was glad to have the opportunity to flirt with Janet of course, and she even joined us in our antics with the Frisbee, where we all showed off our athletic abilities and acrobatics with the flying disc.

That afternoon Janet had asked me about the history of the group of scars that I have on my abdomen. I sighed, sat her down beside me and with a serious expression, told her that two years before Bermuda, I was walking past one of the banks in my home town of Reading, when two masked robbers hurtled out into the street and ran towards a waiting car. Without thinking, I gave chase, but one of the men, armed with a sawn-off shotgun, let fly at me, hitting me in the abdomen. Luckily I was some yards behind him, and the spread-shot had caused painful, but thankfully limited damage. Any closer, I told her, and it would have been far more serious, possibly fatal. Janet's mouth was open in amazement as I related this story.

It was only much later that I told Janet the true story relating to those scars.

When I was eighteen years old, I developed a beauty of an ingrown big toenail – wearing those winkle picker shoes for too long, I was told. Being young and irresponsible I let it go on for far too long before seeing my doctor. The nail had grown through the flesh and had reached the underside of my toe – it was a mess and I was admitted to hospital. It was impossible to remove just the nail, so my toe was effectively quartered and one side of it was completely taken away, nail and all.

I had been in the hospital for over a week and there was no sign of me being allowed home, which jarred me off considerably. I made such a fuss that the surgeon who had performed the operation told me that he would sign me off, only if I agreed to skin grafts being taken and that thereafter, I also promised to use a crutch until I returned for a change of dressing – or however long he deemed it necessary to keep my weight off that foot. The result was twelve pinch grafts from my abdomen. This is a method where the skin is pinched and the fold cut off with surgical scissors giving an oval shaped piece of flesh. They would need to take twelve because not all would be successful; indeed, he told me, there was a possibility that none of them would take, in which case it would be back to square one. Only one of the grafts was successful as it turned out, and although that was enough, it meant that the healing would take longer.

And that was it. The scars were a leftover from the pinch grafts.

Janet had believed every word about the bank robbers, and when I eventually told her the truth, she and the boys fell about laughing, but she knew to take everything from then on with a very large handful of salt.

Ricky had decided to give it another go at chatting Jeannie up that afternoon, which as it turned out was another wasted effort and left him even more determined. Janet had whispered to me that Jeannie liked our pal, but had no other interest whatsoever, and had tried without success to let him down lightly. Jeannie was getting to the stage, I was told, that she was simply going to have to tell Rick to bugger off and leave her alone, but she was reluctant to be that blunt, and besides, she valued him as a friend.

It was later that day when we had all arrived back at the house; showered, fed and relaxing, with our late afternoon drinks accompanied that evening by Mr Bowie and his crew, *Ziggy Stardust, Major Tom, Aladdin Sane,* and the rest, before scooting off to the Robin Hood, when the phone rang. It was me that answered and having listened to what the caller told me, I handed the phone to Rick. 'It's for you, mate.' Then I gestured for Dougie to join me in the kitchen.

'Who's on the phone?' Dougie asked.

'Jeannie. Janet's friend,' I told him, and then outlined what Janet had told me that afternoon on the beach. 'I think she's called to blow him out.'

'She could blow me anytime,' Dougie sniggered.

We gave it a few minutes before we returned to the lounge, where we encountered a down at heart looking Rick. 'What did Jeannie want?' I asked, full well knowing the answer already.

He looked at me sorrowfully and said: 'You had better sit down, Colin.'

Oh really, I thought. What in the hell is going on here?

'The thing is, Jeannie has just told me why she keeps turning me down.' He paused as if trying to find the right words.

'Well go on then, hit me.' I was getting impatient.

'Jeannie is in love with Janet,' he blurted out. 'I think they are a couple of dykes.'

I looked at Dougie and he looked at me, then after a long pause and not able to hold it in any longer, we burst into laughter much to Rick's consternation.

'It's not fucking funny, man!'

'It is at it happens,' I told him. 'I think it's you who needs to sit down and I'll try to explain.' And I did, with Dougie still chortling away in the background. It was Jeannie's way of letting Ricky down lightly, and in the process had come up with a brilliant story, but one that in conscience I could not allow Rick to believe. His face was a picture when I spelled it out for him, with Dougie still sat, nursing his drink grinning like a Cheshire cat that had got the rum, if you'll excuse the blitzed metaphor.

SIXTY-EIGHT

Two of the lads had some holiday time coming up, and having talked about flying down to Jamaica and spending a few days at the Playboy Club Hotel in Ocho Rios on several occasions, they thought it might be a good idea to put our talk into practice. But Dougie would find it difficult to justify taking days off from his workplace, he told us, and it presented a similar problem for me, so the idea was quickly abandoned. It was all of us or none at all we had agreed, besides, the cost would be substantial. So consigning the plan to the pending tray, with a view to resurrecting the boys-only Jamaica trip at some future time, we set-to looking into what was happening the following weekend.

It was Thursday; I had managed to finish work early on what was the last day before a long weekend, with Friday marking Bermuda Day, and therefore a national holiday. I had showered and was relaxing with a long cool drink listening to some relaxing and soothing music courtesy of Cat Stevens and his brilliant *Foreigner* album, when suddenly the front door flew open crashing against the wall, and a blur of denim shot up the corridor heading towards the bathroom. It was Dougie and he was clearly in need of liberating something desperately, then seconds later the door to the smallest room in the house slammed shut behind him. It was ten minutes before a relieved but somewhat worried looking Dougie emerged and he began noisily fishing around in the kitchen cupboards. I put down my drink and asked him what he was looking for. 'A bucket,' was the answer.

'It's outside the back door,' I told him and obliged by going outside and bringing in the required article. 'So what's up?'

'I can't get rid of it,' he said.

'Can't get rid of what?'

'The biggest Richard the Third you've ever seen,' he boasted. The flush on the loo wouldn't do the job it appeared and so he was going to try and sluice it away with a bucket of water. This I had to see, even though the thought of it made me somewhat nervous – especially in view of Dougie's diet.

'Bloody hell, Doug, now what have you been eating?' I asked as I stared incredulously at the *thing* that was wedged solid and standing proud on the water like some gigantic up-ended brownie. 'Hold on,' I said, 'I had better call the Sanitary Department and warn them what's coming down the line – they're gonna need extra staff.'

Ignoring my remark, he moved me to one side and threw the contents of the bucket into the bowl with such force, that water splashed over the rim of the loo. But the Richard held firm, and I had visions of it smiling and winking at Dougie's efforts. This called for some drastic action and Dougie rushed out of the bathroom, with me feeling duty bound to stand guard in case the stool from the black lagoon attempted to escape into the house. Minutes later Dougie returned wielding a spatula and set about attacking the offending article with gusto. The sight of it was too much for me and I retreated to the lounge where my now very welcome and abandoned drink was awaiting my return.

Looking victorious and rather pleased with himself, Dougie duly appeared in the doorway brandishing the… now how can I put this… tarnished spatula, and with my imagination working overtime, it seemed somewhat akin to a latter-day Arthur having pulled a shitty Excalibur out of the stone and holding it aloft in triumph.

'It's gone!' he proudly announced, and then the new slimmed

down and considerably lighter Dougie, grinned and poured himself a drink, and I just knew that here was a story I would be recounting for many years to come.

Later that evening, we met Terry and Rob and decided on the Rum Runners pub to kick off our evening's entertainment, and were lucky enough to latch on to a group of likely looking ladies. They were good company and we shared a lot of laughs as usual, and swopped exaggerated stories of our past lives. One girl in particular had caught my eye and we were getting on like a house on fire (fires being a particular speciality of mine). She was a delightful young thing and I had the good fortune to fix up a date for the Saturday night. Then without warning and within the hearing of my three mates, she declared quite brazenly: 'As long as you know that I don't screw on first dates', which unsurprisingly brought sarcastic 'oohs' and 'aahs' and derisive laughter from the boys, and other patrons who were within earshot and had joined in the fun. After a thoughtful pause I asked: 'In that case are you free on Sunday as well?' which, I was pleased to note, was received with loud cheers of hilarious support from the crowd.

There being no work Friday, Graham, Rick and a few others had joined us and we had got together over a large lunch at the Henry VIII restaurant, which somehow had morphed into the evening without our noticing. It seemed pointless moving on, so we made a day of it, and ordered dinner.

I spent the Saturday morning browsing through cassettes at the Sounds Plus and Music City record stores; met up with Mary for coffee in the Washington Mall, and had a cheeseburger lunch at the Dick and Tickle, which had pretty much been my Saturday routine when I was living at Little Arches. There was an unfortunate incident later as I somewhat theatrically mounted my bike after lunch. I was wearing a fairly new pair of pale green coloured strides and with a sound of rending material, the darn things ripped from fly to rear waistband, leaving me wearing virtually two unattached legs, plus air conditioning to my wedding tackle which was on full display due to the fact I had decided that morning to go commando. It didn't help that the bike had been parked in the sun and the seat was red hot. It was a good job I was on my way home, and I made a mental note to bring up the quality of the slacks to Richard at Gentleman's Quarter where I had purchased them. In fairness though, the fashion for pants at that time was for flared cuffs, but snug fitting around the thighs and rear end, so that the crotch region was always going to be under pressure – especially with me doing a Rudolph Nureyev onto the Suzuki.

The party that night was at a house shared by an indeterminate number of guys, one of whom was Alistair Anderson, a work colleague of Colin Marshall and our erstwhile neighbours in Woodbourne Avenue: David and Ian. I had escorted the outspoken young thing I had fixed myself up with the night before, and the place was still rocking when we left in the early hours, leaving the rest of the gang to it. It was only at the bar of the Robin Hood the following evening that Alistair related a humorous albeit heart stopping incident for him, which had occurred just before dawn after everyone, apart from the usual unconscious-brigade stretched out on the floor and on various items of furniture, had left.

We had noticed that Alistair had been particularly attentive to an attractive female throughout the evening. She was new to me, but Colin M had confided that she was the wife of a colleague at their place of work. The husband had apparently decided not to attend the party and had gone off to do his own thing whatever that was. The telephone next to Alistair's bed rang at around 5am which turned out to be the husband in question. 'Is my wife still there, Alistair?' he demanded.

Alistair stammered that she was, and then thinking quickly added: 'She's just helping us clear up.'

There was a pause, then from the other end of the phone: 'Thank goodness for that, I was beginning to get worried,' then he asked Alistair to tell his wife that he would see her later and hung up.

'Who was that?' enquired the pretty little head on the pillow next to Alistair.

'Your old man!' It seemed they had got away with it, but there followed a feverish rush to get dressed and to see the extracurricular wife safely on her way. And that was that, with apparently no repercussions and Alistair remaining employed with his arms and legs still attached.

SIXTY-NINE

Our friend Rick had revealed to us he had three goals in life that he was determined to attain. Number one to become rich, number two to marry a beautiful woman and number three… well actually I can't recall what that was, but there were definitely three goals. He already had a promising job as comptroller for a large petroleum company based in Bermuda with impressive prospects, and could well lead to the realisation of ambition number one. It had been less than a month since Jeannie had told Rick in a most creative way to sling his hook, but he had soon got over it and was back to his normal fun-loving self, complete with his Friday night tantrums after being regularly trounced at Crazy Eights. So when he announced enthusiastically one weekday evening after work that he had met a gorgeous girl and was taking her out to dinner on Saturday night, it seemed as if he might at last have his foot on the second rung of the ladder to achieving his dreams of marrying a beautiful woman – or a smart tart as Dougie would have termed it. Being Rick's housemates and friends, we quite naturally showed what was, on reflection, a suspicious overabundance of interest, and good wishes for him in his quest. Furthermore, as his *very best* buddies, we declared our keenness in meeting the lucky lady.

Rick eyed us warily. 'No frigging chance,' he told us. The last thing he was going to do was bring her to meet us. 'She's got class,' he added. Then to underline his statement: 'I know you Limey bastards too well.'

We were deeply wounded by that and we told him so. He didn't believe a word of it, so to emphasise the point Dougie and I adopted suitably hurt expressions. But we weren't going to let it go and assured Rick that we knew that he would not settle for anyone less than amazing, and were simply keen to meet her and see for ourselves.

'Yeah right, I'm not falling for that one, so forget it,' he assured us robustly.

'At least tell us her name,' Dougie chipped in, then added: 'How many of our tarts have you met?'... Dougie had such a polite way of expressing himself with regard to the opposite sex.

But this seemed to make Ricky think; the look of hesitation could be seen in his eyes before he pulled himself together. 'How the hell would I know? I can only count to fifty.'

'Exactly,' Dougie continued after a pause to think about it. 'You know most of them, right?' Then quickly backing Dougie up I reminded Rick that we always introduced our girlfriends to him – conveniently omitting the fact that most of them were up and gone before Ricky had clambered out of bed on a Sunday morning. Because that's what friends do, I concluded. The look of doubt deepened on our pal's face, and we knew we had him.

'Right, well... I'm not promising.' Then he weakened some more and told us that maybe, just maybe, he would drop by the house after picking the young lady up on their way to wherever it was he was taking her. Then as a final concession he informed us that her name was Barbara.

'Out of sight,' I said.

'Far out,' Dougie added, with both of us oozing as much sincerity as we could muster.

'But don't you dare pull any stunts you buggers,' was Rick's passing shot as he left the room to get himself spruced up ready for his hot date.

'Wouldn't dream of it, would we, Mr Dewar?' I side-mouthed to Dougie out of Rick's hearing.

'Nooo, course not,' Dougie side-mouthed back. But the cogs were turning.

'But I'm not promising,' was Rick's passing shot.

It's fair to say that lounging around the house on a Saturday afternoon, Dougie and I were less than fastidious about our appearance, and as it took us just minutes to get ourselves ready to go out for the evening, we were still in – how can I put it – a tousled and dishevelled state when Ricky arrived back at Carisbrook. He warily came into the lounge, looking first to the left and then to the right as if expecting some sort of ambush, then showing a look of contemptuous distaste at our appearance, he nervously ushered his new lady friend forward. 'This is Barbara,' he tentatively informed us, and for some reason looked somewhat unsettled. Then placing a hand on her shoulder, he gently eased his new girlfriend into the room. Barbara was indeed what most people would term lovely, with long ebony-black hair down to her waist, an open tanned face and perfect teeth that reminded me of the white keys on a showroom piano and would have been a match for our pal Rob at twenty paces. This was confirmed when she smiled at the two scruffy gits facing her. She was also short and a perfect match for Rick.

We were playing some less than sedate Led Zeppelin at the time, but Rick soon hit the button to stop play, which was fair enough, I guess. It's hard to have a decent conversation if Robert Plant is giving it large with *Black Dog* playing at ear tingling volume.

'Let's have a drink,' Dougie suggested, but as he began to rise from his chair, Rick quickly cut in…

'No, we've got to go,' and looking at his watch a little too keenly, added. 'We're booked in for seven.'

Are we? Was the unspoken raised eyebrow look that Barbara gave him. But Rick was adamant; it was obvious he just wanted to leave while the going was still good. And then it happened.

Still on his feet, Dougie let out a monstrous fart that would have put even the impressive vocals of Robert Plant and the booming riffs from Jimmy Page to shame. What is it with us English and farting? It never fails to entertain and give rise to excessive mirth, and provides many humorous anecdotes and recollections when us boys get together, but this one was of gold medal proportions, and if Dougie had been an Olympic pole-vaulter, he would have just cleared the roof of the stadium. It had everything: volume, an impressive bass tone, perfect resonance and an optimum time span, not short and sharp but perfectly prolonged. Dougie had perfect pitch – it was the Mozart of farts.

My mouth dropped open, not with shock, but with admiration and I have to admit, a certain amount of envy. If there was to be an aroma that matched the intensity of its other qualities, we were all in trouble. But I needn't have worried because it thankfully turned out to be an NBND job… Nuclear But Not Deadly. There was silence for several seconds as we all froze in tableau, then almost as a reflex I said with feeling: 'Aw Jeez, Rick, is this the sort of girl you're going out with now?'

Then catching on in a flash and making the situation much worse, Dougie added: 'Yeah, thought you said she had class,' and we quickly left the room making remarks and noises of disgust and revulsion as we went, like '*urghh*' and '*that's foul*' and '*gawd that smells*'.

We never saw the going of Rick and Barbara, because we were in the kitchen trying unsuccessfully to smother our laughter, with me holding onto the worktop with one hand in an effort to stay on my feet, and holding my private parts with the other to deter the very real prospect of pissing myself; alongside Dougie who was doubled over with both hands clamped to his mouth. It was a fruitless attempt to stifle our hilarity. After we heard the front door slam shut, we just let it all out and loudly laughed ourselves silly. After we had managed to gain control of ourselves, which was some minutes later, we wiped away the tears and, still chuckling, resumed our former positions in the lounge grasping large freshly poured glasses of much-needed sustenance.

'Was that planned?' I asked Doug after a long period of slurping and giggling.

Still finding it hard to compose himself, he answered: 'No it just slipped out.'

'Slipped out!' I spluttered; it blew the bloody doors off.'

It was brilliant timing, and we both agreed that if Dougie had not let go when he did, we would have thought of something else. But there was nothing we could have done that would have trumped the explosive fart. (See what I did there again?)

After a long pause Dougie ventured: 'Do you think he'll be mad?' Not that Dougie looked in the least concerned one way or the other.

'Incandescent I would imagine,' I offered.

'Good word that.' He seemed impressed with my vocabulary.

Then another long thoughtful pause before raising my glass. 'Here's to Rick and Barbara.'

'Yeh, Rick and his tart. Cheers.'

'Cheers.'

We clinked glasses and were wondering already how we could catch Rick out the next time. One thing was for sure; if there was a wedding, we wouldn't be invited.

SEVENTY

I have always been a bookie type of bloke; not the type that accepts bets on horse races you understand, but an avid reader – a bookworm, or if you want to get highbrow, a bibliophile. As previously mentioned, from a very young age I devoured books at an incredible rate. But I have to admit that reading was often the last thing on my mind during the time in Bermuda, and although picking up a newspaper for a cursory glance, or spending the odd half hour on the beach with a title that appealed in between Frisbee sessions and talent watching, it was a relatively rare occurrence. It was the same with TV – which we did not possess anyway – or even the radio. There was far too much going on in our social lives to often have the time to bother. The only exception for me was to regularly purchase the monthly copy of *Playboy* magazine. Now I know what you're thinking, young one-track-minded male; great looking women with no clothes on, fairly typical. But I believed then and I still do, that it was a first-rate magazine and apart from the obvious attraction of naked females, it genuinely was a good read, and of a very high quality... yes alright, the amazing knockers were a definite bonus.

The book reviews were particularly good, and on more than one occasion, I enjoyed a synopsis of a new release so much, I made a mental note to acquire the publication at some undetermined future date when my testosterone levels had decreased drastically (which I hoped would be well into the next century) and my love of books and the time to read them, had returned. There were also segments of established books that were reprinted in the magazine, and I often made a point of reading them when they looked interesting enough and I was prepared to give it the time. One such, was the opening few hundred words from a book called *The Green Man* by the British author, Kingsley Amis. It was a mixture of ghost story, comic novel and according to the *Times Literary Supplement*, 'a moral fable'. (I looked that last bit up.) In any case it was a darn good read and many years later and sometime after the sad demise of Mr Amis in the mid-1990s, I did actually purchase the book.

But to get back to the point of this increasingly tedious build up; another interesting and sometimes perplexing feature of *Playboy*, was the range of advertisements, not to mention the letters page asking for advice of a sexual nature, and which bashfulness dictates that I definitely do not go into here – the contents often bordering on the obscene and with some of the answers even more bizarre. Anyway, there was an advertisement in the latest edition that caught my eye and had stimulated my already vivid imagination... a set of black satin bed linen. I just had to have it and although my birthday was long gone, I saw it as a very belated present to myself, and I duly sent off for this luxury item. Oh, how this would increase my reputation with the ladies, I thought. None of my housemates had anything like this. It was all Dougie could do to actually make his bed once a week and, I have to confess, we were both guilty of leaving the changing of our bed linen, along with our underwear, until the last possible minute when we would make an emergency dash to the Quicky Licky laundromat. We had a foolproof method of determining when our grubby bed linen, jeans and other items of clothing were ready to be bagged up, loaded onto the back of the Suzuki and hauled down to the Quicky Licky, and it was this: if you threw the items at the wall and they stuck, the time was right. I jest of course, nobody could be that squalid... umm... but we did tend to leave laundromat matters until the last possible minute.

There were two beds in my room at Carisbrook, and although not the ideal arrangement for a young sex-mad Jack the Lad, each was larger than the average single and so perfectly adequate for some energetic mattress jiving when the occasion arose. I therefore decided that I would make up one of them with the new groovy set of shiny black sheets and pillow cases for those evenings if and when I managed to get lucky. The rest of the time I would sleep in the other, which was quite adequately adorned with my ageing but still serviceable white cotton jobbies sporting dandelion and buttercup motives... what?

I say sleep *in*, but of course for much of the year the heat and humidity that prevails in Bermuda, meant that sleeping in the buff on top of the bed with the windows full open, was the favourite and most practical way of getting a good night's sleep... as long as mosquito screens were fitted of course. Air conditioning was certainly around then, but most of the houses and apartments – at least those that were rental accommodation and that we had experienced – were often without these handy appliances. And even if they were present, it was often a question of which was the lesser of the twin evils: intense humidity or the grinding noise of one of those early air-con units rattling the window frame in which it sat, as per my experience in Highclere. But I was excited when my purchase arrived and I could not wait to put my new super-duper bedding through its paces.

The eagerly anticipated evening soon came around when Dougie and I got lucky one Saturday night at one of the many summer parties, and we invited two lovely young things back to the house, ostensibly for coffee and a snifter. We had our own definition for snifter of course, and it was most definitely not brandy. It had been the usual Saturday evening routine; a few beverages at several of our regular bars, then armed with a bottle apiece, on to the designated party which, on that occasion, was somewhere in Southampton Parish, just off the South Shore. The girls, who had been with a party of four, had also obviously been doing the rounds and we were all suitably well oiled, extremely jolly and ready to go. Consequently, one thing led rapidly to another and we retreated to our rooms before the coffee was cold, both Dougie and I grabbing a bottle of something from our drinks supply in order to keep the party going. So when I threw the door to my bedroom open, I was thrilled to note the amazed look of approval on the face of my partner when she saw the black sheets expensively lying there in all their satanic glory. As an aphrodisiac it was better than oysters – at least it was for me, and with the black satin, there was the added advantage over shelled molluscs, because there would be no fishy aftertaste and bad breath.

I won't go into the details or build-up, but suffice it to say what happened next you simply could not make up. In an eagerness that seemed to even surpass mine and with the help of a good deal of alcohol, my attractive young partner leapt onto the bed in a sort of giggling swallow dive, slid the full length and head-butted the wall with a resounding crack, knocking her senseless. Oh my God. I was appalled. I mean… my new bed linen. Now I was going to get blood all over the damn things.

As I hastily shoved the girl to one side in order to rip the sheet away, she let out a groan sat bolt upright and pushed me hard, causing me to slither across the bed onto the floor taking the bedside cabinet with me and knocking over the half empty bottle of Cockspur in the process. More expense. The upside was that in fact the pretty young thing on my bed was only mildly and momentarily stunned, partly through the knock on her head but mostly due to her own alcoholic intake, and there was thankfully no sign of blood and apparently no side effects. Booze is a great anaesthetic I have always found. So much so that amazingly once we had recovered sufficiently, we both had a good long laugh at what must have looked pretty comical.

We endeavoured to resume where we had left off so dramatically a few minutes before, but it was a lost cause because any vigorous movement on those sheets simply invited a slipping and sliding that invariably ended with two sweaty individuals in a heap on the deck, having slithered out of the sheets like Quality Street toffees from their shiny wrappers. And the floor is where we ended up, having called time on those deadly sheets, and I am glad to report they were never used again but simply left on the bed as an expensive adornment and talking point, which is exactly what has transpired, allowing me to dine out on *yet another* story on numerous occasions over the years.

SEVENTY-ONE

I can honestly swear on a stack of Playboys, that every day of my time in Bermuda, whether at home or at work, I would spend a few minutes to absorb my surroundings; never take for granted my good fortune, and to remember every precious moment. It didn't matter what the outlook was – there were few locations in Bermuda's nine parishes that did not offer a scenic view or breathtaking vista. It was *all* Bermuda and a reminder, if one was needed, of what would almost certainly be the best period in my life, no matter how long that life turned out to be.

There were also other odd occasions when I would take myself off for a short walk, or find myself sitting alone on the beach when the rest of the crew were splashing around playing silly arses in the warm waters off Horseshoe or Warwick beaches, when I would indulge myself in a spot of inner reflection. How could it be, I wondered, that having experienced the disaster of a broken marriage and the loss of a young daughter, I was now enjoying life so much? And leaving England as I had, with the guilt of abandoning the courageous Stevie to fight her illness alone still hanging over me like a dark cloud, how could life feel so eventful and good? Yes, it had been Stevie's wish that I take up the job offer, and yes, I had been assured by her surgeon that there was no reason why she could not join me at a later date; but it was nevertheless very hard to reconcile my conflicting emotions. I was looking for answers, but was it because I genuinely wanted there to be a rational explanation, or simply that I was looking for a way to exonerate myself and take the weight of blame off my shoulders?

Apart from the one time Dougie and I had opened up to each other perched precariously on the roof at Look Over, I had never shared any of this with Terry and Rob, or the girls. It was something that I needed to keep to myself – Dougie excepted – because it was a dilemma that was difficult to explain, and one that I needed to sort out in my own way. Then much later, an event occurred that changed my mind-set and began to help me put my inner house in order.

It was during my early days in Bermuda, that one evening when I arrival at the Hood at an unusually early hour, Richard Floyd appeared and asked me if I was interested in driving over to Flatts Village in Smith's Parish for a change of scene and a drink or two at the Coral Island Hotel. He was obviously not on duty that night at the Hood, and as he told me, it was good to get away from the business occasionally, particularly with the hours that he and his partners Jack and Tinny put in. I also knew that Richard liked to keep an astute eye very firmly on what was going on with the competition in the rest of the island.

Well, it sounded like a good idea to me, it was still early and I was on my own for a change; Richard P and the girls would probably show up later and possibly Terry, although this was in the early days and Dougie and Rob had not as yet, come into my life. As Richard had said – it might be good to have a change of scene.

I had been to Flatts many times, having thoroughly explored the island within the first few weeks of my arrival, and of course the boozy fishing trip had left from there in those first few months – but I had never been into the Coral Island Hotel.

Flatts Village with its picturesque inlet was, to my mind, one of the prettiest of places in what was an aesthetically stunning group of islands. The hotel was surprisingly quiet when we arrived, although it was early in the evening, not to mention early in the season, and perhaps most of the guests they had were still at dinner. There were a few tables occupied with one lonely figure at the bar and Richard being Richard and knowing just about everyone, introduced me to the guy who, it turned out, was a hairdresser at a salon in Hamilton.

William was another of the many ex-pat workers in Bermuda and we had a pleasant chat about this and that, though nothing that was going to change the world, along with the usual banter when a group of guys get together over a drink. He was engaged to be married, it transpired, which accounted for the fact that I had no recollection of seeing him in any of the usual haunts. Moreover, it was to a Bermudian girl, so he was pretty much assured of a future there in paradise, lucky devil. Then another guy came into the bar who, of course, was also known to Richard. He was another Brit called Jimmy and who, it turned out, was engaged to a young lady entertainer that was resident singer at the hotel, hence Jimmy's appearance. Apparently, she was not working that evening, and Jim was taking her to some restaurant or other for an evening out. The short-term plan, he told us, was for him and his fiancé to leave Bermuda for the US at the end of her contract, which would be coming up shortly, and get married and settle in the US where she hailed from. It was the only time I saw the lady when she turned up ready for the off a few minutes later, and she was a lovely looking girl. Jim was a very lucky man. Wishing them all the very best for the future as they left, I believed that it would be the last time I would see Jimmy and his lady, but I was wrong – at least about Jimmy.

Nine months later, Dougie and I were doing the rounds one night in Hamilton, and had nipped into a bar that we infrequently used on Front Street. It was a very pleasant place but it reminded me of a smart hotel bar, with ornamental mirrors, and overstuffed chairs surrounding glass tables – more a place for lounge lizards. Very nice if you were into that sort of establishment, but not in the same league as the Robin Hood in our view, and one where we would feel embarrassed to really let rip as we often did at the Hood and Rum

Runners. Then just as we ordered our first drinks, who should walk in but Jimmy.

Dougie had also obviously met the bloke somewhere because we both showed our recognition and greeted him. It was Dougie's round so having asked the bar tender for a beer for our new companion, I said to Jim: 'I never expected to see you again, mate; thought you would be married and tucked away in the States.'

'Should have been,' he said. 'But she dumped me.'

The sadness coming out of this guy was palpable. 'What the hell happened?' I asked.

'You tell me. It was the week before we were due to leave and she just said, 'Sorry, I can't marry you' and that was that; no reason, no excuses.'

'Another bloke?' Dougie queried.

'No idea. I never saw or heard from her again. That was months ago.' He was obviously still very cut up.

'So you stayed.'

'What else was there to do? My boss was understanding and the job was still there so, here I am.'

This was only the second time that I had run into the man, but right from that first meeting at the Coral Island, he had come across as a thoroughly nice guy – softly spoken and pleasant. What a devastating blow for him; it was a situation that I could readily relate to. Dougie told me later that he could not remember where he had met Jimmy, but that it had not been at any of our regular haunts. To my recollection I had not run into him since that first meeting, so it appeared he was very much a loner, and that was the distinct impression we got from him that night in the Front Street bar.

That was to be the last time either of us saw Jimmy, because just weeks later we heard that he had been killed in an accident when his motorcycle had gone off the road somewhere on the South Shore. Even before its tragic ending, Jimmy's story had given me pause for thought. A cog seemed to drop into place in my brain and with it came the realisation that the past is the past and we cannot go through life carrying guilt like a heavy coat. The important thing to remember is that we all go through life committing mistakes and at times making the wrong decisions that impact on other lives, but we must accept them, learn from the experience and move on.

Jimmy's story was different to mine with few parallels, but it had somehow been the catalyst that helped put perspective into my mixed emotions and help me move on into a different and more comfortable reality, but never forgetting my bad decisions of the past and the lady and young daughter I had left behind.

It was later that night, having returned to our favourite drinking den, that Tinny McCann, one of the three Robin Hood partners, arrived back at the bar around midnight, having been cruising the rival bars, to weigh up the opposition. Most of the Hamilton establishments, including the Hood, were open until 1am every night.

This was something that he, Jack, and Richard F did on a fairly regular basis, and why the boys were always coming up with something new to offer their faithful regulars.

Tinny told us that when he arrived back, he had seen Ally MacLeod, Matt Taylor's buddy, staggering around in the small bike park at the foot of the Hood's outside stairs, trying unsuccessfully to keep his moped upright. But every time he managed to stand the thing up, he would fall over, taking the machine with him. This happened twice with Tinny watching, then he approached the swaying Ally and suggested, 'Why don't you park the bike here tonight and call a taxi?'

'A taxi to where' Ally slurred, 'I've only just arrived.'

SEVENTY-TWO

One Friday night as a precursor to Elbow Beach, we had all decided to meet in the Rum Runners for a change of scene. The Robin Hood was our first choice of bar on most occasions, but we also paid frequent visits to this Front Street establishment that belonged to two of Richard Pedro's brothers – David and Roger – and had only opened in the preceding year. Whilst the Hood's patrons were, for the most part, made up of young Bermudians and British ex-pat workers, and provided nightly live music from the then resident singer Rod McKenzie, Rum Runners customers were growing in numbers and were a more eclectic mix, with many of our age group who were regular attendees. It also attracted an older clientele; thirty years and upwards. Or so it seemed to us.

Early evening in particular was a very pleasant time to relax after work and perhaps enjoy some first-class food, prepared of course by our good friend Steve Croucher. There was an added bonus that, discreetly stashed under the bar, was a supply of Goslings wonderful 151 proof Black Seal rum, reserved for celebrities and VIPs… aka, us. Gosling's rum is the basis for what is regarded as Bermuda's national tipple, the world famous Dark and Stormy cocktail, which is: Two thirds of Goslings Ginger Beer poured over ice, topped off with one third Black Seal rum and served up with an optional wedge of fresh lime, just as Richard Floyd had instructed the previous year. Whilst the standard ingredient is Goslings 80 proof version of this rum, the 151-proof variety gives the drink a supercharged kick which was very much up the street along which Dougie and I often strolled, so to speak. Although, unlike us, Terry and Rob were not regular rum drinkers, they would occasionally partake when the mood took them, and they did enjoy their samplings of that legendary drink, which is what transpired on that particular Friday evening. Ricky of course, was absent, and off filling his boots somewhere with the new love in his life, Barbara.

The restaurant was yet to become busy, and with several customers in the bar area occupying tables and more enjoying the early evening's warmth on the balcony outside, we four seated ourselves at the bar and greeted our bar tender pal, Larry. Having ordered our first round of 'specials,' as we had christened that potent version of the cocktail, we all expressed our satisfaction after the first taste with heartfelt sighs of satisfaction. We had learned that this was not a drink to be rushed; not only was there a delicious aftertaste that exploded into life at the back of the tongue several seconds after the initial sip, but this was a seriously powerful spirit and it was wise to pace ourselves and savour the superior taste over time.

The topic of conversation was the Arthur Haines show, a British television programme that had run for ten years from the mid-1950s and one we had watched as young lads in the early sixties. As was often the case, the subject had come up entirely out of the blue via Terry who seemed to be able to exist in two parallel universes simultaneously. We all remembered the series with fondness and particularly the Irish actor Dermot Kelly who had a very distinctive way of expressing himself, which Terry was only too happy to demonstrate when Larry the barman asked us if we were ready for refills.

'Oh no I can't do dat, oh no, oh no – I weel,' Terry answered. Larry studied Terry with an expression that said: I'm not sure if he's taking the piss or he needs urgent therapy, but he decided to ignore our friend's version of an Irish accent and began to prepare our drinks with a shrug.

We were still laughing about Dermot Kelly and all doing our bit to impersonate the little comedy actor, when two young Royal Navy sailors staggered in. They were no more than lads and had obviously been painting the town red in the time-honoured matelot way. We had just received our drinks and they overheard Larry announce to us: 'Four specials coming up, guys,' as he presented them on the bar and added the lime wedges with a flourish. He also managed a further suspicious glance with another shrug at the four of us, now all doing our Dermot Kelly impressions.

'Wos that then?' one of the sailors asked, as he nodded towards the four long glasses of two-tone liquid.

'It's Black Seal rum,' I informed him.

'With ginger beer,' Rob added.

'Wos speshul 'bout that?' Jack Tar number one enquired suspiciously.

'It's 151 proof rum,' Dougie told him.

'Right,' his eyes, that seemed at cross purposes, lit up. 'We'll have two large ones, barman,' slurred the sailor. Larry blinked, looked at us, blinked again, and looked back at the half-cut seaman. 'But nothing in it,' the youngster added.

'What, straight up?' Larry blinked disbelievingly.

'Yeah, really,' returned the sailor, misinterpreting Larry's Americanism.

We all looked at each other minus the blinking, before gently explaining to young Hornblower that it would be advisable to dilute the rum with something – even water. For our pains, we were informed that they were members of Her Majesty's illustrious navy, and were therefore used to knocking back copious amounts of rum on a regular basis. They had failed to mention that in fact the traditional 'grog' ration that had once been doled out aboard Royal Navy ships – one part strong rum to two parts water – had been abolished in 1970.

Larry just shrugged his shoulders as if to say, on your heads be it, and began to pour the drinks into double-shot glasses.

The two raised their glasses as they tried to stand to attention. 'The

Queeen!' they bawled, nearly shattering glasses on the shelf behind the bar.

'The Queen,' we all echoed, and then in an act of bravado they downed the drinks in one gulp as we watched with interest. There was an expectant pause; we knew something was about to happen because sailor number one who had hitherto been very vocal, tried to focus on sailor number two, mouthed something inaudible and with a face that was rapidly taking on the aspect and colour of an overripe avocado (we had them in the garden at 'Little Arches', so I know what I'm talking about), he began to keel over backwards as if in slow motion. It was a classic example of the straw that broke the camel's back – but a double 151 proof rum was one hell of a straw – and stiff as a tailor's collar, he hit the floor, bounced a couple of times and came to rest. He lay there inspecting the ceiling with a puzzled half smile on his boyish face as his colleague grabbed the bar in an effort to stop it moving away from him.

It was with a considerable amount of effort that the four of us were able to half carry both lads down the stairs from the bar back to their ship, a Royal navy frigate, which was conveniently tied up further along Front Street, not too far from the now more than aptly named Rum Runners.

The warrant officer and two ratings who were on duty at the gangway, or whatever it is they call it in the navy, simply looked on in a rather bored fashion as if this was the most natural thing in the world, and simply told us to drop them there and they would have them taken aboard.

'This happen often?' Dougie asked one of the men.

'Every port. All the bleeding time,' we were told. 'There's still more than twenty to come.' And with a sigh he informed us that the remaining few would invariably be found at the police stations in Hamilton and probably St George's as well the next morning.

The Arthur Haines and Dermot Kelly piece of nonsense, amazingly, has stayed with us down the years, and even now we always greet each other on the phone, by email or when we reunite from time to time in some part of the world or other, in the same fashion: 'Hello dhere, Mick – how y's doin'… oh no, oi can't do dat, oh no… ', or something in the same vein, much to the astonishment of whoever happens to be in the vicinity. People who hear it regard it as childish, which we take great exception to. We have merely never grown up, which is another thing entirely and something we are all quite proud of.

Whatever… little Dermot Kelly has a lot to answer for.

SEVENTY-THREE

All our birthdays were long gone, but just for the hell of it I bought a fancy looking birthday-type cake that caught my eye in the supermarket. It must have been difficult to sell because it was offered at a knock down price, and I always had an eye for a bargain. I have since learned through much experience that the more attractive and flamboyant the cake, the worse it tastes and the sicklier the icing – but not so then, and drawn to its vivid blue and Barbara Cartland-pink icing (obviously a unisex confection), I took the thing home to share it with my friends.

'Bloody 'ell, looks like the baker was having a bad day,' Dougie exclaimed.

'Beggars can't be choosers,' I told him. 'You pour the drinks and I'll get a knife.'

But Ricky was quicker off the mark: 'I'll get it,' he volunteered, and shot off to the kitchen. Ricky loved sticky confections.

'Best thing is to close your eyes when you bite into it,' was Graham's pearl of wisdom, and he was probably right; it didn't look anywhere near as tempting sitting on our coffee table.

'No cake knife, just this,' Ricky had returned brandishing a spatula… Dougie and I glanced at each other, but it was not *the* spatula. We had obviously purchased a new model since the giant brownie incident. Then with a look of disdain Dougie said, 'Oh sod it, here…' and adopting a martial art pose and yelling something that sounded like HYEEEE!, he double karate chopped into the cake, with the result that we each received a piece of the now multi-coloured wreck, mostly on our shirts and faces, with other fragments splattered on the wall. There was only one way to eat the damn thing after that, and we all piled in with dessert spoons.

Ten minutes later we had pretty much demolished what was left of the cake, and having cleaned bits of sponge and icing off the wall, we were all sitting around discussing the coming evening's entertainment and clutching our obligatory drinks.

'You're out with Windows tonight, aren't you?' I asked Dougie.

'Windows? Who's Windows?' There was a quizzical expression on Ricky's face.

'Windows Willoughby,' I told him.

Graham laughed out loud, 'Who the heck is that?'

'I called her that because she wears glasses with really thick lenses, and she reminded me of a kid in school named Willoughby,' I explained. 'You must have seen her at the Hood.'

'Oh yeah I remember her, bit of a goer I've heard,' Ricky recollected. 'Didn't Rob chat her up a couple of weeks ago? Reckoned he gave her one too.'

'That's her, but she phoned earlier to cancel tonight,' Doug informed us. 'Says she's got an infection.'

Graham nearly choked on his drink. 'Infection… where?'

'Baileys Bay I think,' I chipped in.

'No, I mean…' Graham started to say, then realising it had been an attempt at a joke trailed off. There was a minute's silence as we all pondered the same thing. 'Do you think we should tell Rob?' Graham had voiced our collective thoughts.

There was another minute's deliberation then: 'We would have to be discreet how we tell him,' offered Ricky.

'Right on. How about: "Have you got blisters on your dick Rob?"' suggested Dougie.

'That should do it,' I agreed, and we all took that as the sign to get ready to hit the road.

I was usually the first to get ready for the evening's escapades; I liked to relax with a drink listening to music before leaving the house, and that evening I was cooling out to the *In Search of the Lost Chord* album by the Moody Blues. The track 'Legend of a Mind' was playing when Dougie bombed into the room clutching a pair of his underpants.

'Look at these,' he said. Then holding them up to the light, I could see the problem because they were peppered with tiny holes. 'Some of the others are like it too. Have you checked yours?'

Well, I hadn't, at least not minutely, but I had to admit that unless you gave Dougie's underpants close scrutiny (obviously not something I did on a day-to-day basis) they would have gone unnoticed. Ricky and Graham had heard the latter part of the exchange, and all three of us wandered off to our rooms to inspect our budgie smugglers. Sure enough, several of my own had the tell-tale pin prick holes in them, but also one other thing: a large dead ant – or was it a termite – in the folds. I had no idea which it was but it became obvious who the perpetrators in *the case of the ventilated kecks* were.

Graham and Ricky came back into the room and, shrugging, informed us that on very close inspection (these two guys were meticulous verging on obsession when it came to their clothing) there had been no sign of termite tampering or anything else amiss.

'Just you and Dougie then,' Ricky announced. 'That tell you anything?'

There were several answers to that, but we kept shtum. It was a literal take on the old 'ants in the pants' idiom.

We came across the culprits a couple of days later, when getting ourselves something to eat in our kitchen, Dougie stopped what he was doing and said: 'Listen… hear that?' And I could; something like a faint rustling sound, and it didn't take more than a second to locate the source. Hundreds of large ants had formed a procession going to and from a crack in the wall near the ceiling, carrying away fragments of our opened packet of chocolate digestives that we had left on the worktop. I'm all for hard graft and enterprise that those little fellers exhibited, but this had to be dealt with and quickly. It's amazing what you can achieve with a bit of Polyfilla and a putty knife.

Ricky was off early that evening to pick up the ravishing Barbara, but he was close lipped about what they had planned or where they were heading. Very wise I suppose and we could understand his thinking after Barbara's explosive introduction to us two weeks before. One thing was for sure and that was Rick would not be bringing her back to Carisbrook in a hurry, at least not if Dougie and I were at home. Graham was also doing his own thing in the early evening, but told us he would see us at Elbow Beach staff club later, which was fine we said, but if you see us before we see you, and it's after nine o-clock, and Terry and Rob are there, it will be your round. At that, Graham left us with a puzzled look on his face, still trying to figure that one out.

I noticed that I still had some of the shattered birthday cake on my shirt, so I took myself off to my room for a quick change of clothes.

'Thought you were going to change,' Dougie queried as I joined him in the lounge five minutes later, wearing the same two-toned long sleeve number I had donned earlier…

…*Eye-catchingly elegant yet cool and casual, in cool cream pima cotton with contrasting lapis blue shoulder features, all brought together with premium plastic mother of pearl buttons…*

'Well, I was going to change my shirt, but I changed my mind instead,' I told him. 'Sponged the bit of cake off, blasted it with my hair dryer and it hasn't left a mark. Let's go.'

It had been windy for most of the day, but by the time Dougie and I arrived back at Carisbrook later that night, the wind had increased even more and was now a howling gale.

Dougie suggested we close the wooden garage doors that were rattling violently, to prevent debris being blown in causing possible damage to our bikes. So heads down we dropped onto the drive and heaved the doors closed – this was the first time that we had done so since moving in, and they put up a stiff resistance. But we finally succeeded and then retreated to the lounge for a nightcap. We clambered into our beds having called it a night around 2am – uncharacteristically early for us – then just as I was dozing off, a massive bang from outside the house. *What the…?*

Dougie was at the front door before me, and I skidded into him on the veranda; he was looking down at our housemate Ricky who was lying on the gravel drive, his smoking machine beside him. He seemed unhurt, but spluttering with rage he shouted: 'Which one of you Limey bastards closed the fucking garage doors?'

SEVENTY-FOUR

One of Graham's weekend pastimes, we learned, was indulging in a spot of fishing. He preferred to keep his cards very close to his chest, and we knew very little about it or where he went. As far as we knew, one of his footballing friends, or perhaps a work colleague, had a boat, which was probably the most likely scenario. But it didn't stop us from ribbing him about his apparent lack of success with a rod and line, because we had never seen any evidence of freshly caught fish at Carisbrook. Surely he would bring home any seafood that he caught we reasoned, if not to share, then at least to show as evidence of his angling prowess. And us being us, we often mentioned it in no nonsense ways shall we say. Discretion was not our strong point, and in fairness our mickey taking probably did wear on Graham's nerves. None of it was meant as anything other than good-natured banter, and it was not as if we singled Graham out; poor Rick had to take the brunt of our taunting on a daily basis, but obviously taken in good part because he always came back for more. And it wasn't one-sided because Dougie and I had to endure similar treatment from each other and from our mates Terry and Rob… even Ricky was learning the ropes and dishing out some of his own medicine to the rest of us. We were young guys just doing what young guys do, but the more we kidded with Graham, the further he seemed to distance himself from us and although there were exceptions, he preferred to do his own thing, particularly at weekends. He confided to me once when we were living at Highclere that he didn't feel that he belonged in Bermuda to the extent that the rest of us did, which came as a huge surprise. I mean, how could anybody not embrace the Bermuda lifestyle and devil-may-care atmosphere within the young ex-patriot community? It was sad, and looking back, perhaps our badinage and teasing did not help.

That said, Graham's interests were obviously very different to ours which was fair enough. He was a fit guy and played regular football which was anathema to Dougie and me. We kept fit in other ways and tended to approach life at maximum speed, whereas Graham was a sporty type and a thinker and liked to plan his activities accordingly. Ricky was also different to us in that he was very neat and tidy and paid great attention to his appearance. He often boasted that as a Virgo, he was naturally well-ordered, but we countered that by telling him that with a Virgin for a star sign, it meant he had never had his leg over. But all in all, we were four diverse characters who shared a house and at heart were good pals.

Dougie and I came home from whatever we had been doing late one Saturday afternoon and not having eaten since lunch time, were starving hungry. 'Come and have a look at this,' Dougie shouted from the kitchen as I was sorting out some suitable music. Stuffed inside the fridge, coiled on the largest of our dishes along with newspaper protecting the fridge's innards, was a decent size fish with a note attached.

'What does it say?' I asked Doug.

'It says: Caught by Graham on Saturday.' An obvious message from our housemate with a subtext that actually announced: *See, you tossers – I do catch things!*

I was looking closely at the unhappy creature trying to identify the species. 'You know what this is, don't you?' I said, as I inspected its mouth.

'Yeah, a bleeding fish.'

'It's a shark. Graham's bought home a shark.'

'Can't be, sharks are big buggers, this one is what… maybe a couple of feet long.'

'More like three I reckon, but it is,' I said. 'Look at those teeth.' And I opened its mouth to reveal an impressive set of small but wicked looking gnashers. 'See those spots?' I pointed out. 'Well apparently they indicate that it's probably a young nurse shark.'

'How do you know all that?'

'Fire, one of my workmates told me, he knows all about this stuff.'

'Fire; what sort of name is that?'

'It's because he doesn't move very fast… you know, the opposite of being quick. It's a joke.'

'Well at least it's solved one problem,' Dougie grinned.

'What's that?'

'What we're having for dinner.'

'Right on!' I enthused as the penny dropped. 'You get the chips done and I'll skin the shark.'

'Why skin it; just cut it into chunks and stick it in a pan.'

'Fire told me that you can't eat the skin, it's like leather. He reckons they make ties and things out of it.'

'Far out!'

Fire had got it wrong I later found out; sharks' skin was a generic term for a woven fabric that resembled shark skin, but I didn't know that then and skinned the shark anyway. A two-foot, six-inch shark takes a lot of eating, let me tell you (I measured it to settle the argument between us). The flesh is very dense and meaty, somewhat akin to tuna and swordfish and although I would like to say we managed to consume the whole thing, even my large appetite and Dougie's legendary one, could not manage that amount of nurse shark. There had been a moment's uncertainty from me when Dougie was serving up the fish. 'That's not the fish slice you…?' I trailed off.

'Don't worry, I boiled it for ten minutes then disinfected it with Dettol,' he said, which accounted for the slightly antiseptic taste I thought I had detected. But then he laughed, 'It's the new one we bought, don't you remember?'

I did. Of course. We were going to use it for the technicoloured cake, before Dougie put his hand to it.

We had kept the head and tail of the shark, and I was also careful to preserve most of the back bone with my inexpert chopping and filleting. We placed the parts in order on the same dish in which we had found it, more or less, with one generous shark steak placed in the centre of the skeleton. It was the least we could do, along with a note saying: 'And eaten by Douglas and Colin on Saturday night.'

SEVENTY-FIVE

There had been the strange affair of Amy's doppelganger that I had experienced amongst the supermarket aisles the year before, followed by the one-in-a-million coincidence with Steve Croucher's long lost uncle during our residency at Highclere; and then to complete what amounted to a trilogy of serendipitous events, another strange happening occurred through a chance meeting one night at the Robin Hood.

Mary and Lee were at their usual posts keeping vigil at the bar in case someone had the temerity to occupy their assigned bar stools, and were accompanied by another young lady that I had to my knowledge, never seen before. She was introduced to me as Jenny who it turned out was staying at Horizons where Mary worked, and being a solo traveller, she had been taken under Mary's generous wing and was being shown around. The term 'shown around' to Mary and Lee, was pretty much the lounge and saloon bars at the Hood, where she was being introduced to the regular nefarious crowd. But in fairness, where better to see life and meet some interesting and quirky individuals?

Exactly.

Having done the introductions, the mother hen routine was forgotten, and Mary and Lee, unnoticed by me at first, had quietly slipped away to the adjoining bar where there were probably some interesting new faces to become acquainted with. I really didn't need or want matchmakers in my life, but Jenny seemed a nice girl and we got chatting. She had lived in Los Angeles most of her life, but was actually British born to English parents, so the inevitable question from me was obviously: where in Britain?

'It's a town called Reading,' she told me, 'do you know it?' She had to be joking. Reading? My own home town.

'I don't suppose you remember where exactly?' I asked. She knew exactly where, and when she told me Cressingham Road, Whitley, pronouncing the name Cressing-ham in the American manner, I was floored. She then proceeded to dig around in her purse, eventually producing a grainy photograph of herself as a toddler in the garden of what was obvious from its architecture, a pre-war council house and instantly recognisable to me. This was unbelievable. I was brought up in Whitley, a half mile from the house she was showing me, and in the background of the picture just a few properties along, was the garden of my aunt and uncle's place who had also lived in *Cressing-ham* Road. As with previous episodes, the same question nagged at me: what are the chances, and for what purpose?

We spent a very pleasant hour or so chatting, and she was as amazed as me over the unbelievable coincidence and couldn't wait to get back home and report back to her parents.

I was still mulling over the encounter as I left the bar later, trotting down the steps to my parked bike, and such was the total immersion in my thoughts wondering if there could be a reason for these amazingly frequent coincidences, I failed to notice that something substantial was missing from the Suzuki. It was only after twenty yards or so that I registered an unfamiliar jarring to my rear end, and thinking I must have a puncture, stopped the bike and dismounted. I couldn't believe it. Both rear shock absorbers had been surgically removed. No wonder my backside had received a pummelling. Whoever had nicked the shocks had been good at their job. There were constant comings and goings at the Hood and the small bike park was immediately adjacent to the entrance steps, so the perpetrators had been extremely fast in their act of larceny.

Bastards!

The dealers from whom the bike had been purchased picked the bike up the next morning, following a phone call from me. Then much to my delight, albeit a muted one on hearing what it was costing me, the bike was ready for collection later the same day. It was a very quick turnaround that took me by surprise and the dealership was as fast and efficient as the thieves had been. Perhaps it was they who had knocked off the things in the first place, I mused. If so, here was a cunning business plan if ever there was one. But of course I didn't take myself seriously. Why should I – nobody else did.

But the story wasn't over.

The following weekend I had cause to visit our local shanty version of Sainsbury's on Mount Hill, and chatting to the proprietor about this and that, I mentioned the shock absorber incident and thought no more of it until a few days later when visiting the shop again for a case of selected sodas that we liked to keep in at Carisbrook. The owner reached under the bench that passed for a counter and produced two rear shock absorbers wrapped in newspaper, both in good condition but obviously used… Suzuki rear shock absorbers.

'Got these for you,' he said. 'Thirty dollars for the two. It's a steal.' No truer words had ever been spoken.

I was getting used to strange coincidences occurring, but this was a bridge too far. Were they my original parts? I will never know for sure, and there was not a chance in hell that I would be able to prove anything. And in any case, following our initiation-by-burglary when we had moved in, the last thing any of us wanted was to upset the locals. Explaining that the parts had already been replaced and politely declining the *kind* offer along with the follow-up suggestion from him that they might become useful in the event of a future misfortune, I took my leave. But in spite of myself, I could not help giving a wry smile that stayed with me on the short walk back to Carisbrook.

The cheeky buggers.

SEVENTY-SIX

It's strange looking back, how one of the essentials of everyday life – eating and more specifically the meals that we must have shared after work most days – are strangely absent from my memory cupboard. Probably because they were boring interludes that we had to go through, and were unremarkable and hurried affairs before the important part of the day began, viz, when we left home for the pleasures at our regular watering holes, or if we were lucky, a liaison with some of Dougie's downy thighed young ladies. The exceptions were eating out which admittedly was fairly often when you included Sunday brunches, or attending the occasional dinner party at someone's house or apartment. There was also the regular weekly free spaghetti night at the Hood of course, which we always took full advantage of. Well, it was free... I mean.

Dinner parties in the conventional sense did not occur frequently at our previous places of abode, Highclere and Look Over, or in the early days for me at Little Arches, the one exception at my first residence Netherlands, being the dodgy chicken curry with mashed potato I had prepared for Penny. Any such get togethers we had were infrequent and took the form of parties with snacks or, at best, a buffet thrown in. This was mostly because we lacked the essentials like dining table and chairs, and more than two or three cutlery pieces that matched, but also because we were too darned idle and detested washing up.

But at Carisbrook there was more of an effort and we sometimes held small supper soirées – not that we used such poncy terms – but there was a notable exception when we agreed amongst ourselves to throw a larger than normal dinner party.

I cannot remember the occasion, if indeed there was an occasion, it being more than likely something we just decided to do at short notice. All four of us were involved in a joint effort for once, and it must have been a fairly lavish affair by our standards, because whilst my job was to ride into Hamilton after breakfast to pick up a case of wine, Graham, Rick and Dougie began the early preparation of the food in our gleaming, state-of-the-art kitchen. I mean – we had a smart new spatula, ergonomic, umm… stuff… and running water.

Bear in mind that this was 1974 and our experiences with the delights of the grapevine were extremely limited, which our selection that day bore witness to. Having dedicated long hours of research into the wonders of sugar cane, molasses and their offspring, dark rum, we voted unanimously to purchase a case of Blue Nun, one of the few brands whose name we were familiar with. I appeared to be one up on the others here however, because often on a Saturday evening in England, a group of five or six of us would treat ourselves to a slap-up meal in one of our regular meeting places. Thinking it was the ultimate in sophistication, almost to a man – with very little alternative choices it has to be said and in line with the rest of the population – we would order a prawn cocktail to start, followed by T-bone steak (with chips of course) and Black Forest gateau to finish. All washed down with a bottle of hock – two if we were feeling flush. So that was about it as far as German, or any other wine was concerned. We mostly settled on Liebfraumilch instead of Blue Nun back then, for no other reason than the price. But Blue Nun was a familiar name, and a brand that we assumed was a bit more upmarket, so that's the plonk we agreed upon. Mind you I had stopped drinking Liebfraumilch when I discovered that the translated wording was *woman's body milk* or some such thing. No thanks, I'd had quite enough of that as a baby in 1946 thank you very much. So Blue Nun it was – not Nun's Milch thank goodness

– and I arrived back at the house with the wine and ready to pitch in with the preparations alongside the lads.

Now look, it is simply not possible to be in the kitchen with your mates under the watchful gaze of a dozen bottles of wine, without sampling the stuff. It's all part of the bonding process and so having poured four large glasses – half pint beer tumblers in point of fact, not possessing anything as fancy as wine goblets – we toasted each other and our dinner guests yet to come. As the vino disappeared, the ribbing and laughter increased commensurately. Someone quipped that the proprietor of our local shop had recently branched out into motorcycle spares... bastard! And predictably someone else made the point that more wine was going into us than into the food. Ha, ha, good one.

By mid-afternoon, with much of the preparation still unfinished due to an inexplicable and worrying phenomenon, namely the absence of feeling in our hands and other extremities, and an inability to vocalise even the simplest sentences. Coincidentally we were down to five bottles. We had toasted everything and everybody from our neighbour's ginger cat and Rod McKenzie's guitar, to the Quicky Licky and Hitler's one testicle. Foolishly I volunteered to return to Hamilton in order to replenish our stock, and although I cannot bring to mind the exact conversation signifying my intention, I do remember leaving the house giggling like a schoolgirl, with my three wonderful, bestest, most handsomest friends in the whole world, standing in the doorway waving me off, and me thinking: *Isn't that nice.*

I have only the vaguest recollections of my trip to and from the liquor store in town, but it must have been a success because strapped to the carrier of my bike, was a fresh case of Blue Nun. I still cringe today thinking of that journey and how many near misses there might have been and the strange – even terrified – looks I must have attracted. But the Suzuki returned unblemished, as did I, and I heard nothing further about that maniacal ride. The one thing that remained a mystery however was the fact that apart from the wine, a half bottle of vodka had got itself lodged uncomfortably under my belt, beneath my shirt. I didn't drink vodka.

We could all remember that day up to and including my second expedition into town, but then curiously, not one of us could remember much about the dinner party itself.

Strange that.

As an added attraction at Carisbrook, we perfected silly after-supper games – sometimes simple quizzes, occasionally charades, but mostly forfeits.

The rules of forfeits were simplicity itself. You each wrote out two forfeits on slips of identical paper which were folded and chucked into a container – usually my worthy velvet barrow boy cap – in the centre of the circle of friends, usually plonked on the floor because of the lack of organised seating. For the same reason, we would sometimes eat off plates on our laps as we sat cross legged on the deck, although the alternative of simply collaring whatever seat we could find anywhere in the house was also applied. This would mean that depending on the number of guests, every seat could well be occupied, whether in the lounge, kitchen or any of the four bedrooms. On the only other occasion when we had an unusually high number of bodies in Carisbrook, I found myself eating dinner whilst perched on the loo, with Rick reclining in the waterless bath scoffing a plate of tuna salad and baked potato. To say these dinner and supper jollies were informal would be stretching the definition of the word 'informal' to breaking point.

But back to the game of forfeits.

On the throwing of a dice or more often than not, the spin of an empty bottle of which by this time there were plenty, it was decided who would collect a forfeit. If the recipient did not like what they had selected, they could, if they so wished, carefully re-fold it, throw it back in, re-shuffle the pile and select another which then had to be enacted upon. It can be seen therefore, that a certain amount of caution had to be shown when writing out forfeits, because it was highly possible to select your own. Also by discarding the first choice for whatever reason, the second could well prove to be more demanding than the first. It has to be remembered that by this time, hosts and guests without exception were totally blasted and the word caution simply did not apply. Consequently, some of the suggestions were at best bizarre and at worst staggering.

On one occasion Terry's forfeit was to drink a large glass of gin immediately followed by a half pint of Brussels sprout water left over from dinner that night – it could even have been from the day before, I don't remember. Whatever, on the night in question the brew was stagnating menacingly in a saucepan in the kitchen. Moreover, Terry had to drink each glass straight down only pausing for breath between each one, with the consequence that he sprang to his feet and jetted off to the bathroom at the far end of the corridor. All credit to him that he managed the forfeit, but keeping it down had been a step too far. After several minutes he returned ashen faced, and forcing a smile collapsed on the floor and began unsteadily to write out another forfeit to replace the used one – another rule of the game.

'About bleeding time,' Dougie told him after Terry had returned from the khazi, 'I'm bursting,' and he hurried off to the bathroom, returning minutes later with a selection of undigested food, mostly carrot, nestling in some toilet tissue.

'This yours, Terry?' Dougie asked, holding the gooey mass up for everyone to see. 'This was hanging off the wall in the corridor, thought we'd got new flock wallpaper.' At which point Terry took a couple of audible gulps, and raced off to the bathroom for a second performance. Later Terry blamed it entirely on the gin, whose brand name shall remain unreported in case of legal consequences, but all of us resolved never to touch that brand again and as far as I know we never have. All this in tenuous support of Terry's libellous claim that the alcohol was to blame, conveniently forgetting the role that a large quantity of a species of liquid brassica had played.

On another occasion, and a memorable one for me, was when I drew a forfeit that required me to completely change clothing with

Mary's pal Lee, one of our female guests, who I wish to point out, had worked at the famous Playboy Club in Mayfair, London. We used Rick's bedroom for the exercise which stood opposite the lounge, and gosh it was tricky. It took the best part of an hour to accomplish this very difficult and demanding task. When we emerged fully dressed in our own clothes, we were greeted with boos and cat calls and accusations that we had not fulfilled the requirements of the forfeit.

'Yes we have,' I protested and went on to explain that we had changed as required then changed back again. There was nothing in the forfeit that said we had to parade in each other's clothes.

It turned out that during the hour of our absence, we had missed another interesting albeit very tame forfeit that Dougie had drawn, that involved standing on his head, supported by another member from the group of his choosing, then while upturned sipping large measures of vodka through a straw. It was obvious that our years of state education in the UK had paid dividends.

But there is one evening in particular that, for me, stands head and shoulders above the rest, and looking back I cannot understand why I actually performed it to the letter when it would have been easy for me to fake it and simply report mission accomplished. No that's untrue, actually I can understand why, because the presence of dark rum always seemed to be the perfect nostrum for diffidence and doubt, especially when diluted with a quantity of wine… a very large quantity of wine.

Anyway, the forfeit was this: I was to take off all of my clothes apart from my underpants which I had strenuously negotiated to keep on, jump on my sporty Suzuki, ride the considerable distance into town, do a circuit (the actual route being left to my discretion) and return. And to make sure there was no cheating, my clothing had to be left behind. I still do not know to this day what I was thinking, because having come to the end of our short lane and turned right for the downhill ride to town, I could easily have gone just a sufficient distance in order for the sound of the engine to gradually fade, then stay put for a suitable length of time for my friends to believe I had completed the forfeit – hoping like hell no cars drove past.

But I didn't.

It must have been well after 3am so I was reasonably confident that nobody would be about, but even so, was I mad? Because I rode on into town, being very careful not to break the speed limit of 15 mph – as if this would make a difference – and proceeded to complete a circuit via Par-La-Ville Road on the outward leg and Woodlands Road by way of Church Street on the return. However, my luck ran out in Church Street, because I glanced in my left-hand mirror and spotted a police car that had appeared from nowhere and fell in about twenty yards behind me. Oh please no. I maintained my speed and nothing happened for a further hundred yards or so and then quite suddenly the patrol car accelerated and pulled alongside me and indicated for me to pull over. I closed my eyes and prayed that this was all a dream and that I should have in fact done the sensible thing and laid-up not far from Carisbrook before returning and blithely claiming victory. Who would have known?

But it wasn't a dream, it was a potential nightmare.

I reluctantly opened my eyes only to encounter a couple of very familiar faces in the car – two English cops Dave and Jeff – who frequented the Rum Runners and who I had often shared an hour or so with over drinks and tall stories. Doing his very best to keep a straight face, Dave wished me a good morning to which I responded accordingly, but who the hell says good morning to a near naked motorcyclist at three in the morning as if it's the most natural thing in the world? But that wasn't all.

'We've had reports of a suspicious looking individual, riding around town on a motorcycle… a bit like yours as it happens judging by the description, and possibly in possession of a concealed weapon,' he told me earnestly.

'Oh, right,' I stammered.

'If you see him, do not approach, but call us.'

'Oh right,' I repeated and nodded my head dumbly, wanting

desperately to get rid of them, then as they drove away, I could hear them through the open car window laughing like hyenas at my expense. I returned to Carisbrook triumphant, but I'm not sure that anyone believed me when I related the whole story to them, and most annoying of all, nobody who was at that party seems to remember the incident at all these many years later. Mind you, it has provided me with an amusing story to tell when I have had a few vinos inside me.

Not Blue Nun though, I hasten to add.

It was a blessed escape and on reflection the following day, I thanked my lucky stars that of all the members of the Bermuda police force I could have encountered that night, the Gods of Silly Games had smiled on me and presented me with Dave and Jeff. I have often wondered what became of them, and the only lead I have ever been given was a rumour that they had both married and eventually emigrated to Oz with their ladies.

I wonder if they have ever dined out on the story.

What am I saying, of course they bloody have!

SEVENTY-SEVEN

We were enjoying an after-lunch drink at the Rum Runners; relaxing on the balcony and watching the world go by on Front Street. There had been something of a kerfuffle earlier on, somewhere further along the street, which we had not been able to view. Then two of the bar staff from the Robin Hood, who had also dropped by for a bite to eat, our friends Mark 'Time' Selley and Dave 'I will I' Wilmot (think about it) saw us perched on our balcony and joined us briefly. The tags to their names by the way, had been added by us one silly night in the Hood, and the two had accepted the christenings, with sighs and the shaking of heads. 'What do you expect from those two?' Mark had commented. What indeed.

They told us that the disturbance down below had been an accident involving Matt Taylor and his bosom buddy Ally, another Scot. Matt's bike was lying in the road, so it was assumed he had been hit by another vehicle, or he himself had hit something – it was all a bit unclear, but they had witnessed an ambulance arrive and Ally stopping the paramedics from touching his friend until they had shown identification. Mark and Dave laughed at the memory and Dougie and I joined in as we imagined the farcical scene... only Ally and Matt, I thought.

But then, what about our pal Matt; how badly was he injured and was he going to be alright? That was answered later on that evening when we entered the Robin Hood. The place was buzzing with the story, thanks to the ultra-efficient Bermuda grapevine, and the details were these: there had been no accident, with Matt simply falling off his bike totally and comprehensively pissed. The pair had been on a bender, and although Matt was not injured, he was still comatose when the paramedics were finally allowed, by Ally, to bung him on board the ambulance and be taken to the hospital. Later on, Ally insisted on seeing his mate, who was still sleeping it off in a hospital bed, and checking nobody was around, he removed Matt's tartan kecks, stuck them on his head and took a photograph… actually, I have no idea what colour or pattern Matt's knickers were, but they really *should* have been some sort of tartan, I feel.

It's a story that has stood the test of time, and Matt maintains to this day, that he has never forgiven Ally.

Dougie and I had been dropping casual hints to Ricky and recounting tales of the art of fart lighting for some weeks. We had slipped the subject into the conversation on several occasions, with tales of people we had heard of lighting their emissions, sometimes with spectacular results and telling him that we had indeed witnessed such events. We knew from experience that although Rick had laughed at the implausibility of it all and without us pushing it too far, his curiosity would eventually get the better of him and he would want to know more and perhaps request a demonstration. What Rick did not know was that, contrary to what we had told him, neither Dougie nor I, or Graham for that matter, had ever seen it demonstrated; it was just one of those stories that circulates amongst blokes, with very few admitting they had actually experienced it, and purporting to know someone or other who had. It was possible therefore that it was just another urban myth and a tale that gains the status of folklore through constant retelling.

But it made sense and was logical in a weird sort of way. The body produces methane gas and methane is inflammable, ipso facto it should be possible to ignite a fart. The point is that nobody in his right mind is ever going to volunteer to put a light to his arse, and only a suicidal maniac is likely to experience it by proxy and follow a herd of cows around with a box of matches.

This is where Rick came in.

We had enjoyed a meal out together one Friday night at the Rum Runners as a prelude to our Elbow Beach gathering. Now there was a novelty! Several of us had tried a starter of snails for the first time I recall; or escargot if you want to be poncy about it. It was to be my first and last sampling if I am honest, and I felt that I would never be able to look a snail in the face again without a feeling of guilt. But then, I was yet to experience the destruction of carefully nurtured lettuce and cabbages in my garden in West Suffolk that was to come many years later, and would change my opinion drastically. However, although several of the others seemed to enjoy the dish, for some reason that particular item did not seem to sit well with Ricky, giving rise to certain digestive tremors.

Later, there were the usual dance gymnastics at Elbow Beach and naturally the excessive imbibing of half-priced drinks, which seemed to have a cumulative effect on our little housemate and his excited innards, because when we arrived back at Carisbrook, he was finding it hard to keep the regular gaseous volleys under control, which, paradoxically, pleased him no end. Rick was not known for his ability to audibly break wind and he often expressed his feelings of envy for those that could – mentioning no names of course. Then a gleam appeared in his eyes as his mind seemed to turn to the incendiary possibilities.

'Quick, I've got a real rip-snorter on the way,' he announced, and he hurriedly hoisted himself onto one of the kitchen units and assumed a ludicrous crouching position with both feet on the worktop and leaning against the wall with his rear end pointing outwards. With an expression of gleeful anticipation, he looked like an outsize frog about to pounce on an unsuspecting juicy fly, or a chuckling gargoyle perched on a church roof. Dougie quickly produced his lighter and waited for Rick's final instruction – being careful to stand well to one side, and which I had the good sense to mimic.

I had a sudden thought. 'Don't breathe in,' I told Rick earnestly, having no idea why I should come up with such a ridiculous suggestion.

'Here it comes now!' hollered Rick and he let out a very impressive loud Bermudian trump; not up to the usual *Limey bastards* standard, but nevertheless a creditable first performance. Simultaneously, Dougie clicked his lighter and a vivid blue flame shot out into the kitchen. It was brief but dramatic and would have been even more theatrical, I mentally noted, that had we had the forethought to switch the lights off. But it was undoubtedly a successful experiment with Ricky as the guinea pig, and we had achieved lift off, with a hot blast that could have toasted crumpets. What immediately followed was the distinct aroma of singed fabric and Rick bounding off the cabinet holding his rear end. It was not a blow-back as such, thank goodness, which could have set off a chain reaction, just a regrettable and inevitable scorching of his rear end, and probably the ruin of a perfectly good pair of strides.

Dougie offered up the suggestion that perhaps this was where the word ars-onist originated as Rick simultaneously hissed the all too familiar, *Limey bastards,* as he made his urgent bow-legged way to the bathroom and some cooling water.

I subsequently discovered that the art of setting fire to your rear end is called *pyroflatulence* or *flatus ignition* and I have always wondered if the 60s pop star Georgie Fame's backing group, The Blue Flames, had acquired their name from this dubious and inflammatory practice.

Well, it's possible.

SEVENTY-EIGHT

Angela was not only delightful in appearance, but also a delightful individual inside as well as out. Everyone, both male and female, loved her; she was attractive, gregarious and amusing, and always great fun to be with. Because she was so charming and nice, and was rarely without an accompaniment of friends, perhaps explained why I had never chanced my arm with her. Actually, I have no clear idea why, because although we had attended many of the same parties and other events, it had never occurred to me to progress beyond the level of friend. Until at one particular party.

It was a major shindig at one of the large properties on Harrington Sound and was hosted by the son of the owners who were on vacation somewhere in the Pacific, and who were probably oblivious to the hundred or so people currently abusing their half dozen bathrooms and, it needs to be said, the outside wall of their house. Angela and I both found ourselves unattached and so we quite naturally gravitated towards each other. We were already friends as I have mentioned; she was particularly close to the dynamic trio of Penny, Jane and Sandra and along with the lads, we as a group were part of a large clique of ex-pats who often found themselves in the same place at the same time. And so it was on this particular evening.

We had several dances, and we chatted about our respective past lives in England. I had added to my already substantial intake of Cockspur rum and felt mellow, but on the ball and in complete control, which is important to note. As we talked, I began to hatch a cunning plan of seduction.

It was early morning, but the party was still in full swing. As casually as I could, I asked my companion if she would like to perhaps join me back at the Carisbrook homestead for some more conversation over coffee with a bit of soft music thrown in. No strings attached, I glibly fibbed. And so, with me on my Suzuki trail bike, and her following on her Vespa scooter (long since restored to full health with the aid of Dougie's money), we rode off side by side.

When sparse traffic forced us to adjust to single file, I kept her targeted in my rear-view mirrors. I didn't want to lose her now because she had no idea where Carisbrook was. But the roads were not that busy and I glanced frequently at the panoply of stars spectacularly displayed overhead in the pollution free atmosphere, and wondered how many accidents had been caused by the distractions of the Milky Way… and in the process, almost colliding with a Mini-Moke travelling towards me.

We arrived at Carisbrook and as expected the place was in complete darkness. Leaving a light on to mislead would-be burglars in that neck of the woods, would have been a complete waste of electricity. Not that we had any worries on that score because having become accepted by the local populace, it would have meant dire trouble for anyone from outside the area daring to rip-off a neighbour. They had their principles and a strange set of standards after all. I knew none of the boys were home and in bed because I had counted heads before leaving the party. We had the house to ourselves. Perfecto. Phase one of my wheeze was going according to plan.

Having fiddled nervously around at the front door causing my key to drop to the concrete and bounce off the raised terrace and into the garden beneath, I eventually managed to retrieve it, calm my eagerness, and successfully usher my blonde companion into the house. I put some appropriate music on my Sony twin tape deck – Barry White, in preference to the Steppenwolf tape that was already in the machine – then having ensured Angela was comfily ensconced with a glass of something, I removed myself to the kitchen to make coffee. Apart from the errant front door key, everything was going well.

After our coffees, I mixed more drinks for us both; hers a vodka tonic and mine, a fortifying brandy, and we spent a pleasant hour or so chatting and snuggling closer on the sofa. Then the moment of reckoning and the inevitable question: 'Why don't you stay?' I ventured.

She appeared to mull it over, but then said: 'Thanks, but I'd better go,' which was the not unexpected response.

Then like the gentleman I was, I smiled indulgently and said: 'If you're sure,' and having clinked our glasses one last time before finishing the cocktails, I managed to give the appearance of reluctantly showing her to the door. What Angela did not know was that while I was waiting for water to boil, I had slipped out of the back door, raced around the side of the house to where the bikes were parked, and let the air out of both of her tyres with the aid of a very small screw driver that I knew was tucked away in one of the kitchen drawers, and perfect for tampering with tyre valves.

'You are going nowhere, my beauty,' I whispered to myself, sounding like a panto villain.

Angela paused on the threshold as I held open the front door, and having divulged sensually in my ear; 'perhaps next time,' we exchanged a final semi-serious kiss before she made her way in the darkness towards the silhouettes of the parked vehicles. I wished her a safe journey, then as soon as she had kicked the scooter off its stand and started the engine, I gently closed the door and waited, wearing a lascivious grin. I must have looked like Wile E. Coyote flattened against the door, waiting to jump the Road Runner.

I heard the scooter's engine purr tantalisingly on the motionless bike for a few seconds, and then remarkably pull away. I waited, but the sound of the Vespa receded into the distance. *She must be as canned as me*, was my first thought; my second being concern for

Angela's safety. Perhaps I had not let enough air escape the scooter's tyres? I opened the door and waited some more but once the sound of the Vespa dissolved into the night and then giving it a further few minutes, I closed the door, puzzled. Then the day's excesses swiftly took over as they tend to do once the adrenalin pump reduces speed to an idle, and I made my unsteady way to the comfort of my lonely bed.

I knew nothing more until sometime later that morning when I awoke to the proddings and pokings of Dougie trying to rouse me. 'Are we going to the Coop or what?' he asked. 'And by the way you had better do something about your bike first.' I had no idea what he was talking about, and still rubbing my gluey eyes, I stumbled after him. There, sulking in the drive, was my beloved Suzuki, both tyres flatter than a skinflint's pancake, and following a brief moment of utter bewilderment, realisation slowly dawned. The tyres were not the only ones that were totally deflated!

There is inebriation, and then there is beyond inebriation. Paradoxically my memory of the whole evening was crystal clear and I had felt totally in command, but how far gone was I several hours before, to have been misdirected by my brain and failed to differentiate between a silver-tanked Suzuki trail bike and a red Vespa sewing machine?

Best laid plans.

Angela was completely unaware of the incident at the time, and remained oblivious to it for the next thirty years, when finding ourselves at the wedding of our mutual ex-Bermuda friend Sandra, I took Angela aside and recounted the incident to her. She took it all in and roared with laughter, and it was all I could do to talk her out of grabbing the microphone from the wedding singer, and telling the story to everyone present, including her husband Paul.

SEVENTY-NINE

We have frequently heard over the years that the seventies is regarded as the decade that fashion forgot; though it has to be said that such views often come from so-called male fashion gurus and aficionados, who either advocate stuff that frankly often resembles the product of a panto character's wet dream, or is so dull and lifeless, that even Wurzel Gummidge would be embarrassed to wear it. Indeed, the bizarre design of much of the so-called high fashion for the young, often looks as if it had been donated by The Salvation Army as being unsuitable for their clients. Even winos have their pride. Take the prison-look for trousers; worn half way down the bum cheeks and as baggy as a deflated hot air balloon, whilst at the same time exposing the waistband of underpants, emblazoned with some designer name.

Oh puu-lease!

But in any event, those that decry the seventies could not be more wrong. It was, I believe, a decade of quirky but tasteful eccentricity and colour, as far as fashion was concerned, and reflected the optimism of the time for my generation – in spite of the Cold War and that small concern of being constantly on the edge of nuclear incineration. We were intent on living for the moment and regarded the future as being inconsequential, and that tomorrow would take care of itself. It was not being irresponsible, but simply refusing to worry about things over which we had no control, and as if each day could indeed be our last on Earth. It was our version of pragmatism – a positive statement in an uncertain world.

Those platform shoes, patterned shirts, crazy hair styles and tank tops, totally outrageous at times, but *fun* all the way. I still hanker after those days as several pairs of flares hanging in my wardrobe forty-five years on, just waiting for a recall, will confirm. As do the Cuban heel ankle boots, still in good nick and sitting patiently underneath their bell-bottomed pals; although with my ageing feet now taking on the look of arthritic claws, there is no chance that they will ever again see the light of day.

I remember with great fondness the wonderful loons – light canvas flares, available pretty much in every colour imaginable and sporting twenty-inch bottoms. With our feet totally enshrouded, it looked as if we were gliding along on a cushion of air. And at thirty bob a pair, they were great value, even in those early seventies' days.

We took our cue from the likes of David Bowie and Marc Bolan, and bands such as Roxy Music, Sweet, and Mott the Hoople; and not just the style of clothing, but the fabrics they were fashioned from. I owned a pair of burgundy velvet strides that I wore tucked into knee length leather Cuban heeled boots. Actually, I wore them just once, because having walked into the Robin Hood on one of my very first visits to that establishment, the look of shocked disbelief on the faces of the patrons present, and the sound of stifled gagging, told me in no uncertain terms that Bermuda was not quite ready for that particular experience. To be honest I was not sure about the boots myself, but having only recently met Richard Pedro and purchased several items from his excellent Gentleman's Quarter boutique in Chancery Lane, he had shown me the footwear described and after a convincing sales pitch had offered them for a ridiculously low price.

I had always wanted to try the look, having seen photographs in the similarly named *GQ* magazine some months before in England, but on reflection it had been a bad decision and there had been no repeat performance. My physical appearance did not help. I could have been a model for seaside rock, but definitely not men's fashion. Richard admitted much later that those boots had been hanging around the storeroom for well over two years and he had been desperate to get rid of them. At least I was able to laugh at the memory, albeit through gritted teeth.

Then there was the platform shoe fad. Great, except for the unfortunate incident when Penny sent me shooting off into the void when she stuck one of her chunky items of footwear in the rear wheel of my Honda. But with those two painful exceptions, one to my pride and the other to the Honda and my knees, there was nothing wrong with the trend and combined with those other seventies items of fashion we looked and felt like the Labrador's gonads.

I look back on the many photographs of us all during those memorable years spent in paradise, and it occurs to me that our colourful lifestyles were perfectly matched with what we wore, and is perhaps an indictment of some of today's dowdy and boring clobber.

So let's get this straight... the 1970s. The decade that fashion forgot?

You had to be there!

EIGHTY

It must appear that the whole alcohol-soaked ex-pat squad were in a permanent state of inebriated befuddlement, and well, yes the booze consumption was impressive by anybody's standards, but our capacity had been steadily and expensively building since our entry to Bermuda, and in spite of our nightly expeditions into the alcohol jungle, none of us – at least at Carisbrook, plus our good friends Rob and Terry – seemed to be any the worse for it the following morning. With few exceptions, the accepted definition of drunk simply did not compute and the fast pace of our social lives and the constant raised levels of our metabolic systems seemed to counteract the more disturbing effects of alcoholic intake. Alright, slightly drunk I will concede, and usually by the same suspects, but it was definitely not disorderly.

I had calculated at one point you may recall, that with an unbroken seven day a week attendance at the Robin Hood and other salubrious watering holes (and a few less wholesome establishments it has to be admitted), augmented by at least one all-night Saturday party and a reasonable intake at home; that Dougie and I managed to put away a combination of five bottles of Cockspur and Goslings Black Seal each per week… minimum. But with hand on heart, I can honestly say that we could rarely be described as roaring drunk; slightly unstable, perhaps; giggly, often; but roaring, falling over, obnoxiously drunk…

never (well almost). In fact, there were minutes in the day when we imbibed nothing stronger than my tea.

But for me there was one very notable exception.

I had met the lovely Janet two months before and had managed to *accidentally* meet up with her and husband Robert on several occasions since Janet's birthday evening at Elbow Beach. There were occasions too when Janet, accompanied by her friend and work colleague Jeannie, joined us at Horseshoe Beach, with Robert taking part in some cycling event or other. Moreover, having been introduced to our circle of friends, they seemed to take to our high-speed lifestyle and were happy to join us whenever the circumstances arose, and that of course included the frenetic party scene. As a married couple, they had been part of a completely different clique where dinner parties and days out on boats; games of croquet (I jest) and suchlike were the norm.

They were also both hairdressers and by and large that was also a separate specialist crowd. Consequently, having spent over seven years in Bermuda, they suddenly discovered a new, albeit questionable way to spend their recreational hours with a new bunch of eccentric and completely off-the-wall friends.

There was also a rapidly growing mutual attraction developing between Janet and me, which transcended mere friendship. I had no idea where that was going, and doubted that it ever could be anything other than what it then was – a close and unconsummated relationship – but paradoxically, it was also out of the question for me to believe that I could ever imagine not seeing her again. So when we informed Robert and Janet that there was a shindig coming up way out in St George's Parish one Saturday, they were keen to attend and having given them details, it was agreed we would see them there.

The evening had started with panic stations at Carisbrook. Dougie and I had met in the hallway outside the bedrooms, each of us on the same mission: namely, to borrow a pair of kecks from each other because all of ours were mouldering away in the washing basket waiting to be taken to the iconic Quicky Licky. Graham was away somewhere for the weekend, but Rick was busy tarting himself up in preparation for an evening out with the luscious Barbara, so we converged on his room.

'Rick. We've got an emergency,' I said.

'Yeah, we've got no clean cacks.' Dougie added,

'And?'

'Well, we need to borrow some of yours.'

Ricky laughed, 'I wouldn't let you near any of my underwear, knowing what you two Limey bastards get up to,' he said. 'Ask Graham.'

'Graham's not here,' we said together, then looking at each other for a second or two, the same idea must have entered our heads simultaneously, because we both made off for Graham's bedroom.

'Be careful,' I said, as Dougie and I went through our housemate's chest of drawers. 'You know how tidy Graham is.'

We soon located the appropriate drawer, and selected two pairs.

'Great, he will never know that we have been here, we can put them back tomorrow.'

'Yeah, we really need to get down to the Quicky Licky in the morning,' I agreed. And we were all set for our evening out.

It had been a particularly rollicking night at Elbow Beach the evening before, and going back to a friend's house afterwards for more carousing, Dougie and I had, en-route home, stopped off at the Chicken Coop for breakfast (shock horror), but tired and slightly worse for wear. Nothing strange in that, but a dinner was on the agenda later in the day at the Rum Runners in Hamilton, followed as usual by the entertaining diversions at the Hood before setting off to the St George's party. There was nothing up to that point I had done that had been any different to a normal weekend, but as we drove towards the party in Terry's Mini Cooper, I realised that I felt uncharacteristically crocked and had better shape up if I was going to continue my mission of impressing the delectable Janet.

We duly arrived and finding no parking spaces in the streets around the large house where the party was being held, and judging by the volume of the music and George McCrea giving it large with 'Rock Your Baby' booming out into the night, the rave was in full swing. Terry drove into the grounds, across what had once been a manicured lawn prior to our arrival, and parked amongst some trees. Terry, Rob and Dougie leapt out of the car and made for the house leaving me to struggle, in my inebriated state, to extricate myself from the back seat, an exercise usually executed with youthful zeal like my departing buddies, but on this occasion with a good deal of difficulty. Having managed the procedure, I stood for a moment trying to get my bearings, but confusion reigned. I was lost, and I staggered from tree to tree in an effort to find my way out of the wood, with just one thought – Janet – and foolishly not thinking for one minute that the last thing I should be contemplating was trying to impress anyone, let alone the lady in question.

Seeing double was a common occurrence according to those who were less able to hold their booze and was something that in those days was not a phenomenon that I had often experienced. But on this occasion, I knew that I had reached that dangerously advanced stage of pissedness, because having gone through the seeing-double stage, I found myself viewing everything in quadruplicate. Hence the small grove of trees that we had parked amongst, now appeared as a dense threatening wood, and I felt like one half of the Hansel and Gretel partnership, completely lost and near to panic. I could see the house not fifty yards away and hear the sounds of some serious partying going down, but how to get there had me temporarily bewildered.

When I finally managed to find my way into the throbbing atmosphere of the crowded building and locate my friends, they thought the whole thing was hilarious, pointing out that there were only a dozen or so trees that comprised my 'forest,' which I was already vaguely aware of, and was confirmed much later when we left to return home. Strangely, once inside, instead of presenting myself to Janet as an embarrassingly drunken blob, with slurred speech and uncontrollable eyeballs, I miraculously seemed to quickly regain control and managed to convince myself that it was perhaps something I ate.

'Yeah, sure it was,' Dougie said later, shaking his head, and giving a sarcastic chuckle.

Whatever the cause, Janet told me much later, when I had garnered the courage to come clean and regale her with the whole story, that she had not been aware of my condition. But on reflection, perhaps she was just being nice. Nevertheless, with things going off as well as I had hoped, I came away feeling that we were another small step closer in what could turn out to be a dangerous and clandestine relationship.

Dougie and I arrived home at some unspeakable hour Sunday morning, and before hitting the hay, we kept the promise we had made earlier, and carefully folding the underpants we had borrowed, put them gently back into Graham's drawer.

EIGHTY-ONE

August is a special month of the year. Although strictly speaking it is not the height of the summer, it is the month that many most associate with summer activities past and present. August was the one time in the school year when we had a full unbroken month of freedom from lessons, homework and in particular the sneering teacher Tony Lever, my first-year nemesis at Ashmead Secondary Modern.

Like many other businesses, my dad's factory would close down annually during the first two weeks of August, and every year for the first ten years of my life, we would spend two glorious weeks with my aunt and uncle in Exmouth, South Devon. As a small boy I remember it was the month when we would pack our stuff into well-worn suitcases, lug them onto the trolleybus that took us to the station and from thence to a place of holiday bliss for a fortnight. The number of postcards that my parents sent home bearing the obligatory *Wish you were here* on one side, and a caricature of a be-smocked Devon yokel on the other declaring *Yer Tis!*, probably went some considerable way to helping the Devonshire card manufacturers remain in profit.

Yes, pure happiness. The one month of the year that was completely untarnished with that place that is traditionally described as representing the best days of our lives. The hysterical joy that poured out of us kids as we raced for the school gates at the end of term, gave lie to that particular dictum. It certainly did for me. These days the sheer numbers of tourists accompanied by their screaming broods only goes to remind me of this, but that's alright because solace can be found in those endless G&Ts shared with friends at the setting of the sun – another very seasonal activity – which on rare occasions when I think about it, has also been partaken with the *rising* of the sun. Most importantly for me though, it is the month when, in the summer of 1974 my present wife and I realised that there was the start of something important and life changing, and euphemistically speaking, we got together.

It was on the aptly named, *Cruise of the August Moon.*

The government tender *Canima* was the vessel in question; one of two such craft owned by the Bermudian government and moored at Dockyard in Sandys Parish. They each had a seven-hundred-person capacity, and were used to ferry passengers from the larger cruise liners that were unable to berth alongside Front Street, and bring them ashore at Bermuda's capital, Hamilton. The *Canima* had been chartered by the owners of the Robin Hood for a fun and alcohol-fuelled night cruising the Bermuda islands.

There had been a similar cruise the year before, also organised by the Robin Hood, which had been a success and a lot of fun, albeit without live music. Lessons had been learned about the need for entertainment and other elements, and the 1974 August cruise promised to be something very special, and from the start it was obvious that it was going to be a night to remember.

Dougie and I had volunteered to accompany Jack in the Robin Hood van that was loaded with booze and sundry supplies for the evening, and offload them at the Royal Naval Dockyard where *Canima* was berthed. We collected Colin Marshall, who had also volunteered his services, from his apartment on the way and in typical style we had to drag him from his bed and wait for our hungover pal to throw on some clothes. Such was the number of tickets sold, several trips for the beer and spirit supplies were necessitated. Hundreds of thirsty partygoers was going to require tanker-sized loads of beer and rum, and other alcoholic and non-alcoholic delights. We had no idea how many tickets had been sold, but, later, judging by the line of passengers waiting patiently to board, it appeared there was every reason to suppose that the supposed capacity of 700 had been exceeded.

Boarding was from 7pm at Albuoy's Point near Front Street and embarkation fixed for 7.30. A dozen or so of the Robin Hood regulars had volunteered for bar service, and Dougie, Rob, Terry and I had grabbed the first two-hour shift on each of the two main bars which were situated at either end of the ship. Dougie and I had the added help of Colin Marshall and one other, whilst Terry and Rob had enlisted their own help. We had turned up extra early to prepare the things for the inevitable rush, but several hundred ticket holders had the same idea and we began to serve almost immediately.

It was pandemonium even before we were fully loaded and able to cast-off, which was delayed in any case because one of the groups booked to provide the music – Burning Ice – had not turned up. Word got back to us that certain members of the band were being held at the police station in Hamilton on some charge or other, but Richard Floyd managed to work his magic, the temporary release of the members of Burning Ice was secured. They joined us along with Genesis, another local band, who had also been booked for the night (not *the* Genesis with Messrs Collins and Rutherford it must be stressed), and almost an hour late, we at last slipped our moorings and glided majestically away from Hamilton's dockside.

Genesis had joined the ship at dockyard, and were able to set up in advance, ready for the off, so as we made for open water, we were entertained by the band belting out the reggae strains of 'I Shot the Sheriff'. As an aside, I have never quite understood the thinking of a man who openly confesses to shooting the sheriff, but who is adamant that it wasn't him who wasted the deputy. The gunman is toast anyway, so why keep denying the lesser charge? But I digress.

Most of those who had volunteered to tend the bars were kitted out in *I Made Marion at the Robin Hood* tee shirts, but our little gang preferred to sport our best spiffy ensembles as we always did – at least the small percentage of gear that was not waiting for the overdue excursion to our laundromat. After all, there was a party much later after we had docked, and it would be precious time wasted if we had to return home for a change of clothes. We had worked out our shift rota so that would leave us free to let our hair down, and get stuck into the evening and making sure there would be plenty of opportunity to party-on-down with the other guests. Because of the long delay at dockside, we had worked for longer than our allotted two hours, and when we at last walked away from the bar, the deck was awash with enough spilled alcohol and melted ice to fill several bathtubs. Drinks were priced at a bargain 75 cents and sandwiches at one dollar, so plenty of encouragement to eat, drink and... eat and drink some more.

The Robin Hood had remained open, but as few customers were expected, Tinny and Barbara Ann held the fort. It was strange that we, as regulars at the Hood, were serving drinks to the team of bar staff who had the night off and were given the chance to relax and enjoy the party with the rest of us.

As the name of the cruise suggested, there was indeed a full moon that night, and obviously somebody had been rigorous in their homework when choosing the date and title of the event. To complete the picture, the sky was clear and with the total absence of industrial pollution, a tidal wave of twinkling stars and far away galaxies was spread out overhead in the breathtaking canopy. The air was balmy and the sea like shimmering glass, with the scent of frangipani, jasmine and other exotics hanging in the air, and the clamour from several hundred serious partygoers notwithstanding, it was absolute perfection. With drinks flowing freely right from the start, it was impossible to imagine that it would be less than a memorable night. As the evening wore on, any remaining sober inhibitions were disappearing fast as Burning Ice got into their stride and the *Canima* with its cargo of revellers, rocked into the Bermudian night. This was the stuff of which dreams were made and in our case we all agreed years later, a defining moment in time.

We had finished our first chaotic shifts at our respective bars and were standing off to one side admiring the miniskirts, hot pants and low-cut tops (the girls looked pretty good too) and I inhaled deeply and took in the heady and familiar perfumes on the breeze. 'Smell that,' I said as I tilted my head and savoured the fragrant air. There was a pause as the boys lifted their heads and sniffed dramatically, bloodhound style.

Rob licked his lips. 'Yeah, Acapulco Gold I reckon.'

'Nah, that's definitely home-grown,' countered Dougie.

'I detect a hint of Lebanese hash,' Terry chipped in.

'Not the grass,' I said. Although I had to agree there was a certain fragrance rising up from the crowded deck that was exotic to say the least, and which I personally felt leaned towards Columbian red. 'Go over to the side of the boat and you'll see what I mean.'

'Ship,' Terry corrected.

'What?'

'It's a ship not a boat.'

'Who cares – there, get a load of that,' I said as we reached the starboard side; which is the right-hand side if you are facing forward. I was an expert on that nautical stuff. We had moved away from the intoxicating mist of the herbal substances and tobacco being enjoyed by the revellers, and were facing into the delicately flavoured breeze. Leaning on the handrail looking out on the Great Sound and the small islands dotted around, I believed that we were all thinking the same thing at that moment, silently taking in the splendour of the night, as if we each were locking away the memory for future times.

'Yeah, see what you mean,' Dougie admitted finally as he took a deep breath, triggering great intakes of air from the rest of us.

'Strangely intoxicating,' Terry suggested.

'That's a big word Terry,' Rob said, sounding that he was mightily impressed, although his expression indicated otherwise. It was his new word for the day, Terry told us, and he had simply been waiting for the opportunity to use it.

'What – "strangely"?' quipped Dougie. Terry had access to many big words in his capacity as a newspaper employee, he loftily told us in his ersatz journalistic voice, although we all knew that his job at the newspaper was selling ads and taking occasional photographs.

'Great isn't it,' I enthused, getting back to the subject of the sweetly perfumed air, prompting Rob to ask…

'What is it?… that scent?'

I turned to him, 'that's the smell of Bermuda,' as if that was explanation enough. A heady yet subtle mixture of the many sub-tropical flowers, shrubs and trees – something I could not help noticing soon after arriving on the island many months before, and one that I never lost my appreciation for or took for granted the whole time I was there. It was a bouquet that would come back to me at odd times in the years to come, taking me back immediately to those happy days spent with good friends in a unique place and that one extra special night on the water.

'If you could only bottle it,' Rob murmured, and we all nodded our heads in agreement.

After a lengthy pause of joint reflection – no pun intended – our reverie was broken by a shout from Dougie, bringing us back to the real present.

'Intoxicating,' he yelled, repeating Terry's comment. 'Which Cockspur rum is, and I've finished mine, so time for another drinkie,' and with a collective nodding of heads, we stumped off towards the bar, all hair and flares; pushing through the seething mass of people who were seriously getting down to Bumpy, the vocalist, and his Burning Ice bandmates as they gave their spirited rendition of Edwin Starr's *War*…

'…War-huh… what is it good for?' Bumpy sang out sonorously.

'Absolutely nothing!' The crowd yelled back.

'Say it again… War-huh… What is it good for?' He bellowed even louder, and then pointing the microphone out to the dancing throng, to a man and woman, we roared in response – 'ABSOLUTELY NOTHING!'

We had acquired a number of fat Black Beauties, also known as 'speed,' to get us through the evening and the anticipated party in Happy Valley Road wherever the hell that was, after we had docked in the early hours. This was only Saturday after all and there was still a lot happening the following day that we did not want to miss. Being a chef and required to help prepare breakfast the following morning for the Deepdene Manor clients where he worked, Rob was particularly anxious to keep alert and not miss out on any of the fun. We had popped the capsules earlier after dinner, and by the time *Canima* had sailed, we were feeling no pain and flying at ten thousand feet. At one point Terry pointed out that the three of us were sounding like a tape being played fast forward. What he didn't realise was that in pointing this out, he was also prattling at such a rate, each word merged into the next as if there was a deadline for delivery and he was running behind schedule. When we pointed this out to him, with Dougie telling him that he was like a fart in a colander, the writer in Terry just mumbled (at speed of course): 'I am constantly overwhelmed by my shortcomings.' Mmm, the booze was working. Ricky, who had stumbled up to us at that point and had overheard the last part of our conversation, stopped and with a puzzled cross-eyed look, asked, 'What the fuck is a fart in a colander?'

'It means that you don't know what hole to come out of first,' I informed him.

It still obviously meant nothing to our friend, and after a few seconds of considering my explanation, continued on his stumbling way chuckling and muttering, 'You fucking Limeys kill me.'

I knew that Janet was on board somewhere, accompanied by her friend and work colleague Jeannie; they had approached the bar on several occasions, and I promised to find them once my shift was over. I also knew that Robert would not be there for some reason that I never quite understood, and felt a unique opportunity opening up before me. The problem was finding them both amongst the hundreds of revellers.

I saw my friends Richard Pedro and Lesley chatting with other familiar faces from the Robin Hood along with Vicki, Lesley's housemate at Wallingford, and the girl I had treated so badly at their party earlier in the year. We joined them for a few minutes and although Vicki and I were on friendly terms again, I still felt wretched over the way I had let her down some months before, but was glad that she seemed to have moved on, and if the rumours were correct, had resumed her relationship with Mike – the guy who was the bar tender that had been the subject of Matt Taylor's hostile attention at the same party. Mike was not in evidence that evening, however. I also recalled that it was on the previous cruise in 1973 that I had first met Vicki. She had been impressed, I recalled, when I correctly guessed her star sign, Sagittarius, and gave her some trumped-up rubbish about my star sign Aries being fully compatible with Sagittarius women. It was a total guess – a one in twelve chance – and I had hit the bullseye.

Richard Floyd was doing his regular PR job, chatting to all and sundry and giving everyone the feeling that each of us was a special friend, as indeed I suppose we all were. These days it is called networking, and Richard was the master. In fact, it was Richard who directed me to where Janet and Jeannie were located on the ship when last seen, but the mystery was how he even knew I was interested in finding them as I had been careful to keep my feelings about Janet between me and my three close friends. I should not have been surprised. There did not seem to be a thing that Richard was not fully informed about – the detention of certain band members notwithstanding.

The music flowed over us and the booze flowed through us, as we wove with an element of difficulty, through the crowded deck, stopping to chat to other people we knew and when the chance arose, grab a dance with whoever caught our eye. For me, this included the lovely Angela and I was on the verge of baring all about the tyre incident at Carisbrook – the deflated tyres and the even more deflated me – when I spotted Janet and Jeannie being chatted up by some Jack the Lads on the edge of the dancing throng, and I hurriedly excused myself and made my way over. Janet saw me approach and gave me a smiling wave that had the gang of would-be Lotharios swivelling their heads my way in disapproval. Jeannie, bless her, grabbed one that was to her liking and jerked him onto the dance floor leaving me to give the evil eye to his companions who slunk off to search for fresh possibilities elsewhere. The rest is history, and in fact there is little to tell. Dougie and company were off following their own agendas, leaving Janet and I to spend the remainder of the cruise together. The next three hours seemed to dissolve in a flash. I am tempted to say that time stood still, but that would be too cheesy... but it did. Many close dances later and before we knew it, the *Canima* was edging back into its berth at Albuoy's Point, albeit behind schedule due to the earlier delay. We parted on the quay and for the time being went our separate ways – she to her bed, and me to another all-nighter. It was after 3am, the night was yet young, and in those glorious mid-seventies' days, so were we.

The Happy Valley party was the usual rip-roaring affair that had taken on extra intensity as we and several dozen fellow cruisers arrived, infiltrating the bash and replenishing the rapidly depleting bar with our offerings. The Black Beauties were doing their job admirably and in fact as it turned out, far too well. I was not able to get any sleep for two days, such was their potency, and I was bouncing around for forty-eight hours before, exhausted, on arriving home from work on Tuesday afternoon, I finally crashed out into a dreamless sleep on the sofa still in my work gear.

EIGHTY-TWO

It was very late summer and we had been invited to a party at a house overlooking Warwick Long Bay, which had something to do with Juanitas' family I recall, and there were a number of their American friends in attendance. I had no idea about the status of these people in relation to Juanita or anyone else present, but in any case, as far as the occupants of Carisbrook were concerned, it was just another party and we were there in force, plus the dynamic duo of Terry and Rob of course. The only difference with this party was that it was commencing in the afternoon, which wasn't to say it would not progress well into the night, but there it was, a party is a party after all. A barbecue was in continuous use, and we had all binged on the burgers, sausages, steaks, snapper and king prawns that were being doled out as if there would be no tomorrow.

Feeling suitably replete, I was sitting on a raised lawned area of the garden, and partnered with another large Dark and Stormy, I was having one of my reflective moments. I had been introduced to several of the Americans present who, it appeared, were on vacation, albeit a fairly brief one. Two of those people were Ben and Cheryl Morton from Rosemont, Pennsylvania, and they were very interested in Dougie and me, and England in general. They also liked our distorted English sense of humour, although I suspected that most of it went over their heads. They told us that they were actually 'add-ons' for the trip – a first time in Bermuda for them – and merely friends of others of the group that had Bermuda connections and had invited them along.

It was to be a significant meeting for me, because although I still had some months left of my contract, I had often pondered whether or not to travel to the States on completion, in order to check out the place for possible jobs and even relocation. When I told them all of this, they immediately insisted that I stay with them if and when I made the trip; they had plenty of room they told me, and I could stay for as long as I liked. It was a very generous, and I felt, genuine offer. Little did I know at that point, my stay in Bermuda would come to an unexpected and premature end.

As I sat gazing out to sea my mind skipped back over the last twenty months or so, and random events flitted through my head like photographic slides… our explosive introduction to Ricky's Barbara; the fabulous wheelie at Flamingo Beach; the two bottles of good champagne Richard P had been 'given' at his brother Roger's wedding and which we had taken to an all-nighter after the reception. An incident I had recently been told about after Penny went for water ski lessons, and typically had ended up skimming the water on her back with her ski-bedecked feet in the air, also floated through my mind and I smiled to myself. That was typically Penny. So many happy times and more to come. But fewer than I hoped for, and I would be taking up the Mortons' offer sooner than they or I had envisaged.

Madison, a woman of about forty and another of the American party, was also introduced to us; Ben had whispered to me that she was worth millions, had seen off two husbands who had kicked the bucket whilst suspiciously young, hmm… and lived in Bryn Mawr, a very upmarket township on what is known as the Main Line in Pennsylvania. The connection apparently being that Ben was the vice president of a bank where Madison did business. She was currently single and looking for another victim… sorry, husband.

Not my cup of tea, and Dougie was not keen, not keen at all. 'I wouldn't even go there with yours,' he told me in his usual indelicate way. 'Looks as if she's been in a collision with an oil tanker,' he went on.

'Yes, alright Doug, you've made your point,' then a long pause before I continued, 'Ben tells me that she is a millionaire and unmarried.'

Dougie stopped, looked from me to Madison – who I noticed was now making her way over to us – then back to me, and finally fixing his eyes on the lady, got up and with a broad smile said, 'Hi, I'm Dougie. I'm up for it if you are: let me get you another drink,' turned her around and strolled off with his hand around her waist, steering her towards the bar.

I later made my way back to the elevated seat overlooking the ocean, and turning, I watched in fascination as the sun disappeared beneath the horizon. Apart from the muted sounds of the party going on nearby, there was a moment of relative silence and a feeling of serenity swept over me.

Then the tree frogs broke into song.

EIGHTY-THREE

I had first met Ellie during one of the parties at the house called Wallingford on Pitts Bay Road, and having bumped into her and her friend, another Barbara – an Amazonian female who had the height and build that signalled that she was able to take on all comers – on numerous occasions since, either at the beach or certain of our mutually attended drinking establishments. Ellie was a masseur and at some point, I asked her for a date, and for quite some time we saw each other on a regular basis. We would often meet at the beach, and spend weekends together, and as a massage therapist at Deepdene Manor Hotel – the same hotel where our mate Rob was employed – I had, for a time, a standing appointment out of normal working hours on a Friday evening, to enjoy a free whirlpool, sauna, and full body massage. Ellie was doing this in her own time and had obtained permission to use the facilities from her employers, and I had the pleasure of meeting them one evening when they dropped by to pick something up from their office. It was also somewhat embarrassing – but I am not going to enlarge on that.

It was interesting to note that although I was under the impression the term for a female masseur, was masseuse, a correct assumption it must be said, Ellie insisted on being referred to as a masseur or massage therapist, believing that there were connotations that the word masseuse was associated with. I could see where she was coming from.

Another of Ellie's friends was Juanita whose parents owned the popular and much-frequented Flamingo Beach Club, and one weekend we were invited to have tea with Mrs Matthias, Juanita's mother, at the family house adjoining the resort, and where we had attended the recent party where we had met Ben and Cheryl. I say *we* were invited, but it was Ellie who had received the invitation and had asked if she could take me along.

It turned out to be just Ellie and me, one other couple who I can barely remember, and Juanita with her newly-acquired Australian boyfriend – and of course, Mrs Matthias. Her husband obviously had better things to do, probably in connection with the business, which being the usual busy weekend was in full swing a short distance away. It was all very informal, with the seven of us lounging on overstuffed chairs and sofas in the spacious lounge, where a light and pleasing breeze gently ruffled the curtains at the open French windows. We helped ourselves to the pastries, sandwiches and cakes that Mrs Matthias had laid out for us, swopping stories and jokes as we ate. It was an unconventional Bermuda afternoon, for me, but we were all having a good time in each other's company.

Then Gary, the Aussie boyfriend, reached for his bag that was leaning against the side of the sofa he was sharing with Juanita, whipped out a copy of *Playgirl* magazine, selected the centrefold pages and presented it to Mrs Matthias.

'What d'ya think of that then, Mrs M?' he enquired, sporting a cheeky lopsided Aussie grin. It was obviously pre-planned and designed to embarrass our hostess, and was Gary's warped idea of a joke.

The picture in question was of a good-looking young guy with an expression on his face that said: *Bet you can't beat that*, and displaying the biggest willy I had ever seen. So much so, I thought that it must be a very clever and lifelike plastic prosthetic knob. Whatever its origins, it was a mighty weapon and had me reflexively crossing my legs. I doubt that the centrefold guy would have been able to.

Mrs Matthias, who on the face of it was always the picture of sobriety and primness, took the magazine, adjusted her spectacles, turned the magazine first one way and then the other. Then without cracking her face she handed it back to Gary and told him: 'Average son, average.' This had us all in stitches and was one up to Mrs Matthias, surprising our Australian companion, who had obviously expected to evoke a shocked reaction from Juanita's mum.

The rest of the afternoon continued in the same good-humoured vein and having polished off a large quantity of tasty grub, along with much tea, coffee and beer, Mrs Matthias asked Gary if he had enjoyed his very first Bermuda high tea.

'Bonzer, Mrs M,' he said. 'It was facking great... oh. I'm sorry. I didn't mean t'say that,' he apologised sheepishly in his distinctive Aussie drawl. Juanita just looked on with obvious disapproval.

Mrs Matthias looked unruffled and waved it aside. 'Don't worry about it.'

'Na really, I don't want ya' t'think I go round swearing like that all the time... even though I am an Aussie,' he added with a nervous laugh, obviously thinking that his nationality presupposed he was a filthy mouthed slob and cursing was always expected from Australian men... which of course it generally is.

'Just forget it Gary, these things happen,' Mrs Matthias generously tried to assure him as she got to her feet and brushed off imaginary crumbs from her expensive looking shorts.

There was a sullen pause from Gary, but he still wasn't going to let it go. 'I mean,' he continued, 'I'm goin' out with y'daughter and all, and y'know...'

'Look,' cut in Mrs M much more forcefully this time, 'it's forgotten and let's hear no more of it.' Then she left the room.

Gary still looked crestfallen and let out a deep sigh, before leaning over and whispering conspiratorially in my ear: 'Shit, Col, I feel such a cant.'

EIGHTY-FOUR

I had been given a month's notice from my place of work. It had not come completely out of the blue, because we had experienced major troubles on one of the large contracts we were involved with. For my part, there was certainly nothing wrong with the work completed by me and my regular work companion Nobby. But against my advice, not enough of a certain bituminous product had been ordered, and I had no choice but to use another material that was provided, which in my experience I knew would not stand the test of time. In addition, the builder's work relating to my job was incomplete and in crucial areas, sub-standard, but in spite of requests from me to have these rectified, nothing was done, meaning I could not complete our end of the contract.

As it became more and more involved and me being at the bottom of the food chain so to speak, it was obvious that I was being targeted as the fall guy – not by my own boss, but the powers that be at the American controlled main contractors. I later discovered that a New York-based subcontractor had also tendered for the roofing job, but against the main contractor's wishes (they were obviously old pals) our Bermudian company had secured the work. A representative of the NY company was even flown over, paid for by the main contractor presumably, to find faults in our work, and it was gratifying to hear from him when we met on site, that he could see nothing wrong. What went on later behind closed doors was another matter.

I knew our company was having some problems finding enough work to justify the workforce head-count, mainly because of a temporary government ban on all new hotels and hotel extensions and other related work, which normally constituted a good part of the firm's order book. Those two situations combined, therefore, had brought to a head my contract being terminated.

It was a traumatic and thought-provoking time and gave me cause to reflect about the previous twenty-two months since my arrival. Although I had made a point of regularly reminding myself of my good fortune, and telling myself to not take my circumstances for granted, I now had to reconcile myself to the sudden adjustment I was forced to make, about a life without Bermuda and my good friends.

I had arrived in Bermuda at the beginning of the previous year with mixed feelings and a massive amount of guilt. The trauma of my brief terminated marriage that led to my having to give up my daughter, which in turn was instrumental in my decision to simply walk away. But seen retrospectively, my time on *de Rock* had served as a therapeutic and healing period.

I hadn't been looking for a life partner and I was still trying to come to terms with my feelings with regard to Stevie, and the way things had turned out between us. But as time passed I had slowly come to realise that, as much as the previous months had probably represented the best and most significant period in my life, the prospect of that well-worn term, *settling down*, was perhaps not as unrealistic as it had been, and that maybe I should be thinking of the future. My mind-set had been altered by one, and only one, significant factor that had entered my life at that point, and that was the lady called Janet.

We had spent a limited amount of time together, it was true, but we had been instantly drawn to each other that night at Elbow Beach and beyond, and although neither of us dared say out loud what we both knew to be true, there was a closeness that had developed rapidly and completely, culminating in expressing our mutual feelings on board the *Canima*.

As a hairstylist, Janet had invited me to her and Robert's cottage in Warwick, ostensibly to get her scissors to work on my unruly locks, and as I took in their home and what they had created together in their seven years of marriage, the reality hit me: that this was the kind of life I was now ready for. It was probably out of the question that Janet and I had a future together, but what I was seeing was a template for my own vision of what could lay ahead. I regarded Janet as beautiful, but it came home to me what the important characteristics are for that perfect relationship when I remembered an experience I had the previous year.

When I was still living at Little Arches, I dated a lady I had met in the Hood one night. I shall refer to her as Deidre. She was stunning – tall and slim, with shoulder length blonde hair, and a naturally lovely face that looked as if it received little or no make-up. She had a smile that was warm and a laugh that was infectious. She also seemed completely unaware of how attractive she was.

She fell for my chat-up spiel, and I thought I would impress her by cooking dinner at Little Arches. I went to town (in my own way), preparing the dish that Tricia had treated us to months before: bobotie. I bought the best bottle of wine I could find – the best in my book back then was anything up to five dollars – and dressed the table smartly, à la Chicken Coop plus A Levels – and, although I can hardly believe it now, I even lit a bleeding candle.

And the bottom line? As perfect as Deidre seemed to be, we simply did not hit it off. There was no spark whatsoever with which to take that one step further, viz, the road to a happy, non-committal relationship. We had absolutely nothing in common and the conversation was so one-sided, I was on the verge of holding a mirror to her mouth to check if she was still breathing. It was not Deidre's fault, we were simply and totally incompatible in spite of her wondrous looks and pleasant demeanour, and the evening was cut short with us both returning to the Robin Hood – she gravitating to her friends and me to mine.

With Janet, there was always something beyond the looks, which as I may have hinted at previously, were very special – and a mutual and immediate bond that was impossible to ignore.

EIGHTY-FIVE

My day of departure was fixed, but then Janet gave me the news that Robert would be flying to Montreal in Canada where a major cycling road event was to take place, and although she had been asked to accompany him, Janet had declined, ostensibly because it would be a boring week or so watching spandex-clad cyclists on their expensive treaders whizzing along the road, or round a track or whatever. What she did not know at the time, was that I had received advance notice of Robert's trip, and had altered my flight-out accordingly, meaning that we would have a few precious days together.

I had told Robert about my revised flight times (although not the reason why) and we had arranged to meet in the Rum Runners for lunch the day before his own departure. It would probably be the last we would see of each other. But looking back, I found it hard to believe that Robert was oblivious to the closeness between Janet and me, and after lunch when we were saying our final goodbyes, Robert said seriously: 'Take care of Janet,' and it was almost as if he was sanctioning what was to come.

The boys' final night out together was two days before my actual departure, and was a muted affair. It was the end of an important chapter in my life, and that was to be the final night with my good friends. Naturally we had gathered at the Robin Hood, but the three

Dazzlers were absent, saying that they felt it would be too emotional, so I had promised to call round to say goodbye to Penny, Sandra and Jane, after leaving the Hood that night. Richard Pedro was also not present, and I had arranged to meet him at the shop on the morning of my flight.

I was moved when Rob stepped forward and presented me with a gold Zodiac pendant signifying my April birthday and inscribed on the back: *From All Your Friends in Bermuda*, for which each one of the members of our little tribe had contributed. Rob insisted I say a few words, and I tried to make light of the situation, but it was very hard to keep from showing just how I really felt.

I had other plans for my final night, I had informed Terry, Rob and my housemates Dougie, Graham and Rick, and they understood why I would prefer to have the house to myself. The fact was Janet would be joining me; we had spent several days together after Robert's departure, but we still needed to tell each other things that had largely remained unsaid, and make a commitment to our future which was now clearly inevitable.

And that's precisely what happened. We spent the night together and resolved to meet up in Philadelphia after I had settled in. The following morning was the most difficult time yet, having to say goodbye on the steps at Carisbrook, and watching Janet drive off down Mount Hill. I had made it clear to everyone that I wanted to leave the island in the same manner I had arrived – on my own. Goodbyes were always heart rending, but extending the pain in the airport departure lounge only increased the agony further.

EIGHTY-SIX

As the vibrations of the massive Rolls Royce engines changed pitch, and our Eastern Airlines Lockheed L-1011 began to roll, I was suddenly overcome by an inexpressible feeling of loneliness. The friends I had made over the previous twenty or so months were no longer going to be present and playing a part in my everyday life. I was leaving them behind and the amazing times we had shared would be no more. Times that were filled with laughter and the sheer joy and privilege of being alive in one of Earth's most beautiful locations, was being consigned to history. True, another adventure lay ahead, but the feeling of finality and the irrefutable truth that nothing I would experience in the future could compare with my all too brief Bermuda sojourn, was a fact I was already struggling to come to terms with. My only consolation, and it was a powerful one, was that Janet and I had agreed there was something worth following up between us, and she had agreed to join me in Philly for an extended stay at some point in the foreseeable future, subject of course to my hosts' agreement and the reaction of Robert.

Although I was unaware of it at the time, I was to later learn that Robert had met a young lady during his trip to Canada and was immediately smitten. What was to follow was a mutual and amicable agreement that whilst Janet was with me in Pennsylvania, Robert's new lady would fly to Bermuda from Montreal to be with him. As bizarre as it would sound, and like something found in a Mills & Boon novel, fate it seemed, would be kind and things would fall into place for everyone.

Ricky had kindly offered to take me to the airport in a car he had loaned, and it was not easy saying our goodbyes outside the terminal building. I had called on the three *Dazzlers* the two nights before, only to find that Penny had absented herself in order to avoid an emotional scene. She had become like a little sister to me, and I understood how she felt. I felt it too. It was also very hard to say goodbye to my partner in crime, Dougie, although we both put on a brave face and laughed and joked, pretending we were unaffected as we hugged and said our farewells, promising to keep in close touch. In reality, I wondered when I might see my best buddy again, if at all. It felt as if I was leaving after a frenetic two-year long party, and the future suddenly seemed uncertain.

Once aboard my flight, I had been unexpectedly seated in what passed for first class, and had, I suspected, something to do with Jack Harris who I had seen earlier that morning at the Robin Hood where I had called in to settle my bar tab – not an inconsiderable sum. He had an association with the airline or some such thing I had been told, and there was certainly nobody other than Jack I could think of, who could pull the appropriate strings. I never did find out for sure, but it was a friendly and generous gesture that was appreciated.

Although it meant very little to me at the time, Eastern Airlines was, up to that point, the only airline in the world that flew the new wide-bodied L-1011, commonly known as the Tristar, and featured the new state-of-the-art ultra-quiet Rolls Royce engines. Our pilot welcomed us all aboard his lovely new toy and introduced himself as Bobby Roy Almendinger (that's what it sounded like and how I noted it down) who briefed us on the route we would be taking; the present ambient temperatures in both Baltimore and Philadelphia, and the anticipated time of arrival in each.

I was vaguely impressed by the strangely muted whine of the powerful engines, but I was far too immersed in my own disconsolate feelings to give it much attention. Far more impressive to me soon after take-off, was the endless complimentary supply of free rum-Collins cocktails that were being doled out by the attractive and attentive cabin staff, so much so that when we arrived in Baltimore for a seemingly unnecessary ninety minute stopover and allowed to deplane into the terminal building, I was so chilled and mellow I felt I was floating – as were my back teeth. It was no surprise therefore that I lost all sense of time and geographical direction, and was somewhat surprised to hear my name being announced over the public address system ordering me back to the plane that was waiting to resume its short onward journey to Philadelphia. Thank goodness for the two uniformed gentlemen who made sure I was escorted to the relevant area. Although a bit unnecessarily rough I thought.

Just fifteen minutes out from Philadelphia, I had been recounting those last two years with the multitude of precious memories whirling through my mind, and I marvelled at how much I had crammed into such a relatively brief period. I pondered how much I had changed and what the immediate future held. When would I see my daughter Emily? I tried to imagine how she looked now at six years old. I had received no photographs, but then neither had I sent any of my own. Whichever way I looked at it and whatever my reasons, I had not been a very successful father.

Then there was Stevie. I fervently hoped that she would be happy and have a fulfilled and healthy life. What if I had stayed in England? What if Stevie had been able to move to Bermuda? What if, what if, what if… lives are built, and sometimes lives are ruined on 'what ifs'.

I closed my eyes as the aircraft began its final descent which somehow seemed to symbolise the curtain coming down on a phenomenal life experience, spent in a stunning location that had been shared with a collection of people perfectly placed there as if by a Hollywood casting director...

All the right people, in exactly the right place, at precisely the right time.

EIGHTY-SEVEN

A POSTSCRIPT

The chain of coincidences that had occurred during my time in Bermuda, had one more link to add seventeen years down the line, when a chance remark led to a notable and welcome reunion.

I had secured a job as manager for a national roofing company, working between their Norwich and North London offices, which led to Janet and me settling in rural West Suffolk, roughly midway between the two.

Janet discovered early on that there were many young mums who were tied to their homes because of family, and unable to travel the ten miles into any of the three nearest towns, opening up an untapped market that offered a mobile hairdressing service to the outlying areas. Those were the days when this kind of service was almost unheard of, and Janet began a successful business for people in their own homes that was to last until our retirement many years later.

One of her regular clients lived in a small village called Brockley Green close to Bury St Edmunds, and on one of her frequent visits, the conversation, for some reason, turned to the client's neighbours – a retired couple by the name of *Wight*. A strange way to spell the name Janet and her client thought, the common version being *White* of course.

It was purely by chance that Janet recounted the conversation to me, and she had my immediate attention. My erstwhile temporary friend from early Bermuda days, Ian, also had the same uncommon surname. Could there be a family connection?

I joined Janet on her next appointment in Brockley Green, and cheekily rang the doorbell of Mr and Mrs Wight's smart house. To my shocked delight, the couple were indeed the retired parents of Ian, who they told me was married and doing rather well in Grand Cayman where the rest of the Wight siblings were located.

Through them, and via Ian's wife who neither of us had met, we recommenced a regular correspondence. Then in 2001 we finally met up, after receiving an invitation to Ian's fiftieth birthday event in the Desert Orchid Suite at Kempton Park. He had several horses running that day, and the first two races on the card were named in honour of Ian's half-century on Earth. An excellent meal was laid on for our party of sixty or more that included a number of Cayman Islanders and Wight family members; and on our table a very interesting gentleman who, it transpired, was Ian's Lambourn trainer. There were trips to the parade ring accompanied by Ian as an owner, to inspect his horses between races, and even a tote desk in the suite saving us the trouble of descending to the course and mixing with the hoi polloi to place our bets. It was a memorable day, and Ian, although still recognisable, had become a confident and obviously, highly successful man.

Ian's father had been right, albeit in a hugely understated way... Ian *was* doing rather well.

ACKNOWLEDGEMENTS

To my special ex-Bermie partners in crime, with my grateful thanks for the many adventures and your unconditional friendship down the years: Penny Cameron; Jane Sassi; Sandra Kendall; Rob Waggott; Terry Murphy and the incomparable Dougie Dewar. Together we are the Magnificent Seven.

For lifting me up when I was at my lowest ebb and always being there: Jim Anderson, Ray Lawrence, and Alan Mallia. And for those early happy times: Chris Norris, Baz Gorst and Mick Bell.

For keeping the faith for the last half century:
Dave Revell; Mary Woollett; Graham Blackshaw; Steve Croucher; Adrian Robson; Jack and Mair Harris; Elaine Firth; Rob Henderson; Maggie Moore; Mark Hawrylak, and Graham Cooper.

And to all those friends who helped shape the great Bermuda times:
Colin Marshall; Trish Charters; Linda Francis; Tinny McCann; Val Moffat; Linda Allison; Liz Winter; Anita Perry; 'Nobby'; Pam Craven; Matt Taylor; Neil Morgan; Viv Tierney; Olga Govia; Dave Wilmott; Deidre Lancaster; Jane Rattigan; Mark Selley; Sue Le Strange; Val Cheape; Sue Sanders-Jones; Malcolm Martin;

Ricky and Barbara Correia; the Pedro family; Lee Simons; George Trott; David Panchaud; Ian Crawford; Wendy Boyd; Suzie Lowe; the Matthias family; Barbara Holhouse; Babs Somerville; David and Jean Weedon; Duncan McFarland; Inez Robertson; Jeannie Sims; Barbara Da Silva; Ian Wight; Marilyn Dick; David O'Meara; Cathy Mortlock; James Lindsay; Renee Carol Valentine; Jackie Spark; Sara Kerr; Louise Sunderland; Caroline Catherall; Tahra Richardson; Denise Belvin; David Doidge; Christine Greenslade; Liz Kemp; Barbara Floyd; Robert Tierney; David Walker; Beverley Dyer; Al Ouellete; David Doidge, and the people of Bermuda… **Without you, life would have been poorer.**

Gone but never forgotten:
Stevie Dobson; Ray Lawrence; Richard Floyd; Angela Hasenfus (Wilkinson); Richard Pedro; David Arkle; Colin Thomas; Ron Robinson; Gary 'Prunes' Marshall; Mac Eddey; Michael Correia; Brian Rowlinson; Gibb Todd; Rab Craig; Rod MacKenzie; Chris Crick; Tony Pope; Chalky White; James MacCallan; Nelson Cabral; Tom Belvin and Rick Faries… **Thanks for the Memories**

Special thanks to Maureen Callanan for her pictorial records and advice, and Gerry Chenhall for her generous help and encouragement with that all important first draft.

My thanks and appreciation to all those at Troubador Publishing for your support, guidance and professionalism. Without you, the bones of this book would still be mouldering away in notebooks at the back of my wardrobe.